The Postgraduate Rese

Accession no.
36192566

www.skills4study.com - the leading study skills website with FREE study tips, downloads and advice.

The Postgraduate Research Handbook

Succeed with your MA, MPhil, EdD and PhD

Second Edition

Gina Wisker

LIS - LIBRARY

Date
26.11.2019   War

Order No.
Donation

University of Chester

palgrave
macmillan

© Gina Wisker, 2001, 2008

All rights reserved. No reproduction, copy or transmission of this publication may be made without written permission.

No portion of this publication may be reproduced, copied or transmitted save with written permission or in accordance with the provisions of the Copyright, Designs and Patents Act 1988, or under the terms of any licence permitting limited copying issued by the Copyright Licensing Agency, Saffron House, 6–10 Kirby Street, London EC1N 8TS.

Any person who does any unauthorized act in relation to this publication may be liable to criminal prosecution and civil claims for damages.

The author has asserted her right to be identified as the author of this work in accordance with the Copyright, Designs and Patents Act 1988.

First edition 2001
Second edition 2008

First published 2001 by
PALGRAVE MACMILLAN

Palgrave Macmillan in the UK is an imprint of Macmillan Publishers Limited, registered in England, company number 785998, of Houndmills, Basingstoke, Hampshire RG21 6XS.

Palgrave Macmillan in the US is a division of St Martin's Press LLC, 175 Fifth Avenue, New York, NY 10010.

Palgrave Macmillan is the global academic imprint of the above companies and has companies and representatives throughout the world.

Palgrave® and Macmillan® are registered trademarks in the United States, the United Kingdom, Europe and other countries.

ISBN-13: 978–0–230–52130–8
ISBN-10: 0–230–52130–4

This book is printed on paper suitable for recycling and made from fully managed and sustained forest sources. Logging, pulping and manufacturing processes are expected to conform to the environmental regulations of the country of origin.

A catalogue record for this book is available from the British Library.

A catalog record for this book is available from the Library of Congress.

10   9   8   7   6   5   4   3
17   16   15   14   13   12   11   10

Printed and bound in China

Contents

List of Figures and Tables

Acknowledgements

I have enjoyed working on writing and more recently revising and updating this book and am grateful for all the insights provided by the many research students who have worked with me, using and commenting on the materials as they developed into the book. This revised edition has benefited through comments from the many local and international students who found the first edition useful, and also information, reflection and comments from the many local and international supervisors with whom I have worked since its inception. I have also found that as, inevitably and vitally, research has become much more central to my own work, the second edition owes much to both my own and others' research into postgraduate student learning and supervisory practices. Particular thanks go to the several cohorts of research students from Israel undertaking PhDs with us at Anglia, to my colleagues Dr Gillian Robinson and Professor Vernon Trafford for their advice with materials, and Miri Shacham, Shosh Leshem and Yehudit Od-Cohen for helping me further develop those materials. Thanks also go to Michelle Bernard, Charlotte Morris, Lindsay Barnes and Nicola Skinner for their dedicated hard work on layouts. Especial thanks go to my family, my late husband Alistair, and sons Liam and Kitt for their support and tolerance, as well as their company, when we have travelled to Australasia, South Africa and the Caribbean, while I gave workshops based upon both the first edition, its companion *The Good Supervisor* and my own research. Finally, thanks to Suzannah Burywood and Karen Griffiths during the preparation of the second edition, Margaret Bartley during the first edition, and other colleagues at Palgrave Macmillan who have supported and commented along the way.

GINA WISKER
Cambridge and Brighton

1 Introduction

If you are thinking of starting to research for an MA, MPhil, PhD, EdD or PrD, then this book should help you at each stage of your work. Initially, it will help you to decide what and how you want to research, where you would like to undertake your research qualification and study, and how to work with a supervisor. It will then tackle how to keep the momentum going over time, and how to analyse your findings and draw conclusions from them. Finally, it will help you to see how to produce a good quality dissertation or thesis – which, we hope, will pass – and then consider how to progress with your research (or other) career.

Commencing a research degree is a very exciting and also rather daunting undertaking, because you know that it is a next step up in your learning. You will probably have heard of friends or colleagues who started a large piece of research, took years and years over it but never completed the work. But you will also know people who have really enjoyed and benefited from undertaking a research degree. My own experience as a part-time, female research student – working at a distance from my supervisor and home university as well as combining a full-time job (and commuting) with study – certainly had its ups and downs. It did, however, change my life; it also changed my sense of my own achievements. I have never regretted the work and have always been pleased I gained the degrees (first an MA, then a PhD). It is this experience that prompted me to write this book, as well as the exciting and fruitful work I have been involved in over the past few years with research students and supervisors, particularly a large cohort of professional part-time research students from Israel and supervisors new to Anglia Ruskin University, the university where I worked for many years. The intention of this book is to enable you to see clearly the topic you wish to research, how to go about your research and how to work successfully towards achieving your aims.

The book draws on good practice developed at a wide variety of universities in Australia, the USA and the UK. I am grateful to colleagues from Australia, the UK, Israel and, lately, South Africa, who have engaged in immensely useful conversations with me, pointing me towards local good practice and sharing their own strategies. Historically, this led to a companion book for supervisors entitled *Good Practice in Postgraduate Supervision* (Wisker and Sutcliffe 1999), and more recently *The Good Supervisor* (Wisker 2005) and some of the ideas in those books may also be of use to you in your work with your supervisor.

Naturally, you will receive a great deal of support and guidance from your university and your supervisor(s). However, having this book as a guide should help you to take control of and responsibility for your own learning, and to discover what kinds of questions to ask – which is equally as important as the answers to some of those questions – as you proceed on your research journey.

One of the largest growth areas in higher education is postgraduate work. More students than ever are deciding to continue with their studies, or to return to postgraduate study to research for a qualification after spending time in paid or voluntary work or bringing up children. There is now a diverse group of students seeking postgraduate study and it is no longer only the lifetime career academic who seeks research study qualifications. There is also much international movement, as many research students wish to gain the enriching experience of studying in another country, most commonly the UK, the USA and Australia. The greatest growth in groups of research students is that of women, in particular women returning to study, who must often combine their study with jobs and domestic responsibilities. Many other students undertake research when they have retired from full-time employment. They, too, as so many others engaged in research, are seizing the opportunity to 'do something for themselves at last'. The diversity of research students has helped to bring about development and change in research supervision practices and in universities' practices of support for and recognition of the needs of research students. This book takes note of the differences in demands of students from different cultural contexts and takes into account different social, age and gender backgrounds. It also takes note of the different kinds of postgraduate research study in which students are engaged.

In this book, students embarking on research for qualifications are considered in three related groups: those working towards their Master's, particularly the MA; those working for an MPhil; and those working for a PhD, EdD, DBA or Professional Doctorate these latter qualifications being substantially different from the former for reasons of length, depth and originality. Some students attend tuition at all three levels while others undertake research-based studies. More recently, there has been the development of a professional doctorate, where appropriate, referred to as an EdD (education), a DBA (business) or a PrD (professional practice). These developments recognise the integration of and synergy between professional practice, employment and work-related study and research. They are often different in shape from established research since they frequently involve staged development and the production of progress reports. Doctorates by publication have also recently been recognised. These, too, are different in shape: they entail the collection of previously published works that follow a focus or theme and the production of a theorised 'wrap' or mapping and a theorising, discursive and conceptual section that brings together the published pieces into a more coherent whole. However, all involve research, and anyone undertaking any of these qualifications will find this book useful. We will be looking at these variants and concentrating on what is common between them: for the most part, therefore, I will use the generic term PhD and mean the research and communication that is involved in all the variants. The main element in common for your work towards all these awards is *the process and the practice of research,* which is the main focus of this book.

The book really starts where I did, and where so many of my own research students began, with some basic advice, some questions to answer and things to think about. The opening sections of each chapter outline the issues to be discussed. There are reflective questions to consider and some strategies, plans and exercises to try out that aim to get you to concentrate on planning and managing your research. The more complex developments are in the middle of each chapter and a conclusion sums up the main points covered. The book as a whole follows the line of development of a research project, whether a relatively short-term project for an MA (probably around a year's work) or a longer project for an MPhil or a PhD (between three and six or more years' work, depending on whether you carry out full- or part-time research). You will need to pick and choose your way around the book as different questions arise for you in your work. In other words, treat it as a useful sourcebook, like any other in your research. It is one to which you can refer when you need, but which also provides an underpinning to your study.

Each chapter asks you to become involved in reflective (or active) tasks to help you to focus further on your work. These should aid the reflection on the progress and process of *your research* – activities that in themselves are a key to good research.

● What the book does not do

This book cannot guarantee you success: the hard work still rests with you. As you develop your own working relationships with supervisors, your research area and university, and as you also develop autonomy, you will appreciate that there could not be a manual that successfully guaranteed that at this level. It is a complex, original and creative activity.

This book is specifically addressed at social science and humanities students: it does not aim to guide science students, although those undertaking health-related research should find it useful (and scientists might find some parts useful, too). Nor does it do more than introduce some of the methods you might choose. You would be advised to turn to specialised books on each of the methods for the kind of useful guidance you will need. Some of these appear in the references but you will find more, as this is a growth industry.

● What the book does and how it is structured

The book gives basic advice, as well as signposts to more specialist research methods, and I hope that you will find that it is accessible and clear in its presentation, and includes the basic points you will need to consider in carrying out and communicating your research.

There are four parts:

1 Starting research;
2 Getting going – supervisors, methods and time;
3 More detailed research methods – maintaining momentum;
4 Support, progress, analysis, writing up, the viva, presentations and afterwards.

There are 'things to do' boxes to enable you to consider how research methods could work for you and to help you with your thinking towards your research projects. The book endeavours to direct you towards reading that leads you to further *specialist research methods training*. It does not try to replicate the books that train in the use of, for example, statistics, but instead asks fundamental questions that enable you to make some choices about appropriate methods and underpinning methodologies.

In outline it:

- takes you through generic decisions about titles, areas of study, the methods and methodology of research, timing, structures, and so on
- deals with issues and practices common across different subject areas and levels in the social sciences and humanities
- branches out, where relevant, to consider the different levels of Master's, MPhil and PhD. It defines the kind of difference related to

original work or work that contributes to the PhD, and the issues around contribution to practice and experience which much Master's work now involves. It also looks at how to ensure this all takes place consistently and reflects on the different needs of international students.

You will see the book is structured in relation to the four phases of a research student's work, that is:

Part 1   Starting research

This section concentrates on:

- starting your own research
- choosing universities
- choosing topics
- defining the area and asking research questions.

Part 2   Getting going – supervisors, methods and time

This section focuses on:

- understanding and taking control of your own learning
- getting into good study habits and managing time
- literature reviews (presenting theoretical perspectives in which you engage in a dialogue between your work and that of others in the field, or the underpinning theorists), notes and referencing
- selecting research methodologies, theories, methods and practices
- starting to work with your supervisor – agendas and contracts.

Part 3   More detailed research methods – maintaining momentum

This section deals with:

- maintenance and development of ideas and research practices, restructuring and refocusing issues and practices
- continuing to maintain good working relations and supervisions with your supervisor(s)
- restructuring to take into account findings and new questions, new reading and ideas, and so on
- maintaining momentum
- ensuring pilot studies inform further developments, analysing your data and producing and building on your findings

- recuperating after difficulties with data and respondents
- making a leap in conceptual awareness
- dealing with underlying values, knowledge and structure-based difficulties.

Part 4   Support, progress, analysis, writing up, the viva, presentations and afterwards

This section covers:

- analysing data
- writing transfer documents, progress reports
- supportive research cultures
- building in time for seen and unforeseen problems
- what makes a good quality research piece, especially a PhD
- editing
- re-editing to keep to length
- ensuring that your organisation develops the thesis
- ensuring that the thesis raises and deals with problems
- diagram design and presentations
- protocols
- submission formats
- vivas
- rewriting and resubmission if it goes wrong and as a natural part of completing the process
- conference presentation
- publication
- the difference between MPhil- and PhD-level work.

Outside the research, the writing up and the viva, the book then looks briefly at presentations, conferences and publications – getting your work out into the broader research area – and life after research; that is, what you might do next.

Good luck! I hope you find the book helps you achieve your aims in your research.

● Further reading

Wisker, G. (2005) *The Good Supervisor* (Basingstoke: Palgrave Macmillan).

Wisker, G. and Sutcliffe, N. (eds) (1999) 'Good Practice in Postgraduate Supervision', SEDA Occasional Paper 106 (Birmingham: SEDA).

Part One

Starting Research

2 Starting Your Postgraduate Research

This chapter looks at:

▶ Why undertake a research degree?
▶ Reasons for undertaking a research degree now
▶ Auditing your research skills

● Why do an MA, MPhil, PhD or other Doctorate?

● Is this the right time for you to start and, if so, why?
● What are your reasons (both personal and occupationally related) for going into research?

Research underpins and informs our understanding and appreciation of all aspects of the world, and its insights lead to physical, social and personal growth and change. While, in itself, your research might not seem to make any immediate direct impact, over time, research-led insights, understanding and changes affect everything we do in society. This really matters: postgraduate study is an opportunity for personal skills development and for professional recognition and status. It is challenging and demanding. Being involved in developing and working on a project or, increasingly, in taught courses with a dissertation element that you have chosen (at least partly), is very exciting. You are, at last, able to concentrate on one of the most interesting things in your life and to watch it grow and develop. There is no doubt that this type and level of study requires you to invest a great deal of hard work and time, but it aids your personal growth, helps you to develop a range of skills that are transferable to life and work afterwards, and helps self-awareness and self-actualisation. If it is a clearly and fully conceived project, it will make intellectual demands of you as regards dealing with complex concepts, ethics and issues to do with the handling and interpretation of different kinds of data. It will also demand a high level of communication and skills of self-expression from you because others (everyone from the window cleaner and your mother to the great authority on the subject) will want to know what you are doing, both in informal and formal exchanges. You will need to keep clear goals and clear expression constantly in mind, without letting the desire for clarity lead to undue simplicity.

Research does not suit everyone, nor is it always the only way to develop an interest. One question you could ask yourself is whether postgraduate study is the best way to further your interest in the area or subject in which you wish to research or to develop a deep interest. Perhaps your interests would be better served in a form that required less stringent data management or bibliographical work and did not have to conform to the extensive commitment, deliberation and institutional regulations with which a postgraduate qualification will be involved. Perhaps the project you have in mind might be better served by being explored through a book or a report.

However, postgraduate study might be exactly what you seek now. It is demanding, rewarding and creative, and can help you to develop an alternative sense of identity as you become involved in your work.

It is also a big challenge to your intellect and determination, and you might well fear failure because of the daunting size and depth of the project. It is important, then, that you are sure you want to start this work, know what it entails and can commit to it with enthusiasm and determination, and can be motivated to continue with it. You will need a good support network of others who believe in and will help motivate you, and who are willing to help you use the necessary problem-solving strategies to work out ways of dealing with and overcoming various problems, meeting various challenges and seizing opportunities as you meet them. And you will meet them! That is the nature of research and also part of its stimulating challenge. To look on the negative side for a moment, let us recognise that some people do not complete their research. It could be argued that the only reasons to give up are if the research information is clearly flawed and the hypotheses upon which it was founded are clearly incorrect, or if all the other priorities in your life take over. However, in the former case you could recast the research, and in the latter, formally enquire about deferral. Neither are really reasons to give up. Having said this, you will be surprised how many students do actually fail to finish their research.

If you have committed yourself far enough to read a book on studying and working for a research degree, you are probably already lessening your chances of being part of that group. You are spending time considering the challenges of the tasks ahead and the planning and hard work that contribute to your success. You are also starting to learn more about how *you* learn and study as a research student. This contributes positively to your success because it will allow you to be personally aware of your learning and to take control of this process yourself.

Undertaking postgraduate research is exciting, and personally and professionally rewarding. Success leads to greater self-esteem and, whether or not it eventually aids promotion or the acquisition of a new job, it increases professional credibility and status. You might well be rather nervous about undertaking such a big step, taking on what could, certainly for PhD and MPhil work, be a long-term commitment (MPhils often last three years full time and six years part time, and so do PhDs, while MAs last one to two and a half years). It is certainly true that this undertaking will expect you to take a step up in terms of the level at which you have been working. There will have been previous such steps, between GCSE and A level, for example, and A level or equivalent and first-degree study. You would do well to remind yourself how you recognised the step up, the differences in levels demanded of you, and to consider how you managed the step. You can also remind yourself that you have been successful in making these steps and have already written substantial pieces of work. This will help firmly establish your confidence as well as give you some insight into your own sense of how you work well. There are now many resources to help you to choose the appropriate kind of postgraduate study in the appropriate university for your needs and interests. Most universities have websites that will give you local information and there are some generic websites, as well as specific books, to help you decide. *The Good Universities Guide to Postgraduate and Career Upgrade Courses* (Ashenden 2002) is a useful first step, as is www.thegoodguides.com.au and, for both choice and ongoing connection to issues of postgraduate study, www.grad.ac.uk

If you are undertaking an MPhil or PhD, these questions about research background and skills are absolutely central. Your main activity is research. For MA students, research is a part of each element or essay and is the crucial element to the final dissertation.

Things to do

In order to benefit from your own previous research experiences and draw out your research abilities, ask yourself:

- What previous experience of research do you have? For example, research carried out for a dissertation, for publication, for internal papers, for Master's or other postgraduate qualifications, in your role discovering practices and supporting developments.
- Was it scientific research, social science research or humanities research?
- Was it research to feed into or underpin your daily work, new processes and practices, for a professional activity such as a report?
- Was it research carried out for interest alone?
- Was it market research, research into choices people make, attitudes or behaviours?

- Was it research into the background of something or someone, for work, for pleasure, for your family or for interest?
- Was it teaching and educational research – to underpin teaching practices?
- Was it more general research – to find out about buying a house, about your family tree or local history, to discover different costing and different opportunities in house development or holiday planning?

All of these kinds of research, broadly speaking, use humanities and social science research strategies that involve identifying issues, problems, questions and sub-questions and setting out to investigate them; foraging for information in a variety of sources including literature, the Internet, and from people; asking questions of different data and people in different ways; and coming to some – probably temporary – partial conclusions. They might have led to a furthering and deepening of knowledge or understanding, an interpretation of an area of thought or work, a change in practice, information on which to base a development at work, insight gained into why certain things always happen or certain people did or do certain things in certain ways, and they could have resulted in information presented in many different ways, including reports and information sheets, or even in essays – but this last is less likely unless they were related to an academic context.

● Planning, key issues and suggestions

This section looks at:
- planning your research – the first stages
- contributing to the research culture – originality
- developing a hypothesis and/or questions
- defining research outcomes
- defining each stage of the research process
- suggested research skills.

Planning your research – the first stages

Planning your research and re-planning it as you proceed are essential elements in a good research project and a good research degree. As you begin to define your research area and the kinds of methodologies and methods you intend to use, who to work with, where to work and who can be supportive of you, you need to be clear about why you want to undertake the research and what you hope to find out. Think of your interest, which fuels this research, as a guiding force of motivation. You will need to think strategically and conceptually, and to manage both long-term activities and short-term work. Some of these elements are covered in the latter part of the book.

Contributing to research culture – originality

You need initially to concentrate on the accurate definition and description of the research by selecting an appropriate title and asking yourself why this research is important. What can it contribute to knowledge and/or change? The Swinnerton-Dyer report (1982) comments about postgraduate research:

> the choice of research topic should be heavily influenced by the staff and, where appropriate, also from outside the academic institution; this is to ensure that the topic is a suitable subject for research training, that it is likely to prove a rewarding investigation, that it is of practical benefit where this is possible, that competent supervision is available and that the work can be completed within the time available.

Defining your research area, choosing your title and asking your main research questions are essential points of entrance into the research process. This identification of the importance of working with staff direction is slightly differently interpreted in different areas of discipline, however. With science research and some large social science projects, it is quite normal for students to apply to be part of a research team, be funded, ensure their work forms part of the funded project, and agree a title that fits the project. In arts and humanities and much social science research, the development of an area of research, title and design are more individualistic and open to negotiation with the supervisor.

What the Swinnerton-Dyer report also suggests is that MA, MPhil and PhD research is not an end in itself. It is actually a training ground for researchers. The hope is that you will establish sound practices during your course and transfer these to further research afterwards. Since the Roberts Report in the UK (2002), the Metcalfe Report (2002) and various government decisions in Australia, PhD students are now expected to complete their research and writing up within three years, often even if they are studying part time. They are also expected to undertake a research development programme alongside their studies so that they are able to develop research and other generic skills, which will enable them to move on in their careers following their research. If you are undertaking an MA you will have several sessions, or even a whole module, that focuses on the skills required to undertake successful research and, if you are undertaking a PhD EdD or PrD, you will need to take part in an ongoing staged programme which is recognised in the UK by the Quality Assurance Agency and internationally by the appropriate bodies in each country.

What follows are some initial prompt questions to encourage you to think about your research and the processes for undertaking it. You will find that a whole chapter (Chapter 5) is devoted to the development of your research question.

● Starting to think about developing a hypothesis and/or research questions

As you begin your research you will need to define what you want to find out about, and why, and how to go about finding out.

Things to do

Consider:

Where do your work and your ideas fit in so far? What are you clear about from this list of first stages of research?

- Define your area
- What do you want to research into?
- Decide on a title that gives you enough scope to ask research questions but does not attempt research of too great a scope
- Develop a hypothesis or research question
- Set up a plan of activities and sort out where the resources and information may lie
- Plan the time – and the critical path
- Seek funding and support
- Set up effective supervision arrangements with your supervisor(s)
- Seek a support group or person, if appropriate
- Get started on the literature search, the reading, the initial plans, the first supervision, and the writing up of the first and subsequent drafts of the proposal for university agreement.

Now look at the very first stages.

Consider:

- What will be your research area and title?
- What questions and concerns do you have about developing good research practices in your situation?
- How can you work to overcome any problems? (What might they be? Time? Money? Work demands?)
- What needs do you have to carry out your research?
- Share your ideas and initial plans with a colleague (if you can).

The areas of developing your research are covered fully in the chapters that follow, but it is useful to consider now what you want to research, where you want to carry out your work and what kind of research degree you want to undertake. These thoughts, as well as some idea of the problems and benefits of research, should inform your use of the chapters to follow, and then inform your work.

What follows are some suggestions about key issues in successful research practices, largely originating in Australia. These should provide a guide for good practice and good experience throughout your study.

Defining research outcomes

- The research student should ensure that he/she is engaged on a promising topic that might fairly be expected to produce sound results within the agreed time frame.
- Students should work with their supervisors to develop standards of achievement that will result in a good quality thesis (*University of Queensland Calendar*).

Ask yourself if your research is promising or rich enough and likely to produce sound results. Will it be completed within the time allowed?

It is important that the supervisor works with the student to look closely at the first stages of development of the research project proposal. It is also important that both student and supervisor agree that this is a promising, manageable project that should achieve a good quality thesis. Once you have thought through and settled on your responses to the lists given above, you might want to share them with your supervisor(s).

Defining and managing each stage of the supervising process – systems, problems, good practice

Once your supervisor has been chosen or assigned and contact has been made, there follow several informal interviews or discussions, some of which might be by phone, e-mail or letter. The early development of an outline of your postgraduate research hypothesis, ideas, concerns and research questions follow. It is important also to start to read widely within the appropriate literature and to start to develop a literature research base. You will need to use your own sense of what realistic and good quality research you have worked with in the past, and to consult with your supervisor and colleagues to produce what looks like a viable project based on the quality of the research questions, the methodology, your ability to organise ideas and your discoveries to date. You will need to show imagination and realism, and the ability to change and develop ideas in relation to what you are discovering.

The next stage of the activity is to move towards establishing the procedure for the research, the design of the actual research work you will undertake, which, particularly in a project relating to social sciences or health research, should contain:

- a description of the theoretical or conceptual framework
- a list of potential reading and other sources of evidence and evidence/authority
- the research design and research questions
- the methodology and methods to be used
- an outline of the analytical techniques you think you will use to analyse your data and start to interpret it.

There should also be:

- a timetable for the completion of stages of the work
- a draft set of contents, which helps you to define the major areas of work, and research questions informing the whole.

Some of the stages and some of the responsibilities include:

- network planning or critical path analysis – working out what you need to do when and who might help you in your work
- setting objectives
- putting the research activities into some plan or order
- estimating the time each stage of the research should take
- deciding on and getting hold of the necessary facilities and resources
- drawing up a realistic schedule, which will (of course) be changed with developments, setbacks and changes in circumstances.

See Chapter 11 on balancing demands and Chapter 12 on time management.
  Once this schedule has been decided and planned, it then needs to be actioned. You will need to seek support from your supervisor and other research student colleagues in developing your research. You need to ensure you:

- are realistic about your critical path and schedule, and can plan an appropriate course of study
- meet your supervisor at regular intervals to discuss and guide the progress of your work

- seek opportunities to take part in the university's research culture, attend the research development programme, give papers, consult with peers, attend conferences, and so on
- consider, plan and seek advice from other students, and work with the university's published guidelines on the scope and presentation of the thesis, on format, length, layout, dates and various regulations
- consider and plan publications likely to arise from the work (much of this emerges as you carry out the work)
- agree with your supervisor that he/she will see and comment (helpfully, constructively and critically) on drafts of the major sections of the thesis as these are prepared
- encourage supervisors to comment helpfully, constructively and critically on the draft of the completed thesis before it is submitted.

Being aware of these stages and taking notice of the advice can help supervisor and student develop a harmonious working relationship, with clear patterns of working and clear expectations of each other's responsibilities. However, there are some specific areas in which research students can have problems in their research, or with their supervisor, and these too need considering in relation to working successfully with your supervisor for success in research.

There are many potential difficulties in relation to supervisors and resources. You might like to think about how to overcome some of these (should they emerge!) before embarking on your research. Look also at later chapters (such as Chapter 10) that discuss the managing of your supervisor to consider how to overcome common problems in this area.

Some broad areas that could cause concern are:

- inappropriate/unachievable/excessively complex research questions and/or research plans
- management and planning, if these are unrealistic
- difficulties with acquiring data, or analysing and managing it
- relationships with supervisors
- life outside research preventing a full and successful focus on your work.

There are also some difficulties that could arise because of the kinds of learning styles and approaches that students take – see Chapter 13 for some thoughts and suggestions about this.

Common problems

Research has shown that students have problems with:

- research questions and areas that do not yield enough information or have been inappropriately posed – asking for accumulations of information rather than questioning and suggesting – so that the work becomes dull and descriptive
- access to research subjects, contacts and contexts – often this seems guaranteed at the outset of the work, but situations change. Sometimes the people, information, scenarios, and so on, disappear, or you are no longer in a situation to access them (or, surprisingly, they are refused to you early on or part of the way through your work)
- personality factors: neglect by the supervisor, a clash of personalities, barriers to communication arising from age, class, gender, race, differences in approach to work
- professional factors: a misinformed supervisor or one without sufficient knowledge in the area supervised
- a supervisor with few genuine research interests, or ones that differ fundamentally from those of the student
- organisational factors: the supervisor having too many students to supervise; the supervisor being too busy with administration; the supervisor's inability to manage his/her research group or numbers of researchers efficiently
- departmental facilities and arrangements isolating the student
- lack of a genuine research culture – lack of others to work with and talk to, to share excitement, discoveries, setbacks, problems, developments, strategies and solutions
- inadequate support services and provision of equipment
- difficulties with other life demands and crises that do not allow you enough time to develop the research.

You will need to consider how you might avoid or overcome these potential problems and pitfalls.

Some student dissatisfaction with the development of his/her work and with relations with supervisors can be avoided if there is clear and open communication on all aspects of the project and if, overall, there is structure without a straitjacket; that is, a framework for supervision and studies that facilitates rather than hinders a student's development and creativity. Such a structure will enable students to develop their autonomy, to become sure of the rules and resources, and of the intellectual and systematic support they need to do so. It will also help students to be treated equally fairly when being supervised, even in cases where they have personality clashes with supervisors.

To avoid problems, both research students and supervisors have to make it very clear to each other at the outset where the different responsibilities lie, and agree the roles and responsibilities they will each take on. It is in the spirit of this need that the idea of developing contracts emerges (see Chapter 10): it is in the spirit of an ongoing need for support and discussion – which is not always possible from the supervisor – that the idea of peer support systems and co-counselling has developed (see Chapter 14). There could be some difficulties for distance research students, whether in the UK or abroad, and distance systems should be set up to cope with such problems. A different kind of pacing of agreed activities has to be set up and maintained for supervising relations at a distance. Some of these needs can be satisfied by the development of contracts, and some others by peer support networks and structures.

Research students need to develop autonomy. They need to plan and action their research projects, and use the support of the supervisor and research colleagues to guide them, help clarify difficult issues, test hypotheses and the importance of data, and support and redirect them in crises if necessary.

Autonomy, negotiation and the development of shared responsibilities should result from the establishment of sound research practices and a good, clear relationship with your supervisor(s). This puts the supervisor in a position as facilitator, and you in a position where you are well informed, sure of what to expect in the nature of supervision, well aware of rules and formats, dates, what you can ask your supervisor, and so on. This usually results in successful supervisory relationships. Colleagues in Australia (Ingrid Moses and Linda Conrad) have developed an exercise where students and supervisors debate which of them has the responsibility over various stages in research, ranging from deciding the research questions through to editing the thesis. If you are able to have that kind of discussion with your supervisor, it should be clearer to both of you where you expect support and where the supervisor feels that too much support would prevent you from developing the necessary independence to become an independent researcher in your own right. Alternatively, the supervisor may be rather 'hands off', actually leaving you with too little guidance and too few questions. Negotiation is needed between you for the smooth running of the relationship, development of independence in your own learning and the production of a piece of research and a thesis that you can say is genuinely your own (but is one that has been appropriately supported). Supervisors are very important in the development of your research skills and the thesis, but so, too, are research development programmes, which are now common throughout universities the world over, largely because numbers have increased and also because governments and universities agree that students need support in the strategies of research and the development of research-related skills. You need to make sure you attend one of the research development programmes at your own university.

Important, also, are peer groups: they help students to share ideas and develop a sense both of communicative peer support and of ownership of their work. A useful addition to formal, timetabled supervision sessions, peer- and group-based sessions and systems can make life easier and much more productive all round. A lower drop-out rate and better quality of work are predictable, tangible results.

Things to do

Consider:

- Are there any problems you foresee?
- What can you do to avoid or cope with them?
- What do you need to do immediately to set up good working relationships?

Research skills – are you ready for this?

You might well have underestimated or even overestimated your skills in some areas and you might also think that skills developed so far will not be relevant at this level of research. Be realistic. Think of instances in your study life and everyday life when you have used such skills and could transfer them to a research context. For example, if you have run a family budget, you might be better skilled at calculating than you imagine. If you have carried out literature reviews for an undergraduate essay, or written a journalistic piece, these too are skills that can be developed and transferred. If you find genuine gaps in skills, then seize opportunities to work with others who have these skills. Seize development and training opportunities – develop, build and reflect on your skills as you carry out your research work. Some of the chapters in this book aim to help you develop some of these skills, so you should find the tasks helpful.

Things to do

You might well already have many research skills. You need to assess and measure these, and so you will find it useful to audit your skills. Most universities offer research methods and skills training. Find out if yours does. You might specify needs, such as training with social science research analysis packages (SPSSs). Alternatively, your needs might be more general, for example acquiring and managing knowledge. It is a useful exercise, first, to consider your research skills and needs on your own, then to discuss them with your supervisor, perhaps as part of several different supervisions. You might well find that it is useful for you to take on some specific training which will help you to tackle some of the broader more generalised areas of skills now expected of research students, as well as those that are necessary for the successful interpretation and writing up of the dissertation or thesis.

Here are some of the research skills you will need. Audit them now. Mark the extent of your current skills and your skills needs. [1 = need to develop, 2 = some skills, 3 = quite confident, 4 = confident, 5 = a strength of mine.]

Project planning	1	2	③	4	5
Time management	①	2	3	4	5
Knowledge retrieval	1	2	③	4	5
Knowledge management	1	2	③	4	5
Analytical skills	1	②	3	4	5
Calculation skills	1	②	3	4	5
Interpretation skills	1	2	③	4	5
Evaluative thinking	1	2	③	4	5
Problem solving in different contexts	1	②	3	4	5
Creative thinking	1	2	③	4	5
Reading for different purposes	1	2	3	④	5
Reviewing the literature critically	1	2	③	4	5
Thinking and writing at a conceptual level	1	2	③	4	5
Writing for different audiences	1	2	③	4	5
Writing theses and articles	1	2	③	④	5
Structuring and presenting papers	1	2	3	④	5
Managing discussion	1	2	③	4	5

Conclusion – a few points to remember

☐ Pick the right research qualification route for you

☐ Spot and work to avoid or overcome potential pitfalls

☐ Audit and update your research skills and recognise what you already have experience with in relation to research.

● **Further reading**

Ashenden, Dean (2002) *The Good Universities Guide to Postgraduate and Career Upgrade Courses* (Cambridge: Hobsons).

Metcalfe J., Thompson, Q. and Green, H. (2002) 'Improving Standards in Postgraduate Research Degree Programmes', October (Bristol: HEFCE).

Roberts, Sir G. (2002) *Set for Success: The Report of the Sir Gareth Roberts Review* (London: HM Treasury) (available at http://www.hmtreasury. gov.uk/media/643/FB/ACF11FD.pdf).

Swinnerton-Dyer, H.P.F. (1982) *Report of the Working Party on Postgraduate Education* (London: HMSO).

University of Queensland Calendar (1984) University of Queensland.

Websites

www.thegoodguides.com.au
www.grad.ac.uk

3 Choosing the Right Research Degree

This chapter looks at:

▶ Types and varieties of research degree — and choice
▶ Choosing your university and supervisor

Selecting the right research degree and institution is vital.

● Types of degree

This book largely concentrates on research projects, reports, dissertations and theses, which are all part of MA, MPhil and PhD work. It looks, in the main, at research for postgraduate study. Some of the specific points are more directly relevant to studying in the UK or Australasia, or in the educational systems and contexts influenced by those in the UK or Australasia, while other more general points will suit anyone undertaking postgraduate research.

Before you embark on your research, you need to decide which is the right kind of research degree course for you. It might be that you decide to undertake a degree that offers more opportunity for taught and staged work than concentrating on a pure PhD by dissertation or thesis alone. This is possible now even at PhD level (the EdD, for example). If you choose a partly taught postgraduate degree, you will still need to think about the dissertation or thesis element, and this book can help you with that. Remember also that, in the UK and Australasia at least, you will need to undertake an accompanying staged research degrees programme. Consider which kind of research degree suits you by looking at the definitions and discussions below.

Practice-based doctorates of all sorts – PrD, the professional doctorate, EdD, the Education doctorate; and DBA, the Business Doctorate – also often involve coursework elements or a staged progress report-based process, but include a research-based dissertation. Chapter 18, on practice-based research and action research, also comments on balancing your coursework and your research, should you be undertaking this kind of coursework and/or practice-based postgraduate qualification. The reason for focusing most heavily here on the research element of whatever postgraduate degree you are undertaking is that this most often constitutes a large-scale, new kind of undertaking for students: coursework, although perhaps of a different kind at postgraduate level, is more recognisable and possibly more manageable, resembling undergraduate essay work. The size of the thesis (often 80 000 words) is such a significant leap in terms of mass, extent, depth and potential for conceptual complexity and detail, that it constitutes a real development of a particular kind of study for students and very different kinds of study practices, over time, than do extended essays, even at Master's level (most often these are 5 000 words – more like an undergraduate dissertation than a thesis).

MA

Master's degrees are more usually a taught option. They frequently provide the opportunity to spend some time on research methods that help future research. If you decide to undertake an MA, consider whether a part-time or full-time course would suit you and your other commitments. Do ensure that there is a research-based dissertation or similar, because these are seen as guarantors of the level and quality of the work produced and appropriate preparation for further research. Should you decide to undertake further research, you will be expected to have completed a dissertation to show that you are capable of an extended piece of research work (around 15 000–20 000 words).

MRes

In many universities, there is a specific Masters course in research. This enables you to concentrate on developing your skills in research and research methods so that you are ready to use them in a dissertation, and later on in a PhD.

MPhil

An MPhil is often seen as a stopping-off point before a PhD. The MPhil is actually an opportunity for a very highly focused piece of research, often a single case study. A single issue, problem or concern often provides the focus for an MPhil, which involves research, but without the depth and the wide contribution and research culture of the PhD. They tend to last from between two or three years to five or six years depending on whether it is full or part time (length 50 000–60 000 words or more). Sometimes students aiming for a PhD will be awarded an MPhil instead should examiners feel that the focus is very specific and the contribution to knowledge and understanding more circumscribed than that expected for a PhD.

PhD

A PhD is a contribution to research development culture. It is a significant step forward in the work done in a specific area that is disciplinary or inter-disciplinary-based. PhDs tend to be larger, broader and more original than MPhils; to cover more ground, whether in breadth or depth; and to contribute something new, both factual knowledge and an understanding of the question and the field, that operates at a conceptual level – that is, the level of ideas and meaning. It will also be well founded and grounded. PhDs tend to last from three years (full time) to six or more (part time) and so are substantial time commitments (length 50 000–80 000 words). In Australasia, and increasingly in the UK, students are expected to complete within the three years and to produce not only a substantial piece of research and contribution to knowledge, but also to have developed the various postgraduate skills of communication, project management, presentation and teaching alongside the development of transferable research skills. These latter are gained through completing the PhD and a research development programme, which is fast becoming compulsory in many universities.

● Varieties of research degree

There are now, in many universities (probably mainly the 'modern' universities), real opportunities for doctorate study in particular, that are flexible, responsive and creative, can involve staged progress reports and course work, and which are often also practice-based in many instances.

PhD by publication

Over a dozen universities in the UK, and a growing number in Australasia and the USA, now recognise the PhD by publication. Normally this involves pulling together a variety of small and large publications with a common theme, and supplying an appropriate analytical and critical commentary of about 10 000 words to accompany the submission. The coherence of the submission is crucial: there need to be common themes and arguments running through the publications rather than an attempt to gain recognition for all you have previously published (at whatever level). In this form of PhD, the mini-thesis or commentary accompanying the published pieces sets out to prove the coherence of the whole and links all the work together.

Creative PhDs/MPhils/MAs

Many students now choose to produce something original and creative in response to a question, and to write an analytical discussion of how they see the creative work reflecting and moving forward the concerns, perspectives and needs. In the fine arts, women's studies, performing arts and other creative areas, this is an essential way of recognising the kinds of thought and work that arise in the subject area. A firm theoretical and critical grounding is essential in these theses, which are often accompanied by creative works that otherwise would not be very easily analysable or explicable (sculptures, videos, collections of creative writing, stitch-craft, and so on).

Practice-based PhDs, the professional doctorate, the DBA and the EdD

Several universities across the world, principally in Australia and some parts of the UK, have recognised the usefulness of the practice-based doctorate. In some instances this is an education doctorate (EdD). The professional practice-oriented doctorate has also been developed in several other subjects, chiefly social work, business, management and health practice. Practice-based PhDs involve both a research element and a practice element. Often, the research is into elements of practice and forwards understanding of that practice, leading to change. Essentially, this kind of PhD grew out of the aim for change rather than research for its own sake and so, in terms of shape, the PhD will have a large element of recommendations and action leading from its findings, or will chart and explore reasons for certain practice developments and their effects. Practice-based doctorates are doctorates that 'represent inquiries by professional practitioners (for example, teachers, nurses, civil servants, police, doctors) into an aspect of their own practice' (Winter and Sabiechowska 1999).

This kind of research degree requires a different kind of planning and supervising. It involves coursework as well as research, and it requires supervisors and examiners who understand the practice base and the effective aims of the variant of the PhD. The EdD is an educationally related version of this practice-based PhD.

The doctorate in education (EdD)

Education practitioners in particular often choose to take an education doctorate, an option offered by several universities, including Anglia Ruskin University and the Open University (OU).

It is aimed at professional development, involves much taught face-to-face work, operates using cohorts of student groups, and is assessed by several staged pieces of work, building up to a longer thesis. As such, then, it offers an opportunity to take professional issues, developments or problems and base elements of the research around these. For further details of the OU EdD, see Chapters 22 and 23.

Things to do

Consider:

● Which sort of research degree suits you now? Why?
● Might you want to undertake a further research degree afterwards? Why?

● Choosing your university and supervisor

When you choose your university for your research degree, you need to take several factors into account:

● suitability for your kind of research
● accessibility
● facilities
● reputation for completion
● reputation of supervisors in your field
● reputation for support – training and quality of supervisors
● reputation for quality of research culture – publications, named people prominent in their fields, conferences, and so on
● your own feelings and intuition – can you spend what could be a considerable amount of your time here?

Some students select the supervisor for their specialism before choosing the university, some apply for advertised research bursaries or posts within a research project and the supervisor manages the project – perhaps a project that involves several research students working on different aspects. Some students prefer to remain with the university at which they completed under-graduate study, and others prefer – or are forced – to move to somewhere new.

If you are a research student from overseas, it is also important to ask:

● What are the facilities for overseas students?
● Is there accommodation?
● Is there an international office or its equivalent?
● What is the university's reputation for support for international students?

Look up the university on the Internet or through the central applications system (in the UK this is the Universities and Colleges Admissions Service: UCAS), seek out people who know others who have been there, and visit it if you can. For all students, whether this is a university new to you, your local university or one in which you have already studied, you may already know the answers to many of the above questions, but you might not actually know how well the university supports its research students in terms of:

- Accommodation
- A research structure – training programme. Universities in the UK and Australasia are now required to ensure that students receive research methods training and development, and in the UK this is the subject of Quality Assurance Agency scrutiny. There is an extended curriculum, which not only covers research methods and accompanying research skills, writing, IT and so on, but also more generic postgraduate skills such as communication and teaching
- Peer and development culture – this includes centrally or depart-mentally organised seminars, work-in-progress meetings, the provision of a location for postgraduate students, for example, with comfortable chairs, a drinks machine and a notice board
- Computer facilities, library support and, in some instances, support for English language (tertiary literacy) and editing.

You might also not know about the reputation of the university in terms of the subject area in which you seek to research, and you will probably not know the individual reputation of the supervisors you seek out. Much information can be gathered by looking carefully at university and staff profiles on the university website, and seeing who has published what. Some information, both formal and informal, can be gained by contacting or visiting the departmental office of the department in which you will be based, by visiting the graduate office and by talking with current research students. All of these approaches, as well as published materials, can yield answers to the questions about support, provision and research culture. Then you can make up your own mind. Often, mature students study for their research degrees at their local university and have no other alternative because they need to fit the research in with domestic and work demands. Others can move to universities other than the nearest that welcome them. Nearest does not mean best, nor does it mean worst. Your local university might well be the best for the work you wish to carry out. You need to carry out some research to find out what suits you, what will support you and who can supervise you. There is much specific guidance on the websites of individual universities, and also more generally in *The Good Universities Guide to Postgraduate and Career Upgrade Courses* (Cambridge: Hobsons), www.thegoodguides.com.au, and www.grad.ac.uk

Universities are keen to take on research students for several reasons. Their presence contributes to the development and recognition of a research culture that ensures a high level of intellectual activity, exchange, development and practice within the university culture as a whole, and embraces staff and undergraduates as well as research students. This has been described as a research community of practice and, in some cases, means that research students are involved in contributing publications towards research assessment exercises and teaching other students in the department or subject, perhaps even postgraduates new to research. Staff members are often very keen to take on research students in order to build research capacity and also because the most interesting, high-level, intellectual, in-depth learning conversations they have are, for the most part, with their research students. Good research students contribute to the research assessment exercise (RAE) in the UK and to similar cultures in Australia, the USA and Europe, and so enhance the university's research rating, internationally as well as nationally, which attracts funding and students. Some research students actually come with research funds, and international research students often pay high fees for the privilege of being supervised in their research.

However, some universities do not provide the necessary support to enable research students to engage successfully in their research. Some departments and supervisors have poor reputations for providing the kind of support that helps research students (see Lawton 1997: 5).

Some supervisors take on more research students than they can actually cope with, in terms of giving the appropriate amount of time and attention to each one. Ideally, a supervisor should have no more than ten students at any one time. You might find that the supervisor you choose has too many students to take you on (see Chapter 10).

Once you have indicated your interest in being supervised in a particular university and/or you have actually applied, you will probably be asked for interview and you can ask questions about support and facilities at that stage. You will also be expected to engage in full discussion with your prospective supervisor about your research topic, question and, if it has been drafted, your research proposal.

In many cases, students only present with an interest, or apply for a research position and bursary in response to an advert. If pursuing an interest, that interest will need to be worked up and shaped into a title, research questions and proposals: more commonly in the sciences and engineering,

Things to do

Consider:

- What do you know about the university of your choice? And what is its reputation concerning research students?
- What do you know already about the department and the research culture?
- What do you know about your future potential supervisor?
- How can you go about finding answers to these questions?

the research questions or hypothesis might already be in place, as they will have been developed by the project team in order to achieve research funding from internal or external bodies. In the former case, you will need to develop a research question or hypothesis that creates a sufficiently substantial project at the appropriate conceptual and intellectual level to make a contribution to knowledge worthy of the award.

The same is true if you apply for a research position and bursary, but in that case you also need to ensure that your work fits with the project as a whole and that it will be distinct enough in itself, so that you can be awarded your postgraduate qualification on the basis of the quality of your work, not that of the team. It will, therefore, be very useful to have a sense of the questions you wish to ask, underpinning your research, and the methods you will use in your research. The clearer you are about the questions and methods you feel are central to your work, the more likely you will be to ask appropriate questions, and to be accepted.

Conclusion

This chapter should have helped you to choose:

- [ ] the right kind of research degree for your purposes and time available

- [ ] the right university.

● Further reading

Ashenden, Dean (2002) *The Good Universities Guide to Postgraduate and Career Upgrade Courses* (Cambridge: Hobsons).

Graves, N. and Varma, V. (eds) (1997) *Working for a Doctorate: A Guide for the Humanities and Social Sciences* (London: Routledge).

Winter, R. and Sabiechowska, P. (1999) *Professional Experience and the Investigative Imagination* (London: Routledge).

Websites

www.thegoodguides.com.au
www.grad.ac.uk

4 Choosing Your Supervisor(s)

● Introduction

Managing your supervisor(s) well and developing and maintaining a supportive, positive, constructively critical relationship over time is essential to help you produce a good quality thesis. The relationship between you and your supervisor or supervisors is a very important one and it is essential that you can get on with them personally, without necessarily being the best of friends, and can respect them in terms of scholarship, academic credibility and their practices. Many students select a specific person to be their supervisor because they know their work. You need to set up contacts in advance and develop a working link with such a prospective supervisor. Some students even cross the world (or move around the country) to be able to work with the supervisor they want. Often, however, you have little choice over who can supervise you because of the limited range of specialisms available or the specific nature of the research project and, in the case of Master's programmes, supervisors are often allocated later on in the research process.

In other instances, you could find the department and university normally match students with supervisors based on university knowledge of specialisms. If you have selected one or a number of possible universities (perhaps because of location or if other family members and friends study there or live nearby) you could find out about potential supervisors and their specialisms by looking up departmental web pages, which usually indicate research and publication interests. For international students, in particular, this can help provide a 'flavour' of the department and narrow down on or save on costly visits. If you can take an active part in the selection of who supervises you, you need to take some of the following issues into consideration. Do remember that sometimes the most eminent person is the busiest and can afford the least time for supervision, while the least experienced might give you more time. Sometimes we pick our supervisors for their specialist knowledge, at other times for their experience in the dominant methodologies we are going to use. If you are expected to have several supervisors – that is, a director of studies, a second supervisor and even an external adviser/supervisor – it is as well to think in terms of balancing the characteristics of a good supervisor in this choice; that is, accessibility, communication skills, research skills and reputation.

Things to do

In relation to your project, consider a supervisor:

- who is eminent in the field and so would be well aware of the latest reading, contacts and ideas
- who is using the kinds of methodologies you want to use and can help you with these
- who has the time and commitment to supervise you
- who is reliable, trustworthy and clear in his or her relations with you
- who is dependable
- with whom you get on professionally
- who is available
- with whom you can actually keep in contact, even if he or she is not close to you geographically.

● Choosing your supervisor, and internal regulations

In the outlining and development of your initial proposal and the scheme of your project, you will need to follow the internal regulations. In many of the new universities, it is common for there to be a director of studies, first supervisor, and a second internal supervisor plus an external supervisor. In other universities – the University of the West Indies, for example – there is a research committee that oversees the student's work. The first supervisor – director of studies – might be in a position to suggest the other two or more, or you might have some suggestions, or they might be assigned by the department or school. If you do have any opportunity to do so, it is a good idea to pick someone who is interested in the same ideas and area but who can perhaps also contribute different skills, for example, methodology, methods skills and different contacts. The external supervisor is also useful for his or her relative objectivity and other contacts and angles on the research.

You will need to draw up a credible and viable research outline and a discussion of whatever length is required by the internal processes. You will need a clear initial idea of the methodology you intend to use to inform the research design and underpin the methods you will use to gather the necessary data, and you will need to ascertain the kinds of research questions or hypotheses, the kinds of outcomes expected, and the probable skills needed, such as data-gathering and processing skills. You will need to spend some time on considering your underpinning beliefs and ideology, and the theory and concepts you wish to use and can foresee.

Things to do

Consider:

- Who do you think you can ask to be your supervisor, or who have you been allocated?
- What do you know about the supervisor's specialisms, the number of students he or she is supervising and his or her personality?
- Have you already met, and started to plan your research?
- When can you meet the supervisor?
- What do you feel you need to know immediately?

Once you have approached a supervisor and/or a supervisor has approached/been allocated to you (whatever the process is in your case and that of your university), you need to establish a clear definition of how much and how far your supervisor can and will work with you on your project, and contract with him or her over responsibilities.

Often the second supervisor is chosen for:

- expertise in methodology
- expertise in methods
- overall knowledge of university processes.

● Working with your supervisors: initial contracts and contacts

Title and scope of the project

Discuss the overall project with your supervisor and ask for his or her support in defining and clarifying the research title, the research questions and getting started in terms of reading and contracts. Remember how important it is to get your title right. If you are working on a joint project in the sciences or social sciences, it is possible that your title will be allocated to you, in which case it is important to talk over the implications and directions, and to feel you are really interested in and engaged with the title in order to undertake the project.

Good practice working with supervisors – regularity and kind of supervisions, at what stages

You need to draw up a formal or informal learning contract with your supervisor. A learning contract is like a legal contract (but less punitive and mostly informally binding) that you agree between you and which sets out what you each expect of the other in terms of work, communication and responsibility. As you discuss your roles and draw this up as an informal contract, it helps you to make explicit your expectations, the frequency and kind of supervision, and what to avoid.

Try and agree on a clear plan of when you will see your supervisor and what stages of work are expected and when. It is important to set up regular supervisions in the early stages of your work; these will probably become less frequent once you are fully engrossed. After the first stages, you will need to see your supervisor regularly (at not too close intervals) to keep a check on what you are involved in, to ask questions and to hear about further sources and contacts. The supervisor will also need to be closely involved when you are developing complex concepts, to check whether your interpretation of the reading and data is seemingly appropriate and successful so far. It is important that you remember that, although you are under the direction of a supervisor, your research is your activity. The autonomous student who nonetheless ensures that he or she abides by the rules, keeping in regular communication, checking results and writing up appropriately, is the student who is genuinely undertaking his or her own research. You need to keep a firm balance between managing necessary autonomy and individual, independent research, without losing touch with your supervisor and the demands of the university regulations.

● Managing your supervisor

This section covers:

- getting on with supervisors
- what can go wrong
- what you can reasonably expect
- managing difficult and changing relationships.

Students have problems with:

Personality factors:

- neglect by supervisor

- clash of personalities
- barriers to communication arising from age, class, race, gender, and so on
- differences in approach to work.

Professional factors:

- a misinformed supervisor or one without sufficient knowledge in the area supervised
- a supervisor with few genuine research interests, or interests that differ fundamentally from those of the student.

Organisational factors:

- a supervisor having too many students to supervise
- a supervisor too busy with administration
- a supervisor's inability to manage his or her research group or his or her numbers of researchers efficiently
- departmental facilities and arrangements isolating the student
- inadequate support services and provision of equipment.

Research suggests that students' dissatisfaction with the development of their work, and with relations with supervisors, can be avoided if there is clear and open communication on all aspects of the project. Also, overall, there needs to be structure without a straitjacket; that is, a framework for supervision and studies that facilitates rather than hinders students' development and creativity. A sound structure helps students to be aware of rules, demands and constraints, time limits and protocols. Within this structure they feel supported intellectually by supervisors and can develop their own individual, independent research as far as is possible. Structures also ensure fair play and provide systems for dealing with problems such as personality clashes, and misunderstandings about roles and work responsibilities (see Wisker, Robinson, Trafford *et al.* 2003).

To avoid these kinds of problems, both researcher and supervisors need to make it very clear to each other at the outset where the different responsibilities lie and agree what roles and responsibilities they will each take on. It is in the spirit of this need that the idea of developing contracts emerges. It is in the spirit of an ongoing need for support and discussion, which the supervisor cannot always supply, that the idea of peer support systems and co-counselling has developed. It is in the spirit of recognising the need to develop ways of overcoming the difficulties of distance research students, whether in the UK or abroad, that distance systems to cope with such problems and a different kind of pacing of agreed activities have to be set up and maintained. Some of these needs can be satisfied by the development of contracts, others by peer support networks and structures.

Research students need to develop autonomy. They need to plan and action their research projects, and use the support of the supervisor and research colleagues to guide them, help clarify difficult issues, test hypotheses and the importance of data, and provide support and redirection in crises if necessary.

Autonomy, negotiation and the development of shared responsibilities should result from the establishment of sound research practices and good, clear relationships with supervisors that put the supervisor in a position as facilitator and the student in a position where they are well informed. A student needs to be sure of what to expect in the nature of supervision, well aware of rules and formats, dates, what he or she can ask of the supervisor and where peer groups can help him or her to share ideas and develop with a sense of both communicative peer support and of ownership of his or her work. As useful additions to formal, timetabled supervision sessions, peer- and group-based sessions and systems can make life easier and much more productive all round, and a lower drop-out rate and better quality of work are predictable, tangible outcomes. Some of the problems that have emerged, and are noted in the literature, include clashes of perspective and approach based on methodology, and other more fundamental differences such as gender, ethnicity, values, age and a variety of other differences. In some other instances, the relationship itself is seen as less than supportive or developmental, being rather one of power and authority. Indeed, however friendly and professional your relationship with your supervisor becomes, it is important to remember that the supervisor is in a position of authority in deciding the quality of your work, as well as a position of advocacy in helping to support you and your work in communications and relationships with university authorities, outside bodies and future employers or colleagues.

Things to do

Consider:

- Are there any problems that you foresee?
- What can you do to avoid or cope with them?
- What do you need to do immediately to set up good working relationships?

● Things to ask/not to ask your supervisor(s)

What you can reasonably expect

It is good to have a clear relationship with your supervisor, with clear parameters. Here are some of the situations in which you can or cannot reasonably expect help:

- asking the supervisor to help clarify stages of the research
- asking the supervisor to put you in touch with information, people who can give you information and books that he or she knows of.

However:

- do not expect the supervisor to do the research for you
- do not let the supervisor do the research for you
- do not be steamrollered into something totally irrelevant to your project but topical for the supervisor.

Before supervisions, decide:

- what questions you need to look at
- what problems you have
- what you feel you can ask from the supervisor
- what outcomes you have in mind; for example, what you would like to achieve from this particular supervision at this point in your research. It might be assurance that your direction is right, that your data is interesting and valid, or a chance to test out a hypothesis, consult on a problem, or it might be to check out parts of what you have written with the supervisor to see if he or she feels that it makes sense, is fluent, and is written for the right audience.

Drawing up an agenda for each meeting, however informal, can help you both to focus on the important current and longer-term issues. If possible, consult with your supervisor beforehand to see what is on both your agendas, and so start the process of concentrating on the work to be discussed in advance.

● **Planning to get the most from your supervisor**

- Try to agree on well spaced-out supervisions, properly timetabled, not ad hoc chats (these are helpful, too, but should not be confused with proper supervisions).
- Get clear instructions.
- Get hold of the rules and regulations, and check with other researchers.
- Make sure you understand about length requirements, protocols, timings and facilities.
- Try and get on with your supervisor without becoming too friendly, so that you can both be honestly (constructively) critical.
- But remember that the supervisor has lots of other people to work with – other students, other pressing calls on his or her time – so ensure your time with him or her is quality time.
- This is high-level work – you are largely autonomous, but the supervisor shares ultimate responsibility for the quality of work – so you need to negotiate decisions and quality throughout.
- It is important to ensure clear communication and understanding of what is expected, in terms of levels of thought, practice and product. All these elements need to be checked out at the start, throughout the project, and at the end before it is written up.
- Do not take anything for granted.
- Find out anything such as regulations or dates for yourself as well, so that you are not too dependent. You need to know these things as they affect your timing, and your work overall.
- Check with other researchers about stages, problems and quality.

● **What research students can expect of supervisors – a brief summary**

While this is not an exhaustive list, it can give you an idea of rights and responsibilities. Knowledge of these expectations and interactions can help form the basis of a mutually successful supervisory relationship. You can expect your supervisor(s):

- **To supervise** – guide as to structure, scope, decisions about methodology, and so on. You can expect to be told if your work goes off course, seems misguided, is likely to be too adventurous and enormous in scope, and so on. Supervisors cannot give this kind of guidance without seeing and discussing the work in progress. They should be asked for this kind of guidance.

- **To read your work thoroughly, and in advance** – It is important, then, to agree a time for the supervision, select the work on which you would like advice and comment, send this to the supervisor and, if possible, indicate in what areas you would like this advice and comment. It is important to send selected items, but mention the areas that need curtailing and shaping.
- **To be available when needed** – They need mutually to plan regular supervisions, but students need to know that their supervisors are approachable in between these more formal sessions, if necessary, in order to ask key questions through a 'surgery' or other system.
- **To be friendly, open and supportive** – Academic issues need discussion, but it is important to establish a consultative, supportive relationship as well.
- **To be constructively critical** – Students can expect praise to be given where relevant and criticism, toned to the constructive rather than the harsh, to enable change. If you do not receive helpful information and feedback you might become discouraged. Gradually you will need less of it, as autonomy and judgement develop.
- **To have a good knowledge of the research area** – If the supervisor is not an expert, provided the student has access to others who are, and the division of responsibilities between first and second supervisor is clearly made, a supervisor whose specialism is related but not absolutely centred on the student's exact topic can still supervise and support.
- **To structure the supervision, and ongoing relationship** – so that it is relatively easy to exchange ideas.
- **To know how to ask open questions, how to draw out ideas and problems, and how to elicit information, even if the student finds communication difficult** – Some of this can be facilitated by working for some of the time with more than one student present, to aid discussion. If a student works with a supervisor who does not ask useful questions the student should learn to ask them themselves, and elicit information and comment in that way. You might also need to interact with other students supervised by the same supervisor, or on a similar topic, and discuss these kinds of questions and share information and ideas. This is particularly useful if the supervisor is not very practised in asking useful questions and prompting you.

- To have sufficient interest in the research to put more information, such as reading, resources and contacts, your way.
- To encourage you to attend appropriate conferences and introduce you to others in their field – Supervisors should encourage students to publish parts of their work and support them in the writing and editing processes. However, it is important to measure the amount of work put up for publication, and you should seek advice on this. Too much work published from the thesis before submission might endanger the originality of the thesis itself, and too many publications on only tangential topics will probably take your mind off your main focus. A balance needs to be kept between publishing and saving the work for the thesis, and supervisors should advise on this.
- To be sufficiently involved in your success to help you focus on directing your work later for a publication, promotion or job – However, supervisors are rarely able to provide the job themselves, so depending on them too much on this area can be an error. They can always be asked to be referees, and to give advice on jobs sought later (see Moses 1989).

Some of these expectations are really a description of how supervision can enable the student to enter the research culture and gain from its opportunities; others are about the precise direction, teasing out of complex conceptualising and research questioning, and editing of parts of the written thesis, which are probably the major parts of the supervisor's role. In some instances – such as science students working in research labs, or social science students on project groups working daily alongside their supervisor and others – it is difficult to insist on a complex and conceptually taxing supervision when you meet all the time. However, it is important to focus just on your own work. Arrange specific times for supervisions, with the kind of agenda discussed above, at different stages in your research. There is now a burgeoning literature on the role and practices of supervisors. Angela Brew and Tai Peseta from the University of Sydney note, for instance:

> In our work with research higher degree supervisors we asked them: 'What's special about your supervision?' Some people thought their supervision was good because they were solicitous of the needs of their students. Others pointed to the way they integrated their students into an international community of researchers. In other words, some supervisors were thinking of supervision as research and some were

> thinking of it as teaching. We know from research on supervisory practices that the main influence on how people supervise is how they themselves were supervised. Supervision development has traditionally been about tips and techniques, yet this does nothing to change supervisors' underlying views of supervision. ... it is important for supervisors to move to a more theorised/more considered position. We have concluded that it does not particularly matter if supervisors think of supervision as teaching or as research. However, it does matter what conception of teaching or what conception of research the supervisor has and it does matter that they can articulate these within an overall a rationale for supervision (Brew and Peseta 2005).

You are developing as a researcher and it is important to engage with research communities. Your supervisor can help you with this whether he or she perceives the work with you as teaching or as a research activity in itself. Working closely with your supervisor, it is more probable that he or she will suggest conferences and opportunities for publication, sometimes the kind of joint publication that helps a student gain a reputation from the coupling of his or her name with that of the established supervisor. Be careful, in such instances, that you are not having your work merely 'stolen'.

● Stages of supervisions – what you might expect at different stages

At different stages of the supervision process, supervisors should support students' work and advise in different ways, while maintaining a close but not too intrusive eye on the general way in which the work is developing. If it feels helpful, it might be an idea to check with your supervisor whether he or she is happy to take the following responsibilities and elements of the role on board, and what is expected of you in your work. This, too, will form the basis of a formal or informal learning contract, and give each of you an idea of what to expect from the other.

The beginning of the supervisory process

Supervisors should be expected to:

- help define and clarify a title
- suggest and evaluate proposed methodologies
- ensure students carry out any necessary preliminary other skills development and study; for example, research methods, statistics training

- help shape initial plans
- help refine and define the field, methodology, scope and nature of the research
- encourage realistic approaches and hopes
- put contacts and reading your way
- encourage early outlines, and the refining of these outlines
- encourage the development of good time-management habits
- set up a pattern of supervisions early on, which can be modified with need
- put you in touch with other research students
- help design useful learning situations for you, and take advantage of openings that could help you develop.

Ongoing – in the middle stages of your work

The supervisor should be expected to:

- stay in touch but not be overly intrusive, unless necessary
- care about the development of the research and work on it
- encourage conversations that enable you to conceptualise and deal with difficult underpinning ideas and constructions of knowledge
- establish a role model of modes of research, ethical decision making, commitment and perseverance, being realistic, and so on
- teach the craft of research – that is, ensuring students are aware of the importance of setting up well-defined ethical experiments, managing data appropriately and fairly, producing sound reports and a well-argued, well-documented, well-evidenced thesis
- read your work thoroughly
- consider your questions, and the questions you should be asking
- help tease out difficult issues and problems
- give constructive criticism
- wean you away into autonomy gently and gradually
- encourage your academic role development
- encourage you to keep very good notes and references
- support you realistically through any crises in the work.

Towards the final stages of your work

The supervisor should be expected to:

- encourage you to start to write up as soon as you can, and alter it if necessary (but not leave it too late)
- encourage you to edit

- encourage you to disseminate at conferences and through publications as soon as you and your data are ready, and help you with this without taking over
- encourage you to produce a well-presented final thesis
- encourage you to prepare thoroughly and fully for the viva, to believe in yourself and to consider possible questions
- encourage you to move on further, as appropriate, in the field when you have achieved your postgraduate qualification.

The relationship with your supervisor(s) is a long-term one and is essentially designed to help you to become a sound and successful researcher. You need to ensure that you do not depend too much on the supervisor(s), and do not take too much for granted. It is essential to be open and frank about mutual expectations and needs. Consider what Ingrid Moses has to say about the start of the project in particular, from the supervisor's point of view:

> Becoming a supervisor is a two-way process. Openness in the initial discussions may prevent years of frustration for you and the student if your personality and learning/teaching styles are mismatched and no common style or ground is found. Openness about your own and the student's competence may prevent the student from withdrawing or failing (Moses 1989: 10).

Things to do

Consider:

- What do you really want to achieve in your research?
- How can your supervisors help you to achieve this?
- Who else can help you?

● Planning work and supervisions

Considering some of these issues and practices should help you with the planning and managing of your research and your supervisor. You have a right to adequate and good quality supervision (see Delamont *et al.* 1997). You will also find it useful to get into good working habits with your supervisor(s) and maintain good relations so that you can exchange ideas, seek and use suggestions, and avoid any personality clashes. You will also find it useful to ensure that you get in touch with other peers, seek and maintain peer support

Things to do

Consider:

- What kind of agenda will you need to sort out with your supervisor at the early meetings?
- What is essential in a learning contract between you?
- What do you want to ensure happens?
- What do you want to ensure does not happen?

for research in progress work (see Chapter 10) and troubleshoot. But it is up to you to manage your project and your time, and to have a clear idea of what your goals are. You should also be realistic with what you plan; how you work; when things are going wrong and how to readjust; when things are going well; and how to ensure that you produce a sufficiently conceptually complex, well-researched, well-expressed and argued, well-presented postgraduate research project that genuinely contributes to research in the field. This can, and should, be a very satisfying process and experience.

Things to do

Consider:

- Who can you approach to be your supervisor(s)?
- Who might advise you on supervisor(s) to approach?
- Have you already been allocated a supervisor?
- Does the supervisor you have agreed to work with/think you will be working with have the right mix of methodologies, time, willingness, and so on? If not, who could be brought in to balance this lack?

You will need to have these issues clear in your own mind before you start to work with your supervisor(s) so you know what to aim for, what to avoid or overcome, and what kind of help you will find useful. Of course, some of your needs will change during the project and you will need to continue and develop a supportive/constructively critical dialogue with your supervisor(s) to enable you in your work.

Decide on how you want to and need to develop your skills, what to ensure happens and what to avoid. Concentrate on what you can you do in terms of:

- time management
- project management
- self-management
- management of your supervisor.

Before going to the first supervision you need to decide what kinds of activities you will be involved in with your supervisor(s) in the first supervision, what your agenda is, what your short- and longer-term aims are and how you would like the supervisory relationship to work. It is important to set the tone right at the first meeting, and to establish a formal or informal contract between you about mutual working practices, and expectations from the supervisory process.

You might well plan to set up a learning contract with your supervisor(s) on your first meeting. These greatly enable smooth working practices between you and clarify what kinds of 'ground rules' of expectations and behaviours you will be working towards over time (it is a long-term relationship, remember).

Conclusion

We have looked at:

- [ ] Choosing your supervisor

- [ ] Working with internal regulations

- [ ] What you can and cannot expect from your supervisor

- [ ] Potential difficulties with supervisors and how to avoid them.

● Further reading

Anderson, G., Boud, D. and Sampson, J. (eds) (1996) *Learning Contracts: A Practical Guide* (London: Kogan Page).

Brew, A. and Peseta, T. (2005) 'Is Research Higher Degree Supervision Teaching or Is It Research? What Difference Does it Make?', Paper presented at the Society for Teaching and Learning in Higher Education (STLHE) Conference, University of Ottawa, Canada, 16–19 June.

Delamont, S., Atkinson, P. and Parry, O. (1997) *Supervising the PhD: A Guide to Success* (Buckingham: Open University Press).

Leonard, D. (2001) *A Women's Guide to Doctoral Studies* (Buckingham: Open University Press).

Moses, I. (1989) *Supervising Postgraduates* (Sydney: HERDSA).

Wisker, G., Robinson, G., Trafford, V., Warnes, M. and Creighton, E. (2003) 'From Supervisory Dialogues to Successful PhDs: Strategies Supporting and Enabling the Learning Conversations of Staff and Students at Postgraduate Level', *Teaching in Higher Education*, 8 (3), July: 383–97).

Wisker, G. (2005) *The Good Supervisor* (Basingstoke: Palgrave Macmillan).

5 Research Questions and Hypotheses

This chapter looks at

▶ Turning a fascination
  or a professional prac-
  tice or development
  issue into a research
  area or topic
▶ Turning a research
  area or topic into a
  hypothesis or questio
▶ An introduction to
  gaps and boundaries
▶ Moving from topic to
  title
▶ Starting to define the
  research design

firststage

This chapter looks at the first stages of your work, defining and recognising your methodology, and turning research ideas and interests into research questions or hypotheses. Your hypothesis or question is the first real step in developing the ideas and interests you have into something that can be researched and enquired about in a manageable, well-shaped way. The defining of a good research question (and then sub-questions to help you get at or ask your question) leads to the development of research designs that are workable and can be expressed in a research proposal, which can be seen as a kind of map or pattern for your developing work.

Students choose to undertake dissertations or theses for many different reasons. The dissertation is a compulsory part of most honours degrees and MAs, so, clearly in most cases, in the first instance, you might undertake the research because it is a compulsory part of a course. However, what you decide to research and why can be governed by a host of reasons, including work demands, personal choice, what is available, what has been successful to date, and your own desire for personal development. You might be expected to research a topic that a manager or a scientific team leader feels will fit in with developments and needs at work, or with the overall research project being undertaken by the team. Alternatively, you might be free to choose an area that fascinates you. The different contexts and drives to undertake the research project to some extent affect the kind of area and research question asked or hypothesis developed and tested. For students undertaking research related to their profession, it could be that quite a limited focus is expected, or a focus that could result in the development and evaluation of a change, with recommendations – all of which would be more suited to a report based on a project and might actually not have the theorising and problematising necessary for a thesis or dissertation. If you are undertaking research as part of a science or social science group project, you might find your focus limited to a straightforward and specific experiment with limited generalisability. Some students choose research topics that will enable them to pursue cultural, intellectual, emotional and personal fascinations. Some choose research projects they know they can manage, some deliberately stretch themselves into new skills, new topics, new areas, and perhaps into creativity. Some want to develop their skills as researchers, their abilities as people and see undertaking research as a personal development – a mission, maybe.

Whatever your reason for undertaking this research, you will need to think about what your hypothesis or question is, how you can ask and answer (or address it) using what methodology/ies, design and methods, and what your findings might contribute to human knowledge and our developing understanding of the area in which you have researched.

● Developing research questions or hypotheses for research proposals and the research

Some of the first supervision sessions with your supervisor – often even before you have actually registered for your award – will be spent on activities of definition and clarification; the development of appropriate, focused research questions or hypotheses to drive and underpin the research throughout; and the early development of conceptual frameworks to the research – that is, the identifying of the concepts, the ideas and the theories that underpin the work. We will look at conceptual frameworks in Chapter 7.

Let us look, first of all, at the difference between research questions and hypotheses. Partly, as with all research, the choice between whether you are exploring a research question or testing a hypothesis depends on a mixture of your worldview and the specific piece of research that you are undertaking.

Hypothesis

Scientists and social scientists that have observed or experienced certain patterns, and would like to try out whether there are logical and causal relations between events and/or things, are likely to want to construct and test hypotheses. A hypothesis is usually used in scientific research as well as in some social science, health and organisational or related research. From the Greek (υπόθεσιζ), it means to suppose, or suggest, something that can then be tested or tried out. A hypothesis consists of either a suggested explanation for a phenomenon or a reasoned proposal suggesting a possible correlation between multiple phenomena. The scientific method where a hypothesis is more commonly found is based on the testing of a scientific hypothesis which will have been based on extensions of scientific theories, previous experience or observations.

Research question

If you believe that knowledge is constructed rather than provable through testing, you are more likely to ask research questions than to construct testable hypotheses. You are likely to problematise given information and beliefs. You will be asking about relationships between people, incidents, contexts and events, and you will be interpreting what you discover in relation to underpinning theories and concepts. Your research design and processes will set out to explore, address and enquire, and try to construct some responses rather than final fixed answers, all of which are to be interpreted in context, sometimes generalisable to a variety of contexts and instances and sometimes more specific and local to the context and focus of this particular instance of research.

In this chapter we will discuss:

- the type of research you are undertaking
- research processes – questions and hypotheses
- kinds of research
- ensuring research ethics are followed.

To qualify for the award of Doctor of Philosophy the candidate must:

(a) Present a thesis on the subject of his or her advanced study and research and satisfy the examiners that it contains evidence of originality and independent critical ability and matter suitable for publication, and that it is of sufficient merit to qualify for the degree of doctor of philosophy.

(b) Present him or herself for an oral examination and satisfy the examiners therein and in such other tests as the examiners may prescribe.

(Extract from 'Regulations for Higher Degrees at a University', 1993, Anglia Ruskin University).

When you begin to research you need to decide what kind of research you are involved in; which sort or sorts would best suit your aims and outcomes; and then how to acquire, handle and process the information produced in your research. You will, of course, need to ask the appropriate research questions first and interrogate the information as you acquire it.

Methodology underpins and informs our research, while methods act as the vehicles to help you ask your question. Chapter 6 should be read in conjunction with this chapter because the methodology needs to be understood as you develop the kind of research question or hypothesis for your research: the underpinning methodology and the methods you can use inform and then action your research, and help produce and interpret findings.

● The research process

Research is about asking and beginning to answer questions, seeking knowledge and understanding of the world and its processes, and testing assumptions and beliefs. Research is based on enquiry methods, questioning and hypotheses or assumptions that you need to question and test. It contributes to our fund of knowledge about the elements and areas of the world with which we are involved in the research. Other knowledge might well be produced during the course of the research, not least among which is self-knowledge on the part of the researcher.

The basic process of research is based on inquisitiveness. The cycle can start with experience or a problem; a theory or hypothesis; or a question; a fascination with trying to see how, why, if, in what ways, why not, what if? The shape of a research process can often be seen as either:

(a)
- problem/experience/observation/interest
- in a more scientific or social science hypothesis, does this happen? What if this was tried? It is expected that if this happens then this will happen, let us see ...
- investigation and experimentation to test the hypothesis

or

(b)
- asking a research question – looks at effect of, interactions, interpretations, how and why things happen and work (or not), how they might ... and so on
- constructing knowledge and believing that knowledge is constructed rather than trying to prove it and believing it is provable, the world knowable and fixable
- searching literature and engaging your own ideas and work in dialogue with theorists and experts

- development of research design, choice of methodology/ies and the methods, vehicles that help you ask and address your question.

Both forms of research therefore involve

- data gathering
- data analysis and interpretation of the findings
- confirmation or disapproval of the hypothesis

or

- addressing or answering the question
- producing conclusions
- advancing our understanding and our awareness of the interpretations of meaning in the field, as well as our knowledge.

This leads on to further questioning, problematising, experimentation and data acquisition, and analysis and interpretation, or, can feed directly into findings, and changes in practice, depending on the subject area and intended outcomes, research design, methodology and methods of the research.

● Stating your title

Choosing a title can be difficult. It is important that the title makes a statement or outlines an area of study that can be explored, opened up, questioned. The title should pose a question; suggest an area, an idea, a part of a field of study that can be questioned; make a suggestion or propose an innovation; and suggest that you will check for its viability and success. At postgraduate level, it is not a 'say all you can find out about ...' kind of title. It needs to excite, suggest scope for enquiry and reflection, and indicate that it is complex and 'meaty' or sufficiently extensive for your exploration.

During the course of your preparation towards the submission of your research proposal, you will find that you develop and refine your title. You might even find that it changes during the research, if the findings and focus of your work shift due to what you discover or how the field itself shifts. (This is especially likely with longer-term MPhil and PhD projects.) You might well also find that your research question or questions change with time, becoming more refined and focused in light of what you start to read and discover.

Things to do

Note down the key terms of the area in which you want to work. What are the issues, questions and problems that interest you? Try to turn your notes into a question or an issue to be explained.

Some examples of titles:

The dysfunctional family as a vehicle for representation of social change in the work of Thomas Hardy

The relationship between religion and national identity of West Indian immigrants to Britain, 1948–1968

The professional socialisation of social work in Russia

These titles, by indicating relationships and developments in context, can easily develop into specific research questions that lead to research. A title that indicated the coverage of a huge area, without any underpinning issue of question, relationship and time frame, would produce work of a rather encyclopaedic nature – a great deal of information not easily organised into issues, questions or findings, but merely presented. For an MPhil and an MA, it is more likely that the work will be restricted in terms of questions, area, depth and scope. Some MAs are asking complex questions, but answer them in a more restricted time frame than do MPhils or PhDs (a one-year project rather than a project of three or more years).

So, the title:

The experiences of mature students in Higher Education: A case study at one university

would be an MPhil proposal because of its scope – limited to one university and descriptive in nature. It investigates, but does not pose a really deep question:

The history of GM fertilisers from 1950 to 1990

would also be at this level because it accounts for and documents, rather than asking leading questions. Both are limited in different ways, and are possibly limited because of the nature of the area the researcher seeks to study, rather than anything related to the researcher.

● Research questions

How do you turn an area of interest, a problem, a desired development, an area of enquiry, into a hypothesis to be tested or a research question? Because this book is mainly concerned with the social sciences, education, health, the humanities and arts we will not be spending a great deal of time on hypotheses but will mainly focus on research questions.

Research focus and question prompts

You need to think about really being interested in what you will be researching. Even an undergraduate dissertation – probably because it is the first piece of research – seems a very long project, and interest is needed to gain focus and to keep motivated. It could be a new or a long-standing interest. It also needs to be turned from an interest, fascination, or topic area into a sharper, focused hypothesis or research question. Both enthusiasm and organisation will help you sustain your interest and maintain momentum through this enjoyable, often frustrating research journey ahead of you, even in the darker days of dearth of data or drowning in data, and of writing up. First, we will consider how you identify the important concepts or ideas underpinning the area in which you are interested, about which you want to develop a hypothesis to be tested or a research question to be asked. Then, we will look at developing research questions. In looking at developing a research question, and in doing so, we will also look at gaps, boundaries and contributions to knowledge.

● Key stages – developing a hypothesis or research questions

During the research, there are several key stages and issues that need addressing.

One of the first stages is that of planning the research. We will look at this in further detail in later chapters. However, it is important to think about it generally now. Once you have decided on a title, you need to 'unpack' it and think about the questions and areas that need investigating in order to address the title:

- state the research problem or issue or question: introduction – nature of problem, why it is important, how research will contribute to its solution
- state the research question or hypothesis, in the form of an inter-

rogative question asking the relationship between variables, phenomena, events, and definitions of terms
- decide on subsidiary questions.

Asking research questions – setting out to solve problems

Much research starts out from asking questions, considering and trying to solve problems, or constructing a hypothesis about how someone or something behaves or could behave; and then testing out, trying out, working on these problems, hypotheses, and so on, using research methodologies and methods. It is essential when you go into research to decide exactly what your research questions are (or you will find that you could merely collect data).

One essential approach is to identify your topic and question, and the concepts or ideas within it. You then proceed to consider and break down a concept – asking questions about how it is constructed, how it works, what its implications are, what it affects, the theories that can be used to find out about it. The research student is trying out ways of measuring aspects of the idea or concept, so they break it down into fundamental questions and aspects and ask questions about these.

● 'Operationalising' a concept

If we asked research questions about the concept of 'family', for example, we would ask questions about what constitutes a family? Upon what theories of relationship, inheritance, blood ties and responsibilities, social justice and economics is the concept of family based, and can it be questioned and interpreted? Some of the questions asked which help open up, action or operationalise a concept are quite theorised; others are more practical and factual. So, we might ask whether family members have to be related? Sub-questions could involve questions that narrow down particular definitions in order to look at elements of the concept – you want to find out some things about family against the theories of what a family constitutes, so you ask questions about content and relationships – for instance, the number and ages of chil dren, number of parents, whether it was an extended family, with grandparents, and so on, or a nuclear family with parents and children, and then state why this matters in relation to your research question. Operationalising a concept or idea means putting it to work for you – opening up and questioning what seems an idea we just take for granted; problematising something that seems to be accepted by everyone; and then breaking it down into issues and questions about which one can ask further questions and observe interesting contradictions, elements, problems, changes, opportunities and ideas about which you can seek to research.

Asking questions about a concept or an idea – moving further

You need to consider your assumptions of what the concept or concepts – the main ideas underpinning your research area – are, and then form the research questions, the main question you are asking in your research, breaking it down into the fundamental issues and questions involved in it. You might ask more sub-questions, pose research problems and use them as elements of difference to help you differentiate between patterns and categories when you analyse your data. Categories, themes and patterns help to show similarities and differences between elements explored and discovered in relation to asking your question at the data gathering and interpreting stages.

It is through identifying differences and variations that the specifics, the individual elements of knowledge, perhaps those of your findings, stand out. So, the elements that vary and that matter to your research, once you start to interpret your data and produce findings and then conclusions, might be parts of the idea or concept, some might be parts of the population, some parts of the time frame or other elements of interest in the research.

For example, investigating and asking questions about the concept of higher education might include asking questions about what constitutes a student as such. This could lead to defining the field by finding out about numbers of students; their gender, age, class and ethnicity; their fields of study and study habits. It might involve moving beyond questioning what a student is to considering how higher education is funded; how the country does or does not invest in its students; revealing and exploring funding tensions – whether high fees prevent students from starting to study or prevent them from devoting their time to study because they have to work, or, just because they do work, whether they can develop work-related skills that will be useful alongside the studying; kinds of different higher education institutions; the ways in which programmes of instruction are constructed, managed and advertised; the subject areas taught in higher education; the numbers of staff; locations around the country; admissions; quality assurance; qualifications and so on.

The researcher then moves further to construct hypotheses (to be tested) or questions (to be investigated and the information discovered, interpreted) about the relationship between aspects or different elements of the concept of higher education. If they matter to the research, if their influence causes variation in the results and the findings as interpreted, then they are considered to be variables. So, a researcher looking at why students pick certain subjects to study and in what proportions they pick them might ask a question about the relationships between the variables of gender and subject choice, or between the location of universities and numbers of students attending to study what kinds of subject areas. These variables are part of the construction of the field and of the knowledge interpreted from the research data.

Things to do

Please look below, reflect on and respond to these prompts:

Picking the right research question

- Start with an area of research and a real interest – this is a long-term project
- What interests you?

Your research question needs to be of interest to you and to others – this is a long-term project, interest sustains enthusiasm and hard work.

- What is the current state of research and discussion in this field/area? What are the key debates and issues?

Sometimes it seems no one has written in the area in which you wish to research – maybe not directly, but there will be theorists and critics, experts, and other researchers who will have written about similar themes, used similar theories or methods, approached similar questions perhaps from different angles – you need to establish both that your work contributes to these ongoing discoveries and debates, and that you have found a 'gap', an area that has not yet been directly researched.

- Why is it topical?

Even if the area you are researching is ancient history, there needs to be a reason why you and others might want to look at this anew, or for the first time in the light of other developments and interests now – examiners also will want to know this eventually.

- Are you going to develop a hypothesis that you will be testing? Or a question that you will be asking?

This is a question that causes you to think about your view of the world as knowable through collecting facts and measurement, or through interpretation and relationships between things and people. It causes you to think about methodology and methods, as well as about your discipline or subject area. If you are undertaking scientific or scientific-related social science or health research, you might well be testing a hypothesis, an assumption that needs to be tested rigorously and proven or disproved using facts.

● Boundaries and gaps

As you develop your research area and question, you need to define the gap in knowledge that your work will fill and the boundaries to your work.

It might help to do a mind map, which identifies (i) the whole possible field of study; (ii) the area in which your work will fit, the gaps it will fill.

Here is an example on the subject of 'avoiding and preventing aggressive behaviour in the school playground'. The student wants to use dance at playtime as a means of avoiding this bad behaviour and developing children's abilities to express their energies and enthusiasms in a more productive way.

Example

Previous work on:

    Bullying
    Poor behaviour
    School discipline
    Music as a therapeutic practice
    Dance and body movement.

Concepts (main ideas to be problematised, asked questions of, ideas that underpin the research and which are often taken as understood)

    Behaviour and behavioural change
    Child discipline
    Development
    Dance and music as therapeutic and developmental processes
    Learning the aligning of body and mind
    School as a locus for development of socially acceptable behaviour

Theories (larger ideas that have developed from research and experience and which are backed up by bodies of knowledge that involve argument and ways of seeing the world – usually related to key theorists who have developed these arguments which underpin the ways we make meaning of the world) concerning:

    Identity

The gap in knowledge so far in this field relates to using dance as a way of controlling and altering poor behaviour, so that pupils can be seen to become more socially responsible: playground behaviour in schools, per se, has already been the subject of several studies. The boundaries to the work would be defined by the exact shape of the research but, plainly speaking, boundaries show us what we are NOT researching and methods we are NOT using, and limitations to our study – that is, things that, for some reason, we cannot do, ask or know, maybe because you cannot ask these things directly.

It is often helpful to look visually at defining your area of study, the gap that your research should fill and the boundaries beyond which it will not extend. Consider your research as resembling a slice of cake, where the whole cake would be the whole field of study, all the questions you could ask of all the people involved, or all the situations and theories involved. In all instances (impossible to do, of course), defining what your slice of the cake can be seen to be, what is manageable and just enough to be coherent, not too much to be confusing and too far-reaching, and something from which you can actually research and produce interpreted findings, some contribution to knowledge and meaning.

Boundaries

Whatever your research area, there is bound to be the moment when you discuss the focus with your supervisor, or think about it yourself, noting other questions you could ask, other data you could collect, other experiments, other approaches. If you did not define the boundaries to your research, it would lack focus: and so possibly, as you pulled together this vast ongoing data – which you would be collecting if you had no boundaries – you would find that you could not say anything coherent, it would not be full, merely overwhelming. So, it is important to be sure of the research question that will start to help define exactly what your research hopes to ask and answer, the gap in knowledge, and also the limitations or boundaries to the area in which you will work. You could explore some other questions and areas of information later; and after this research you can take your work further: post MA or PhD. Other researchers also might be inspired and focus on another slice of that overall cake, explore some part at which you have only hinted or have left unresearched. There is plenty of time for that, later. For now, you need a manageable-sized piece of research to do, in the time allowed, and to do it so that others can grasp what it set out to explore and ask, try out and discover, argue. They must be able to grasp how the evidence you produce can genuinely fit the claim you finally make about what the research has found, what it contributes to meaning. If you ask too much and do too much, you cannot hope to be that clear!

Figure 5.1 illustrates the analogy of the slice of cake and reminds you 'Not to bite off more than you can chew'.

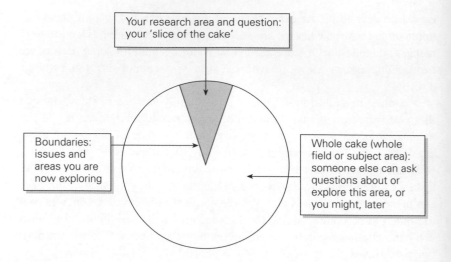

Figure 5.1 Your slice of the 'research cake'

From topic to title

- Keep it tight and properly boundaried – your 'slice of the cake': others can ask other questions and explore other areas and issues
- Do not set up a purely descriptive dissertation/thesis
- Set yourself:

  – a problem, or
  – a set of critical questions, or
  – a set of contrasts (for example, contrasting arguments about or approaches to …)

- You are contributing to ongoing debates and entering a dialogue in the academic community.

When someone else – an examiner perhaps, or the reader of your book – looks at your research question, he or she will probably think of interpreting it according to his or her own interests and discipline area, and with the methodology and the methods with which he or she is familiar. He or she might well think of asking it in ways that differ a great deal from those you intend to use. Bear this in mind as you refine your question and sub-questions, and develop a research methodology and design that will enable you to address the question. You will need to defend and explain these in your thesis or dissertation, and understanding that there are many different ways of approaching a question helps you to appreciate the best ways for you in your research. See below for some thoughts about the kind of research you might be undertaking.

● What kind of research is yours going to be?

You need to think about the kind or kinds of research you will do, what your research approaches are going to be, before finally deciding on your methodology and methods. Some of this will depend, as does the choice of methodology, on the way you see the world – as a problem, filled with facts, testable; or to be interpreted by different people, different ways, explored, responded to with an individualistic or social response, a creative response, and so on. Do please look at some of the views and approaches below. Our research, in this instance, might well be a combination of some of these. If most of it is merely descriptive, however, it will not be at postgraduate level because, in effect, the question it would be asking would just be of factual record, without conceptualising or problematising. It could add to the sum of knowledge but it would not expand our understanding or meaning   it would not be conceptualised. There is a deal of description in the early stages of note taking, investigating and collecting data, and even in writing up, but your work will need to move beyond this eventually to be of postgraduate level.

Things to do

Take an area you might be interested in researching, for example, divorce rates, drug abuse among the young, international students studying in the UK, religious worship, mature students, and so on.

1 How can you 'operationalise the concept', that is, break it down into fundamental issues and underlying elements and questions?
2 How can you ask research questions and take the different research approaches that would produce data about this area of interest?
3 What would be the questions you would ask, what variables might you take into account, how might you gather information and data using:

- descriptive research
- exploratory research
- predictive research
- explanatory research
- action research?

> Now look at research methods, as described in Chapter 16. This identifies dimensions of research.
>
> You might find it useful to consider and identify where in your research you are, for example, measuring, and where you are speculating and defining meaning – how much your research concentrates on gathering information and how much it concentrates, or perhaps should concentrate, on asking questions, criticising and analysing, generalising and coming to (tentative) conclusions.

This exercise aims to make you think about clarifying the dimensions of your research, and probably also extending them. Research in the UK tends to ask questions and critique as well as, rather than merely, detail, record and inform.

● Stages of asking the research question

Topic – fascination – work directive or development

↓

Research question – asking a question problematises and focuses your interests

↓

Gaps:
What has already been asked and discovered in relation to this area?
How?
Where can my work fit in and add new knowledge and meaning?

↓

Ensure it addresses a gap in knowledge.
Ensure it is significant – sufficiently important for the level (MA, MPhil, PhD etc.) of the research.

↓

Boundaries:
Decide on which elements to focus and what to leave for later (either for yourself or others).

Activity

Please consider:

- Could you use these questions and analogies about areas of your work?
- What example of research areas and questions might you work with?
- What sorts of issues about approach and interpretation arise, depending on the kind of research question and paradigm (see Chapter 7), research methods and methodologies chosen to explore it?

Conclusion

This chapter has looked at:

- [ ] Turning fascinations, directives, topics, broad areas of interest into research questions

- [ ] Identifying suitable and appropriate, important and significant 'gaps' in knowledge, so the research to address these is worth carrying out

- [ ] Identifying what kind of research this will be

- [ ] Identifying what the research cannot or will not cover, that is, the boundaries (for someone else to address, or the researcher to look at later)

- [ ] Examples of moving forward, through focus on area of interest, to a workable research question and design of study.

● Further reading

Denzin, N.K. and Lincoln, Y.S. (1998) *The Landscape of Qualitative Research, Theories and Issues* (Thousand Oaks, CA: Sage): 185–93.

Greenfield, T. (2002) *Research Methods for Postgraduates* (London: Arnold).

Holloway, I. and Walker, J. (2000) *Getting a PhD in Health and Social Care* (London: Blackwell).

Hughes, J. (1990) *The Philosophy of Social Research* (2nd edn) (New York: Longman).

Hussey, J. and Hussey, R. (2003) *Business Research* (2nd edn) (Basingstoke: Palgrave Macmillan).

May, T. (1997) *Social Research: Issues, Methods and Process* (Buckingham: Open University Press).

Miles, M. and Huberman, M. (1994) *Qualitative Data Analysis* (London: Sage).

Morrow, R. and Brown, D. (1994) *Critical Theory and Methodology: Contemporary Social Theory* (Thousand Oaks, CA: Sage).

Piantanida, M. and Garman, N. (1999) *The Qualitative Dissertation: A Guide for Students and Faculty* (Thousand Oaks, CA: Sage).

Robson, C. (1993) *Real World Research* (Oxford: Blackwell).

Salmon, Phillida (1992) *Achieving a PhD: Ten Students' Experiences* (Stoke-on-Trent, UK: Trentham Books).

6 Research Methodologies

This chapter looks at:

▶ Introduction to different methodologies in research

● Choosing research methodologies

As was explored in brief in the previous chapter, research methodology springs, to some extent, from the way we see the world, as well as the subject area in which we are working and the specific research area and question on which we are working.

Some people, in some instances, believe that the world is essentially knowable; that it consists of knowable facts; and that, if we ask the right questions in the right way, use the right research methods, carry out the right kind of experiments and processes, we will discover these facts or truths. This is often called 'positivistic research methodology' and tends to be found most appropriately in the sciences. It can also be found in some social sciences, including organisational research, where a hypothesis is generated, then tested and – where experiments can be carried out to prove that something is the case – results are collected and data gathered to argue that case, prove a point. Carrying out certain procedures many times increases their reliability and makes the research activities replicable in other instances. An effective experiment or procedure can be reproduced, replicated in another instance, and the same results will emerge (unless the context and/or other variables have changed). For scientists this is essential. Before releasing drugs, new cars or other products onto the market, they need to feel secure that they know how these will behave. This kind of research is positivistic, based on a belief that the world is describable and provable, measurable and deductive, because the research tests a hypothesis or assumption and typically would use quantitative methods to collect the data, because large amounts of replicable data are sought to ensure that the particular research activity or vehicle, or methods, are reliable for future use.

In the social sciences, one of the closest examples we have of such rigorous, reliable research would be that which is based in the theory of behaviourism (underpinned by theories informed by the work of, for example, Skinner or Bandura based on Pavlov), where human behaviour is considered (like that of elements, metals, gases or programmed animals) to be predictable in specific situations. Pavlov trained dogs to salivate when their food was presented and a bell was rung, then to salivate when they expected the food and heard the bell. The conditioned response has been useful as a way of training for certain procedures, such as swift action in first aid and loading guns, where quick, conditioned responses are appropriate. The research underlying behaviourism is essentially positivistic – people are seen as behaving mechanically and predictably, as do elements in science. Not all of the questions we ask of the world are predictable – many are to do with human interactions, perceptions and interpretations; many are based on a form of constructivism rather than something predictable and proven. Your research questions and subject area will also dictate the kinds of research methodologies you use to underpin your work and the methods you use in order to collect data.

If you believe that the world – and, particularly, human behaviour – is definable, fixable, provable, and can be discovered and described in a manner somewhat resembling rigid and unchanging facts, you might well be undertaking positivistic research, which sets out to prove things. However, if you feel that the world is essentially indefinable, interpreted, shifting in meaning based on who, when and why anyone carries out and adds the meaning – then you might be undertaking postpositivistic research of some sort. In this case, it will be your belief that, instead, we can ask questions but never gain absolutely final answers; that all data collected will need to be interpreted in context; that we make meaning rather than discover it as a fixed entity; that we understand through making links, interpreting contexts, and perceiving; and that our understanding of the meanings we determine from the findings produced by our research could be differently interpreted in different times and places by different people. They are relative. Such research is more likely to be inductive, that is, it makes theory and contributes to meaning rather than testing theory and meaning. It is more likely to be using qualitative methods. The latter, the testing, is deductive – positivist research　and more likely to be using more quantitative methods.

● Methodology

The choice of methodology and the methods for your research follows on naturally from your worldview and philosophy, and from the clear definition of a title and of the research questions that underpin your research. Different disciplines tend to favour different methodologies, but the choice is also dictated by the way in which you see the world and believe that you can know about the world, the kind of information you wish to discover and the ultimate outcomes of the research. There are numerous weighty volumes and shelves full of journals and works that will take you through the stages of research using each of the methodologies outlined here. This is an intro-duction to some of the most popular methodologies used most commonly by those researching in the social sciences and humanities. There is a separate chapter on action-centred research, which is used in health and social sciences, education and subject areas where practice is both the key concern and the source of the research data, and practice in the area into which the research results will feed, causing change.

> Achieving a methodological approach which is consonant with one's own values and concerns typically involves the longest struggle in research work and the deepest kinds of engagement (Salmon 1992: 77).

The methodology you use is a philosophical approach governing research practices.

Methods are the vehicles and processes used to gather the data. Chapter 16 explores these distinctions further.

For social scientists, the range of research approaches includes posi-tivism, interpretivism, structuralism, postmodernism, poststructuralism and constructivism. Methodology includes the following concepts in the context of a particular discipline or field of enquiry:

1   A collection of theories, concepts or ideas;
2   Different approaches;
3   Critique of the individual methods.

Methodology is the rationale and the philosophical assumptions underlying a particular study rather than a collection of methods, though the methodol-ogy leads to and informs the methods. You will need to define, explain and defend your methodology, and also the methods that you have chosen to action the methodology. Our chapter on methodology and methods will explain your ontological or epistemological views.

Ontology This means 'being in the world', self, subjects – how you experi-ence and perceive yourself in the world, whether you believe, for example, that the world is knowable and we all share the same sense of reality, and personal solidity, or whether we perceive differently, although we might agree to communicate as if the world were fixed and reality the same for all of us. Many philosophers have developed views about ontology, including, in the early part of the twentieth century, phenomenologists such as Husserl, Merleau Ponty and Jean Paul Sartre, who each debated how we experience and construct a sense of self in the world.

Epistemology is knowledge, most particularly of the ways in which different disciplines construct, interpret and represent knowledge in the world.

Methodology affects:
- the research questions you ask
- the kinds of research you carry out
- the methods used
- the modes of analysis used on your data
- what you can argue as findings from your data.

Methodology is the rationale supporting the choice of methods and is based on a researcher's worldview. The continuum of beliefs that underpin and inform the chosen methodologies, and therefore the methods and interpretations of data, ranges from perceiving the world to be fixed and knowable (positivism) or constructed (constructivism).

Table 6.1 illustrates the two main paradigms of research – positivistic and postpositivistic – and outlines the approaches and methods that they involve.

Positivistic paradigm	Postpositivistic paradigm
Concerned with hypotheses testing	Concerned with generating theories
Uses large samples	Uses small samples
Data are highly specific and precise	Data are rich and subjective
Produces quantitative data	Produces qualitative data
High reliability	Reliability is low
Low validity	Validity is high
Generalises from sample to population	Generalises from one setting to another

Source: Adapted from Hussey and Hussey (2nd edn) (2003)

Table 6.1 Features of the Two Main Paradigms

You will need to consider which paradigm better describes your own research since, from that, flows the design and methods used, the data analysis and its validity or reliability.

It is also useful here to explore briefly some of the main 'isms' of social science research: positivism, interpretivism, constructivism, structuralism, poststructuralism, postmodernism.

Positivism

- Positivism depends on beliefs that: human society, like the natural world, is subject to fixed laws; behaviour can be determined; and there is little room for choice or multiple interpretations
- Is associated with 'empiricism', 'behaviourism', 'naturalism', or the 'scientific approach', and tends to attribute 'scientific' status to social research
- Is most often used in research in economics, psychology, management studies, marketing, some health related (non-clinical) research
- Argues that knowledge and truth exist insofar as they can be proved.

Interpretivism

- Human beings are subjects and have consciousness or a mind; human behaviour is affected by knowledge of the social world, which exists only in relation to human beings
- The mind interprets experience and events, and constructs meaning from them – meaning does not exist outside the mind and the agreement of human beings.

Constructivism

- Based on similar beliefs as interpretivism, believes that human beings construct knowledge and meaning from experience and from relationships between things, people, events.

Structuralism

- All knowledge is historically and socially contingent – that is, based on its context and mediated by power relations, law and language
- Objective, rational laws inform human activity, the mind, language, behaviours, identity formation and interpretations.

Poststructuralism

- Like structuralism, sees language as divorced from things and events; relations agreed on by human beings (or not) in a context where there are no stable meanings, reality or laws

- All knowledge is constructed, interpreted, in a system of relations.

Postmodernism

- Similar assumptions to poststructuralism
- Knowledge and experience are fragmentary, and humans impose meaning and order upon them
- There is debate between beliefs about the construction and control of subjects in context or the existence of a decision-making human subject.

Things to do

Consider:

- What kind of assumptions about the world, meaning, subjectivity, interpretation, do you have?
- What assumptions and beliefs underlie the research you are going to undertake? Where along the axis from positivism to postmodernism might your own work lie?
- What do you understand now about methodology, methods, ontology, epistemology?
- Do these matter in terms of your research and its design and processes? And, if so, how?

● Research approaches

Below is an exploration of research approaches:

Research approaches – which are yours?

- Theoretical exploration
- Reflection on experience
- Empirical research
- Ethnographic
- Experimental
- Descriptive
- Exploratory
- Predictive
- Explanatory
- Practitioner- and/or action-related
- Creative

You need to understand that your research could be a combination of some of these; however, you also need to determine what your research approaches are.

It is perfectly acceptable to carry out a theoretical research project. A dissertation/thesis expanding and arguing the different ideological constructions underlying your perceptions of, for instance, something as serious as the position of refugees would produce several different angles and, thereby, different theoretical perspectives. Here are some examples: being a refugee/the refugee problem is a social construct; is due to political clashes and problems, defects; is a choice for a freedom from oppression or to gain the benefits of a society that is not the one you were born into; the refugee problem is one that cannot be cleared up by social policies; is a symptom of an uncaring global society; the refugee problem is humanitarian and needs dealing with in humanitarian ways.

You can take questions as theoretical and philosophical, as contested views about the existence of God or the arguments within different theoretical approaches to learning. Each of these can be approached using different theoretical perspectives and probably/possibly different methodologies and methods:

(a) Perhaps it is a piece of empirical research in the real world, using field data about how refugees survive, their numbers, their views, views of others about them, social provision, prejudices, practical resolutions, politics;

(b) Or, if you are looking at the existence of God, you could ask people about their belief systems, practices, the social role of religion, and you could research the work of individual ministers.

Things to do

Read on through the following descriptions and define *your* research type(s). What kind of research is yours? It will probably be a mixture of two or more of the following kinds of research.

Descriptive research

Descriptive research aims to find out more about a phenomenon and to capture it with detailed information. Often the capturing and description is only true for that particular moment, but it still helps us to understand and know more about the phenomenon. The description might have to be repeated several times and then further exploratory questions asked about the reasons for its change or stability. An example of (completed) descriptive research might be:

Achievement of pupils

> ... the Government released ratings for the achievement of
> GCSEs and A levels in schools in the UK which gives readers and
> parents an idea of the proportion of pupils who are entered for
> numbers of exams and the proportion who pass.

Clearly this description would have to be repeated, probably yearly, so
that stability or change could be noted. It tells us something about the
achievements of pupils in schools and about schools that have low and
high achievement rates. The research that led to the data collection
and publication was not aimed at asking 'why?' questions but, rather,
'what?' questions, and so these tables and results tell us about a situation, but not its causes. This data does not tell us anything about why
the schools have these rates of achievement, and so any reasons for
choosing certain schools over others or rewarding them with increased
funding, or whatever, might result from the publication of the list,
would only truly be possible and fair when other questions had been
asked of the reasons for the data. This questioning would lead us into
exploratory research, which often goes alongside descriptive research.

Exploratory research

Exploratory research asks both 'what?' and 'why?' questions. It begins
with the question 'does X happen?' followed by 'why does X happen?'
and sets out, using a variety of methods, to discover whether what is
in question is true or not. Essentially, it explores both simple and
sometimes also complex issues.

Sometimes the ostensibly simple issues turn out to be complex
because a seemingly straightforward question such as:

> Do women shop in supermarkets in the high streets more
> frequently than they shop in smaller shops specialising in meat,
> fruit and vegetables, and so on?

has many underlying subsidiary questions and complex causes.

Other factors than choice or availability are involved, and these factors
affect or bias the experiment you might carry out to explore your
research question. For example, in this instance, the age, occupation,
social class, culture and beliefs of the women might affect where they
shop and why. They might be older, or single, and so perhaps prefer to
shop for small items regularly and so choose small shops, or have
large families and/or full-time jobs and find a large, weekly shop an
easier option. An exploratory study, which could gather information
about these variables (and others), would be both more interesting and
more useful for any further assumptions or action.

Exploratory research is commonly used when new knowledge is
sought or certain behaviour and the causes for the presentation of
symptoms, actions, or events need discovering. Returning to the
published lists of achievements in schools, we might use

exploratory research to ask more about the locations of the schools, their intake, class size, staff–pupil ratios, and so on. These variables will affect the achievement of pupils, it could be argued. The argument would need to be supported by the exploratory research. It could also be aided by explanatory research.

Explanatory research

Explanatory research also asks 'why?' questions. It specifically seeks to look at the cause-and-effect relationships between two or more phenomena. It can be immensely helpful when description and simple exploration have come up with a number of variables that confuse rather than clarify the assumptions and hypotheses.

Explanatory research might, in the instance of the schoolchildren and school achievement rates, compare different sets of variables. It might, on the one hand, ask questions and collect data about the class size, school teaching and learning methods, qualifications of staff, quality assurance controls and the attainments of the children. On the other hand, additionally, it might ask questions about the class of pupils, their background in terms of income, location, housing and living space, the number of other children in the family, whether parents are in or out of work, on income support or not, and the diet and health of the family. Tho one set of variables relates to quality in the school's delivery and the other to the background of the pupils. The two sets of variables need matching against each other before conclusions can begin to be drawn. Such research might be carried out to answer questions about:

> Why women in some African countries find opportunities to publish fiction and poetry while there seem to be no publications by women from other African countries

or, for example,

> In the UK, why it seems that fee-paying public schools with largely middle- and upper-class children from the Home Counties gain better grades at GCSE and A level than comprehensive schools with large classes in, for example, the north-east, where there are high levels of unemployment, ill health and poverty.

This could try to determine, perhaps, something rather more subtle about the quality of teaching and learning being delivered in each of the schools, related to input and output. Clearly, this kind of research could cause social and political argument! But it is certainly fascinating and much more complex than merely stating something about league tables of achievement or publication rates. It can also lead into or relate to predictive research.

Predictive research

Predictive research takes several variables and tries to predict an outcome. It asks 'what if?' questions. The hypothesis is based on data already collected and considered on knowledge and ➡

conceptualisation, as well as, probably, past experience. Predictive research is based on probability and can, for example, be used to predict: the likelihood in England, Europe or elsewhere in the world of seaside towns being full of day trippers on a hot summer bank holiday. It is based on predictions, which themselves grow out of repeated actions and events that have been studied. Predictive research takes several variables into account. For example, as above, the proximity of a hot summer day to a holiday from work, and the attractions offered at holiday towns near the coast, plus the usual habits of English people (and other nationalities) to visit holiday destinations on hot summer days when they are themselves on holiday, act as variables which all add up to a predictable result. If, however, the prediction were unfulfilled, other variables would have to be questioned.

Predictive research works by using knowledge gained from past research and events. It is also possible, in many instances, to experiment with predictive research and to control some of the variables to test whether the results change. Predictive research is based on identification of relationships between variables, so changing one or more variables could, it is predicted, change the outcomes. You can then deduce the effect of that variable on the outcomes, to some extent.

Action research

Action research explores and informs practice. It also asks 'what if?' questions. It is experientially based and usually set up to try and solve a problem, or try out a hypothesis that could improve a practical situation. Teachers, social workers, medical practitioners and other practitioners working with human subjects carry out versions of action research each time they try out an innovation in their work in order to solve a problem, or develop a new and useful practice to achieve a developmental practical outcome. It involves collaboration with its subjects, and seeks to research practice. Action research focuses on bringing about the change process defined by Sherman *et al.* (1991), 'doing research and working on solving a problem at the same time'. (See Chapter 18, which is focused on action research.)

● Methodology, worldview, methods, data and research

If you find your research demands that you collect quantitative data, you are probably measuring variables and verifying existing theories or hypotheses, or questioning them about different variables. One's colleagues are often much happier about the ability to verify quantitative data, as many people only feel safe with numbers and statistics, which seem to relate to hard facts. However, collections of statistics and number crunching are not often the answer to understanding meanings, beliefs and experience, which are better understood through the gathering and interpretation of qualitative data. Quantitative data, it must be remembered, are not mere reflections of a single established world of facts, they are also collected in accordance with certain research vehicles and underlying research questions and so are themselves touched and affected by the research question and context. Even the production of numbers is guided at base by the kinds of questions asked of the subject under scrutiny, so it is essentially rather subjective, although it appears less so than qualitative research data.

Qualitative research is carried out when we wish to understand meanings, interpretations, and/or to look at, describe and understand experience, ideas, beliefs and values – intangibles such as these. Here is an example:

Example

An area of study that would benefit from quantitative research would be the large-scale survey of students' satisfaction or, rather, their response to their Higher Education experience. The National Student Satisfaction survey was launched in the UK in 2005 and yields a range of information taken from large numbers of students. The survey can focus on learning environments, assessment, staff–student interaction and a variety of elements of student learning life, over different subjects and different institutions, and can act as a measure and a way of making comparison. An example of an appropriate use of qualitative research would be that of research into students' learning styles and approaches to study, which are described and understood subjectively by students, interpreted in terms of individuals' preconceptions and experiences, in interaction (see Chapter 13).

● Using qualitative and quantitative research methods together

Although we have just described the different worldviews that underpin the inductive and deductive approaches, and the quantitative and qualitative methods in their service, nonetheless many researchers combine both, using both quantitative and qualitative research methods and vehicles. The results of qualitative research into students' learning, as described above, can be measured to some extent in quantitative data, too, as the numbers of students choosing certain closed responses in a questionnaire or survey about their approaches can be set against the results they achieve in assessment tests, and the numbers produced can be quantified. The statistics produced do not, however, tell us all about how and why students succeed in their learning. There are so many variables – such as the kind of teaching and learning methods, types of assessment methods, timing, student ability, and so on – that it is difficult to make assumptions that some kinds of learning approach lead inevitably to success or failure in higher education assessment tests.

Subjectivity exists in both kinds of research methodologies, as it does also in what could be termed 'pure', scientific research where scientists carry out well-managed and well-documented experiments. Their choice of experiments and, to some extent, the questions they ask of the data in order to interpret it, are based on essentially subjective research questions, a need to know some things rather than others. This can be determined by different times and places, different needs and abilities, the opportunities for different kinds of study, and different subjects.

The most important issue to remember when developing your research methodology and deciding on the research methods is to ensure that these can really help you ask your research question. Research designs differ because of the ways we see the world, and the appropriateness of certain methods to help us ask our questions and get us somewhere near something like an answer.

Conclusion

☐ This chapter has considered research methodologies based on worldviews, and looked at the ways in which you might approach your research, the methods you might use, in relation to the methodology you are using.

● Further reading

Greenfield, T. (2002) *Research Methods for Postgraduates* (London: Arnold).

Holloway, I. and Walker, J. (2000) *Getting a PhD in Health and Social Care* (London: Blackwell).

Hughes, J. (1990) *The Philosophy of Social Research* (2nd edn) (New York: Longman).

Hussey, J. and Hussey, R. (2003) *Business Research* (2nd edn) (Basingstoke: Palgrave Macmillan).

May, T. (1997) *Social Research: Issues, Methods and Process* (Buckingham: Open University Press).

Miles, M. and Huberman, M. (1994) *Qualitative Data Analysis* (London: Sage).

Morrow, R. and Brown, D. (1994) *Critical Theory and Methodology: Contemporary Social Theory* (Thousand Oaks, CA: Sage).

O'Leary, Z. (2004) *The Essential Guide to Doing Research* (Thousand Oaks, CA: Sage).

Piantanida, M. and Garman, N. (1999) *The Qualitative Dissertation: A Guide for Students and Faculty* (Thousand Oaks, CA: Sage).

Robson, C. (1993) *Real World Research* (Oxford: Blackwell).

Williams, D. (2005) *The Essential Guide to Postgraduate Study* (Thousand Oaks, CA: Sage).

7 Conceptual Frameworks

This chapter looks a

▶ How do you clarify
   what is meant by a
   conceptual framewo▪
   or underpinning
   concepts and theorie▪
   which will then help
   scaffold, underpin an▪
   weave through your
   work?

▶ How can you define
   and clarify the
   concepts (ideas,
   issues) that underpin▪
   your work? How can▪
   you problematise
   concepts that seem
   be taken for granted
   so that you are ques▪
   tioning what is given
   and genuinely asking
   conceptualised ques▪
   tions, rather than
   merely gathering da▪
   and being 'busy' in
   your research?

▶ How can you ensure
   that you work conce▪
   tually as well as disc
   sively throughout yo▪
   research and writing

▶ How can you ensure
   you have conceptua▪
   as well as factual fir
   ings?

▶ What do we mean b
   research perspectiv▪
   How might they
   inform and help sha▪
   your research ques▪
   tion, design, metho▪
   ogy, methods, data
   analysis and finding▪

In this chapter we examine the development and maintenance of a conceptual framework to your research. It builds on earlier work on methodology for research and considers perspectives that inform your conceptual framework and underpin your work.

● Research paradigms and perspectives

A research paradigm is the underlying set of beliefs about how elements of research fit together, how we can enquire of it and make meaning. For fuller thoughts and explanations of how your work might lie in relation to positivism, postpositivism, constructivism, poststructuralism and so on, see Chapters 5 and 6.

What are the major paradigms and perspectives driving the research?

We have looked, earlier, at the kinds of research you might be involved in and how it is useful to consider research paradigms. A research paradigm, or perspective, is the underlying set of beliefs about how the elements of the research area fit together and how we can enquire of it and make meaning of our discoveries. Some research projects combine methods. Denzin and Lincoln (1998) offer useful explanations of different research paradigms.

How do we construct and interpret knowledge? Critical theorists with, for example, Marxist or feminist research perspectives have given us new insights into the different ways in which versions, values and knowledge are produced. Their knowledge of the world (epistemology – see Chapters 5 and 6) is transactional (recognising that one set of actions causes other interactions and responses). The methodology required is dialectical and dialogic, recognising that as different readings and arguments are presented and set up against each other, knowledge and versions of the world move on through this interaction and dialogue, producing different understandings and expressions. Poststructural, postmodernist, feminist and cultural studies theories spring from, and are attached to, these methodologies and epistemologies. Much of their tasks aim to show that constructions of knowledge and of value, representations of versions of readings of the world and lives, are relative to whoever is doing the constructing and representing, where and when. To explore these particular research perspectives and worldviews further: their construction and representation have particularly focused on any group defined by the dominant normalised group as 'other' – women, Black people, the working class, gay men and lesbians, and so on. Critical theorists seek to produce transformations in the social order, in the way things are in society, and produce knowledge that is situated historically. It is both historical and structural, and relates to the possibility of causing change. Many feminist theorists and ethnic theorists grow from these constructivist and critical theory bases, some developing an interpretive perspective examining ways in which gender, race, sexuality and so on are repressively inscribed in everyday life and everyday representations. This is done in order to critique and expose these inscriptions as not 'normal' and 'essential', that is, the way reality is, but as interpretations, as constructions that could be interpreted and constructed differently (because they are relative – to time, place, paradigm, the interpreter and their cultural group and positions) (Denzin and Lincoln 1998: 191).

You might like to consider whether your research is positivist, that is, whether it has an underlying positivist paradigm that suggests that people/events/things are logical, linked and predictable. Or is it, for example, based on a paradigm or underlying belief/knowledge-constructed theory so that meaning is created through relating things, that is, is it interpretative – interpreting events and relations, or dialogic – showing a debate between different interpretations?

Any topic can be approached in a variety of ways, and so can be a particular kind or kinds of research. Sometimes sharing fields of enquiry and questions with other students or critical friends early on helps you identify whether the research is theoretical or experimental (trying, setting out and measuring results), or based on your own experience. If you approach their field, area, or question from as many of these approaches as possible, you could see how you might theorise differently, open up your area of questioning and use a variety of methodologies and methods to get at asking your question. It helps to open up the boundaries of your work before choosing the exact area you want to research and enables you to defend exactly why you have chosen this. It also indicates how to carry out the research, whether it is a theoretical study using documentary research, or an empirical study using interviews, questions and so on.

Different approaches and conceptualisations of the problem might or might not be equally valid. I think, as a supervisor, that it is my job to work with the student to develop a research question, a conceptual framework – that is, a framework of ideas, concepts, and a design of the study – that can be put into action and yield interesting, useful and achievable results. I also believe it is of great importance to ensure that the student is engaged with the development process, owns it and can be empowered to take it forward.

● Some examples of areas

How could you develop research questions and conceptual frameworks for these areas and intended outcomes?

1   'I am interested in researching how first world countries help third world countries to develop and to adopt the successful practices of the first world countries.'

2   'I want to find out why hospital nurses, who know about safe practices, still do not take appropriate precautions in their work.'

3   'I would like to look at writers who are interested in writing about representing the self – modern ones, a bit like Virginia Woolf.'

4   'I want to find out how effective my programme is to help stroke victims overcome physical and psychological problems, and get back to health and work.'

These are quite vague and need some prompting to become focused and boundaried – you cannot ask all the possible questions or explore everything in the field. You are filling a gap in knowledge – not merely reproducing someone else's research or synthesising other people's work.

Example

Let us take an example of a research interest or area and turn it into a question with the beginnings of a conceptual framework. You, or another student, might present your supervisor with the following example of a social science piece of research:

I should like to explore homelessness in Cambridge – its origins and range of examples, and ways in which we might tackle it.

One of my first questions as a supervisor is:

- Why is this interesting, and interesting now?

Then I want to know:

- What do you mean by homelessness?

These questions prompt thoughts about the conceptual level of your work. It problematises the concept of 'homelessness' (see earlier chapter on asking research questions). You are, here, questioning terms and ideas that are often taken for granted and so, as you ask your research question, you are more likely to uncover a rich range of ideas. Assumptions and beliefs, ultimately, are more likely to contribute not only facts, but also understanding and some enrichment of meaning.

When we ask questions about what we mean by 'homelessness', we begin to identify the theories and areas of reading that will underpin our questioning, and we also begin to see what methodology and methods would enable us to answer our research questions. An understanding of 'homelessness' that merely meant 'without a home' would miss the full richness of the concept – which implies being outside social structures, on the margins socially, economically and physically. It also sometimes implies a marginal state that relates to or springs from mental health problems, economic and emotional deprivation, and leads to economic and social stigmatisation.

I should like to discover:

- What is it about it that interests you?
- Does your research include the aim of producing a theoretical exploration into the range of its effects?
- Will you be looking at examples using documentary evidence (for example, newspapers)? Have you had first hand experience? Do you know someone who has?

● What angle are you taking?

Let us discuss some of the issues and practical implications around these areas of questioning.

The exact question will dictate the kinds of theories and concepts used to underpin the research, the methodologies and the methods used to ask the research question; the design of the study itself; and the ethics. If, for instance, you intend to find out first hand how homeless people live, how they became homeless, what strategies and policies are in place to support them, what opinions and beliefs there are around about homelessness – all of these areas of questioning would involve different research methods to attempt an answer. Your angle might be quite different depending on your own experience or even your job role. You might be involved in a development programme, or in investigating the working of an organisation. In order to ask your research question in these instances, you might ask how could you have access to the organisation, programme or sample? In addition, how could you deal with what might emerge in terms of information, blocks, confusions? You might observe, use a questionnaire or, alternatively, you could interview (confidentiality emerges here as an issue). If you are pursuing your question about homelessness, we might need to know who you would interview, whether you had experienced this yourself and what theories you were using to enquire (mental health, social policy).

● The nature of the question affects the theories and concepts.
● The nature of your questioning and understanding of the concept affect the ways in which you can ask your question and use your methods.

You might need to read in a range of areas to find current and established work and theories to ask your question.

Among others, narrowing the question, introducing those key questions about topicality, gaps in knowledge, boundaries and fitness for the purpose of a doctorate, will help the question itself become more focused. It is then more likely to be asked, and to some extent, answered by the conceptual framework in action, and articulated through the method and approaches taken.

After a series of such questions, the research begins to narrow down to something that is more manageable, although it is important to ask:

● Is this a general survey or an in-depth study?
● How can you gain access to this information? And, if you do gain this access, could there be a problem of confidentiality, since there

are many ethical issues and issues of access to the sample or population of this (or any other) research?

You will need to address those questions in order not only to narrow your question down, but also to get at, get into, access and action your question in practice. Working on an area with a conceptual framework in order to address a range of issues and problems, and turning that framework into a question for study so that it can be asked, is a time consuming activity. You need to work conceptually (at the level of ideas and issues) and in a down-to-earth practical manner, asking the questions in terms of the ideas, and also in ways that can yield answers (that is, are manageable, doable and practicable). This kind of work is systematic, thoughtful and quite obsessional, requiring skills of focus and persistence, and also knowing when to let go and realise there are some things people will not tell you, that you cannot find, and that are perhaps not there, or maybe they are not absolutely necessary to the research study, although interesting in their own way. Asking research questions is a finely tuned management of issues in practice to do with context/access, theories and concepts in action, appropriateness of methodologies and methods.

If you asked this question in a deductive manner, for instance, you would be testing a hypothesis, checking out in your research, perhaps, a belief or idea you already have and, so, carrying out largely quantitative research to test your ideas in practice. The resulting deductive piece of research would probably involve you in a questionnaire and analysis of documents. If the research is inductive, you are more likely to be asking questions, interviewing, observing, conducting focus groups to discover whether what you suspect is so, and, if so, how people respond to it. You can then build a model of perception and response from the inductive, largely qualitative research you have carried out.

Further work on asking your questions appears in Chapter 5. Focus on analysing data and working conceptually appears later in Chapter 24.

Once you have developed your conceptual framework, you need to ensure throughout your research and writing that you are working both at the factual level (data gathering and management, descriptive presentation and summarising) and at the conceptual level (questioning, problematising, contributing to understanding and meaning). Writing conceptually as well as factually throughout the thesis or dissertation is an issue we discuss in Chapters 22 and 23. Finally, the writing of the conclusions is an important issue, since you need to contribute both factual and conceptual conclusions. The former are a furthering of our factual knowledge, statistics about this, facts about that, instances of this, examples of that, while the latter help us ask what does this mean? How does this complicate or clarify our under-standing about the key issue and questions in the research? In terms of the question about homelessness, factual conclusions would probably round up the findings from the research and summarise in order to remind us of the facts we have learned from the data gathering and interpretation. They would, therefore, detail numbers, kinds and origins of homeless people in a particular location, the stated reasons for their homelessness, and the exis-tence of schemes to support them. Conceptual conclusions would be more likely to move a stage further, look a little deeper. They would enable us to ask questions about the worldviews and practices that inform the construc-tion of the idea and practice of homelessness, and its management. They would enable us to see that the origins of homelessness spring from certain social and economic forces at work in society that marginalise some people, and perhaps also empowering them to live on the margins, but also exclud-ing them from alternative life choices. Any solutions, as such, would then be seen as more complex than a 'quick fix' of more shelters.

Various works have focused on the development of 'threshold concepts' or absolutely key crucial concepts that unlock the way you think and see the world and ask questions about it in a specific discipline or subject area (Meyer and Land (2004, 2006), Margaret Kiley (in Wisker *et al.* 2006), Shosh Leshem and Vernon Trafford (2006) and some of my own work, among others). Our work has also looked at conceptual frameworks as modes of enabling the asking and answering of questions at a conceptual level throughout postgrad-uate research in particular (although some undergraduates also work at this level). We have also observed the importance of asking yourself questions about what things mean, how we can understand them, what key questions need to be answered throughout the research, within this framework of asking questions, approaching the analysis of data, writing through your thoughts and findings in a dialogue with previous work, and finally contribut-ing conceptual conclusions that add to and enhance meaning and under-standing. It is this conceptual level that makes the research a really worthwhile, even major, contribution and, arguably, the conceptual level must be present, in addition to the demanding management of facts in order for research to be sufficiently important to gain an award, most particularly a postgraduate award.

Conclusion

☐ In this chapter we have examined the development and maintenance of a conceptual framework to your research and have considered perspectives that inform your conceptual framework and underpin your work.

● Further reading

Cousin, G. (2006), 'Threshold Concepts, Troublesome Knowledge and Emotional Capital: an Exploration into Learning about Others', in J.H.F. Meyer and R. Land (eds), *Overcoming Barriers to Student Understanding: Threshold Concepts and Troublesome Knowledge* (London and New York: Routledge).

Denzin, N.K. and Lincoln, Y.S. (1998) *The Landscape of Qualitative Research, Theories and Issues* (Thousand Oaks, CA: Sage): 185–93.

Leshem, S. and Trafford, V.N. (2006) 'Overlooking the Conceptual Framework', *Innovations in Education and Teaching International*: 43 (2), December.

Meyer, J.H.F. and Land, R. (2004) 'Threshold Concepts and Troublesome Knowledge: 2 Epistemological Considerations and a Conceptual Framework for Teaching and Learning', *Higher Education*, December.

Robson, C. (1993) *Real World Research* (Oxford: Blackwell).

Salmon, Phillida (1992) *Achieving a PhD: Ten Students' Experiences* (Stoke-on-trent, UK: Trentham Books).

Wisker G., Kiley, M. and Aiston, S. (2006) 'Making the Learning Leap: Research Students Crossing Conceptual Thresholds', Paper presented at the Quality in Postgraduate Research Conference, Adelaide.

8 Ethics and Confidentiality

This chapter looks a

▶ The importance of
ensuring that your
research is ethical,
causes no harm and
retains the confiden-
tiality of those who
participate in it

In the twenty-first century, most universities expect
anyone undertaking research to consider ethics and
also to seek formal ethical approval for the research
before undertaking it. Achieving the balance between
ensuring that ethics are taken into consideration while avoiding being overwhelmed by bureaucracy is difficult, especially in universities that are only
beginning to ensure that full approvals are sought and given before the work
starts. In some respects, it could be argued that the procedures for ethics
clearance could be so onerous and the bureaucracy so labyrinthine that you
might be put off carrying out research that involves human subjects,
however harmless and benign it might clearly be. You will need to seek
some support from your supervisor in gaining ethical clearance for your
work if it does involve human subjects, even in the social sciences, rather
than in a clinical or scientific situation for which situations ethical clearance
first developed. The main point to remember is that it is important to protect
those who provide you with your information, to protect the innocent and
vulnerable, and to protect both yourself and the university from harm and
litigation – albeit that you cannot see any possible harm.

● Typical procedures and their history

Ethics in research

Research ethics have been a major issue since the Second World War when,
following unethical research on human subjects, the horror of the infringe-
ment on human rights initiated the insistence that all research should be
ethical. Historically, researchers undertaking research that involved human
subjects in terms of medical or health procedures would, as they still do, be
expected to seek formal ethics approval for their work. The aim of this is
straightforward – to ensure that no research processes infringe on human
rights, cause any kind of harm, or reveal the confidential nature of the individual participant's involvement. Much health research can be covered by

the Helsinki agreement which, when complied with, protects human subjects.

Whatever kind of research you are involved in, you will need to ensure you take ethics into account. Since scientific research has always claimed to be free from any issue of morality or amorality, and 'pure' in its concentration on pushing forward the frontiers of knowledge, whatever the issue and subsequent cost (think of the development of the atomic bomb and germ warfare, for example), the introduction and maintenance of ethical watchdogs has been a key factor in regulating research.

Ethical guidelines insist that researchers should not do physical or psychological harm and that, where human subjects are involved, the participants should give their fully informed consent before taking part. In some instances – such as in feminist research, or some action research for example – even though participants gave consent initially, they should be able to withdraw at any time and to deny the use of their information in the research. This refusal, should it happen, can be a considerable problem when writing up, so it is definitely advisable to cover all the ethical issues and answer all the questions on any ethics form, and ensure that all your subjects are fully aware of their rights and what it means to give consent. In this way, you will avoid or minimise later problems.

Other areas than those involving human subjects also raise issues of ethics, for example, those involving animal research, although, clearly, the animal cannot give or withhold consent. In this situation, an appeal to a broader concept of ethics is needed. It is also essential, if ethics are thoroughly taken into consideration, to think of the longer-term effects of the research. This is certainly the case with much scientific experimentation, and also some social science enquiry. Even if the actual experimentation seems to harm no one (this would apply to the development of bombs and instruments of warfare that are not actually being tested on people), the results of the experiments must be fully considered. If your enquiry and exploration in a piece of social science research destabilises your participants or their community, then you might well cause lasting harm (or perhaps lasting positive change? – you will need to think seriously about this). Other researchers now also need to comply with much stricter regulations. Students undertaking action research are made fully aware of the need to involve their research subjects (not objects) as fully aware participants who collaborate in and jointly own the results of the research and any interpretation or use of it. In much feminist research, the same kind of processes of agreement, openness and shared ownership are also commonplace. Students engaging in research into text analysis are less likely to find they need ethics clearance before carrying out their work. However, more students are involved in multidisciplinary research, for example, text analysis accompanied by interviews of the authors would be a case in point. This latter, using human subjects (in interview), would need some kind of ethical clearance together with evidence that details are kept confidentially and/or are approved by the participant(s) through informed consent to enable those details to be used in the thesis or dissertation.

Universities have codes of practice and most now have ethics committees who oversee ethics approval. You will need to talk with your supervisor or student advisor about whether your work needs full ethical approval; if it does, you will benefit from their support in completing what could be a very lengthy form. You will need to do this in advance of the actual data collection because it cannot be collected until any required approval is given. This could mean you have to wait for months for the next sitting of the committee. If referred for clarification, this could hold up the entire research. It is a good idea to seek ethics clearance as soon as your proposal has been accepted so that you can start to read, build the research methods, and can alter the design of your research if necessary when the results come through. In most universities, now, some of the decisions are involved with special, small groups of individuals, so it might not take as long as it once did.

There are apocryphal tales of students on Master's dissertations (for example, six months) who just gained their ethical clearance at the point of submission. For PhDs there is at least a longer lead-time. One of the effects of filling out an ethics clearance form – which asks you to explore and explain your methodology and methods, and your selected research processes – is that you are forced to scrutinise the way in which your chosen methodology and methods can help ask your question. Sometimes, at what seems quite a late stage (post proposal), you realise that some of what you expected to achieve is not possible and that other methods or vehicles would better help you ask your question. Sometimes, you also realise there is no way you can actually access the population or sample you had in mind, so the process makes your research more robust and more 'doable' in the end.

There is much debate in the sector about the terminology and the attitudes towards research implied in the terminology. Paul Oliver (2003) takes up the issue of whether to call those who are providing the data – are its sources – 'participants' (implying they take a full part in the process) or 'subjects'. In discussing the use of the term 'subject', he considers that this perhaps implies experimental manipulation, something being done to someone. However, in feminist research it is preferable to 'object' because it implies choice and engagement on the part of the one involved, from whom the data is being gathered. Oliver looks at philosopher Immanuel Kant's notion of the categorical imperative to guide ethics more generally. Kant argued that, in our choice of actions, we should act as if this could be a general principle – the transfer to the general meaning that ethical issues would be more visible, the effects of the action more obvious (for further discussion, see O'Neill, 1993).

If you arc using human subjects in any way at all, you will be asked to produce:

(a) A letter explaining the research aims and processes, and the final use of the results (participant information letter);

(b) A consent form for participants to sign that indicates that they give consent for the data to be gathered and understand how it will be used (participant consent form). You need to give assurance that data is kept confidential and that it will not be released after the research for any other processes or use without approval from the participants.

(c) An example of an ethics checklist for such research projects as are:
- not merely library- or documentary/literature-based
- not being carried out in schools as part of a Higher Education teaching course where the project is to be approved by the appropriate school/college authorities.

The completed checklist would go to someone related to the University Research Ethics Committee. If the person decides that he/she does not agree with you about the lack of need for clearance and that he/she needs fuller information, then the full form would need to be completed in consultation with the Ethics Guidelines, which most universities publish on their Graduate School or similar websites.

Here is a typical, more formal and specific element to an ethics questionnaire:

Example

Section B

If the research involves contact with, observation of, or collection and storage of confidential information about human subjects, then you may need ethics approval. Complete the following questionnaire and then follow the accompanying flow-chart to help you decide.

1 Does the study involve participants who are unable to give informed consent (e.g. children, people with learning disabilities, unconscious patients)?

2   Are drugs, placebos or other substances (e.g. food substances, vitamins) to be administered to the study participants?

3   Will the procedures use human tissue or include the penetration of a participant's skin or body orifices by any substance or device?

4   Will participants be presented with painful stimuli or high intensities of auditory, visual, electrical or other stimuli?

5   Could participants be required to undergo long periods of sleeplessness, confinement, sensory deprivation or any other form of stress?

6   Is there any foreseeable risk of physical, social or psychological harm to a participant arising from the procedure?

7   Will deception of participants be necessary during the study?

8   Will the study involve more than a minimal invasion of privacy, or accessing confidential information about people without their permission?

9   Will the study involve NHS patients or staff?

(http://www.apu.ac.uk/research/gradsch/gshome.shtml)

Even if the answer throughout is 'no', you should still send the checklist to the responsible committee member, or the committee, if you are a postgraduate. Undergraduates may possibly be able to avoid this procedure, but all must comply with the university's ethics rules – about causing no harm, confidentiality, participant compliance, data protection and so on.

Typical questions on a request for ethics approval form

Each of these questions would have a space for completion. If you complete this as part of a supervisory discussion, it actually helps you to focus on your research. Often, sections can be completed by copying and pasting in parts of the proposal. It is also, ultimately, a useful meta-learning activity: it helps you to be objective about the research design, acknowledge flaws in it and so change the design to be more manageable.

You would additionally be expected to use a 'participant's information sheet' and contact letter, as well as a participant agreement/consent form.

You will be expected to keep human subject data confidential and either under lock and key or on a password-protected computer.

Request for ethics approval

- Briefly describe the rationale for and state the value of the research you wish to undertake
- Suitability/qualifications of researchers to undertake the research
- What are the aims of the research?
- Briefly describe the overall design of the project
- Briefly describe the methods of data collection and analysis
- Describe the subjects: give the age range, gender and any particular characteristics pertinent to the research project. (*For experimental studies in the inclusion and exclusion criteria*)
- How will the subjects be selected and recruited?
- How many subjects will be involved? For experimental studies, specify how the sample size was determined. In clinical trials, a Power calculation *must* be included
- What procedures will be carried out on the subjects (if applicable)?
- What potential risks to the subjects do you foresee?
- How do you propose to ameliorate/deal with potential risks to subjects?
- What potential risks to the interests of the researchers do you foresee?
- How will you ameliorate/deal with potential risks to the interests of researchers?
- How will you brief and debrief participants? (*Attach copy of information to be given to participants*)
- Will informed consent be sought from subjects? Yes (*Please attach a copy of the consent form*)/No
- If there are doubts about subjects' abilities to give informed consent, what steps have you taken to ensure that they are willing to participate?
- If subjects are aged 18 years or under please describe how you will seek informed consent
- How will consent be recorded?
- Will subjects be informed of the right to withdraw without penalty? Yes/No.
- How do you propose to ensure subjects' confidentiality and anonymity?
- How and where will data be stored?
- Will payments be made to subjects? Yes/No
- Modification of proposal

- Has the funding body been informed of and agreed to abide by, e.g., Anglia Ruskin University Ethics Procedures and Standards? Yes/No
- Has the funder placed any restrictions on (a) the conduct of the research (b) publication of results? Yes/No
- Are there any further points you wish to make in justification of the proposed research?

(Taken from http://www.apu.ac.uk/research/gradsch/gshome.shtml)

Things to do

Look back at your research area and the questions you are asking:

- What ethical considerations do you need to take account of in your research?
- Are you using people in your research?
- Are they in any kind of work relationship to you?
- How and why would this matter?
- What would you need to take into consideration?
- If they are already dead – and so you are conducting historical research – are ethics and permission still involved?
- What if the data people presented is very old? Are ethics still involved?
- Are animals involved in your research?
- What else might relate to ethics in your research?
- How can you gain the consent of your participants?
- How might you fully inform the participants?

You will need to make quite a full statement about having taken ethics into consideration when writing your proposal.

You will need to continue to consider ethics in your research and to revisit the rules around confidentiality, consent and harm should problems arise.

You will also need to write up about the process of seeking approval, and of confidentiality when you write up your thesis. This part usually appears before the methodology and research design chapter, and you will most certainly be asked at any viva about what ethical issues presented themselves and how you dealt with them.

Revisiting ethics in practice

Before you fill out an ethics form consider:

- Will participants agree to take part? How are you asking them?
- Can you share information and results with them?
- How can you protect their interests?
- How can you protect yourself?
- Are there or could there be any personal issues of access, interpretation, etc?
- How can you manage these? Give and take advice
- How are you managing the information and data? Storing data
- Analysing data and drawing conclusions – how are ethics issues involved here?
- What happens to your research afterwards? Are there any ethics issues here?

You might find it useful to consider come of the ethics issues I have met with and discussed with supervisors round the world – the situations are described below and I will offer some of the resolutions I and other supervisors developed as suggestions.

Please consider these ethics cases:

1 Ruth has discovered her questioning of her population is causing them distress.
2 Mira has so far been refused access to her sample because she is an outsider to that group.
3 If Jamal uses extensive quotations or provides any full information about his sample it will be obvious to a reader who it is.
4 Ben has found out some information important to his research that it could be dangerous to reveal.
   – What would you advise them to do to ensure sound ethical practice?
   – Are there any implications for your own practice arising from this for YOUR work?

Conclusion

☐ In this chapter, we considered the importance of ensuring that your research is conducted in an ethical manner, causes no harm and retains the confidentiality of those who participate.

● **Further reading**

Buchanan, D., Boddy, D. and McCalman, J. (1988) 'Getting In, Getting On, Getting Out and Getting Back', in A. Bryman (ed.), *Doing Research in Organisations* (London: Routledge).

Horn, R. (1996) 'Negotiating Research Access to Organisations', *The Psychologist*, December.

O'Neill, J. (1993) *Ecology, Policy and Politics: Human Well-Being and the Natural World* (London: Routledge): chs 1–2.(1993)

Oliver, P. (2003) *The Student's Guide to Research Ethics* (Berkshire: SRHE and Open University Press).

Smith, L.T. (1999) *Decolonizing Methodologies: Research and Indigenous Peoples* (London: Zed).

Websites

http://www.anglia.ac.uk/research/gradsch/gshome.shtml

9 Writing a Research Proposal

This chapter looks at:

▶ What does a good research proposal look like?
▶ Stages and elements of a research proposal
▶ Submission and revision of your proposal

Your research proposal is the main base upon which a supervisor and a research degree committee can begin to judge the value or potential of your research work. Many universities now demand a great deal of work prior to the submission of a research proposal; in the past, little more than an indicative title might have been required.

Drawing up a research proposal is the first main task you will be involved in with your supervisor, after you have agreed on your research question or hypothesis. Depending on your university's regulations, the norm is to register for your research degree if it is an MPhil or a PhD, develop the proposal, and then have registration confirmed when the proposal is accepted. This could be a process lasting anything from three months to a year, in some instances. However, some postgraduate students will answer an advertisement that seeks researchers for a funded project in which they can complete an element of or the entire research project for their PhD. In these instances, most usually in the sciences and some social science projects, there has already been a research proposal drawn up and agreed. In this situation, external, or perhaps internal, funding has depended on a good proposal, and the supervisor is probably the project director. Your role, then, is to make sure that you understand and can action the proposal, and can also see which part of the overall project you are involved in that can lead to the achievement of doctoral level work, so that you not only fulfil the work requirements of the project but also obtain your qualifications.

For students studying for an MA or other Master's and writing a dissertation, you will already be on the course, and drawing up a proposal with your supervisor is an ongoing, somewhat swift process, usually with an early deadline to begin the work and a set deadline to hand it all in. Do check on university regulations well in advance as you enter your research degree, whatever its length and scope.

Before you submit your research proposal formally, you will need to carry out a substantial amount of early research work, some literature reviewing and searching, and to identify the theoretical and methodological underpinnings to your work.

What are the theoretical bases and contexts for your work? With much PhD research in particular, and some MPhil and Master's work, the often interdisciplinary nature of the research means that there will be several theoretical contexts and areas to which your work will be related and out of which it will grow. You need to determine and focus on underpinning theories that help you to ask your question and place your work in the context of underpinning ideas, ongoing debates and previous work. You will also need to determine how your work can be carried out, the methodology you will use, and thereby the beliefs and ways of constructing and discussing knowledge and ideas with which you will need to be familiar, and then the active elements, the methods, that will enable you to ask your question. You need to be able to show you can work with theories, methodology and methods held together in a research design in order to achieve your research outcomes.

You should seek support from your supervisor in the development of a proposal of sufficient quality that will convince a research degrees committee that you have the potential to carry out research at the level you seek. Master's research proposals often go before field or subject committees, while MPhils and PhDs go before full research degree committees (or whatever body carries out that function in your university) where they will be read carefully by internal and external readers and by the committee. The latter can raise some very helpful points about questions, aims, methods, theoretical underpinning and that fundamental question – so what? That is, to what will this piece of research lead or contribute?

The research proposal is a carefully crafted piece of work. It is also a very useful foundation from which to develop your ideas and arguments. You will be able to use it to help you plan your work and study programme, and to draft your chapters. Some of the problems you might encounter in your early literature review or work towards the theoretical perspectives chapter could lead to central underpinning questions running throughout the research. The issues you deal with in order to write the proposal will also run throughout it. It is a stage, and a substantial piece of work, from which you will draw in the future. You will also have to recognise that it is a compromise. Of course, by producing a detailed plan like this, you might well feel you are in a 'straitjacket' and this should be avoided. You will discover other information and arguments; you will find that some of what you seek is not there; you will change your mind and your emphases; and you will also find that the time planning slips, changes and so on. But the proposal is a draft outline and it will be worked with in the future in a dynamic way. For the proposal acceptance process, it is absolutely essential.

● What do you want to research? How you can draw up a good proposal

You might find it useful to look at Chapter 5 on devising a research question, then at Chapters 7 on the conceptual framework, 15 on theoretical perspectives, 6 on methodology and the chapters on methods in order to clarify the different elements in your proposal.

When you embark on your proposal, you are expected to identify your main research questions and sub-questions, to clarify elements of the research for yourself and for those judging the likelihood that it will be manageable, and significant.

Proposals tend to have the following sections:

- Abstract
- Introduction
- Theoretical perspectives/literature survey
- Methodology and methods
- Design of the study including what research is carried out when and how; what analysis is carried out when and how
- Timeline of work to be completed
- Some sense of the outline of the draft chapters
- Justification for the level of the award
- Biography of major sources.

Drawing up your proposal

In drawing up the proposal, you need to reflect and decide on the following general contents and the focus of each of these sections, and of your research and writing:

Abstract – This is a short summary of what you are researching; why it is topical and important; the ways in which your work will make a contribution to knowledge; your research question; the main theories underpinning and informing your work; and the methodology and methods you will use to undertake the research. (In your final abstract for the submitted dissertation or thesis you explain all of this and also add what contribution is made to knowledge – why the research matters.)

Introduction – This outlines the context for your research – new or established developments; topicality; any changes that make this important work now; your position and reason for this being a topical, useful, meaningful question to ask/piece of research to conduct.

Research question – Be precise and clear, and identify sub-questions.

Gaps in the current knowledge – So that your work can address this gap in knowledge, ensure it is significant – important enough for the level (BA, MA, PhD) of the research.

Boundaries – This should be an indication of what you will not be covering in your research; decide on which elements to focus and what to leave for others/later.

Theoretical perspectives/literature survey – The theoretical perspectives/literature survey element of the proposal is a shortened form of a literature review or theoretical perspectives chapter that indicates the major theories and theoretical positions, and the main arguments and work, in the area in which your own work is situated. It should suggest how your work will contribute to the dialogues and debates in the subject area. You need to consider which theories and theorists engage with these areas for your research; which theorists and practitioners have written about this broad area; and the underpinning ideas that inform understanding and questioning of the issues in your research and can be used to underpin, inform, and drive the research.

Conceptual framework – Here, you also explore the concepts or main ideas and understandings that underlie your work: concepts might, for example, range from profit/loss in economics, homelessness, pupil violence, adolescence in education, self and change; ideas should cover things we take for granted but which need to be questioned and problematised in the development of a thesis or dissertation.

What are the key concepts or ideas underlying this question? How can you develop a piece of research that will work not only at the level of gathering facts, but also at the level of asking questions about meaning, about concepts and working conceptually?

The conceptual framework should include evidence of your having searched the literature. Where have you discovered your theories – from what kind of framework? What are the underpinning theoretical perspectives informing your ideas? For example, you might use feminist or Marxist theoretical perspectives and work on organisational analysis, phenomenography, and so on. Be careful to indicate not only which theories and theoretical perspectives inform your work, but also how they are combined and how they relate to and direct or drive your unique (or relatively unique) piece of research.

Reviewing other literature on the topic in a dialogue with your own work is important here. Set up and explore arguments and link these with both question and argument. Ongoing throughout research for the thesis, theories inform all work

Methodologies and methods – You need to consider here which methodologies and methods inform and can enable you to ask your research question. Here, you argue for and define the worldview and the methodology/ies that will enable you to address your research question.

What is the research methodology, or research methodologies underpinning your research? What methods or vehicles and strategies are you going to use and why? How do they link with and help inform and develop each other?

You will need to know exactly why you have chosen the methods you have chosen, for example, questionnaires or interviews, because of the way they can help you get to and find out about your research object. Your questions and your conceptual framework need explaining. You should be able to indicate clearly how your chosen methods should enable you to investigate your chosen questions and subject area. The sample, your timings and methods of analysis need defining.

Research design – design of study

- Decide on methods and vehicles
- Decide on timeline
- Decide on population/primary sources
- Decide on data collection and analysis

How will you go about collecting information and carrying out each element of your research work, for example, literature searches and data analysis? Provide an outline of the different activities you will undertake at what points in your research and do a critical path analysis of this, that is, first, activities (usually a literature search), and then the research activities.

Ethical considerations

Many dissertations and theses have ethical considerations, and these will be particularly complex when you are using human subjects. Obviously, if you are involved in medical research this would be so, but it is also true of protecting the identities of those who give you information from question- naires, focus groups and interviews. You will need to take care when asking certain sorts of personal questions or using documents that refer to people, alive or dead. You also need to indicate due care and concern for procedures when dealing with those who are dead, and with certain topics. Some research – for example, that of nurses in hospitals – might already be covered by an established code, such as the Helsinki Agreement, so you need to say so. There will probably be other issues to take into account that specifically relate to your work. Other ethical issues arise when working with animals, with confidential material (however old) or with children. Look up your university's code of ethics for guidance. (See Chapters 16 and 24, which have sections on ethics.)

Outline plan of study

This part of the proposal asks you to indicate what you think would be:

(a)   the timeline for your research activities, and
(b)   the main features of each of your chapters.

It would be useful to revisit this at different points in your ongoing research and consider how they are developing and whether any early findings are changing these. It cannot be rigidly adhered to, but it is a useful scheme.

Justification for the level of the award

An MA, MPhil or PhD usually involves this question in any proposal. You will need to describe and discuss what you feel your research will contribute to the field of knowledge, the development of arguments and the research culture. What kinds of practices or thoughts and arguments can it move forward? How can it make a difference? Why does it matter and why is it obviously at this level? Is it serious, broad, deep questioning and is it suffi- ciently original?

Bibliography – primary references

Ten or 12 of these will be included in your proposal submission. Do make sure they represent key texts, the range of your theoretical areas, and some up-to-date examples. The reason for this is to show you are reading in the field, both in the seminal texts and right now in the current contributions and arguments.

You need to be in agreement with your supervisor about your proposal, as it forms the basis of your future work. You also need to be agreed about the

Things to do

- Produce a draft proposal/plan.
- Look carefully through this draft plan and discuss it with a reliable colleague or friend.
- See if you can justify and explain each part of it to your colleague or friend/to yourself.
- What questions and gaps do you have?
- What is still to be fleshed out?
- Draw up a plan of action to work on the elements that are not fully developed.
- Draw up your own draft proposal under the following headings. Remember these are as yet notes which that you can flesh out.

Draft proposal

1 Indicative title
2 Introduction – aim and focus of the study

  – Questions
  – Sub-questions
  – Context for the research

3 Theoretical perspectives and interpretations
4 Research methodology and methods – design

  – Research methods
  – Research design (stages of your work – over time)
  – Ethical considerations

5 Outline plan of study
6 Timeline for activities in the research

  1 from .... to ....
  2 from .... to ....
  3 from .... to ....
  4 from .... to ....
  5 from .... to ....

7 Draft chapters and areas
8 Justification for level of award
9 Bibliography primary texts

proposal before it goes before any research degrees committees, as it will be thoroughly read – probably by both an internal and an external referee, who will have points to make about the viability, the expression and the methodology. It is tempting, if the research proposal is accepted, to ignore the questions asked at a research degrees committee. However, some of the questions about contexts, methods and so on are going to be very helpful, probably in the formation of arguments and in the discovery of information and ideas, so they are useful to take on board. While early supervisions should help develop the proposal, a supervision after the committee has commented will help refine it further, so you can make a formal start on your research. At the same time as committees consider proposals, students usually begin reading more and focusing clearly.

Conclusion

We have considered how you go about putting together a research proposal. At all levels, such proposals are needed, sometimes in a formal (PhD, MPhil) and sometimes a shorter or less formal shape (MA). Writing them helps you to be clear about how your research questions and conceptual framework (of ideas, arguments, theories and methods) run throughout your proposed research. For MPhil/PhD most universities demand a lengthy proposal (about four pages), and this could take up to six months to refine and perfect. You will be researching alongside this writing, but probably will have your proposal agreed (and probably changed a little or a lot) by a research degrees committee before you are formally and finally registered. Sometimes registration can be backdated. Sometimes you might have to resubmit the proposal. This is perfectly normal. You need to get it right, as it informs all you do – so don't be too upset if it is sent back for rewriting – it will encourage you to be clearer, more coherent, and more likely to produce a successful piece of research which matters.

● Further reading

Allan and Skinner (1991) *Handbook for Research Students in the Social Sciences* (London: Falmer Press).

Bell, Judith (2005) *Doing Your Research Project* (4th edn) (Buckingham: Open University Press).

Cryer, P. (1997) *The Research Student's Guide to Success* (Buckingham: Open University Press).

Davies, M.B. (2007) *Doing a Sussessful Research Project* (Basingstoke: Palgrave Macmillan)

Phillips, E.M. and Pugh, D.S. (1994) *How to Get a PhD: A Handbook for Students and Their Supervisors* (2nd edn) (Buckingham: Open University Press).

Walliman, N.S.R. (2005) *Your Research Project* (London: Sage).

Part Two

Getting Going – Supervisors, Time and Community

10 Managing Your Supervisor(s)

This chapter looks at:

▶ Meetings
▶ Learning contracts
▶ Supervisory arrangements at a distance
▶ Ongoing arrangements

● Planning work and supervisions

Considering some of these issues and practices should help you with the planning and managing of your research, and your supervisor. You have a right to adequate and good quality supervision. You will find it useful to get into good working habits with your supervisor(s) and maintain good relations with them so that you can exchange ideas, seek and use suggestions, and avoid any personality clashes. You will also find it useful to get in touch with peers. Their support is most helpful with regard to research in progress and troubleshooting (see Chapter 14 on peer-support systems). But it is up to you to manage your project and your time, and to have a clear idea of your goals. You should also be realistic with what you plan, how you work and how you will readjust when things are going wrong, when things are going well, and how to ensure that you produce a sufficiently conceptually complex, well-researched, well-expressed and argued, well-presented post-graduate research project that genuinely contributes to research in the field. This can and should be a very satisfying process and experience.

Before going to the first supervision, you need to decide what kinds of activities you will be involved in with your supervisor(s) at the first supervision, what your agenda is, what your short- and longer-term aims are, and

Things to do

Consider:

● What kind of agenda will you need to sort out with your supervisor at the early meetings?
● What is essential in a learning contract between you?
● What do you want to ensure happens?
● What do you want to ensure does not happen?

how you would like the supervisory relationship to work. It is important to set the tone right at the first meeting, and to establish a formal or informal contract between you about mutual working practices, and expectations from the supervisory process.

You might well plan to set up a learning contract with your supervisor(s) at your first meeting. These greatly enable smooth working practices between you and clarify what kinds of 'ground rules' of expectations and behaviours you will be working to over time (it is a long-term relationship, remember).

The first supervision will take place before you have submitted your proposal and had it accepted by the research degrees committee, or whichever group at your university makes decisions about the viability of research degree proposals. You need to draw up your own agenda for this meeting concentrating on:

- Getting to know each other
- Sounding out the supervisor with regard to their availability and suitability, their enthusiasm and their initial responses to your project
- Drawing up an initial draft proposal in outline
- Drafting a title (see Chapter 5 for details on how to go about these last two activities)
- Talk through the aims and outcomes you have in mind, the kind of methodologies you intend to use, and any of the needs or problems you foresee (see Chapter 9).

In your first supervisory conversation, you can judge your supervisor's initial responses to your ideas and ways of thinking, and the extent to which he or she can offer further reading, contacts and suggestions about methodologies and their viability. For instance, it might be at this very early stage that the supervisor advises you to go beyond simply using a questionnaire for data collection, or asks you some thought-provoking questions about controversies in the subject area in which you are working, or tests your responses to how to deal with ethical issues, and so on.

It is important that your first supervisor/director of studies also includes your second supervisor at an early stage so that there can be some development of agreement as to the different, complementary roles they will play in relation to your work, and how you and they are going to work together. If these working relationships are not made clear early on, you could find that you receive contradictory advice and are caught in the middle of their debates. This needs to be handled with sensitivity.

At the first meeting with your supervisor, you can also decide together what form your future supervisions could take, their frequency and, in this first instance, the next stages towards preparing the proposal. A learning contract can help to clarify and formalise some of these working practices.

● Learning contracts

Research students are undertaking a long piece of work with many stages, at any one of which they might need guidance and help. Sometimes you work closely with your supervisor, or see them frequently, but sometimes supervisors and research students hardly cross paths and you might both be unsure of how often you should be meeting. It is important, for the sake of clarity and equality, that there should be learning contracts, clearly defining how much time, and what kind of support the supervisor(s) can offer, and what the expected behaviours of each of you are. Learning contracts can be drawn up to specify, for example, frequency of supervisions and the production of stages of work. These contracts can help everyone involved in the supervisory equation to manage their work and to point out problems from an objective viewpoint. A learning contract is like a legal contract (but less punitive and mostly informally binding) agreed between you, and will set out what you each expect of each other in terms of work, communication and responsibility. As you discuss your roles and draw up this informal contract, it will help you to make explicit your expectations of the frequency and kind of supervision, and outline what to avoid. Another shape to a learning contract is less about expected roles and behaviours or 'grand roles' for the supervisory relationship and more about ensuring you have clear goals and outcomes, and a clear idea of how to achieve these. You will need to decide what sort of contract enables you and your supervisor to establish ground rules and working procedures. You might decide to use the contract for just yourself and merely mention it informally to your supervisor.

Why use learning contracts?

Research has shown that when adults learn on their own initiative, for reasons of personal development (see Brookfield 1986, Rogers 1989 and Tight 1983), they can do so within a loose structure. However, when the purpose is to improve competence in a job, engage in a profession or develop a longer-term project (such as a research qualification), then the needs and expectations of other groups must be taken into account and the structure needs to be more explicit.

Learning contracts (see Anderson *et al*. 1996) also provide a vehicle for the mutual planning of learning experiences by the research student and supervisor. By participating in this process, the research student can feel that he or she owns the plan and therefore can be more committed to the learning.

Guidelines for developing a learning contract

Once you have agreed a learning contract, you need to fill it out in some detail for yourself.

A learning contract can be thought of as having six stages: learning needs, learning outcomes, learning resources and strategy, evidence of accomplishment, review, and carrying out the contract and evaluating success at each stage.

Learning needs – The learning needs are the gap between where you are now and where you need, or want, to be. The gap to be bridged for you as a researcher involves both training to equip yourself with research skills (such as IT skills, presentation and viva skills, as well as statistical analysis and library research skills, and so on) and the various stages of the research that it is hoped will yield the findings useful for your research degree submission.

Learning outcomes – The next step is to specify exactly what you need to learn in order to fill the learning gap. This involves describing what will be *learned*, not the strategies adopted. This is an account of the specific skills and levels you need to develop to be successful in undertaking your research – quite apart from whether you discover what you seek in the work.

Learning resources and strategy – Work out what materials will be needed and who might be involved to help you meet each of these outcomes. Note what approaches will be used. You need to identify stages of the research, who can help you, what is needed, what needs to be in place, who needs to be involved, and so on.

Evidence of accomplishment – You will need to decide what can be counted as evidence of achievement of the stages of the research and the outcomes. You could point to various findings and analyses for the research and also to publication, conference presentations, and so on. The transfer document or research report (depending on which you need to complete) will also be evidence of achievement of certain stages in your work.

Review – Review the contract with friends or colleagues to check how clear, appropriate and convincing they find it, and whether they think anything has been omitted.

Carry out the contract and evaluate your success at each stage – One such learning contract for research degree supervisions could take the form of the one below (but there are many alternatives, and you will need to decide on what suits your situation and that of your supervisors). You might find it useful to start to fill out the blank learning contract from your point of view before your first meeting with your supervisor. To be sensitive to the relationship, it would be a good idea to ask if a learning contract might help clarify the way you will work with supervisors and then show them an example, rather than arriving with one half completed. It should be negotiated between you, but is *not* a necessity.

Learning contracts

Here is a bare outline of the kind of contents to be found in a typical contract:

- Defining goals, aims and outcomes
- Agreeing goals, aims and outcomes with the supervisor
- Recognising and planning appropriate learning tasks, activities that will help achieve these goals, aims and outcomes, for example involvement in research seminars and training courses
- Drawing up/finding/agreeing a specific time plan for activities that contribute to stages of the research and to training, presentation, and so on
- Drawing up/finding/agreeing a set of achievement measures that will enable you to measure off your achievements – in training and in stages of the research
- Evaluating – reflecting on further needs for learning – both training for the research and stages of the research work.

Agreement between learner and supervisor

This is a very prescriptive learning contract. You might want to develop a more open-ended one that largely concentrates on defining the ends/outcomes you wish to achieve, and then negotiates (with your supervisor) and defines the routes you will take to get there, also specifying how you will know when you have achieved your outcome. Obviously, achievement of the research degree will be the major outcome, but there will be others along the way and these are important to try and identify.

A working example of a learning contract

Research student:

First supervisor/Director of studies:

Second supervisor:

External supervisor:

Title/research topic:

Date of registration:

Approximate proposed date of completion:

Agreed frequency of supervisions:

Research student
I agree to:
- agree meeting dates and attend meetings well prepared
- maintain a steady working pattern
- send chapter drafts/work as agreed two weeks in advance of each supervision for comment and discussion
- suggest issues, questions and concerns for discussion arising from work in progress or contained in the chapter drafts for an agenda for the supervision
- seek, consider and take advice on aspects of conceptual issues, reading, methodology, progress, writing up, publication and presentations, as appropriate, from the supervisor
- inform the supervisor(s) immediately of any major problems in the research, changes in workload which affect the research, and personal issues which affect it, for example, house moves, job changes and so on
- provide draft progress reports every six months to aid scheduling, replanning and monitoring of progress.

Supervisor
I agree to:
- agree meeting dates and prepare to consider key issues, overall work and future developments
- read and comment on chapter drafts/work as agreed in advance of each supervision for comment and discussion
- suggest issues, questions and concerns for discussion arising from work in progress or contained in the chapter drafts for an agenda for the supervision
- offer advice on aspects of conceptual issues, reading, methodology, progress, writing up, publication and presentations and so on, as appropriate
- suggest appropriate reading, contacts, and methodologies

- inform research student immediately of any major problems in the research, changes in workload which affect the research, and personal issues which affect it, for example, sabbatical absences, job changes, and so on
- ask for and comment on draft progress reports every six months to aid scheduling, replanning and monitoring of progress
- advise on writing up, conferences, opportunities for publication and presentation, and so on.

Signed ....

Date ....

Addresses and contact points:

Research student:

First supervisor:

Second supervisor:

External:

Learning contracts are a learner-centred way of encouraging students to identify and be involved in their own programme planning, recognising their learning outcomes and objectives, and becoming fully involved in their own learning. In this way, students become able to recognise and develop their learning approaches and styles, make the most of their learning opportunities and monitor their own learning needs and achievements. As such, then, it is a key, new learning strategy related to experiential and work-based learning, and personal monitoring and management of learning. Certainly, if you are involved in a work-based or professional doctorate, you will want to develop a learning contract. It is also useful for all those undertaking research work, since it causes you to plan in negotiation with your supervisor and to make perfectly clear what the time, tasks, roles, outcomes, assessment and products look like at each stage.

If students are to develop the skills of planning and carrying out a self-directed learning project, then they need not only the empowerment to do so, but also a framework in which to learn. This framework is the learning contract.

A learning contract can be:

- informal
- formal
- an implicit self-contract.

See p. 112 for a draft learning contract to complete.

Involving your supervisor(s)

There is also often concern about how much supervisors are actually involved in the work their students carry out. They are important in helping to shape and structure the work, and in providing support, information and guidance, but they must not actually do the work for the students. When the

Things to do

Your draft learning contract (please complete)

Draft learning contract

Name: ....

Supervisor: ....

- Defining goals, aims and outcomes.

    Agreeing goals, aims and outcomes: (a) training; and (b) stages of the research:

    (a)
    1

    2

    3

    4

    5

    (b)
    1

    2

    3

    4

    5

    6

    7

drafts of the thesis finally come in, it is important that the supervisor encourages some of the editing but that the student undertakes it. Discussing fundamental theories and the meaning of what has been discovered is helpful, but final expression and editing is not. It starts to take the ownership of the work away from the student. The supervisor is the repository of

Recognising and planning appropriate learning tasks.

Tasks and activities:

1

2

3

4

5

Time plan for activities.

Dates: Activity:

Dates: Activity:

Dates: Activity:

Dates: Activity:

I will know I have achieved these outcomes when:

1

2

3

4

5

Evaluating learning and reflecting on further needs for learning: (complete this when contract completed – a self-reflection exercise)

Agreement between ....

and ....

Date: ....

knowledge about rules and regulations concerning expression, layout and so on, but it is important that you have the written information about these details and access to central information as well, as supervisors can forget and give erroneous or sketchy information at times. With information and formalised rules and systems of support established, understood and available, you are then empowered and responsible to make choices, develop and express ideas and, finally, to check that expression yourself in the final draft of the thesis.

Getting on well with your supervisor(s), establishing and maintaining good working relationships while avoiding personality clashes and coping with absences

Some of the concerns that research students have voiced are to do with personality clashes, for example with the recalcitrant or interfering supervisor who will not let them get on with anything and checks their every move. Maintaining a steady rate of work can be difficult in these instances. You need to ensure that you have clear working relations with your supervisor, do not intrude on his or her personal life, and manage to keep the balance between friendship and a professional working relationship so that neither of you relax too much and forget to concentrate on the timing and management of each aspect of the research. If you do not get along with your supervisor, it is important to remain cordial at least, because social impasses will affect your work adversely. Interpersonal relations need handling with sensitivity. You also need to make sure that preoccupied supervisors still concentrate on your work; that very eminent supervisors who travel to conferences and go away a great deal still give you the time you need, as agreed; and that those whose working situations change (sabbaticals, retirement, new job responsibilities, and so on) renegotiate their working relationship contract with you to enable you to continue with their support. If he or she retires/leaves his or her job and cannot continue to supervise you (the two do not necessarily follow), then the supervisor needs to ensure that someone else with equal commitment takes on the supervision process.

Questions
- What would you do if you found you did not personally get along with your supervisor(s)? Does this matter?
- If your supervisor left for a sabbatical year/six months abroad, what would you do?
- If you realised that good practices of meeting for supervisions had lapsed, what would you do?

● If you developed disagreements about the emphasis of the thesis, interpretation of information, underpinning concepts, and so on, what would you do?

To avoid these kinds of problems, supervisors have to make it very clear to students at the outset where the different responsibilities lie, and agree with them what roles and responsibilities they will each assume. It is in the spirit of this need that the idea of developing contracts emerges. However, there can always be changes, either in working relationships or access.

It is important to:

● ensure that your right to adequate supervisions is not jeopardised because of staff absence. In these instances, you might need to discuss with the supervisor(s) who will replace them in their supervision of you; whether, in their absence, they can continue to support you through visits and regular e-mail and phone contact; or whether they have a trustworthy, like-minded colleague who could take the supervision over.

● ensure that you get on with your supervisor(s) but make it clear, politely and assertively, when you disagree with good reason; when you need clarification and they do not seem to have been fully clear with you; when you need information and guidance and this is not forthcoming or you have not fully understood; and when there are certain developments which you believe they seem to overlook or undervalue. If you actually 'fall out' or have quite strong disagreements, you will need to sort this out. Write a letter and then make an appointment to resolve the difficulties. Again, ensure you are assertive but polite – do not lose your temper, but get a fair deal. If there are extreme working relationship problems with your supervisor, you need to ensure you discuss these with the supervisor confidentially, then with the subject leader or research head, as appropriate, so that your work is not jeopardised by a clash of personalities or clash of emphasis in the work.

It has been acknowledged that a supervisor cannot always supply the support and discussion required, which has led to the development of peer-support systems and co-counselling (see Chapter 14).

Supervisory arrangements at a distance

There are many successful practices, and also difficulties, for distance research students, whether in the UK or overseas, and distance contact and supervisions systems need setting up to cope with any problems. A different kind of pacing of agreed activities has to be set up and maintained. Some of these particular needs can be satisfied by the development of contracts, and good distance supervision and contact systems, and others by peer support networks and structures. If you are working at a great distance from all your supervisors, you need to ensure that you maintain regular contact and update them on your work; ask the necessary questions; and discuss conceptual issues, data findings, the directions of the research, and so on. Some of this will happen in face-to-face supervisions, arranged well in advance, and just as straightforwardly as it would for supervisors and students who work closely together. You can phone, e-mail and/or write to set up supervisions in line with the learning contract you have drawn up. Often, distances ensure that when you do meet it is true quality time, because it has been quite an investment on your part to find the time to travel the distance. The supervisor is making an investment here, too – he or she will prepare for supervisions by reading your work, finding useful current writings, and setting aside his or her time for you.

Videoconferencing

In some instances, students can be supervised through videoconferencing. This is more face-to-face than an e-mail contact but much more complex to set up. There are some supervisory teams who meet regularly by videoconference, with the supervisor fielding questions, causing and facilitating debate between the research group and updating them all on developments. This can support a research culture and lead to a well-managed work rhythm. Some of these videoconference links are European and international.

Good practice with videoconference supervision

For supervision by videoconference, you and your supervisor need to do the following:

- Plan commitments to meeting at specified times
- Book videoconference rooms, preferably with refreshments
- Send work – drafts, plans, questions, reading between you in advance for a focus
- Settle on an agenda – time is precious
- Ensure a friendly technician can be called on for help if the line goes down
- Keep good eye contact – start with social comments, then ask specific questions
- Give the supervisor time to pause to think before answering

- Try not to talk over each other – because of time lapses and the lack of interaction possible in videoconferencing, this is more likely to happen than in face-to-face supervisions
- Agree what you have decided and repeat it back (you cannot show it to the supervisor unless you have a visualiser connected to the videoconference system)
- Ensure a clean, friendly end to the videoconference and 'sign-off' as you switch off (as it becomes either messy, or rather abrupt)
- You could fax or e-mail agreed points immediately after the videoconference.

E-mail supervision

In order to keep a regular discussion going, it is useful to use e-mail. There are many distance discussions that take place by e-mail or fax, backed up with some visits for full-blown supervisions. If the supervisor is in another country, then e-mail contact is essential, as the face-to-face supervisory contacts will be condensed into the periods when you can both be in the same country. Make e-mail contacts lucid, short and precise, with some friendly tone to establish a personal touch. Try not to get involved in excessively chatty discussions but concentrate on asking questions, seeking information and reporting on findings for comment.

E-mail is quite an insistent medium. If you make contact too frequently, the supervisor will feel harassed. If you make contact too infrequently, the supervisor will feel guilty (and so will you), wondering what you are up to. Regular brief contact with some very full discussions on work in progress at regular intervals will maintain a sense of a working relationship over time and space.

Good practice with e-mail supervision

- Keep regular contact for both social comments and progress checks
- Try to test out the kind of tone that enables you and your supervisor to be both (a) friendly; and (b) focused in your exchanges
- Send short messages with explicit questions
- Reply to questions in texts sent to you by interleaving in capitals (or bold, or in colour)
- Send chapters in draft, by attachment. Ask for comments back by interleaving text (in bold, capitals, or in colour)
- Print off exchanges as a record to refer to where necessary
- Send draft materials to both supervisors; also send copies of questions and comments to both, indicating where a response is needed.

Group/project team supervisions

Videoconference group supervisions are not the only group supervisions that are logical and useful. In some subject areas – for example, practical science or medicine – there are likely to be several students working on a related project. In these cases, it would be useful to hold regular group project supervisions at which students could share ideas, problems and questions. Group supervisions are also helpful to the supervisor, as comments concerning learning outcomes, length of the thesis, time, protocols, question framing, strategies, reading and so on need only be made once, rather than to each student individually. In other subject areas, there might be only one student working in a specific area, but there will probably be a few working in cognate areas or areas that are related in some other way, whether in terms of methodology being used, or in terms of subject or discipline. It would be just as useful in these instances to bring these students together for group supervisions, either occasionally or regularly. This is not so as to substitute for individual supervisions but rather to augment them and provide a sense of sharing, support and peer responsibility. You and the other students will often get as much (though sometimes different things) out of sharing your own questions, ideas and work in progress with each other as by discussing it with the supervisors. Also, the group session enables you to keep updated on progress and gives you the opportunity to ask questions and seek to develop ideas. What can also be encouraged is meeting together in self-help peer-group sessions (see Chapter 14 on self-help groups and self-managed sessions).

Key points

1 Find the right supervisor(s). It is important to find supervisors who have the time, the right knowledge and the commitment to work with you productively;

2 Abilities and expertise can be shared out among a supervisory team. You need a director of studies/first supervisor, and possibly also a second supervisor and an external one;

3 Initial contacts and contracts are important. Establish workable learning contracts so you decide and agree on the regularity and shape of supervisions, and your commitments to an agenda, work production, and so on;

4 Ensure you discuss the title and scope of the project at your first session;

5 The nature of the supervisory relationship is important. Set up regular sessions, make relationships clear, ask for help with planning the scope of the project, reading, contacts, and so on;

6 What you can expect from your supervisor(s) needs clarifying. You can expect support, clarity, direction, support over sharing information, management of ideas and concepts, ideas about presentations and publications, and guidance over the examination process;

7 Stages of the supervisory process need clarifying. The supervisor(s) are involved at every stage: the title, planning, literature search, methodology, draft data collection and pilots, drafting, presentations and publications, writing up and editing, viva and after;

8 Do establish and maintain good working relationships to ensure full support through all of these stages. Handle any difficulties in relationships with sensitivity and assertiveness;

9 Supervisions at a distance are a possibility. Set up e-mail contacts, video links, regular contacts and visits, quality time;

10 Also, ensure peer group support is in place.

Conclusion

We have looked at:

☐ Managing your supervisor(s) well, and developing and maintaining a supportive, positive, constructively critical relationship over time is essential to help you produce a good quality thesis

☐ Ground rules and learning contracts are vehicles to help this, but less formal agreements can serve the same ends

☐ Students studying at a distance and/or part-time – possibly in an international context – need to establish good contact systems (for example, e-mail) and set up a support network at home/amongst their peers.

● Further reading

Anderson, G., Boud, D. and Sampson, J. (eds) (1996) *Learning Contracts: A Practical Guide* (London: Kogan Page).

Blaxter, L., Hughes, C. and Tight, M. (1993) *How to Research* (Buckingham: Open University Press).

Brookfield, S.D. (1986) *Understanding and Facilitating Adult Learning: Comprehensive Analysis of Principles and Effective Practices* (Milton Keynes: Open University Press).

Moses, I. (1984) 'Supervision of Higher Degree Students – Problem Areas and Possible Solutions', *Higher Education Research and Development*, 3: 153–6.

Rogers, J. (1989) *Adults Learning* (Buckingham: Open University Press).

Tight, M. (1983) *Education for Adults. Volume 2: Opportunities for Adult Education* (London: Routledge).

Wisker, G. (2005) *The Good Supervisor* (Basingstoke: Palgrave Macmillan).

11 Managing the Balancing Act

This chapter looks at:

▶ Balancing the demands, pleasures and problems of research, home, social/leisure and work
▶ Transferring skills from one sphere to the other – or not
▶ An audit of demands, skills, pleasures and problems
▶ Relating research to home and work demands

'If you want a job done well, give it to a busy person.'

The old adage about giving jobs to busy people certainly rings true when we think about the variety of tasks and roles we have to balance, especially when embarking upon part-time research. You could be reminded of a circus performer balancing and twirling plates, keeping each one twirling just fast enough so that it does not fall and smash into pieces.

Being able to manage a variety of roles and tasks at any one time is a feat of flexibility and diversity. We have to be careful, however, that it does not become a millstone around our necks, and that we do not hamper our own quality of life or the quality of our work by trying to do too much at the same time. Balance is essential. Some of the issues we need to think about, then, are stress and time management, identifying the kinds of roles and needs that are in the balancing act for each of us, learning to support each other and developing coping and planning strategies for ourselves and others. We also need to learn to say 'no' sometimes when there are too many demands placed upon us at home or at work that will make our research impossible. Similarly, there will be times when the research has to take second place to home and work demands. In order to minimise the stress and the disappointments this can bring, you need to plan ahead and spot the clear moments of conflict of interest and effort so that you can negotiate and balance your activities.

If you are intent upon becoming an academic of some sort after your research, or continuing to research, write and publish, you will find the skills you develop for balancing your different roles and demands absolutely essential in the future, too.

● Balancing what?

Most part-time researchers in higher education balance at least two other roles quite apart from that of researcher. They have a job, full- or part-time, and a set of domestic responsibilities: family, parents, partners, and sometimes a host of pets and close friends besides. For international students working on their research in another host country, there can be the stresses of homesickness and demands that are difficult to meet caused by distance and the occasional, perhaps unforeseen, need to return home. We all need to juggle a variety of demands. Many of us also balance various roles within our jobs, for example, coping with the complexities of balancing teaching with administration, and both of these with research. Increasingly, more demands are being made on us to take on and develop the various roles related to our jobs. If we are academics already, there is increasing pressure to research and, if we wish to further our careers, we have to take on more administrative responsibilities whether we teach and research as well or not. Other balancing acts include juggling the demands made by the various people to whom we report; those whom we supervise; those with whom we work closely; other administrative and support staff; personal assistants; secretarial, clerical and technical staff; and other staff with whom we work. The tensions and demands of these often tend to build up at the same time, so that we are faced with a variety of heavy demands at particular points during the year.

If you are not actually involved in working in an academic environment, then this can be both a blessing and an increased difficulty. On the one hand, others might have little or no idea of the kinds of demands and stresses (as well as the joys and celebrations) associated with your research work. They might envy you for it, be distanced from you because you have developed an alternative 'other' life, or simply fail to see why you bother. All of these responses undermine our sense of the value of our research and, at worst, they can be augmented by some deliberately hostile or destructive behaviour.

At work

- It is important to negotiate with those with whom you work and to explain the demands of the research in which you are involved without boring them or requesting special privileges.
- It is also important, if the research is work-related, that you negotiate some support and time in which to assure your colleagues that the work is not just for personal satisfaction but also for the good of the company/organisation/workplace.

At home and socially

- Try and gain the support of family members and friends for the research you are involved in – explain the demands to them, negotiate the pressures and support needed.
- Try not to let your involvement in research undermine your relationships.
- Try not to let your involvement in research take all your time or you will find you lose your friends, alienate your family, and become rather boring company. You might well get bored with yourself too – so it is a good idea to try and balance the pleasures and demands rather than putting aside all your social activities and your domestic responsibilities. When involved in research, it is often very pleasant to be able to escape and become another person, enjoy yourself, talk, socialise, relax, become involved in sport and leisure – all these interests use different parts of your brain and your energy. If you do not have any other pursuits and interests, you might think of developing some to relieve the tensions and stresses, and to provide different stimuli and rewards.

● Varieties of roles and activities – an audit

In order to begin to review the variety of role demands and elements involved in the act of balancing research, work and home/other, it is useful to identify where particular responsibilities and activities, strengths, rewards and demands lie in our lives. One way of doing this is to look at the skills, activities, roles, demands and pleasures identified under the three interesting categories (see Figure 11.1) of home/other, work, and research.

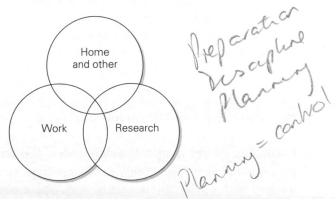

Figure 11.1   Balancing spheres of activity

Things to do – audit

- What skills, problems, demands and strengths, or rewards, and so on, appear in each of the circles?
- What overlaps are there?
- Are there any strengths and enjoyments that appear in one area that could usefully be developed and used in another, for example a skill in home activities, time and task management (sorting out a family – food, domestic management, rota of jobs, and so on) – which could be built on to help you handle those specific developments and demands in your research?
- Then, consider whether there are any specific outlets and areas of relaxation, personal development and enjoyment that appear in 'home', 'other' or your work which can balance some of the tensions and demands of the research. These will let you develop such skills or provide an opportunity to do something completely different.
- The clue is to decide what role these areas play in your life and note the ways unstressful, sporting or social activities, or alternative demanding roles help to offset the stresses and demands of the research, those of your job, and so on.
- If you find that there is an overload of similar demands or of damaging conflicting demands in the various different strands and areas of your life, you will probably need to think about changing things, about how to cope with the clashes.
- Sometimes merely recognising potential clashes and benefits is enough to help you start balancing and appreciating each for its own merits.
- A successful research project can, for example, provide you with a long-term sense of identity and fulfilment set against an undemanding or unrewarding job.

Once you have started to fill in your own version of this figure, you need to ask yourself some questions to work out ways of balancing demands on you, and recognising the kinds of pressures and also the skills and enjoyments that appear in each sphere, those that could either be usefully cross-fertilised or kept very separate (you will need to decide this for yourself).

● What kind of balancing act suits you?

Balancing, rather than collapsing under, the stress

We are all different people and the kinds of balancing acts we can cope with will vary as much as do our personalities. The main point is to recognise what you thrive on, and what to avoid. I know that I thrive on variety but with some overlap. If I am involved in many different activities, if some of them have a common theme of skills or interest, I can carry out a certain balancing act because the overlap and the interfaces will help me to keep various activities all running at once. There are dangers in everything being connected and everything relying on the same sorts of skills and contacts, producing the same sorts of demands and responsibilities, however, in case the collapse of one area affects all the others. When I was studying for my own PhD, it had very little to do with my work life or my home life for much of the time, and provided an alternative way of thinking and behaving, an alternative identity for me. The research I carry out now is of both sorts, sometimes coping with everything, sometimes very definitely an intellectual escape.

You will also need to review the role different kinds of leisure activities play in your life when you are involved in research. Not everyone you meet will want to hear all about your latest discovery or how you file your index cards. You will probably want to keep some leisure interests separate and develop others related to the research. Many people make friends in the university library, the coffee room, the lab. However, the fact that you might make these friends could be a concern for friends and family, who will wonder whether your social involvement in a research culture will take you away from them intellectually and emotionally. You will need to put yourself in their shoes and consider how to handle this possible friction.

Balancing research and teaching – for academics involved in research projects

If you are expected to carry out both research and teaching, you will probably also have those other domestic and outside responsibilities going alongside to consider, but let us look at the research and teaching issues first. There are contradictory findings about the success of various balancing acts. Margherita Rendel's research (Rendel 1986) suggests that women with domestic responsibilities actually produce proportionally more research and published papers than do single men: an interesting example of a successful balancing act that gives some of us heart. This is contradicted by Over (1982) in his study of psychologists, but there are subject differences, which could account for the overall differences in these two sets of findings. Shirley Fisher (Fisher 1994) comments that domestic responsibilities may play a big part in the discrepancies found between publication and research rates of men and women: 'The difference in publication rates may reflect the dual role of women in that rearing children even with back-up services may create overload' (p. 58). However, currently there are increasing loads being placed on both men and women. More and more, in higher education, we are being asked to publish and to research, and always on top of heavy teaching and administrative loads. Fisher (1994) looked at the difficulties university staff have in managing the different demands on their time, and divided up groups of academic staff in relation to their expectations, their role demands, and the stress these caused. Staff members were grouped according to their sense of identity as researcher/administrator/teacher, teacher/administrator/researcher or administrator/researcher/teacher, each role balance reflecting how the staff member saw his or her priorities and the demands of the job. Asking academics what caused stress for them in this complex balancing act, Fisher found that research was frequently prioritised as the activity academics most wished to be involved in. However, it was also the area that caused most stress because it could only be performed in very congenial circumstances. As demands increased to produce research output under the research assessment exercises, pay-offs increased, but so did stress, at least for some.

Your success in balancing the various elements of your work, research, domestic and other commitments will depend to a great extent on your time management, and on the support of others around you. It will also depend on your determination to carry on with the research. Sometimes research work has to take a back seat because of work or domestic demands – do not worry about this. Keep it in your head, review it from time to time, and promise yourself that you will get back to it. Plan this into your programme, and get back to it. It is an important part of your identity and you cannot let it go without a personal sense of loss. So, work on retaining it beyond the crisis or crises – but do not be put off. Most part-time and many full-time researchers have a succession of demands and problems that prevent them from putting all their efforts all of the time into the research work.

Conclusion

We have looked at the following key points:

- [ ] Why you need to balance work, home and research demands

- [ ] How to plan and balance.

● **Further reading**

Fisher, S. (1994) *Stress in Academic Life* (Buckingham: Open University Press).

Over, R. (1982) 'Does Research Productivity Decline with Age?', *Higher Education*, 11: 511–20.

Rendel, M. (1986) 'How Many Women Academics, 1912–1977?', in R. Deem (ed.), *Schooling for Women's Work* (London: Routledge).

12 Managing Your Time and Tasks

This chapter covers different ways of planning your time and also time, task and stress management on a one-year (MA) or three-year-plus research degree (MPhil or PhD full- or part-time). We consider how to fit in not only research, but also domestic and work pressures where appropriate. (See Chapter 11 for further consideration of managing the balancing act of research, work and domestic and other responsibilities.)

Undertaking research for a postgraduate qualification is a very time-consuming activity. However, it will probably have to be carried out alongside many other commitments, such as full- or part-time work, and responsibilities to home, family and other domestic matters. It is essential that you use the time available to you well, and that you gain support from others in doing so. You need to ensure that you plan the stages of the research carefully so that the longer-term activities – such as experiments, ordering materials, travel abroad or around the country, and presenting the final written draft in perfect condition – are all costed out in terms of time. There is no point in wasting time awaiting materials or results when you could, with good planning, be getting on with other elements of the research. There is also no point in rushing because of bad planning, because a rushed piece of postgraduate research usually lacks a conceptual underpinning that has been carefully considered throughout, with clear organisation and sound referencing and expression. It will also lack that final presentational polish, which helps to convince its readers and assessors that this is a piece of work of quality, one which can contribute usefully and well to knowledge and understanding in the field.

● Good planning: long-, medium- and short-term management of time

It is essential that you plan well and manage your time carefully:

- Look back over the information on stages of the research project and the kinds of demands involved.
- Develop a plan and programme that considers your overall project and the ultimate aims.
- Outline your long-term planning aims and outcomes.
- Outline your long-term activities and end results.
- See the whole project in outline.

Not all that you predict will actually happen, but you need an idea of the whole project in terms of the time and stages of activities involved in order to use time effectively, to revise plans if necessary, to develop, and to spot problems. To do this, it is helpful to look towards the end results of the project and track backwards, putting in place different elements of research activity, support, acquisition of materials and resources and writing.

Now look more specifically at long-, medium- and short-term planning, carrying out a critical path analysis to help you to spot points at which there will be too many things to do, potential problems and waiting time so that, once identified, these times can be used effectively.

● Overall planning and the cycle of research

It is helpful to think about the research in terms of a cycle that moves on, progressing at each stage and informing each stage with the experiences of previous stages of the cycle. This can be set against the rather linear time-planning activity already completed and so can help you to plan your time effectively.

The research cycle is somewhat like Kolb's experiential learning cycle, which underpins action research (see Figure 12.1).

Eventually, this leads to conclusions and writing up. In full, the development process looks more like the following:

Stage 1
- Initial ideas and hypotheses
- Title and research questions to structure the research activities

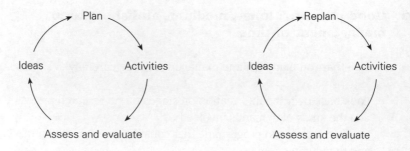

Figure 12.1   Kolb's Experiential Learning Cycle (Kolb 1984)

- Plan
- Carry out various preliminary activities, for example, literature searches.

Stage 2
- Alter plan – firm up stages
- Carry out activities – for example, reading, interviews, drawing up and using questionnaires, or other experiments, in stages
- After each stage reflect, evaluate, see how it shapes the whole research
- Write up any findings in draft form
- Reflect.

Stage 3
- Replan and move on
- Draft
- Carry out research activities
- Reflect, evaluate
- Get ideas, findings and arguments in perspective, modify if necessary
- Produce results.

Stage 4
- Write up and edit
- Final write-up
- Submission of thesis
- Examination and viva.

Both your supervisor and any supportive research group of which you are a part can help you at each of these stages, in different ways. Other colleagues, unrelated to the research, can also be helpful sometimes in putting contacts or reading your way, or suggesting other approaches or interpretations. Friends and relatives can provide a different kind of support and help. When you see the different stages, you can also spot what kinds of support you need to seek: it may be support in clarifying methodology, interpreting data, learning new skills, talking through difficult concepts, overcoming intellectual hurdles, helping to solve problems, helping to spot issues that have not been taken into consideration, thinking of other ways of finding out answers, or providing professional, psychological and emotional support in times of pressure or when things are not going very well.

Time and task management and planning – action

- Draw up plans – start this process now.
- Although you probably cannot produce a refined plan at the beginning of your project, start the process off and then spend time finishing off the plans for long- and medium-term planning as soon as you can. Take advice from colleagues or partners to whom you might show the plan.

Things to do

Consider:

Long-term planning – What needs to be done over the next few years? Where are the high points, suspected moments of difficulty and over-load, and where do other activities in which you are involved produce time-consuming work or demands that will affect how much work you can put into your research?

Medium-term planning – Draw this up on a chart, track it in stages of actions in a diary/on a calendar. Perhaps look at a single year. This way you can spot:

- forward planning needs
- some of the problems
- some of the really hectic periods
- some of the quieter periods
- what activities need to be carried out over the next few months
- what other activities will make demands on your time coincidentally.

This kind of planning helps you to visualise the work needed, to take control over the time and not feel overwhelmed or pressurised by so much to do in so much time. Planning gives you control. With medium- and long-term planning in place, you can usefully manage time to fill the quiet periods with more routine activities or activities that need completion at some point and can be carried out in quieter moments. You can also plan ahead and carry out some small preparatory tasks, such as continued reading, ordering resources, ringing up people you need to make appointments with, and sorting and cataloguing data, all of which activities will help you manage the more hectic moments, so that you do not feel overwhelmed.

Look backwards from your **long-term plan** to see when:

- stages of activities can be slotted in
- contacts can be established
- things/activities can be bid for, organised or agreed
- visits can be made
- materials can be ordered
- people can be consulted
- problems of different stages can be addressed.

In this context plan **medium-term activities**, for example:

- fixing up supervisions
- gathering data
- managing money
- setting up experiments
- organising visits
- producing and processing questionnaires
- organising interviews
- piloting stages
- drafting parts of the thesis
- presenting to colleagues in progress seminars and sessions – presenting parts of the work to others at conferences
- writing up some elements of the work into publishable papers.

Critical path analysis can help both your long- and short-term planning.

Consider when other pressures might upset your research plans and plan ahead to leave some space, to avoid crises, to tackle problems in advance.

Use systems of 'bring forward' dates in diaries to remind yourself when to order something, start a process, and start to clear time and space for a difficult piece of work coming up. Then start to write up certain elements and book space with your supervisor in advance for him or her to see your work.

Critical path analysis

This is an example of a critical path analysis, in this instance, planning towards the delivery of a presentation. Look at how the different stages of work are fitted in around foreseen and unforeseen demands and problems. (This example does not actually include domestic and full-time work demands and the problems that you might well have to include.) When you have considered this example, it would be useful to draw up your own critical path analysis, possibly in the form of a small chart (see Figure 12.2).

Now draw up and plan your own critical path analysis. Choose the period you wish to take into consideration. You might like to consider the full planned time for your PhD/MPhil/MA, or just until the end of the year, or some other appropriate slice of time.

Consider what demands, activities, pressures and problems could affect your time in relation to:

- the research work itself
- other work – paid or unpaid
- domestic and social responsibilities
- the work loads and demands of those who work with you/for you/who you work for in relation to the research – for however small an amount of time (for example, technicians, reprographics, media)
- anything or anyone else connected with the research – subjects, animals, plants, calls on machinery and equipment.

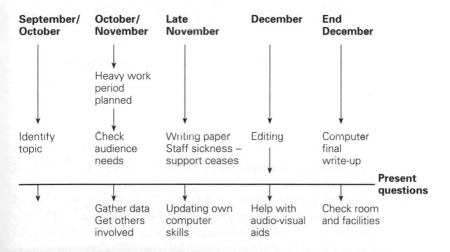

Figure 12.2 Preparing a presentation – a model critical path analysis

Seeing the critical path visually will probably initially be something of a shock – there never seems to be enough time and there are many pressures involved. It will help you to plan realistically and to avoid real pressure points (and so relieve stress and help ensure better quality deep learning and work).

Consulting others

Now that you have begun the process of long- and medium-term planning, discuss it with a colleague or partner.

Things to do

Ask yourself and ask each other:

- Is it realistic?
- Is it full enough?
- What moments of pressure have been overlooked?
- What essential ongoing activities have been left out?
- Who else needs to be brought in, at what stages?
- What resource needs are not yet planned for?
- What crises have not yet been identified?
- Is too little time left for certain activities that might need repeating or checking, or which could go wrong and throw the planning out?
- Have you given any thought to when you might be able to see your supervisor and for what kinds of meeting?
- What else?
- Co-counselling – give each other advice on refining the longer- and medium-term plans.

Managing time with domestic and other work commitments

You will already have been planning some of these into your critical path analysis work. In order to help you consider their importance it is useful to consider:

- Who are the main people in your domestic and social life to whom you have commitments of time?
- How much can you negotiate with them for specific and ongoing periods of time in which to work?
- Can you organise rotas for chores and visits, make deals with others to be involved in domestic and social activities – particularly at moments of 'quality time', and keep other times clear for your work?

Most research students find that their work encroaches on their domestic and social life, so you will need to take this into consideration and weigh up the respective benefits of domestic and social activities and those of your research. You will need to relax as well as fulfil commitments, and will possibly tend to resent the research if it dominates all aspects of your life to the detriment of others that stimulate, relax or entertain. Everyone's circumstances are different but you might find it useful to consider demands on your time in relation to sets of overlapping circles, pinpointing where demands impinge on each other and where there are clear spaces and trade-offs.

Short-term planning and 'to do' lists

With the longer- and medium-term plans visualised and in place (although they will certainly change over time) you will be able to plan short-term activities for tomorrow, this week, the weekend, and so on, with further elements of your research work in mind.

You will need to produce 'to do' lists that you can fill in daily/weekly with a variety of small, large, deep or relatively trivial and yet essential tasks:

- List and define parts of the daily or weekly main research tasks, such as distributing questionnaires, continuing a literature search, writing up explanations of statistics, conducting focus group interviews, and so on
- Parts of essential ongoing regular activities, such as checking sources and monitoring experiments
- Small, tedious but essential activities that could otherwise hold up your work, such as buying paper for the printer, keeping your card-index of sources and references tidy and up to date
- Small parts of larger tasks, sometimes because large tasks cannot be completed unless smaller tasks are completed first, for example, learning how to operate software, phoning people back
- Tackling parts of a problem that has been broken down into manageable sections
- Continuing to think through difficult ideas, and read and discuss them with colleagues.

Things to do

Consider (and then, if possible, discuss with a colleague):

- Do you already use 'to do' lists?
- How could they help you in your organisation and planning of the research work?

Draw up a 'to do' list for tomorrow in relation to fitting your research development work so far in with your other work. Consider things you need to find out, questions to ask, thinking and reading to do. When you have drawn up this draft list, assess its usefulness.

Conclusion

We have looked at the following key points:

- [ ] You will need to manage your time and tasks carefully in relation to the clear stages of your research

- [ ] Managing commitments to domestic and other work areas alongside your research commitments will lessen stress and clarify your different areas of demands. Do not give up all your domestic and social interests, but do learn to time and schedule them into your programme in rela-tion to your research, so as to ensure that they do not cause more stress and you do fulfil commitments

- [ ] When planning do not forget that other people's time, commitments and skills will be involved, so do plan these in too

- [ ] Draw up and continue to map your work against your criti-cal path analysis, which you should also update. Working with this in sight can often help you to see how you have progressed and what different parts of the work need to be set in motion when. It also helps you to re-plan and cope realistically after crises and difficulties.

● **Further reading**

Bell, J. (2005) *Doing Your Research Project* (4th edn) (Buckingham: Open University Press).

Dunleavy, P. (2003) *Authoring a PhD* (Basingstoke: Palgrave Macmillan).

Kolb, D.A. (1984) *Experiential Learning: Experience as the Source of Learning and Development* (Englewood Cliffs, NJ: Prentice-Hall).

Roesch, R. (1998) *Time Management for Busy People* (New York: McGraw-Hill Professional).

Walliman, N.S.R. (2005) *Your Research Project* (London: Sage).

13 Learning as a Research Student – Learning Approaches, Styles and Pitfalls

This chapter looks a

► How do you approac
your learning?
► How do you concep
alise your research?
► What possible pitfall
could arise from a
mismatch between
learning approaches
and the demands of
your research?
► Using the research a
a learning question-
naire, as a learning
vehicle

When you start your work as a research student, you are making a great leap upwards into a more complex and demanding level of learning, just as you did when starting a degree, or the work that preceded it. It is, therefore, very useful to find out more about the learning demands of research-as-learning and about your own preferred or usual learning styles, strategies and approaches in relation to those demands.

We do not know very much about how students learn, and even less about how research students learn, but some of the theories and vehicles for finding out about student learning can help you to define your own learning style, your learning conceptions and approaches, and help you to work out how to learn from a variety of opportunities. These opportunities include experiences, information, events, situations and other people. This informa-tion can help you identify your current learning style and indicate how you might refocus this to learn from people, documents and experiences from which you would not normally learn. It will also indicate when you should adopt learning styles and approaches with which you are not familiar. It will help you to adapt your learning style and to recognise some of the potential strengths, weaknesses or pitfalls in your learning style and approach in rela-tion to certain kinds of research activities.

The following areas of questioning will help you to think about:

- why you carry out your learning and research, that is, what moti-vates you (such as parental examples, a sense of duty, a sense of fulfilment)

- how you conceptualise your learning (such as seeing learning as accruing more knowledge about the world or enabling you to fit new understanding into a conceptual framework and link it to your experience)
- what kinds of learning and research approaches you take (such as accumulating information and data, relating ideas and information holistically)
- what sort of outcomes you seek (such as gaining status for yourself, seeing the world differently, bringing about creative change).

See 'Reflections on Learning Inventory' (Meyer and Boulton-Lewis 1997, discussed in relation to postgraduate learning), Meyer and Kiley (1998) and Wisker (1999).

It is interesting to clarify these kinds of issues and practices for several reasons. Because learning as a postgraduate, rather than an undergraduate or a professional, makes new and different demands upon you, you might need to develop your learning strategies to cope with this. If you are an international student, culturally influenced learning expectations and behaviours might well differ in your research university from those at home. Increased awareness of current learning approaches and the demands on learning approach development made by postgraduate studies can lead to your developing the appropriate variety of learning approaches and behaviours demanded at this level. Research into student learning (Entwistle and Ramsden 1983, Marton and Säljö 1976, Ramsden 1979) has suggested that students broadly take one or more of three approaches to their learning.

● Learning styles: deep, surface and strategic learning

Established research into student learning identifies two main learning styles – deep and surface learning (Marton and Säljö 1976, Ramsden 1979). It is suggested that 'traditional teaching' largely encourages surface learning, particularly in science subjects, but that deep learning produces better results and longer lasting learning for the students.

Surface or atomistic learning – this approach tends to see knowledge as the acquisition of a number of facts; tasks and objectives are seen as discrete, as are the stages towards completion of a task; time is very important; and any personal relation to the work is considered inappropriate and even misguided. This kind of student relies a great deal on learning and memorising because they are not uniting ideas and facts, and they are not fitting new information into already developed learning or concept 'maps'.

Deep or holistic learning – this approach searches for the meaning that lies beyond or within the specific task; relates any discrete information given to a general, already established learning or concept map; and relates new ideas and learning to prior experience and prior learning, moving this on as new information as ideas are added. It personalises learning tasks and integrates them. It sees the whole problem, the general ideas and the main concept, and fits the learning activity into these frameworks of understanding and of personal experiential reference.

Strategic learning – this has been identified as a third category of learning. This approach focuses on the end product – the marks, with the main aim being to pass. It means the student merely chases grades and only learns what looks necessary, thus there is no linking and little retention.

● **Disciplines**

Different areas of discipline, and different parts thereof, might be taught in a way that encourages either surface or deep learning. Ramsden (1979) shows that students can switch strategies to suit tasks, whilst Thomas and Bain (1982) argue that students develop a certain learning style and do not change it. Biggs and Rihn (1984) show that while students might show tendencies for either sort of learning, it is both possible and desirable to encourage the development of deep learning approaches, because these are overall the most successful learning approaches. Depth of processing implies meaningfulness in learning.

The empirical evidence would support these implications

A deep learning strategy, based on wide reading, reading and adding new knowledge to what is already known, and so on, results in better learning. 'Better' is described as being a complexity of outcomes (Biggs 1978, Marton and Säljö 1976); satisfaction with performance (Biggs 1978, ch. 6); and self-rated performance in comparison with peers or examination results (Schmeck 1988, Svensson 1987, Thomas and Bain 1982, Watkins and Hattie 1981): 'not only does consistency exist over such varied ways of defining good quality learning, the measures of depth of processing are also quite diverse' (Biggs and Rihn 1984).

It is recognised that science students more usually adopt a surface approach – and that the sciences tend to call for this – but research carried out by Svensson (1987) suggests that those who learn to adopt a deep approach gain better exam results in the end (or become better learners).

A useful learning activity to encourage is the development of an awareness of how you are learning.

These arguments show that learners who contextualise their learning relate it to themselves and their own world. They concentrate on how they are learning as well as what they are learning. They are higher achievers than those who are less aware of, or consider irrelevant, such consciousness and contextualisation. These learners concentrate, instead, on the acquisition of fairly disparate facts and the achievement of discrete tasks and objectives.

Students' approaches may differ at different times and in different learning situations. This may produce a diversity of learning cues for supervisors. Difficulties could arise if, particularly at postgraduate level, you adopt a consistently surface approach: accumulating information rather than integrating it into a cohesive interpretation that changes the way you see the subject or the world. These notions of broad approaches to learning have developed into fuller and more complex studies of students' learning systems and their variants. Your learning relates closely to the way in which you see the world, and to the reasons for your undertaking research and the kinds of outcomes you seek from it. It is useful to consider why you are researching, how you conceptualise your research, how you go about it and what outcomes you seek. For example, if you find you are largely taking surface approaches, you could be left with the accumulation of large quantities of disparate data and no developed idea about how to fit it all together, or make meaning from it.

Things to do

- What kind of learning approach/es do you normally take (deep, surface or strategic; or a combination)?
- What approaches do you seem to be taking as you start this new research activity?
- Do you feel you might find it useful to develop some strategies now and, if so, how and why?

● What kind of learner are you?

There are other theories that suggest tendencies towards learning styles, and identifying these in yourself can help you understand why you find it difficult to learn from some situations and in some contexts, and easier in others. When you have such knowledge about your own learning, you can choose to plan to your strengths and/or to work on your weaknesses and develop further the learning styles that are not the most obviously successful for you. You could ponder which of the following four main styles seem to suggest your kind of learning (see Honey and Mumford 1986).

Please consider Honey and Mumford's definitions of learning styles. If you want to complete their questionnaire and analyse your results for a more 'accurate' picture, this is readily available in their book *Using your Manual of Learning Styles* (1986).

Learning styles

Each style has its own strengths and weaknesses. There are no 'good' or 'bad' styles. Your major styles will tell you what strengths you have as a learner, which things make it easier for you to learn and what you need to be wary of. For example, studying car mechanics will tend to favour pragmatists and English literature will tend to favour reflectors.

The greatest variety of learning opportunities is available to those who can, to some extent, operate in all styles, but who are clear, when facing a problem, which style is most effective for them.

Activists – Activists learn best from constant exposure to new experiences. They like to involve themselves in immediate experiences and are enthusiastic about anything new. They tend to act first and consider the consequences later. They enjoy new challenges but are soon bored with implementation and consolidation. They learn least well from activities that require them to take a passive role.

Reflectors – Reflectors learn best from activities that allow them space to ponder over experience and assimilate new information before making a considered judgement in their own time. They tend to be cautious and thoughtful, wishing to consider all the possible angles and implications before making a decision. They often spend a good deal of time listening and observing. They learn least well from activities that require rapid action with little time for planning.

Theorists – Theorists learn best from activities that allow them to integrate observations into logically sound theories. They like to think problems through in a step-by-step way, assimilating new information and experience into a tidy, rational scheme. They are good at analysis, and are comfortable using theories and models to explain things to themselves and others. They are less comfortable with subjective opinion or creative thinking. They learn least from situations they are unable to research in depth.

Pragmatists – Pragmatists learn best from activities that have a clear practical value and that allow ideas and approaches to be tested in practical settings. They tend to be down-to-earth people who like to get on with things. They also tend to be impatient with open-ended discussions. They learn least from situations where learning is not related to an immediate purpose.

Things to do

Consider:

- Which description(s) of learning styles best fit you and your learning?
- Are there any situations or modes of research behaviour that you find you are naturally happier with? How do they relate to learning style? (For example, if you are a theorist and low pragmatist, you might tend to read excessively before starting any fieldwork or beginning to draw conclusions from findings.)
- Are there any learning styles you find you do not seem to be happy with or learn easily from?
- If you notice such an approach or research learning behaviour and, for example, find it difficult to learn from focusing deeply or reading and understanding complex theories, what might you do to strengthen your learning behaviour approach to carry out this kind of learning more successfully?

Although you have one or more supervisors, much of your research as learning will actually be carried out on your own, or on your own in a team. In order to be successful at MA, MPhil or PhD level, your research will need to have a great deal of self-direction, motivation and sticking power. You might find it useful to consider the theories of self-directed learning. How do these apply to your research-as-learning as a researcher? Research students are by definition adult learners. You might well be combining a professional context and/or professional experience with your research. You will certainly need to develop reflective practice and you are involved in lifelong learning – your research work will probably carry on in your own life and is usually a result of a certain thirst for learning.

Self-directed learning

One of the aims of good learning experiences and activities is to encourage learners to become self-directed and lifelong learners, their self-direction indicating that they understand, own and control their own learning. Self-directed learning is defined as 'the adult's assumption of control over setting educational goals and generating personally meaningful evaluative criteria' (Brookfield 1986).

Self-directed learning is not a set of techniques but rather a process of learning that, by its very nature, fosters the critical questioning and reflection that should be the purpose of adult education.

These several related theories and practices of lifelong learning (experiential learning – Kolb 1984 – (reflective practice); Schön 1983 – (self-directed and lifelong learning) feed into basic assumptions and guidelines underlying success in learning, in the setting up of learning experiences and in the monitoring, evaluating and evidencing of learning.

Learners are able to make use of their own experience as a starting point for new learning and as a reference point throughout the learning process.

- Learners are aware of their individual differences in learning styles and how to build on these or improve on their learning strategies and overcome their weaknesses.
- Learners exercise some control and responsibility for the direction of their own learning. These kinds of choices help them to become more self-directed and self-aware of their own learning needs and achievements.
- Learners are given opportunities and guidance for reflecting on their experience – whether from life, work, or the more formal learning situation – making it explicit and turning it into learning.
- Their learning is task- or problem-centred; in other words, learners are dealing with problems and issues that have immediate relevance and application.
- Their learning is active – they are able to learn by doing, with an opportunity to apply theory in practice.
- Learners are able to share ideas, feelings and learning experiences (past and present) with other people, and to learn from their experiences and ideas.
- Learners are in a climate and learning context that is reassuring and conducive to learning. The learning programme needs to make

outcomes, processes, expectations and criteria explicit so that anxieties about assessment procedures, fear of critical or punitive attitudes from tutor or group members, and lack of confidence in the purpose of the learning programme are avoided. These negative elements are not conducive to a good learning climate.

- Learners are involved in negotiating the learning, at all stages; learners should be encouraged to accept a share of the responsibility for the planning, operating and evaluation of a learning programme, and preferably have some choice over learning and assessment methods. With these suggestions in place, learners are more likely to be self-directing in their approach to learning tasks, to own and take responsibility for their learning, and to work effectively with others in developing and sharing learning. They are also more likely to relate their learning to their experience both in everyday life and in their work and practice, and become true lifelong, reflective, self-directed and active learners.

Things to do

Consider the above descriptions of self-directed learning.

- What are the benefits to you of being a self-directed learner?
- How might you develop your skills as a self-directed learner?
- What could you ask from your supervisor to better enable you to become, and continue, as a self-directed learner?

You could:

- ensure you base your research work with your supervisor around the explicit use of a learning contract
- keep a log, diary or reflective journal of your research plans, problems, activities and findings
- recognise your own current and previous experience, where relevant, as a valuable contribution to your research processes; for example, if you manage a home or an office, you could transfer those organisational skills to record keeping and management of the research. If you are a keen observer of others you could develop this as a research strategy.

What other specific ideas do you have about your own self-directed learning as a researcher?

Experiential learning

Kolb (1984) in particular (following Dewey 1963) developed a model for experiential learning, which can be used to help learners recognise and build on:

(a) their experiences in everyday life, drawing learning from these; and
(b) their learning experiences, both individual and in groups, in more formal learning contexts. The latter range from academic class-rooms through to workplace training contexts.

Kolb defined experiential learning as 'the process whereby knowledge is created through the transformation of experience'. He also developed (1984) a useful diagram that explores how learners start from experience, move through stages of reflective observation and abstract conceptualisation, and then on to active experimentation. After this, they begin a new cycle, and on again, building in each cycle on both their experience/experimentation, and their reflection and abstract conceptualisation (see Figure 13.1).

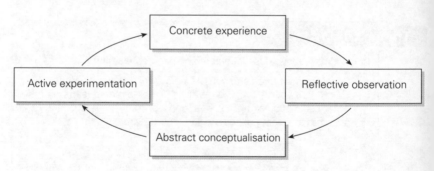

Figure 13.1 Continuous learning (after Kolb 1984)

Continuous learning offers the opportunity for fresh, deeper meaning to develop. Other theorists add to the idea of experimentation that of 'play', or a creative release and exploration of ideas and practices (Gordon 1961, Melamed 1987). This could involve the use of imagination and emotions, metaphors, games and simulations, and other creative modelling processes, as well as releasing creative energies in brainstorming or problem-solving activities. During the activities themselves, adults often have flashes of understanding and insight, 'a-ha' moments when ideas and experiences fall into place. When reflected on, these activities can lead to self-reflection and personal transformation (Mezirow 1985).

Reflective practice

Donald Schön, in *The Reflective Practitioner* (1983), establishes a theory of how professionals and practitioners learn from experience by arguing that professionals respond to and reflect on the varied experience that arises in their work. They then seek development and change. These reflective practitioners are more than merely technical solvers of problems. They use 'artistry' creatively to draw from a set of past examples and precedents to transfer from one situation to the next continually, and create and learn anew in each situation, bringing their past learning to bear on the new situation. While professional work and practice generate experience and knowledge naturally, it is important to make this learning explicit in a learning situation, so as to encourage learners to reflect on and articulate their learning from practice and from their work (see Evans and Varma 1990, and Winter 1995). For your own reflective practice, this will involve being able to draw out from your professional work and practice the learning experiences that relate to the research work you are undertaking.

Consider:

- How might you develop your reflective practice? Is this relevant to your work as a researcher?
- How might experiential learning be used in your research? How might you build on your own experiences in your research?

Example

A PhD student wants to research how the use of a particular piece of art therapy affects patients.

- She starts with her own concrete experience. This experience, from several years' practice, has given her hunches and insights.
- She moves to *reflective observation*, studying the therapy pattern and its effects on patients, analysing its elements.
- She then produces some *abstract conceptualisation* of the way the patients work; the kinds of behaviours before, during and after it; and what this means for the patients' response and development.
- She reads theoretical works and feeds these insights into her own thinking and work.
- She uses the abstract conceptualisation to stand back and develop a *model* of patient treatment.
- She then tries it out, in active experimentation. This is a piece of concrete experience.
- She notices what happens and studies it in *reflective observation*.

The development is a cycle.

You could actually base the start and progress of your research around Kolb's experiential learning cycle. See how and where you might enter the cycle, and how your research progress can be changed, by working out how you move through it.

You can use the cyclical approach in the actual research process by capturing it systematically and using theoretical underpinning and appropriate research methods.

Research-as-learning: a specific learning styles questionnaire/activity for researchers

Look below at some of the definitions of conceptions of research and learning approaches in which postgraduates and researchers are involved. Can you complete the questionnaire and think about what this tells you about your own research strategies? Looking at your research topic and your proposed methods, could there be any moments of contradiction or any potential clashes?

Clashes are likely to take place, for example:

1 when an accumulation approach is largely adopted but a transformative aim is sought (how to move from accumulation of data to interpretation, analysis and decision-making, leading to recommendations for action if there is little obvious connection between the stages);

2 when adopting a holistic or negative postmodern approach (Hodge 1995). In this, it seems that everything, such as findings and theories, is linked to everything else, but there are no clear sets of meanings or obvious routes of interpretation. You could easily flounder amongst masses of fascinating data that link everything to everything else but provide little hint of how to make a decision or bring coherence and order. You may be unable to suggest and argue any one interpretation through the information and theories over any other (a kind of problematic relativism in the face of excess).

There are two very clear potential difficulties that can be identified when scrutinising the research project on which you are engaged: your behaviour and your approaches to your project. There could well be many others. It will be useful for you to consider potential clashes, limits and blockages, and think about how you might develop your research proposals. Or possibly you could limit the area of your study, the variety of your research vehicle, or change the kind of research vehicle you are using from, for example, a largely quantitative approach to a mixture of quantitative and qualitative methods.

- How are you going to process, analyse and interpret the data that your research vehicles will produce for you?
- How might you direct the vast mass of information you are gathering and link ideas together?
- How are you going to make decisions about what to say about your findings, how to interpret them, and make recommendations and suggestions for change and development as a result of these findings?

The following set of thoughts and two-part research-as-learning questionnaire should help you with this.

The research-as-learning questionnaire: assumptions and questions – constructions of research in relation to self, understanding, beliefs, knowledge and the world

These are introductory ideas lying behind the questionnaire that suggest some researchers' beliefs underlying their approaches to research as learning.

Beliefs underlying research approaches and strategies

These could include:

- beliefs about knowledge and experience
- beliefs about personal subjectivity
- beliefs about categorical classification and pinning down of proof and real answers
- beliefs about involvement
- beliefs about the importance of creativity and originality rather than recording
- beliefs about the importance of research contributing to the improvement of human life.

What approaches and activities might different sorts of researchers take?

- Positivistic researchers might record and expect solutions
- More holistic researchers might look at living responses, variables and the whole context
- Professional, practice-based, creative/morally engaged researchers might seek some answers to effect change
- More predictive/descriptive researchers are positivistic, believing everything is discoverable, and they might take a more pragmatic approach to the right questions to produce the 'right' answers.

Questions about postgraduate research styles

Things to do

Complete the following questionnaire and then consider your pattern of responses.

Context: The aim of this short set of questions is to find out about you and your research so that you might understand your approaches. It will help you to gain insights into your beliefs, practices and approaches.

Title of research proposal (so far):

> What are your main research questions? What are you seeking to find out?

Part 1

What is research?
Answering this question gives hints as to:
- beliefs
- values
- personal learning constructs
- worldviews
- team-based interpretations of experience, approaches and findings – the way groups/cultural groups make meaning.

Part 2

In carrying out your research, which of these descriptions describes your activities? Please score them from a range between:

1 – 'this does not describe my approaches and activities' to
5 – 'this describes my activities clearly'.

I believe my research is about/is concerned with:

1 Describing – finding out information about an event,   1 2 3 4 5
   a set of relations between variables or a situation
   and carefully describing it/them in detail.

2 Exploring – looking for reasons why certain things   1 2 3 4 5
   have happened and what might have caused
   problems/developments/situations.

3 Right answers – if there is enough exploration and   1 2 3 4 5
   recording, there will be discoverable right answers
   to important questions which can then be recorded.

4 Experimenting – starting with a hypothesis and   1 2 3 4 5
   through trying out something, seeing what happens
   next, looking at the results and linking them back
   to the experiment.

➡

5 Prediction – predicting the links from things, events   1   2   3   4   5
   and reactions in the past, similar to your area of
   research, or setting up conditions and activities
   and speculating and predicting about what could
   happen in the future.

6 Weaving, interrelating – believing that aspects of   1   2   3   4   5
   areas are related both distantly or closely to others,
   even across disciplines, and finding out about
   these links and overlaps.

7 Metaphorical links/leaps – using metaphors/creative   1   2   3   4   5
   comparisons between the imaginative and the real,
   across disciplines, in order to spot relations and
   similarities; making often imaginative or philosophical
   mental leaps across areas which possibly seem
   logically unrelated.

8 Being creative – trying out a new activity or change   1   2   3   4   5
   mechanism, exploring 'what happens if ... ?' and
   producing something original and creative/helping
   others to produce something original and creative.
   Pushing forward the boundaries of creativity and
   making something new.

Is there anything else you would like to add about research?

Things to do

Now that you have completed the questionnaire, look back at the
questions and the points posed above.

- What do the results tell you about your conceptions of research,
  your approaches and any potential problems or clashes? If you
  detect any difficulties, how might you now overcome them?
- Look also at your research area, questions and intended methods.
  You might find that you see research as leading to changes, and
  being creative and individual. You might see your own research as
  numbers 6, 7 and 8 in Part 2, that is, interrelating areas and disciplines, metaphysical and creative, but you know that you are planning to use largely quantitative research methods. You might then
  find that it is difficult to make the leap from the accumulation of
  data to creativity, and change outcomes.
- There could be other dissonances, contradictions or problems.
  What could you do to handle such a discrepancy?

These research-as-learning questionnaires have been a useful aid in action research with groups of postgraduates (such as Israeli PhD students at Anglia Ruskin University).

Reflection on your own learning and research as learning should feed into your insights and practice:

- when planning and carrying out your research, analysing findings, and so on
- when reflecting on the programme of the research
- when diagnosing and coping with contradictions and problems – getting stuck in some parts of your research where this relates to how you go about it as a learning activity
- when researching the learning of those you work with or teach.

Some research into postgraduates' learning has been carried out and is accessible in Wisker and Sutcliffe (1999). For international research students, it is also written up in Wisker (2000).

Conclusion

In relating learning to research we have looked at:

☐ Student learning approaches:
   – deep
   – surface
   – strategic

☐ Student learning styles:
   – activist
   – reflective
   – theorist
   – pragmatist

☐ Reflective practice, self-directed learning, experiential learning – implementations for you

☐ Research as learning: identifying and seeking to overcome potential clashes or dissonances.

● Further reading

Biggs, J.B. (1978) 'Individual and Group Differences in Study Processes and the Quality of Learning Outcomes', *British Journal of Educational Psychology*, 48: 266–79.

Biggs, J.B. and Rihn, B.A. (1984) 'The Effects of Intervention on Deep and Surface Approaches to Learning', in J.R. Kirby, *Cognitive Strategies and Educational Performance* (London: Academic Press): 279–93.

Brookfield, S. (ed.) (1986) *Self-Directed Learning: From Theory to Practice* (New Directions for Continuing Education 25) (San Francisco: Jossey-Bass).

Dewey, J. (1963) *Experience and Education* (New York: Collier).

Entwistle, N.J. and Ramsden, P. (1983) *Understanding Student Learning* (London: Croom Helm).

Evans, P. and Varma, V.P. (1990) *Special Education* (London: Falmer).

Gibbs, G. (1981) *Teaching Students to Learn* (Buckingham: Open University Press).

Gordon, William J.J. (1961) *Synectics: The Development of Creative Capacity* (New York: Harper).

Hodge, B. (1995) 'Monstrous Knowledge: Doing PhDs in the New Humanities', *Australian Universities' Review*, 38 (2): 35–9.

Honey, P. and Mumford, A. (1986) *Using your Manual of Learning Styles* (Maidenhead: Peter Honey Publications).

Kolb, D.A. (1984) *Experimental Learning: Experience as the Source of Learning and Development* (Englewood Cliffs, NJ: Prentice-Hall).

Marton, F. and Säljö, R. (1976) 'On Qualitative Differences in Learning. I – Outcome and Process', *British Journal of Educational Psychology*, 46: 4–11.

Melamed, L. (1987) 'The Role of Play in Adult Learning', in D. Boud and V. Griffin (eds), *Appreciating Adults Learning: From the Learner's Perspective* (London: Kogan Page).

Meyer, J.H.F. and Boulton-Lewis, G.M. (1997) 'Reflections on Learning Inventory', University of Durham.

Meyer, J.H.F. and Kiley, M. (1998) 'An Exploration of Indonesian Postgraduate Students' Conceptions of Learning', *Journal of Further and Higher Education*, 22: 287–98.

Mezirow, J. (1985) 'A Critical Theory of Self-directed Learning', in S. Brookfield (ed.), *Self-Directed Learning: From Theory to Practice* (New Directions for Continuing Education 25) (San Francisco: Jossey-Bass).

Ramsden, P. (1979) 'Student Learning and the Perception of the Academic Environment', *Higher Education*, 8: 411–28.

Schmeck, R.R. (1988) *Learning Strategies and Learning Styles* (New York: Plenum Press).

Schön, D. (1983) *The Reflective Practitioner* (San Francisco: Jossey-Bass).

Svensson, L.G. (1987) *Higher Education and the State in Swedish History* (Stockholm: Almqvist & Wiksell).

Thomas, P.R. and Bain, J.D. (1982) 'Consistency in Learning Strategies', *Higher Education*, 11: 249–59.

Winter, J. (1995) *Skills for Graduates in the 21st Century* (London: Association of Graduate Recruiters).

Wisker, G. (1999) 'Learning Conceptions and Strategies of Postgraduate Students (Israeli PhD Students) and Some Steps Towards Encouraging and Enabling Their Learning', Paper presented to the Quality in Postgraduate Research Conference: Developing Research, Adelaide.

Wisker, G. (2000) 'Good Practice Working with International Students', SEDA Occasional Paper 110 (Birmingham: SEDA).

Wisker, G. and Sutcliffe, N. (eds) (1999) 'Good Practice in Postgraduate Supervision', SEDA Occasional Paper 106 (Birmingham: SEDA).

14 Developing a Supportive Research Culture Locally and at a Distance

This chapter looks at:

▶ Seeking support from colleagues and other researchers
▶ Setting up support groups close by and at a distance
▶ Work-in-progress and seminar presentations
▶ Building academic communities of practice and sustainable development in different cultural contexts

Research students are expected to work largely autonomously, with supervision. Remember, however, that you are entering a large local, national and international 'community of practice' (Lave and Wenger 1999) when you begin to research. With increased international communications and the Internet, we can all be so much more in touch with each other, supportive, exchanging ideas, contacts and work in progress. One of the most helpful and supportive elements of your work and contacts with others in the broader research community is that of actually seeking support from colleagues who are other researchers. There are many queries that can be cleared up, considerable stress that can be relieved, and much clarification gained by working together in various supportive peer groups, either close by or at a distance. Ultimately, beyond your current research, you could be setting up research partnerships for the future from such support groups. It is possible that you will be working with a group of others on a joint research project (more usual in the sciences) or, if on an MA/MSc, a staged EdD or PrD, you could have a natural peer group with whom to share your developing work. Often, however, it is up to the research student – that is, you – to set these groups up and maintain them, so it is important to look out for others who are working in similar fields to yourself and network with them.

Some supportive groups develop because they are working together in a research team. More often, they develop because students decide to set up groups to exchange questions, developments and progress.

● Group/project team supervisions

In some subject areas, such as practical science or medicine, there are likely to be several students working on a related project. In these cases, it would be useful to encourage your supervisors to organise regular group project supervisions at which you can share ideas, problems and questions. An added benefit of group supervisions is that the supervisor can pass on information to the group in a single statement rather than having to address each student individually. This ensures that issues about learning outcomes, length of the thesis, time, protocols, question framing, strategies, reading, and so on are dealt with proficiently.

It is not merely scientific researchers who work in research groups, however – although they are more likely to be working alongside each other, involved in the same experiments. Often, there can be a social science or an educational research group with research students looking at different aspects of similar areas (housing, childcare, gender and schooling, and so on) in a research group. They, too, are easily brought together in regular work-in-progress meetings as a natural part of their research.

In other subject areas, there might be only one student working in a specific area, but there will probably be a few working in cognate areas or areas that are otherwise related, whether in terms of methodology being used, subject or discipline. It would be just as useful in these instances to bring these students together, regularly or occasionally, for group supervisions. This should not be a substitution for individual supervisions but rather to augment them and provide a sense of sharing, support and peer responsibility. It is important that research students take the initiative here. If it seems unlikely that a supervisor or group of supervisors will bring you and colleagues together, start a student research group of your own for mutual support and comment. You will derive as much benefit (although perhaps of a different kind) out of sharing your own questions, ideas and work in progress with each other as you would discussing it with the supervisor. Additionally, the group session enables you to keep updated on your progress, and gives you the opportunity to ask questions, make supportive suggestions to others that also feed into your own thinking, and seek to develop ideas.

Often, initial methods training sessions or modules for MA students, and methods training programmes for MPhil, MRes and PhD/EdD/PrD students can be the basis for your groups. Ask at such a session if there is a group, or if anyone would like to help form one.

Things to do

Consider:
- Who would your natural supportive peer group be?
- How can you help set up a support group?
- Is there one you could join?
- Are there peers with whom you could work and exchange ideas, work in progress?

Self-managed groups and networks

It is not only groups who are naturally working together on similar projects – perhaps with the same supervisor or close colleagues as supervisors – who can benefit from supportive group activities. All research students can benefit. If there is no natural grouping of research students around a project, then it is important that supervisors, you and other students work to bring about such a grouping. Meeting together in self-help peer-group sessions can provide support, ensure there is an extra social element to the work, and could, in more formal terms, lead to a system of research-in-progress seminars. At such seminars you each share your research questions and development, and seek ideas, critical questions and suggestions about analysis or further reading from each other. When you present your work to the group it must be in a comprehensible shape; this forces research students to start to organise and clarify their thoughts, and order the kinds of data and results they are discovering. The presentation to peers is a marvellous opportunity to use the intelligent critical thinking of others who are working in similar areas or using similar methodologies. Their questions about questionnaire wording, the viability of research samples, how to interpret focus group and interview data, or whether some recent piece of writing on the subject is credible and important, all can help give you a clear focus. They will ease you out of any ruts in your thinking, and give you new angles and new ideas when you need them. Presentation at a work-in-progress seminar is also a practice or 'dry' run for later conference presentations, and even the viva if you are undertaking a UK or European PhD. Working together in supportive peer groups, you can also move beyond the PhD or Master's in itself, and can circulate information about conferences and publication opportunities to each other, thus expanding a research culture that could extend beyond this particular project.

The sharing of key questions about procedures, systems and ideas – depending on the context – can be immensely useful for students who might otherwise feel rather isolated. Self-managed groups help students feel supported, promoting the discussion of issues, developments, problems and breakthroughs. They also provide the perfect opportunity for the exploratory talk we all value so greatly at undergraduate level that is often so sorely missed just when it is absolutely essential to the development of enquiry, the testing of hypotheses and the sharing of discoveries at postgraduate level.

Self-managed groups can be immensely helpful in supporting each other, meeting regularly to discuss questions in each other's research, sharing skills in terms of how to do literature searches, pilot questionnaires and so on, and hear reports on each other's work in progress, providing useful feedback and sharing ideas.

Networks aid the dissemination of skills and information, and keep students in touch with each other. With this kind of communication, not only can they support each other and discuss ideas, findings, and so on, but they can also keep students in touch with each other on issues of dates, regulations, passing the hurdle of transfer to PhD from MPhil, and other such potentially threatening, often confusing and ill-informed experiences.

International students may find that the international office – or the postgraduate school, if there is one – may have set up a self-managed group in advance. If not, you need to help set one up with your peers. Some international students could find research life very lonely, and a support group is a social as well as an intellectual 'lifeline'.

Even if the supervisor plays a key role in setting up these self-managed groups and networks to begin with, the groups should be able to run on their own, driven by the students, because they are useful to the beneficiaries. This is essential supportive networking and it is up to you as research students to work together to establish and continue it.

● Peer pairing

Supervisors can be asked to set up systems of peer pairing. In this system, research students are put in touch with each other to work together supportively in pairs. They do not have to be working on the same project, but should be involved in similar subject areas or using similar methodologies. They might both be students of the same supervisor or of her/his colleagues. For the new research student, being paired with another can be most helpful. You will, of course, make your own contacts and friends, but the supportive pairing ensures that you meet regularly and compare notes. Information can be shared regarding the way you can work usefully in the university on your research, issues to do with policies and practices, dates and availability of materials and resources, and so on. With a formalised peer pairing system, everyone has someone else to talk their work through with from the beginning. This relieves some of the initial burden of work from the supervisor, who can then concentrate on supervising the project proper and its needs, rather than spending time repetitively informing different students about policies, and so on.

Things to do

Consider:

- Do you have access to others who are working in the same subject area or using similar methodologies? Could you have?
- Are you already part of a research group that can develop further to support each of you in your research?
- What kinds of supportive systems and structures are present in your university or home base?
- Where, how and with whom could you set up supportive peer-pairing links, or groups, whether supervisor-led or peer-led?
- What would the specific benefits of such supportive peers or groups be for you?
- How can you set up self-help supportive groups and research groups?
- How will you use them?
- How can you keep in touch?
- What can you do immediately to help set up or maintain such supportive relationships?

● Peer support systems over a distance

An increasing number of research students are carrying out their studies in a country different from that of their supervisor. This is for a variety of reasons. Sometimes the expertise lies in another country, and it is far too expensive and disruptive for the researcher to move in order to work with the supervisor of their choice. Sometimes the second or third supervisor is external to the university home base of the student. Sometimes the student wishes to be registered with a distant university because there is nowhere locally with which to register, and they wish to study in a recognised and accredited university culture and context. Some students studying part-time will necessarily work away from their supervisor's base. Sometimes supervisors move jobs, but wish to maintain supervisory contact with their students rather than passing the students on to someone else to supervise midway in their research. Many international students study at a distance for all or part of their MA, MPhil or PhD.

Traditionally, in these circumstances, contact with the supervisor will often be by e-mail, Skype, visit and phone. With the advent of e-mail, videoconferencing, Skype and webcams, it is possible for supervisor and research student – and for research students in a group – to be in contact over long distances, either in specifically arranged sessions by videoconference, or together through a chat room or a discussion list. WebCT and Blackboard online course management systems provide opportunities for this. Chat rooms, which you can set up yourselves, and Yahoo or other instant messaging systems also afford you the opportunity to speak together synchronically (in real time). These relatively hi-tech contacts are invaluable for students wishing to maintain that necessary support from peers, as well as supervisors, and to further their studies.

If you are carrying out all or part of your research at a distance, do ensure that you stay in touch with others involved in MA, MPhil or PhD research at your university. Exchange e-mails, download Skype, and keep each other updated.

● Using electronic and video links to support research students in their work

Research supervision aided by e-mail and videoconferencing was explained in Chapter 10. With the use of videoconference links, groups of research students or individuals can become involved in a multimedia videoconference.

Videoconferencing links provide the opportunity for groups to work with their supervisor or for students in different locations to offer each other the kind of peer support and research in progress that has been described previously. In this instance, the kind of information and ideas exchanged will probably not be about local systems, but will concentrate on joint or individual research issues and problems, and on trying out ideas and developed projects with each other. Here, the peer comments and support can be invaluable, especially to the more remote or isolated student. The quality of comment from peers across the world cannot be underestimated, as there is a fascinating breadth of knowledge and approaches that spring from the different learning cultures of students of different nationalities. Students can put each other in touch with reading materials, resources and links in a number of countries, as well as keeping valuable contacts that could be most useful in the years after completion of the research.

● Different modes of contact explored

Audioconferencing can also fulfil many of these aims and objectives, both for supervisors and for groups of research students. With these practices, research students can book audioconferences with each other to carry on work-in-progress discussions without the presence of the supervisor.

A third, and possibly the easiest, contact is by e-mail. For groups of students, access to e-mail can provide a valuable discussion forum. The formal e-mail discussion group can be set up and joined by researchers around the world by their subscribing to be involved. As anyone who has used e-mail discussion groups will know, it is possible to be involved in heated discussions with a group over a period of time, which is immensely profitable on the spot. Much of this immediate discussion is best facilitated through instant messaging and in discussion groups using synchronous chat activities. A version of this that supervisors and students might use, or which might well facilitate student-to-student discussion is Skype, which can remain open for hours and provides discussion and even webcam links between people across the world.

Synchronous discussion and asynchronous discussion are useful for keeping in touch. A useful and slightly more distant involvement can also be maintained, where you read others' comments and only contribute if you have something to say, but remain in touch nonetheless. This is an asynchronous discussion which would be enabled by being connected through WebCT or Blackboard. Asynchronous discussion is also possible if you have a specific request for ideas and information or solutions to a problem. In this instance, an e-mail discussion group can be most useful for making specific suggestions to questions put out over the discussion group. Learning conversations of a high order can result, and the research student can select the information he or she finds useful, probe further and credit the provider. This takes place rapidly and over great distances. Subscription to specific mail groups can also be a way of obtaining more information from a wide number of people, by sending out a request for information and ideas, or describing a problem and asking for responses over the broader e-mail mail group.

Another version of the e-mail discussion group is the chat room, or virtual tutorial discussion space. Students can post comments on work in progress and ask for support and tips from others in their research group or others engaged in similar kinds of research – whether on similar topics or using similar strategies. The supervisor of a group of students can occasionally join in and help solve some problem or provide tips, but the main discussion and support comes from the students themselves, to each other.

Things to do

Consider:

- Do you, or could you, have access to videoconferencing or audio-conferencing for distance tutorials and supervisions?
- Do you, or could you, have access to these conferencing methods for discussion with other research students?
- Do you or could you use e-mail to discuss your work with your supervisor? How?
- Do you or could you become involved in an e-mail discussion group, or join a mail-base discussion group or WebCT (or other) chat room?
- Do you have access to instant messaging, or Skype?
- If so, which ones are likely to be helpful and appropriate for you?

How might you best use these different forms of contact?

● Other peer-support systems – establishing a research culture

A key peer support system, and a very good one for developing the skill of research, is the more formal research seminar series. During this, both staff and students alike give research-in-progress seminar papers, followed by discussions. Here, questions can be asked and methodology, practices, discoveries, theories and problems all aired and discussed, with a coherent base of a seminar paper upon which to build.

The establishment and maintenance of a research culture is a sensitive and complex issue. If you work in a learning environment that has always had a research culture, active research, and the exchange and mutual respect of research ideas and findings, then you might take this culture for granted. Do ensure that you discover its opportunities and make the most of them. If, on the other hand, you are starting to carry out your research in a university whose tradition of research is not as old as Oxbridge and some others, or you are researching part-time and only visiting the university, or you are researching at a great distance from it, the existence of (and your support and contribution to) a research culture are essential. At its best, a research culture is one that comprises respect, resources, activity, funding, mutual trust and sharing, and support for productive research (and occasionally – in the less successful moments – unproductive, frustrating research).

Some universities have research offices, postgraduate facilities and social activities, well-stocked research libraries and equipment, and a widely shared respect for the kinds of time demands, flexibility and pressures involved in carrying out successful research in all subject areas. Other universities need to develop these cultures. It is important that you work towards such development. Research is fundamental to the creation and development of knowledge and skills. It motivates those involved, and enables them and the subject area to move forward and develop. It provides a firm underpinning for what is taught in a university and also, often, for how teaching takes place (depending on the area of the research – see, for example, action research). It contributes to our understanding of how others work, learn and behave, to our linking between knowledge, theory, experience and practice. Going outside the university, research contributes to moving forward human knowledge skills and development more generally.

Everyone benefits in the end from successful research that is shared and feeds into development and change. Clearly some subject areas can claim this direct relationship more obviously. Those working on Aids, cancer, and experiments to do with making aircraft safer, buildings stronger, TVs more hi-tech, are much more likely to be able to point to the direct effects of their work or work to which they have contributed. But even the most esoteric research contributes to the fund of human knowledge and development if it is shared and used. We need to ensure that other colleagues know we are involved in research and respect that, without arrogantly parading the fact. It is also our duty to ensure that the research findings are indeed shared and eventually used. Communities of practice – local and international – can be established and maintained beyond the life of your research project. In many instances, academic research can, through some communities, cause real change in certain contexts, leading to the sustainable development of research, changes in a variety of practices and so have a real impact on culture, society, behaviour and human knowledge.

Conclusion

We have looked at:

☐ Support for research locally and at a distance

☐ Peer-support groups and research methods groups

☐ Use of video links, instant messaging, Skype and e-mail

☐ Work-in-progress seminars and groups

☐ Building academic communities of practice and sustainable development in different cultural contexts.

Further reading

Burkitt, I., Husband, C., McKenzie, J., Torn, A. and Crow, S. (2001) *Nurse Education and Communities of Practice* (London: ENB).

Gibbs, G., Wisker, G. and Bochner, B. (1999) *Supporting More Students* (Oxford: Oxford Brookes University).

Hildreth, P., Kimble, C. and Wright, P. (2001) *Computer Mediated Communications and International Communities of Practice*, Proceedings of Ethicomp '98, March 1998 (Erasmus University, Netherlands).

Lave, J. and Wenger, E. (1999) 'Legitimate Peripheral Participation in Communities of Practice', in R. McCormack and C. Poechter (eds) *Learning and Knowledge* (London: Paul Chapman Publishing).

Wenger, E. (1998) *Communities of Practice* (Cambridge: Cambridge University Press).

Wenger, E. (2000) 'Communities of Practice and Social Learning Systems', *Sage*, 7 (2): 225–46.

Wenger, E. and Lave, J. (1991) *Situated Learning* (Cambridge: Cambridge University Press).

Part Three

Carrying Out the Research and Starting to Write

15 Carrying out a Literature Review – Developing the Theoretical Perspectives Chapter

This chapter looks at how you develop your engagement with the literature and debates in the field, setting up good habits early on in your research and maintaining them throughout. It also looks at how you can write the literature review chapter, referred to here as the 'theoretical perspectives chapter' because it suggests an engagement in a debate with theories, theorists and experts in the field. Your research is seen as a contribution to knowledge in the field and it needs to indicate, therefore, that there is awareness of what that knowledge comprises, and what the various debates, disagreements and key theories and concerns are in the field. Your own contribution to knowledge and to meaning, constructed in a dialogue with the experts and the theorists, is important in a literature survey or review, so that you are seen to enter the academic discussion about your topic and subject area with those who have developed the theories and those who have put them into practice and written about them.

The reasons for literature reviews or surveys are twofold. You need to read yourself into the field of study in order to gauge where your own ideas fit, what can inform them, what others think and have discovered, and to define where and in which ways your area of questioning, your research and your findings could contribute to existing knowledge and extend meaning and understanding. Your own work both engages with the known literature and adds something else. This might seem a tall order, because you cannot possibly read everything that has been written about your field of study or everything about your particular area, unless it is very specialised. It also seems rather daunting at first because, in the early days of your research, you might well feel that everything has been said by the theorists and experts already, and that you will never have anything else to add. By searching out the literature, and therefore the debates to which your own work will contribute, you are not trying to cover and summarise everything. This would be an endless, daunting and ultimately pointless task. Yours is not a role of summariser of everyone else's thoughts and discoveries, but one of engagement in *dialogue* with what has been written and what is to be written and discovered by others. You need to read the background literature to contextualise and underpin your own work rather than substitute for it. This indicates to readers and examiners that you know the field, and also that you know you have something to contribute to it. I prefer the term 'theoretical perspectives chapter' to that of 'literature review' (or survey) because it suggests that you are discovering the previous and current work, and determining the debates, discussions and disagreements, as well as the key theories and examples that have put some of these theories into practice, in the work of experts and others. The term 'theoretical perspectives' gives the sense that there are debates and areas of work to which your own work can contribute, rather than that you are reviewing a finished, dead set of texts and theories. It is dynamic: you will have much to contribute, even if this only becomes clear to you as you read; first, summarise; then start to synthesise – that is, bring ideas together focusing on their patterns and the varied debates, see arguments and different theories and points of view emerging so that, as your own work develops, you can see what you have contributed.

● A literature review/theoretical perspectives chapter

- ● Not a dead list with annotated comments about texts only in an early chapter

BUT

- ● an ongoing dialogue with the experts, theories and theorists underpinning your research.

You will need to:

- ● Read widely (more than you need) for contexts and debates
- ● Take careful note and record sources

● Summarise only in order to engage in a critical debate – your arguments arise from, relate to, and are underpinned by the experts – content and methods.

Various practitioners have discussed the different stages leading to a literature review. Chris Hart (1999) outlines these as: clarifying and reading research; argumentation analysis; organising and expressing ideas; mapping and analysing ideas. Searching, assessing, integrating and writing up are also seen as key stages. There are a number of useful books and websites that can take you through versions of the stages and provide useful tips (see 'Further reading' on p. 185)

Things to do

● Read one or two examples of essays in your own subject area that use a wide variety of literature – you can tell this is the case by looking at the bibliography, which should be extensive and range over several years, using primary essential texts and some newer ones that take the various arguments on further
● You are not reading for the sense as such, but for the ways in which the authors have responded to and worked with the literature, and added their own new knowledge or understanding and interpretation of that body of literature, suggesting ongoing debate

In order to judge whether this is a live literature review/piece of theoretical perspectives writing you need to ask:

● How do the author and the essay use the literature?
● Is it a dead list; is it organised into themes, debates, disagreements; or are the texts to which they have referred only listed or summarised without pulling together the main themes and debates?
● Is it vague? Too broad? Too narrow? Disorganised? Leading too widely to too many ideas so that a common thread of argument is not clear?
● Do they summarise the key points of key tests, developing patterns in order to add to debates about the issues – or not?
● Do the essays really engage with the arguments that have been developed by the author, or are these arguments merely stated?

Literature reviews/surveys or theoretical perspectives chapters are a really important part of your thesis because they enable you to work at a high conceptual level with other people's work, and to see how your own contributes to knowledge and meaning. They enable you to work conceptually, identify your developing contribution to knowledge and meaning (which ensures your work is on the right level for the award), and they enable you to engage in a dialogue with the work of others. This developing chapter ensures you are NOT merely going into detail on what is said, what you find and how you carried out your research, but are instead showing how your research develops from and engages with work in the broader academic community, that is, how dynamic it is. Theoretical perspectives chapters are also something you work on from the start to the finish of your thesis and they involve hard, busy work. They depend, in the first instance, upon extensive literature searching. Some of this is undertaken before the research question is posed and the proposal written, so an early literature review helps to establish the field, arguments in the field and how this new piece of research should be able to contribute to debates. Next, most of literature reviews or theoretical perspectives chapters are ongoing, taking place alongside the research throughout. Literature reviews or theoretical perspectives chapters usually appear as a separate chapter, although some of the ideas and arguments also form a part of the introduction to engage the reader in the theories and arguments of the research. The main texts, theorists and argument will reappear throughout the thesis as you engage your own work with that of previous and established theories and work in the field.

Theoretical perspectives chapters indicate previous work in the field, the context into which your own work fits, and the different theories from which your own work springs and which inform it. You will be reading in areas of the field, of related fields, of critical and theoretical questioning and approaches in order to properly inform and drive your own work.

While the theoretical perspectives chapter contains the developed arguments, theories, themes and ways in which your own work contributes to knowledge and meaning in the field, you continue to refer to key themes, texts, writers and experts as and when their work informs and relates to yours throughout the thesis or dissertation. So, from the point where you analyse your data and start to interpret it and determine findings to the moment where you draw your factual and conceptual conclusions, you will still be underpinning your points and arguments with reference to the key theorists and the experts in the field whose theories and practical work underpins your own.

● **International students – some particular issues**

If you are an international student you will most probably find that you need either: to seek a translation of the work of international theorists, critics or experts you hope to use in your own arguments and research; or provide your own translation of the quotations you use, if they do not publish in English. If your university allows you to present your work in your own language and assumes that it can be examined in your own language, you will clearly not have to do this (but you would probably be translating the work you find into English). However, most UK, Australian, US and other English-speaking universities do expect the dissertation or thesis to be presented entirely in English. You might also find that it is an unusual challenge to go beyond summarising and noting the work of experts to identifying the debates in the literature, and realising that your own work can contribute to these debates and even critique some of the previous work undertaken by experts. When you first start your work, you might feel you will never have anything substantial or new to contribute, and that you have no right to debate the idea of experts. However, your work will start to become your own original contribution and this is partly achieved by just that understanding, synthesising, and debating with the experts.

The theoretical perspectives chapter sets the scene for the research questions, the major arguments of the research and thesis, and then for the work itself, taking different elements of the thesis argument on in different places and providing a coherent thread of reference for key arguments and ideas. In theoretical perspectives chapters, it is sensible to keep reading throughout the research. There could be really important new discoveries or key texts that appear even quite close to the end of your own work, and you will need to acknowledge these, even to say that they could not be incorporated into the research design because of when they were produced. This shows that you have awareness of the field and of the learning conversations taking place within it, and can see what your own work contributes. Most people still refer to this chapter as a literature review (as I have explained above, I do not think this is a helpful term).

> The process of the literature review involves the researcher in exploring the literature to establish the status quo, formulate a problem or research enquiry, define the value of pursuing the line of enquiry established, and compare the findings and ideas with his or her own. The product involves the synthesis of the work of others in a form that demonstrates the accomplishment of the exploratory process (Andresen 1997, adapted from Bruce 1994).

Theoretical perspectives chapters establish the background and the context, and involve consulting and engaging with primary sources of all sorts – and secondary sources too, or, rather, other researchers' and academics' contributions to the field of discussion. They involve reflection, analysis and comment on contributions to the field of study, acknowledging that you are aware of what has been found, the methods of research, and the underpinning arguments in your field:

> A literature review uses as its database reports of primary or original scholarship, and does not report new primary scholarship itself. The primary reports used in the literature may be verbal, but in the vast majority of cases are written documents. The types of scholarship might be empirical theoretical, critical/analytical, or methodological in nature. Second, a literature review seeks to describe, summarise, evaluate, clarify and/or integrate the content of primary reports (Cooper 1985: 8).

The purposes of literature review, according to Andresen, are:

- becoming familiar with the 'conversation' in the subject area of interest
- identifying an appropriate research question
- ascertaining the nature of previous research and issues surrounding the research question
- finding evidence in the academic discourse to establish a need for the proposed research
- keeping abreast of ongoing work in the area of interest (Andresen 1997, part 3: 48).

The literature review is an essential part of planning your research and helps you to develop your own line of thought. As an ongoing process, it also helps you to keep abreast of developments in your subject and field, and possibly enables you to get in touch with others working in the same field, in that you can contact other researchers and discuss work with them. Your examiners will be looking for how far your thesis contributes to knowledge in the field, to which the literature review element of your work is central.

● Carrying out the literature review

There are several activities associated with handling a literature review, leading to a theoretical perspectives chapter:

You need to scour your main library and associated libraries, probably using a computer to help in your search, but not substituting it completely for looking around the shelves in the area where you may find a useful book. We often find other related texts in close proximity. Look in the reference sections of key books and articles you are using and of others' theses on similar topics. Here, you will find what might be minor references for others' work but possibly either background or really key references for your own, depending on the different slants and lines of argument taken in these sources.

Literature searches: using the library and the Internet – a brief introduction

Every researcher needs to become familiar with the use of the libraries available to them – not always your local library, but often a specialist library, perhaps at a distance – and also to make good use of the information available on the Internet. Using e-mail and the web to keep in touch with other researchers and your supervisor is also important (see groups/support materials in Chapter 14), not merely because of peer support but also to exchange information sources and start to develop your own discussions about key texts, new ideas.

There are now some highly developed search engines, such as Google scholar, which can help you find out not only the ordinary everyday information you would find on Google, Yahoo, and so on, but also the academic journal articles.

Your own university is probably subscribed to many of the journal article databases that you need, so it is best to go into the academic journal archives through your own university library, which will enable you to access much more than is readily available on the web. Sometimes, it is possible to determine whether a book or article is right for your purposes by reading the abstract online or by reading excerpts that are made available by publishers. If it looks right, you can then send off for the full text, either through the library, perhaps through the Internet or by purchasing it yourself. This saves a great deal of time reading inappropriate materials. Much of what you read will either repeat or slightly build upon those key essential texts. It is NOT necessary to document every example of a comment on the main theories themes and issues; instead, identify the key theorists, practitioner/writers, key texts and the ongoing arguments.

Trawling for information is fascinating when you know how – and many of us do this every day. However, there is often too much information, and on the Internet it is not likely to be organised in the way you need it, so be careful with copying it. Do manage it, organise and sift it, selecting what is important and necessary. There is a real concern with students at all levels merely downloading topical material from the Internet. This is plagiarism, as serious as merely copying from a book. The other problem with material on the Internet is that it is put there without any quality control checks, and some of it is incorrect and poorly written.

You have been warned!

You will also need to consider how to handle the information you gain in your literature searching throughout the research. This depends very much on the way in which you are comfortable and successful in your own research strategies, but it might also mean you have to develop more focused, rigorous and organised methods.

One model suggests that you acquire a great deal of information,

Things to do

Consider:

- When have you used libraries, CD-ROMs and the Internet for research?
- Which libraries will you use?
- Which libraries might you need to join?
- Will you need to develop skills in using the Internet? Or are you already comfortable with online journal searching?
- Will you need to update these skills?
- What experience do you have of accessing subject indexes and abstracting databases?
- Do you have good access and, if so, where?

In considering these questions, note down an action plan for:

- improving your library access. Will you need to ask for a letter of reference signed by your supervisor in order to gain access to another local university library, for example, in your home town?
- improving your Internet access. Will you need to take a brief training course to use the Internet for literature searching/to use the online access computers in the library, or at a distance, and to access online journals though academic links rather than merely looking at what is available on Google, Yahoo and other search engines (often of dubious quality)?
- finding the subject indexes and the abstracting databases, and conducting a trial search. Do you have experience in this? Or can you conduct a trial search to give you an idea of advice you need to seek?

Action points

Your search of the literature leads to the incorporation of ideas, quotations, arguments and references into your own work. You will need to establish a sound set of study and working strategies to make full use of this. Try the skills audit. This will help you evaluate your position.

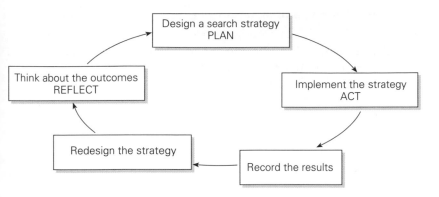

Figure 15.1 Reflective literature searching model

summarise the key points, keep careful references, and write the introductory literature review or theoretical perspectives chapter from this.

Another suggests that, as the literature review and theoretical perspectives process is ongoing throughout your work, you will need to keep returning to the field and reviewing and rereading, certainly catching up on new texts and new areas of study, which become more obviously relevant as your work proceeds. A reflective approach to literature searching is the most useful, that is, one that enables you to go through a cyclical model – searching, recording, processing and researching as new sources or new ideas and developments become clear (see Figure 15.1).

Things to do

What skills needs do you have?

For example:	Good	Quite good	Needs practice
Quick and effective reading	1	2	3
Note taking	1	2	3
Summarising	1	2	3
Finding and using subject indexes and abstracting databases	1	2	3
Reference keeping	1	2	3
Interweaving your reading into your arguments and discussions	1	2	3

Abstracting, noting and summarising

You can usually take one photocopy of a journal article under copyright law. You will need, however, to take notes from and 'process' journal articles and books, chapters and other sources. Try the 'SQ3R' method for rapid and effective note taking:

- Survey – quick read through
- Question – what was that about?
- Read/reread – look through it all/read it carefully and reread, but only if necessary
- Record
- Take notes under main key headings (having identified these main points in your survey); take full quotations and full citations of other references you will need to follow up
- Summarise major arguments and quote the key points made; always indicate with references the sources from which the ideas and the quotations come
- Make some sub-notes and discussion points alongside your notes; underline in colour the main ideas and arguments
- Start to structure your notes and process the arguments
- Review – quickly look back at the chapter/article, and so on. Have you caught the most important points, the main arguments, all you need for your own work? Have you recorded the references appropriately? Are the quotations correct? What have you missed?
- Consult some of the good study guides available to remind you of these effective practices (Cottrell 2003; Dunleavy 1986).

Filing and retaining

You need to keep full, informative notes of all the sources you consult, your contacts and correspondences. These are best kept in card indexes or on your computer. See below for comments on computer or card index storage. End-note and similar packages will help you to collate the various references you discover as you read and research for later use.

Learning journals and logs

You could also use a learning journal or learning log to write up the main ideas, the key arguments and your thoughts about how these relate to your work and how your work contributes to them for use in your ongoing literature search, review/theoretical perspectives chapter. This helps to show the shaping of your arguments and the shaping of your use of your reading, how it informs your investigations, research questioning and interpretation. If you are a part-time student, it also helps you to return to the key questions and findings after periods away from your study – for example, on work projects, family holidays, house moves, with new babies and so on.

Good research habits

You need to ask yourself regularly:

- Have I updated my literature search and review?
- Have I returned to key sources to investigate further what emerged as important issues?
- Have I fully recorded the references I have found?
- Have I been writing up and using what I have found? Have I been using the ideas and spurring on more of my own ideas?
- Have I been leaving information to stockpile (and possibly go stale)?

Management on a computer

Programmes for management of literature include Endnote, Procit, Notebook and Reference Manager, among others.

Establish a list of headings that fits your research – subjects, questions, methodology, methods and so on.

Read papers and parts of books as soon as you get them and assign headings to the material so that you can record these and later access the reference from those several appropriate headings. Consider headings of:

- author
- title
- methods
- key words and areas
- what they contribute to the argument – whose work they disagree with, or agree with, main points
- page, date and place of publication.

You need to link these headings and areas to the file management system so that when the system is interrogated, it indicates work collected under the appropriate heading/author/date, and so on, as required.

This is obviously more sophisticated than a card index, which tends to force you to keep information under author in alphabetical order, so that you are not immediately able to go to the repository of information on a subject area. Card indexes, however, are portable, cheap and can be marvellously idiosyncratic. You will need to find the system that suits you and which you can manage. The most important element of each kind of storage system is that you have the information you need to retrieve. So ensure that you have:

- author
- title
- place of publication, publisher, date (the citation format which is required by your university) and page numbers, if appropriate
- areas of interest and importance – subject headings
- some key quotations
- where the source came from – for example, library, inter-library loan, the Internet, a friend's collection.

Are all recorded? Otherwise you will find that towards the middle of the thesis you cannot locate those wonderful early pieces of reading, and at the end you will have to spend days in libraries trying to track down the books and the journals with the full references in them. This is a frustrating waste of time.

For sophisticated computer users, Carol Tenopir and Gerald Lundeen's *Managing Your Information* (1988) is a full source of how to create your own database and which systems to use.

Things to do

- Select a journal article that relates to your area of research.
- Process it using the SQ3R methods (see p. 178).
- Now write down the key points, the full citation details, the author, subject and so on, on an index card.

Decide where/under what headings – for example, author, key words, area of argument, methods, and so on – you would want to store the information so that it can be retrieved when writing chapters.

● **Writing the theoretical perspectives chapter**

Theoretical perspectives, research activity, academic thinking and good writing

We have looked so far at the importance of gathering and managing your sources, in order to begin to engage with identifying the main issues developed or developing from theories, critics and practitioners. We have considered critical reading and reading that helps you to identify main points. We have also considered ways of taking notes to enable your own responses to start to emerge from the main points and quotations. Now, let us look at the actual writing of this important chapter. The theoretical perspectives chapter is often the most difficult to write well.

- Critical thinking is crucial in postgraduate research
- Much of this involves questioning and problematising accepted ideas and information
- Much of it involves engaging in a dialogue with others who have developed theories or carried out research
- Creating a dialogue between theoretical perspectives and research activity is necessary so that you avoid dead lists, and make the most of your contribution to ongoing debates and to knowledge.

Reading – and writing the chapter

- Reading, arguing and writing are carried out in different ways for different purposes
- Reading on the topic – accumulating information and establishing the field – provides facts and basic underpinning ideas you can use in your work and writing arguments
- Contrastive reading – identifying discussions, debates, disagreements and different positions helps you to critique others' work and ask questions, then argue in a dialogue between experts/others/your work
- Analytical writing and reading – What is it made of? What lies behind it? How does it fit in or not? Is it coherent? Why does it matter? Take it to pieces, find conflicts and arguments
- Consider how topics developed into research questions
- How are concepts and critical issues identified?
- What theories are needed to underpin and ask questions of the field/sample/area?
- What reading and what activities need to take place?

Using theorising to start researching and writing

Once you have carried out much of the initial reading, identified key themes and points as a topical contribution to these, gathered and organised the notes, in order to draw out the different strands and competing arguments you could:

- with colleagues, restate your research questions so that you are very focused on what you are reading
- unpick ideas, concepts, problems, theories and contradictions in the texts and express them visually as a diagram
- visualise – use diagrams to identify contradictions and patterns of ideas and arguments
- start to build your arguments from the visualisation – explain to colleagues
- identify research strategies to approach questions, complications, contradictions and research activities.

You will probably find it helpful to think about reading and writing in several different ways to write this chapter and use the literature later in your thesis. There are several stages – relating to the reading, the thinking and finally the writing – that take you through from merely describing and summarising to pulling the thesis together using different perspectives and arguments. Then, you move on to differentiating between them and determining the key theories and themes, and the key debates that are emerging. At that point, you start reflecting, evaluating and contributing to the arguments yourself. Finally, you know where your work can fit in and take the field forward, and you can contribute at that level. This kind of thinking and discussion emerges later in your research but, when you write up, you talk about it early in the thesis, as well as throughout, because the thesis is a finished product that is recording the development and the findings, the contribution of the research. It is NOT merely a record of stages of your own progress.

Stages of moving into writing your theoretical perspectives chapter

- Describe
- Summarise
- Synthesise
- Reflect
- Evaluate
- Determine competing debates
- Contribute to the argument
- Write something new that takes meaning and understanding further forwards.

When you think about how you can read and write this work up, you might find it useful to look further ahead at Chapter 21, which deals with the writing up, but at this stage consider briefly that the work you are reading is by or about:

Theorists – key thinkers in your field, who may well come from different aspects of the field or from different fields than that in which your work is placed

or

Critical practitioners – people who have taken the underpinning ideas of the theorists and engaged with them in their own research – thus developing arguments from evidence about the application of the theories in practice, in their research.

So, for example, if you are looking at researching management in geriatric hospitals and, in particular, the caring nature of such management, your work would be looking for theorists of:

- organisation
- human worth and care.

And the critical practitioners would be working in the fields or concerns of something closer to your own areas of interest – although you might indeed find that no one has combined the theories and fields and contexts quite as you are doing in your research: this is a major feature of your contribution to knowledge. Critical practitioners and researchers might have written about:

- management behaviour in organisations
- geriatric study
- emotional intelligence
- emotionally intelligent nursing and hospital management
- care and caring practices
- human dignity and worth.

Theorists can be thought of as first stage authors, and they will probably NOT be talking about the same area of work in which you are dealing but, instead, have ideas, approaches, questions, values, and so on that can be used to underpin and inform your work. Second stage authors can be defined as those critical practitioners who are working closely within your field or interest and who have used some of the ideas of the theorists in their own work. In the instance mentioned above, some might look at a variety of work on hospital management, or the treatment of the elderly, perhaps ideologically engaged management, emotional intelligence and public services. You could even narrow this down to work in a similar area, perhaps the management of schools or old people's homes rather than hospitals, so that your own work is taking a different focus. Alternatively, you might consider the areas in which these other second stage authors or critical practitioners have been working and writing and select for yourself a different group, a different context, asking slightly different questions at different times. You will find that you can use: (a) the theorists to underpin the theories you are using (of organisational care); and (b) the second stage of writers' work to engage with ways that they use the theories to underpin their work – which deals with similar areas and questions to your own, but probably in different contexts. You should find that, although there is probably no work that directly engages with the questions, contexts and issues with which your own is engaged, this broader approach helps you find similar work that can be used as a focus in dealing with the issues, arguments and difference in the work that you are undertaking.

It is heartening to see no one else has done exactly what you are doing, but it is very unlikely, indeed, that no one has asked similar questions, looked at similar issues, used similar theories, albeit in different ways. You need to use this work to underpin and inform your own, setting it in a debate while also ensuring you are indicating how unusual it is in terms of focus, angle, context or population. See Chapter 22 for advice on writing this inlay, and in an ongoing fashion throughout.

Good practice in literature reviews/theoretical perspectives

What lessons have we learned about good literature reviews/surveys?

- They are more than dead surveys
- The theoretical perspectives chapter is an early chapter which uses the literature to establish context, underlying theories, main themes and debates, the main argument and the contribution that your work will make to these theories in practice, to these themes and debates – all a dialogue between established and current texts, and with your work
- You continue to draw on the literature/theoretical perspectives base throughout the thesis – it does not merely appear at the start of the thesis
- Theories, arguments, main texts need to appear early in the thesis and be referred to when you are engaging with your data analysis, findings and, finally, in the drawing of conceptual conclusions.

Conclusion

We have looked at:

- ☐ The function of literature reviewing to form the introductory context and theoretical underpinning and to integrate with your own research throughout

- ☐ How to carry out literature searching

- ☐ How to take notes, process and make the information and ideas your own

- ☐ Storage and retrieval.

Further reading

Andresen, L.W. (1997) *Highways to Postgraduate Supervision* (Sydney: University of Western Sydney).

Cooper, H.M. (1985) *The Integrative Research Review: A Systematic Approach* (London: Sage).

Cottrell, S. (2003) *The Study Skills Handbook* (Basingstoke: Palgrave Macmillan).

Dunleavy, Patrick (1986) *Studying for a Degree* (Basingstoke: Palgrave Macmillan).

Hart, C. (1999) *Doing a Literature Review: Releasing the Social Science Research Imagination* (London: Sage).

Tenopir, C. and Lundeen, G. (1988) *Managing your Information* (New York: Neal Schuman).

Websites accessed

http://www.gwu.edu/~litrev
http://www.ecu.du.au/ses/research/CALLR/Writing
http://utoronto.ca/writing/litreview.html

16 Methods in Brief

This chapter looks a
▶ An introduction to both quantitative anc qualitative methods:
▶ Why use question-naires?
▶ What are their pros and cons?
▶ How can you use them?

As we have previously seen, your choice of research methods depends upon the methodology you are using, and the research questions you are asking. It also depends to a great extent upon the discipline area in which you are studying and your view of the world. An argument that sees a dichotomy or polar opposition between positivist methodology (deductive, quantitative data collection and interpretation) and the postpositivist (which is inductive, develops theory, and uses qualitative methods) is an easy rule of thumb to determine worldviews and approaches. However, this is actually an over-simplification, as some researchers combine across the inductive and deductive, qualitative and quantitative, and some research projects are built in stages which, for example, begin deductively, then develop inductively (or vice versa). Let us begin with the overly simple distinctions and then move on to recognising how researchers and research combine across them.

In a very straightforward simplistic reading of research, should you be a scientist or a positivistic social scientist, you probably believe that the facts of the world are provable through trial and error, experimentation and measurement, and that the repetition of studies ensures their reliability, as does the collection of carefully managed data from large numbers. You are likely to be testing theory and testing a hypothesis. For the most part, the beliefs, disciplines and methodology are enacted by quantitative methods, which seek large numbers for statistical validity, and generalisability, which comes from large numbers of trials. On the other hand, should you believe that the world is largely known only in terms of the ways in which we look at and interpret it, that knowledge and understanding are constituted, you are likely to be developing, and will probably be undertaking, more qualitative research. For some research questions, it is both helpful and more robust to combine across the quantitative and the qualitative research methods.

Because of the vast amount of excellent books and good examples on both quantitative and qualitative methods, we shall only be looking at each in a very introductory fashion here, with more emphasis on qualitative methods – particularly interviews and focus groups.

Quantitative research methods – designing and using questionnaires

You are likely to be using questionnaires if you seek responses from large numbers of respondents, as they can be counted, measured and statistically analysed. For this reason, questionnaires are favourites among those with a positivistic worldview and methodology, who seek to test a theory (deductive rather than inductive). However, although questionnaires are favourites among those who seek a weight of numbers to prove a hypothesis, test a theory or discover something, other researchers with a more postpositivistic worldview, who seek to develop rather than test theory (inductive rather than deductive) can also use questionnaires. Their questionnaires are likely to be more open-ended, delivered in written or oral question-and-answer form to fewer people. Inductive researchers seek fuller, more varied responses because they are looking not for statistical significance but rather for richness of information.

If your immediate impression is that a questionnaire is the only real method or vehicle open to you in your research, think again. Many of us rely too heavily on them, and it is possible, if you need real in-depth discovery of people's attitudes, that an interview would be a much better method.

Questionnaires gather information directly by asking people questions and using the responses as data for analysis. They are often used to gather information about facts, attitudes, behaviours, activities and responses to events, and usually consist of a list of written questions. Respondents can complete questionnaires in timed circumstances, by post, or by responding to researchers directly, who, armed with the questionnaire, can actually ask them the questions directly. It is a method of gathering large numbers of responses, although the response rates are quite frequently not high because many people become rather irritated by questionnaires and refuse to fill them out. You need to ensure that your questionnaire has been perfected when you use it with your sample. It is important to take advice, to pilot questions thoroughly and then finalise the questionnaire. Unless you intend to show changing responses over time, you usually have just one attempt at a questionnaire with your sample. It is rarely possible to return to the sample with a more developed version of a questionnaire, not least because having completed it once they will not be able to respond in a natural and genuine manner.

You need to ensure that your questionnaire is:

- kept confidential
- trialled, piloted and refined
- really able to ask the questions you want to pose
- unambiguous and avoids multiple questions
- entirely clear in its questions and layout.

When setting out a questionnaire you need to:

- clear the use of it with your sponsor, or whoever is allowing you to use it
- code the questions first, so that when you analyse responses you can easily collect the data from each question and fit the data into each underlying informing category upon which the questions have been based. Yes/No and Lickert scale-type questions (on a range of 1–5, where for example 1 = strongly agree and 5 = strongly disagree) are easier to code than long open-ended questions. While open-ended questions produce fuller responses, you will need to have an idea of the themes or categories for which you are looking and develop the coding to deal with expected areas of answers. In this way, when the open-ended question responses come in, you can code, sort and analyse your data. Also, if there are sufficient responses, you will be able to carry out some statistical analysis, since questionnaires are most often used to suggest the response of a significant number of people in terms of percentage and proportions.

When sending out questionnaires you need to:

- explain what the purpose is and guarantee confidentiality
- explain who the sponsor is/who it is for
- provide a return address and a time for the return (if it is to be posted)
- explain that the responses are voluntary
- thank the respondents for their time in completing the question-naire.

Layout

This is a complicated science. Questionnaires should not be too long, or they will get a lower response rate; people become bored and irritated, and fail to complete them. Use single-sided paper and quality production, do not crowd the questionnaire, and try not to repeat questions too often (although this is useful for cross-checking, it irritates respondents).

- Number your pages as well as your questions.
- Whatever kind of questions you pose, you need to include a coding box, probably on the right-hand side, so that you can code the responses when you have gathered all the questions together. Make sure this is an integral part of the questionnaire as you develop, pilot and print it, or there will be a lot of tedious work inscribing boxes and coding them afterwards. Some questionnaires can be computer read.
- Make sure your questions are very clear and unambiguous. Respondents should be willing and able to answer the questions so they should be properly targeted, not insulting, not vague and should avoid unnecessary assumptions.
- If you provide consistent kinds of questions with a consistent scale – for example, 1–4 – your respondents will be more able to focus on the questions without worrying about the format. Unfortunately, they are also more likely to coast along on the columns, ticking the same response for several questions, so beware of and identify 'respondent boredom'. A scale with a mid-point, for example, a 1–5 scale, will tend to attract responses in the middle and these are considered by many to be a lazy, indecisive response, and so can often be discounted. A 1–4 scale, however, forces respondents to choose.
- Do put the most simple and obvious questions at the beginning. Questions can become more complicated, if necessary, as the questionnaire proceeds. This keeps your respondent with you and does not confuse him or her at the start.

An introduction to analysing your questionnaire data

Once you have gathered in and labelled your questionnaires, coding them and removing those that are incomplete, you will need to analyse them. You can do this by counting responses, coding the open-ended response and quoting from them wherever appropriate. Alternatively, you can enter the coded and numerical responses into the computer using statistical packages such as SPSS, which then work to produce a frequency analysis for you.

Your reader *will not want to be given your data raw*. You need to read it carefully, look for patterns and categories, themes and counter-themes, discontinuities as well as continuities. Above all, it is crucial to remember your research question so that the questions you ask of your questionnaire results, the way you categorise and thematise the results, is all related to the question. There is a great deal more information to be gathered from any questionnaire than that which relates directly to your question, but you could be overwhelmed by information that is not actually relevant, should you comment on all you find.

Laying out the information from the data

There are many different ways to treat the data. One thing to remember is that the presentation must be appropriate, useful and accessible to readers. It must also be translated for them in a way that is interesting, not merely laid out.

Here are a few words of advice about the use of tables. It is probably advisable to lay out any statistics and data in an accessible form, whether analysed into pie charts, rows of columns, bar charts, or in quotations, and label it – ensuring it is part of your discussion. You need to use it integrally as you develop an argument based on your research question and underpinning theories. The data, analysed and interpreted, is used as evidence of your argument as it develops. If you feel that you need to reproduce vast tables (totally unnecessary, most of the time), they should be in the appendix, not the body of your thesis or dissertation – no one can read huge data tables, neither can they read and manage large questionnaires or narrative and discursive responses. Do the work for your readers: analyse, categorise, seek patterns, make claims and use the responses as evidence to back up your claims, but save the full data tables for the appendix, using what you need in extract form, with discussion, in the body of the text.

As with interviewing, you will soon discover that there are questions you employ that cannot be asked directly, such as those about personal hygiene, sexual relations, spending habits and bad habits. This is because people will not want to be entirely honest and will boast or lie to some extent.

Observation will be dealt with in terms of its application to produce both quantitative and qualitative data towards the end of this chapter. Observation can be carried out in a largely deductive, quantitative manner where the mass observation of human behaviours is involved. In mass observation examples, large numbers can be used to produce statistical data about frequency and kind of behaviour. Additionally, observation schedules for smaller numbers of observations might look at a limited number of interactions and behaviours, and so be able to count and measure responses.

Many researchers choose to combine both quantitative and qualitative methods to enable, for example, a statistical base in a questionnaire to deter-

---

Things to do

Prepare a practice questionnaire. Decide on a topic – this does not
need to be related to your research – for example, student responses
to the facilities provided for postgraduates around the university
campus. Select a variety of questions – closed (Yes/No, 1–4) or open
(for longer discursive responses).

Consider how to word these questions very carefully. Defend your
reasons for those choices. Try the questionnaire out on yourself or
preferably on a friend/colleague/relative, and ask him or her:

- Can you actually answer these questions? Are they clear?
  Ambiguous? Leading? Insulting? Irrelevant?
- Do you think that they enable the researcher to elicit information
  on the purpose of the study?
- Are some of the questions going to be unhelpful because they
  have been wrongly phrased, or have I asked wrong questions that
  just do not produce usable results?
- Then consider: How would you code, analyse and then present the
  data?

---

mine some key questions to be asked in depth of a few individuals in an
interview, or a pattern of responses from a questionnaire to underpin a focus
group interview about attitudes, and so on.

● Qualitative research methods – interviews, focus groups and observation

In this section we are looking at:

- developing, carrying out, writing up and analysing interviews
- when and how to use focus groups, running them, writing up and
  analysing
- kinds of observation – planning, managing, analysing and writing
  up
- ethical issues.

If some or all of your research methods involve capturing people's opinions,
feelings and practice, their experience and the kind of atmosphere and
context in which they act and respond, then you are likely to be carrying out
positivistic inductive research – that is, theory building – then interpretive-

based research and qualitative research methods are likely to form a large part of your exploration and your research. This chapter gives a brief introduction to interviews, observation and focus groups. There are some more in-depth explorations of each of these in various excellent books devoted to research methods (see the Bibliography).

Interviews

You need to decide whether the outcomes you seek for your research would be better served by going directly to people you can access, who could give you in-depth comments. Decide how you can select whom to interview and how to gain access to them. You need to ask their permission to be interviewed (see Chapter 8 on ethics and confidentiality – you will need a participant consent form), whether you approach them in the street with a clipboard (a rather accidental sample) or visit them at home (a more controlled sample).

Why decide to interview?

Interviews give you the opportunity to meet the subjects of your research. They can provide both the detailed information you set out to collect and some fascinating contextual or other information (not all of which you can use). However, they are most certainly time-consuming. You need to bear in mind that, should you decide to tape an interview, it is likely to take six hours or more to transcribe what you have taped, and considerably more time besides to analyse and then use what was said. Not all interviews are worth such an expense of time (and perhaps money, if someone else is transcribing for you), but they do provide rich data if used appropriately and sensitively in a focused way. You might decide to interview if you are looking for:

- information based on emotions, feelings, experiences
- information based on sensitive issues
- information based on insider experience, privileged insights and experiences.

Interviews can be used to gather information:

- to supplement information provided in a questionnaire
- to help pilot a questionnaire – interview a few people to test out the areas and questions
- to follow up a questionnaire – select whom to interview for in-depth or variety of responses following the broader information produced in a questionnaire

- to add to a variety of other methods, such as observation and documentary analysis, by closing in on a smaller sample dealt with in-depth.

Processes

- Decide on an interview as a method – why?
- Decide on and find your sample, and decide if and how you can gain access to them. Do not try to do too many interviews, as they are very time-consuming. You might want to gather a variety of responses from very different kinds of people or a number of interviews with the same kind of interviewees.

For example:

- a selection of external examiners in a variety of different subjects and different universities
- three external examiners who have indicated previously that they support the role staying as it is, and three who would wish to change it in line with the Quality Assurance Agency recommendations.

These two kinds of samples would clearly yield very different sorts of information, so you need to be clear from the outset what it is you wish to enquire about in order to get the right sample (and ask the right questions). Do be careful to ensure that you can locate your sample and gain access to it.

Sensitivities

One thing to keep in mind is that behaviour and wording are culturally inflected. If you are interviewing someone from a different cultural, gendered or class background, you will need to be careful to observe their rules of behaviour, check out their context, check out the meanings of what you ask and what you are hearing, to avoid cultural confusions. You will also find that where the interview takes place, how you dress and sit, are affected by cultural differences and affect your respondents. Do some research into this before setting up and running an interview – you do not want your interviewee to be awkward or embarrassed, and you do not want to be awkward or embarrassed yourself. Equally, you do not want cultural misunderstanding either to limit what is discussed or to cause misinterpretation.

Go on to explore the needs in terms of setting up and running these chosen interviews.

What kind of interview?

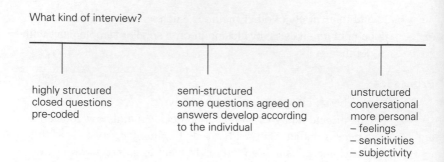

highly structured	semi-structured	unstructured
closed questions	some questions agreed on	conversational
pre-coded	answers develop according	more personal
	to the individual	– feelings
		– sensitivities
		– subjectivity

Figure 16.1   The interview continuum

Kinds of interview

There is a continuum of interviews which ranges from the informal and conversational interaction, which flows with the thoughts and feelings of both interviewer and interviewee, and the much tighter, more structured interview. There are pluses and minuses to all kinds of interviews along the continuum.

What kind of interview do you have in mind? Would you want interviewees to give Yes/No or Lickert scale 1–5 answers, which you fill in yourself? Or would you want to collect all that they say, and afterwards code the kinds of answers you get? The first kind of interview questions produce results very like a questionnaire (it is a questionnaire – administered orally!) – and can produce statistical data (although you are unlikely to be able to carry out quite the number of interviews as you would be able to send questionnaires). Alternatively, they can be highly qualitative conversations between you and the interviewee, which, as they go on, reveal interesting new insights into the topic. In the latter instance, with the longer in-depth interview, you read through transcripts, listen carefully to tapes, read through your notes, and decide on the themes and issues that are emerging in relation to your area of enquiry and your questions, coding the responses accordingly.

Structured interviews rely upon the interviewer completing a set of structured questions with multiple-choice responses, and asking questions according to the order of these questions (rather like a questionnaire, but completed by the interviewer after questioning the interviewee). A structured interview with closed questions can guide the responses clearly, making analysis simpler, but can be too guiding and limiting – it might not gather feelings.

Semi-structured, open-ended interviews manage to address both the need for comparable responses – that is, the same questions being asked of each interviewee – and the need for the interview to be developed by the conversation between interviewer and interviewee – which is often very rich and rewarding. With a semi-structured, open-ended interview there is a series of set questions to be asked and space for some divergence, with the interviewer then returning to the structured interview questions.

Unstructured interviews have been variously described as naturalistic, autobiographical, in-depth, narrative or non-directive. Whatever the label used, the informal interview is modelled on a conversation and, like a conversation, is a social event with, in this instance, two participants. As a social event, it has its own set of interactional rules, which may be more or less recognised by the participants (Holland and Ramazanoglu 1994: 135).

An open-ended, conversational interview may be rich in gathering feelings, following the thought and discussion processes of the interviewee, but could go very much off the point and be difficult either to transcribe or to analyse and compare with other interviews. You might find you have incomparable data that is rich in itself but not easy to start to draw conclusions from in relation to your project.

Interviews may seem like conversations but, in fact, they are more complex, structured, interactive and controlled. Some interviews develop a strange kind of antagonism between the interviewer and interviewee, probably due to the power invested in either side, and to the prying that an interview seems to suggest. Others make the interviewee feel flattered; his or her opinions are being sought, and these matter. In both unstructured and more structured interviews, the real words of the interviewee are used rather than merely his or her responses to closed questions.

Ethics

You need to explain carefully to anyone you intend to interview exactly what you will do with the interview material. While some short interviews of the Yes/No clipboard variety are unlikely to yield very sensitive material, others are more personal. It is assumed that what is said in an interview is 'on the record', but some participants may choose to remain anonymous or to vet the script of the interview before you use it. This is something that should be offered to them – agree to send the transcript to them before you use it (see Chapter 8 on ethics).

Organising the interview

Interviewing needs to be as carefully thought out and structured as any questionnaire, even if it does sometimes appear to be rather like a conversation.

Contact – Contact your interviewee in advance and introduce yourself by letter/e-mail, following up with a phone call. Explain the reason for the research and what your aims are in interviewing them (but do not give all the questions away).

Time and place – You need to agree on a time and place that is mutually convenient, and indicate how long the interview is likely to last. Try to ensure that the environment will be free of interference. Since the interviewee is giving you his or her time, it is a good idea to fit in with the interviewee's plans. This can involve awkward hours and travelling. In interviewing external examiners, I travelled all over the country and met them when it suited. One met me in the early evening, just before he boarded a train, another in the early morning before he started teaching. Both required my travelling at difficult times. Do avoid interviewing someone when he or she is walking somewhere else or not fully concentrating.

Recording the interview

A small, sensitive tape recorder is necessary, but the most expensive tape recorders are not always the best, so try them out first. Do not forget to have enough tapes ready, and to ensure the batteries are fully charged (sometimes there is a battery in the tape recorder and a separate one in the microphone, so check this). Place the tape recorder somewhere unobtrusive but point it out. Your respondents will soon ignore it (hopefully – sometimes they seem to speak directly to the microphone in a rather stilted fashion. Do discourage this!).

You might feel happier taking notes – but this is also rather obtrusive. Do not rely on memory alone. Do either write up notes or transcribe recordings as soon as possible after the interview so that you can contextualise and make sense of the responses.

Asking interview questions

Open-ended questions can enable the interviewee to expand, with prompting, and allow you to follow up with questions that refine an area if there are misunderstandings. However, they can also be misleading and provide a large amount of information you cannot then use. Closed questions can limit interaction and creative exploration, as well as the opening up of the interview, and its subsequent richness.

Some questions are more sensitive than others. The framing of all questions should be carried out very carefully.

What is said and what is not said

In an interview there are areas that people are prepared to discuss and those they will not, areas of which they are aware and areas they hide or are unaware of. Think of what can be discovered as lying somewhere along the axes in the boxes shown in Figure 16.2.

For example, X is an area you and the interviewee can discuss openly: they know about and can reveal, for example, 'Where do you live?', while XX is an area of which they probably are unaware or are repressing, and which they will not directly reveal, for example psychological or behavioural disturbance due to traumatic experience. You might suspect this area, but you cannot ask about it and would need to use 'what if?' questions, choices between scenarios, and other methods of information gathering to really find out (if you can).

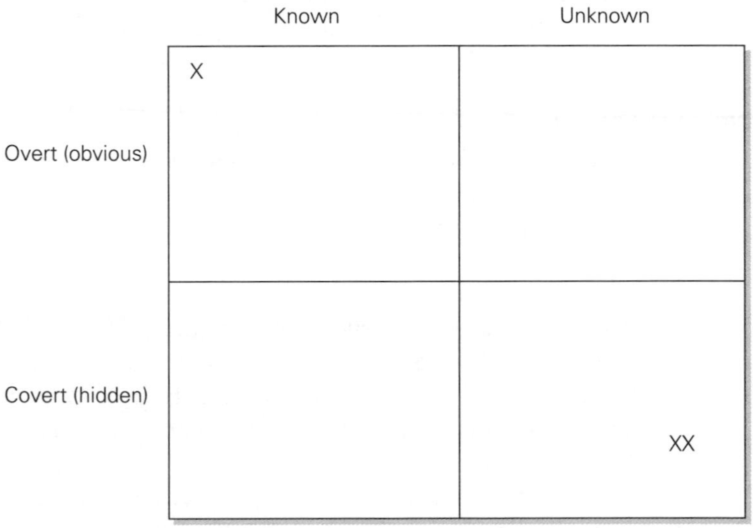

	Known	Unknown
Overt (obvious)	X	
Covert (hidden)		XX

Figure 16.2 Interview interactions

Honesty

Do not make any promises you cannot keep, and do not mislead the interviewee about how the information will be used, when or where. Agree to let the interviewee see a transcript, if this suits you. Sum up your notes and check them periodically with the interviewee if you have been talking for a while about something complex.

Be polite and pleasant and thank the interviewee for his or her time.

Questions and behaviours to avoid

- Do not appear threatened or bored.
- Do not ask:
- excessively long questions – the interviewee may only remember part of the question
- multiple questions packed into one – this will confuse the interviewee and he or she might answer only one part or run several together in a way you cannot use later
- questions using excessive jargon or technical terms – explain what you seek in ordinary language
- questions that lead or suggest bias and prejudice – such as, 'Why have you chosen to retire?' (it may be he or she has not chosen to retire?); or 'Don't you agree that mobile phones are a nuisance in the street and on trains?' Rephrase these to capture a range of possible responses and not just to gain Yes/No answers (which actually halt the thought and interview processes).

Questions and behaviours to use

- Do stay in control and appear friendly and responsive
- Do use prompts and probes
- Probing questions or behaviours can be as simple as smiling and nodding, with an indication that the interviewee should go on and say more; or 'mmm?'; or repeating part of what has been said, which usually makes the person carry on (the Queen is said to do this when interviewing: for example, 'What is your occupation?', 'I am a greengrocer', 'Oh, so you are a greengrocer?', 'Yes, and I sell vegetables and fruit', 'You sell vegetables and fruit?', 'Yes, and ...')

All of these are affected by age, gender, ability, ethnicity, religion, class and a number of cultural differences, so do be careful. If in doubt, consult sensitive others from a similar cultural background to that of your interviewees.

The shape of interviews

Interviews are interactions, whether they are open, semi-open or fairly closed. There will be a momentum and rhythm to them, as with any other interaction. You need to manage this well. They often run along the following lines:

- Introductions
- Social comments about time and place

- Background information to the interview and explanation of how it will be conducted, what you are seeking, and so on
- The interview itself:
  - variety of appropriate questions and some space to let answers develop
  - ways of prompting and probing to expand, if the answers seem to be leading in an interesting and useful direction
  - a way of closing down and moving on if the answers are rambling or not focused
  - more formal movements to and from necessary questions to ensure they are not missed out and are fully answered
  - perhaps even rephrasing questions if they seem misunderstood or ignored, or returning to them if ignored
- Winding down
- A few straightforward questions to finish the interview off and some information about use and contacts
- Closing down – thanks and goodbyes.

Things to do

- Choose a colleague to interview. Decide why you want to interview him or her, what you want to find out about, and decide on the schedule of questions and the setting.
- Develop your interview schedule and compare it against the checklist below. Think through your responses to the items in this list and share them with your colleague.
- Develop some questions you could ask.
- Ask your colleague the chosen questions.
- Collect the responses in notes or tape them.
- Reflect on the process – how successful was it? What worked and what went wrong?
- What would you do differently next time?

Debrief and evaluate what you did, what you discussed, what worked well and what did not. Discuss with each other how you might improve the interview.

Checklist for developing interviews

- Why do you want to use interviews?
- Is this the best method to gather the kind of information you need?
- How will an interview fit in with the rest of your research methods?
- What kind of sample would best suit your needs?

- What kind of an interview is it to be? How structured, free flowing or semi-structured do you want your interviews to be and why?
- Are there any cultural sensitivities you will need to take into account? How can you do this? What should you avoid or ensure happens?
- Are there any sensitive areas of questioning you need to use? How will you ask these sensitive questions?
- Will you need to tape the interview, transcribe or analyse it, tape it to use as back up for notes? Will you take notes while you interview, read them through and firm them up afterwards, then analyse them?
- How will you analyse them? Will you listen and annotate a transcript? Will you use a computer programme such as Nvivo or Nudist (programmes that thematically analyse qualitative data)?
- How will you analyse the data you acquire?
- Decide on your questions, trial run them with a colleague or friend, refine them and collect them on a clipboard, cards or in some other useful form – what will you do?
- Prepare an interview schedule: consider the order of the questions, especially those that must be answered. Prepare some prompts – such as photographs, other questions, samples or examples – in case your interview does not move from one point to another as expected. Which questions and which prompts?
- Pilot your question schedule: Does it work with a friend? Do the questions seem to flow more smoothly in a different order? Have you been able to overcome the problems associated with those more sensitive questions? Are you missing some of the sensitive questions? What can you do to make them more accessible?

Can you now start to draw up a series of questions that you could use for the body of your own interview *for your own research*? Try out a couple of key questions.

Pilot them with a colleague and ask:

- Are these too vague?
- Too probing?
- Embarrassing?
- Closed?
- Will they cause the interviewee to ramble?
- Are they clear?
- Do they follow on from the questions already asked?

- Can they really give me the information I am after?
- Are they not really going to capture that information?
- Are they misleading?

Discuss and advise each other on exact wording.

Creative interviewing

Areas of feelings, interactions, emotions, deeply hidden fears and desires, and so on are very difficult to discover through straightforward interviewing. You could try to use creative interviewing. This involves using interview techniques and a creative visualising exercise. To gain a response about traumatic experiences, a sensitive emotional development or a feeling, for example, about someone's relationship to a group or organisation, asking the person to draw, point or act out his or her response can release creative energies. This is termed 'synectics' and is the use of creative metaphors or imaginative comparisons to capture sensitive responses. For example, someone trying to describe how he or she is being ostracised in an organisation could visualise him- or herself as a weed in a flower patch. You can then discuss with the person how he or she (or others) might move towards a more positive image. In this way, a creative interview captures feelings and can also start to effect change (if that is one of your research areas).

Focus groups as group interviews

Focus groups can be a good way to capture the responses of a small group of people. One popular use of focus groups is to ask to meet a selection of students/clients/interviewees several times over a certain period to gauge their responses to a changing situation. In this way, they become familiar with the research, with you as a researcher, with the context and with each other. They often feel valued because their views are being sought in relation to a development or change, and they often also change and become more self-aware and reflective because of being involved in the focus group. This latter point could affect the kind of information you acquire, but could also be very developmental for those involved in the focus group.

If you use focus groups, you need to follow all the guidelines also suited to an interview, that is:

1   Decide if it is open-ended, semi-structured or structured. It is unlikely that a fully structured interview will work over time with a focus group because it is too closed. However, the use of some structured and clear questions in a schedule does help the group to stay on the point and to focus clearly and specifically. The main

problem with a focus group is that, like any other social group, it can dissolve into social discussion or go off the point, and it does need to be *focused*. If you are meeting the group over time, you will also need to prepare questions that match the developments over time, rather than asking the same questions over and over again, or just letting them talk;

2   Take cultural context and difference into account in what you ask, where you ask it, how you ask it and how you respond;

3   Ensure you have a suitable method of recording the focus group interviews, such as a tape recorder in the middle of the table with the group clustered around. They will need to say their names when they speak, certainly until you are familiar with their voices (on the tape). Videoing the discussion is another option. Both methods could inhibit the group initially, but as a group they are more likely to ignore the methods after a few sentences and get on with the discussion and answering questions.

Unlike individual one-to-one interviews, focus groups need firmer or clearer 'ground rules', such as:

- taking some responses in turn so that one person does not dominate
- prompting each other to speak
- being polite, as in conversation people tend to cut in on each other
- remembering to let the other person finish what he or she was saying (without cutting off the creative interaction that could lead to development, exploration and a higher level of thinking and articulating, as with group work with students).

Focus groups with undergraduates working on identifying how they learn, and what teaching and learning activities enable them in their learning have, in the past, dissolved into a discussion about 'horrible' rooms, the modular system and how much they hate a particular subject. Other focus groups, nurtured and prompted to stick to the questions while developing their answers, have built up sensitive responses over time to the same set of questions, and their belonging in the group has in itself caused these students to be more aware of how they learn – that is, it has developed their 'metacognitive' skills. If the focus group work is part of an action research project, this development of the students will be a very valuable product.

Focus groups have been used by market researchers and housing groups, people seeking responses to building and social changes, to media developments and so on – any situation where the responses of members of a group interacting with each other can provide a rich sense of people shaping feelings. However, because they are engaged in a group activity, they need managing in terms of group dynamics – and there is a special value placed on the collective responses and views. In order to manage this, it is important to set the group up carefully and to agree ground rules about behaviour. Silence and dominance are two behaviours that could inhibit general discussion. The researcher can act as a facilitator for the group and use triggers, prompts or specific questions to develop the discussion. One set of focus groups has revolved around the use of 'trigger tapes' – which are short video extracts – to prompt responses to areas in relation to discrimination and attitude. Managing these has helped both to discover attitudes and to help attitudinal change. They can enable the more silent participants to say more because, as with other group activities, they are prompted by the contributions of others. They are better managed over non-sensitive issues but, as is suggested by the trigger tapes, they can also be used to gauge responses to sensitive issues. Set them up with clear channels of communication over time.

Observation

Observation can be a rich source of information for the researcher. It enables you to capture what people actually do rather than what they say they do. You can observe them in context and relate to your research questions while you observe.

There are two main sorts of observation, defined by Lacey – *participant observation* and *non-participant observation* (1976: 65).

Participant observation involves the researcher becoming a part of the group they observe. As Lacey notes, it involves 'the transfer of the whole person into an imaginative and emotional experience in which the fieldworker learned to live in and understand the new world'. In *The Organisation and Practice of Social Research* (Shipman 1976), he explores his experiences of working for three years observing classes and talking with teachers and pupils at Hightown Grammar (quoted by Judith Bell 2005). The author Zora Neale Hurston worked with Frederick Boas, the anthropologist, and lived with loggers in a camp, getting herself beaten up by a jealous logger woman who thought Zora's interviewing of her partner was too intrusive. There are dangers to participant observation. You cannot be a participant observer unless you are a member of the group – so no one except a kindergarten child can be a participant observer of the activities of kindergarten children. However, you can be an observer whom the group accepts, rather than someone entirely detached (see p. 204).

Benefits – You use yourself as the equipment for this research. You are fully involved and taking part, and can register the experiences and behaviours at first hand from the inside.

Problems – Situations can be quite dangerous, depending on whom you are observing. Lee (1995: 1) comments: 'Researchers often work in settings made dangerous by violent conflict or in situations where interpersonal violence and risk are commonplace.' Lee also notes that it is often the violence that the researcher is observing. This can be risky: one social scientist carried out participant observation with a biker gang. Clearly, not all of us could fit in this situation, so participant observation depends on not sticking out as too different from the group you are observing. It also requires that you do not become a thoroughgoing member of the group. This is particularly important if you are observing criminal behaviour or dangerous activities (as undercover police have found out, to their disadvantage!). It could seriously disturb and even invalidate your findings, and could be dangerous.

Semi-immersed observation takes place when:

- some of the group know you are an observer, and they are therefore a 'part of the secret'
- *the group accepts you as an observer* – someone who does not become part of the group itself but is tolerated. The different levels of immersion affect the kinds of information you can collect, as they affect the context and personal influence on the events.

In all kinds of observation:

- You will need to win the trust and confidence of those with whom you are working.
- You will need an observation schedule that records not only actions, but also your personal responses to them, your feelings and changes, because you are part of the equipment and also part of the subject matter.
- You will need to keep careful field notes, during and/or after events.
- You need to work out how much your presence affects the events and people with whom you are involved in the observation.
- Do make sure you are observing for long enough, not capturing a biased snapshot of activities.
- You might well find it useful to keep a diary, log or journal of your experiences and responses to what you see, so that you can chart

changing interpretations and separate out what you see, what you seek and what you interpret.

Non-participant observation is less intrusive but involves observing the actions of others. You can either observe from a distance, perhaps hidden, or you can observe while you are taking part in the event that is being observed. In either instance, ethics demand that you gain consent from your participants or, if they cannot give it (too young, with mental health issues and so on), it needs to be given by someone with the appropriate right and authority.

All forms of observation require careful planning to determine what exactly is going to be observed and what fundamental or underlying issues and questions are going to be addressed by the observation. They require parameters to be set – observing others is so rich that an enormous amount of data can be collected and yet be of no use at all to the study. On the other hand, collecting data and making field notes sometimes produces unexpected results, so being too rigid and structured in your approach might limit you. You might miss something surprising that could be revelatory in your research.

Direct observation is a key to both kinds of observation. You, as researcher, directly observe what your subjects are doing and saying. You can collect real-life data that becomes part of *your fieldwork*. You are conducting first-hand research from empirical data – that is, data that comes immediately from experience rather than books or notes made by other people. However, your own experience and perception will colour what you observe. Your previous experience of observation and of observing something similar will affect how you 'read' situations and behaviours. While this can lead to insights, it can also skew or affect what you see in an unhelpful manner. As it is unavoidable, you need to reflect on it and take it into account when you describe and defend your research methods, and when you analyse and make inferences from your analyses.

Your role is to observe rather than intrude; to decide on time, place and whom to observe; under what conditions; and to take these conditions into account:

- Limit the events and people
- Decide on what you want to observe so that you narrow the field
- Take careful field notes
- Find ways of testing out assumptions about context and observation to help interpret these field notes.

If you carry out observations of a series of people or events over time, be careful to have a structured observation checklist – what you are looking for, the time and place, and ways of collecting data – so that you can match your samples. If someone else is helping you with your data collection, you will need to work closely together not only to collect information to the same schedule, but also to discuss your framing and interpretation of what you find, since this will inevitably be affected by experience and feelings.

Organisation and use of observation

You might find the following useful:

- Develop an observation schedule that enables you to record certain things and the time you notice them, their frequency and so on.
- If you pre-categorise and pre-structure your observation, you will not be overwhelmed with too much information. It would, however, be useful to observe initially in a more general manner and see what kinds of behaviours or responses appear, then develop your structure and categories.
- Find a way to be unobtrusive, to not join in fully and change the behaviour of those you observe. With participant observation this is very nearly impossible, so you will need to find ways to take into account the changes your presence could cause.
- You need to concentrate on observing.

Observation schedule

An observation schedule should include:

- Events, actions and responses that are noticeable and recorded, the times, frequency and duration of the events.
- Practices, issues, events and actions that are clear, relevant and recordable. You cannot jump to conclusions and record what you do not observe, although you will need to analyse what you observe afterwards and can also record your thoughts and concerns about what you see.
- If you are keeping a very systematic observation schedule, you might like to keep a separate *research diary*, in which you collect your hunches and thoughts about what you see in order to help you monitor your own responses and to manage the data from the observation later, when analysing it.

Non-participant observation

In order to carry this out you will need to:

- be unobtrusive – do not make your presence obvious or you will alter what happens
- be aware of the full context
- be able to sift out irrelevant data. Do not record everything – record what you are looking for, and the context
- ensure you carry out your observation over a reasonable period of time, and preferably repeat it several times to ensure that the data is relatively stable.

Things to do

Look at this example of a non-participant observation schedule and discuss/think:

- why it might have been set up and what it might help us to discover
- what else would need to be taken into consideration in starting to interpret the data.

Observation schedule

Behaviours of colleagues arriving at work in the morning

Colleague	Arrival time at car park	Parking space found?	Arrival at desk
A. Wendy	8.10 a.m.	Yes	8.20 a.m.
B. Steve	8.20 a.m.	Yes	8.25 a.m.
C. Ann	8.35 a.m.	Yes	9.00 a.m.
D. Alan	8.40 a.m.	Yes	8.50 a.m.
E. Angela	8.50 a.m.	No	9.30 a.m.
F. Andrew	9.00 a.m.	No	9.35 a.m.

What might this observation schedule be seeking to discover? What can we deduce from analysing this data? What else would we need to know about the context in order to interpret the data?

In this instance, the decision has been made to observe arrival at the car park in order to work out at what kind of peak time it becomes impossible to find a car parking space on a normal morning, and how long it then takes people to get to work if they have to park elsewhere. In order for this schedule to be useful, the observation would have to be performed over several 'normal' days, since the time in question might well be a day either in the middle of the holidays or when there are many visitor spaces booked, or some other factor might affect the parking.

Interpretations – some thoughts and problems

With this car parking study, you need to know more about those you observe and the context in order to interpret what you have observed. At first glance, you could deduce that Wendy is punctual and efficient while Angela is disorganised (she does not park, she gets to her desk late). However, it could be that Wendy has no dependents and lives close by, and so minimises possible traffic congestion delays. Angela might have to drop children at school, a partner at the station and drive in from the countryside. You will need to find out more in order to use what you have observed, and more still before making decisions about, for example, extending or cutting car parking. Having special places for longer-distance commuters with dependents might make Angela's 'efficiency' soar!

Observation – a continuum

As with interviewing, observation practices can be seen along a continuum from the highly regularised, factual and scientific to the more sensitive and subjective (Figure 16.3).

Where along this continuum might your intended observation take place?

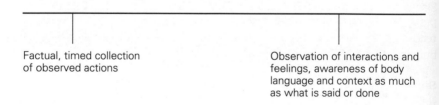

Factual, timed collection
of observed actions

Observation of interactions and
feelings, awareness of body
language and context as much
as what is said or done

Figure 16.3 Observation continuum

Recording interactions among people in groups

Some students studying social interactions between members of groups might find various published observation schedules and categories most useful – see those developed by Bales (1950), Flanders (1970) or the Open

Things to do

Your own observation schedule

On your own, or with a colleague, decide on:

- a topic/subject – something you might like to observe, such as shopping behaviour, car parking, people eating, children playing, the number of people coming through the front door, in whatever way, at work, or some other such easily observed activity
- what you would like to ask the subjects and what questions you might ask about the activity
- a design for an observation schedule that will let you observe the behaviour of several people over time, possibly (preferably) several times
- what are you looking for and why
- how you will observe it
- how you will take notes and of what. Do not forget to keep a time log, if this is appropriate.
- whether you need a diary for comments, too.

Carry out the observation and then discuss your findings, how you might analyse them and what kind of deductions you might come to, once the analysis is concluded.

University (OU) D101 course's simplified version (see Bell 2005). The problem with both Bales and Flanders is that there are many complex categories and sub-sections in which to record different behaviours, and personal choices about what and how to categorise has an effect on the recording. The OU example follows the Huthwaite Research group, which builds up a system to study management skills and behaviours.

Summary

We have looked at:

- the reasons for using questionnaires
- the kinds of questions to ask
- organising and laying out questionnaires
- analysing questionnaire results and laying them out visually
- using interviews, both structured and unstructured
- focus groups interviews
- observations, including participant and non-participant observations
- combining approaches and methods.

We have been looking at quantitative methods and qualitative methods set in the context of the straightforward, overly simplified dichotomy between positivistic deductive research and postpositivistic inductive research. It is possible to combine across these, and the research design of many projects needs to do so. Consideration of Case studies 1 and 2 offer clarification.

Case study 1

Naomi wishes to explore the ways in which middle managers behave in education colleges. She has some thoughts about leadership, stress, role conflict but she is not, as such, testing assumptions and hypotheses. Instead, she has a research question that focuses on exploring their experiences in relation to awareness and management of role.

Stage 1
She uses qualitative data gathering methods – principally focus groups and interviews with open-ended questions – and is working with an inductive, theory developing research design.
Naomi discovers patterns to the responses she receives, and sees some direct links between gender and role conflict amongst middle managers. She develops a theory about the connectedness of these variables.

Stage 2
This work is now deductive, as she wishes to test her theory, and so asks a different and expanded set of middle managers about role conflict in relation to gender, and does so using a questionnaire.

Case study 2

Hamid works with learning theories that have been proven to indicate direct links between students who have little organised idea and practice as to how they go about or understand their learning, and their actual results; and those with a confused or dissonant study orchestration gaining poorer marks than those with an organised study orchestration.

Stage 1

He issues a questionnaire to large numbers of economics students and matches the results of their organised or dissonant study orchestration against their exam results. He discovers there is a direct correlation, and so has some powerful statistics to work with. He is working deductively, theory testing and using quantitative methods of data gathering.

Now he wants to explore how aware individuals are as to how they go about their learning and how, or whether, involvement in the study development programme changes their metacognition or awareness of themselves as learners, so that they might take more control over their learning and hopefully improve their marks. He needs to study this over time and to involve the students in the development, so that they own the learning themselves.

Stage 2

This stage is inductive and uses qualitative data gathering methods. Hamid works with a group of students for a year using action research strategies, involving them in focus groups, conducting interviews, trying out different activities with them and asking about their responses and awareness of development. Each cycle of his research feeds into the next, and the students are full collaborators in the process.

Conclusion

We have taken further some of the issues and arguments about methodology, research design and methods in practice that were introduced in Chapters 5 and 6. Here, we explored in detail a variety of quantitative and qualitative methods, and also indicated how they might be combined in some research projects.

● **Further reading**

Bales, R.F. (1950) *Interaction Process Analysis: A Method for the Study of Small Groups* (Cambridge, MA: Addison-Wesley).

Bell, Judith (2005) *Doing your Research Project* (4th edn) (Buckingham: Open University Press).

Flanders, N.A. (1970) *Analysing Teacher Behaviour* (Reading, MA: Addison-Wesley).

Holland, J. and Ramazanoglu, C. (1994) 'Coming to Conclusions: Power and Interpretation in Researching Young Women's Sexuality', in M. Maynard and J. Purvis (eds), *Researching Women's Lives from a Feminist Perspective* (London: Taylor & Francis): 125–48.

Lacey, C. (1976) 'Problems of Sociological Fieldwork: A Review of the Methodology of "Hightown Grammar"', in M. Shipman (ed.), *The Organisation and Impact of Social Research* (London: Routledge & Kegan Paul).

Lee, R. (1995) *Dangerous Fieldwork* (Thousand Oaks, CA: Sage).

O'Leary, Z. (2004) *The Essential Guide to Doing Research* (Thousand Oaks, CA: Sage).

Walliman, N.S.R. (2005) *Your Research Project* (London: Sage).

Websites accessed

http://www.qualitativeresearch.uga.edu/QualPage/

17 Using Grounded Theory, Case Studies, Journals and Synectics

This chapter looks at:

▶ What is grounded theory and how to use it
▶ How and why to use case studies
▶ The use of personal learning journals for reflection and as part of the research
▶ Using synectics to enable creative thought

This chapter concentrates on reflective methodology and the qualitative research methods of grounded theory, case studies and the use of personal learning journals – to record your own experiences and decisions as a researcher – and the use of journals as research material. It also looks at the use of synectics, or creative metaphors, to prompt clarification, new ideas and developments.

● Grounded theory

Grounded theory is really what it says it is – theory grounded in experience(s). Rather than starting from theory and developing a research idea and question, the researcher starts instead from his or her own or others' experience and grows theory from that experience in action. Inappropriately cited as a rather loose and unstructured way of approaching observed experience, it provides the grounding for the development of theories. Grounded theory, however, is really used in practice to ground the theory (small-scale rather than large-scale theories) in experience, observation and practice, probably in small samples. In 1967, Glaser and Strauss published *The Discovery of Grounded Theory*, which lies behind current use of the term. This book provided a sound basis and framework for years of qualitative research. The authors offer an approach that has space for the different personal and professional perceptions and strategies of different social science researchers. They suggest that a rigid set of rules for approaching social science research would hamper and constrain the discovery of and focus on the object of the research, which is often itself shifting and being transmuted because it is based in human interactions and behaviours. The authors argue that 'a standardisation of methods (swallowed whole, taken seriously) would only constrain and stifle social science researchers' best efforts' (Strauss 1987: 7). Theories are generated empirically from the data, and constantly checked and tested against that data. 'Good qualitative social science research, according to the principles of grounded theory, involves a constant checking of the analysis (theories, concepts) against the findings and a constant refinement of the concepts during the process of research' (Denscombe 1998: 215).

> A grounded theory is one which is inductively derived from the study of the phenomenon it represents. That is, it is discovered, developed and provisionally verified through statistic data collection and analysis of data pertaining to that phenomenon. Therefore, data collection analysis and theory stand in reciprocal relationships with each other. One does not begin with a theory, then prove it, rather one begins with an area of study and what is relevant to that is allowed to emerge (Strauss and Corbin 1990: 23).

The researcher using grounded theory begins with a fresh perspective and some insights, but also a willingness to develop and change his or her views. Understanding the research produces new evidence and information, feeding into the development of theories. Because the situation he or she is researching is constantly evolving, the researcher cannot usually define the constraints of the research design and focus, or say how large the sample will be. He or she often needs to set out with 'theoretical sampling' in mind – a sampling of incidents, actions and events directed by the theory as it evolves. However, this does not mean that the research goes on forever, since once the information seems to continue to confirm the analysis, to repeat, then the sample can be closed, as it has reached the point of 'theoretical saturation' – rather than real exhaustion. It is theory that is not suited to the study of evolving situations and people and, as such, it is:

- based in fieldwork observations
- produces explanations suitable for those carrying out the research, or from whom it is directed
- produces limited explanations based on immediate evidence
- works from an evolving design which adapts to suit the situation as it develops – but does so appropriately.

Strauss and Corbin (1990) suggest it is:

- a scientific method of investigation used by researchers
- inductively derived from the study of the phenomenon it represents

- discovered, developed and provisionally verified through systematic data collection and analysis
- representative of the reality that has been researched
- comprehensible to the persons who were studied
- comprehensible to those who inhabit the area that was studied
- specific to the phenomenon that has been studied
- capable of providing generalisation when the validity of the theory has been established.

Grounded theory is not an excuse for laziness or vague interpretations; the data needs to be substantiated and argued in terms of reading meanings from them. However, as the basis for much qualitative research, it offers the opportunity to enquire and ensure the data and analysis can be rich, and that it can enable the exploration of contested readings and interpretations. It does tend, however, to be rather more selective, localised, and not as generalisable as strict scientific experimentation could be. Research findings 'constitute a theoretical formulation of the reality under investigation, rather than consisting of a series of numbers, or a group of loosely related themes' (Strauss and Corbin 1990: 24). Concepts and relations are generated, and then tested as well. It is related very strongly to the subject or self who directs it, decides on its aims and focus, its use and methods, and its interpretations. It is a flexible, sensitive approach, that needs to be very clearly set out and explained at each stage of the research, so that limitations and constraints are expressed, and findings seen in context.

Things to do

Consider:

- Is your own research based in grounded theory?
- How might grounded theory help you in your research?
- If you are going to use it, what is the situation in which you will use it?
- What kind of theory do you think might be generated from your research? (You cannot be exact, of course, as yet, but you might be able to say, 'I aim to be able to develop a theory about how people in failing organisations ...' or 'The theory I wish to develop concerns how those suffering trauma after war incidents could engage with and deal with the trauma and carry on with normal life ...'.)
- How can you use grounded theory to explore contextualised meanings?
- Where are you in the research?
- How will you carry out your fieldwork?
- What kinds of methods do you think would be suitable at the outset of your research?
- Can you foresee any problems?

● Case studies

Case study as a method has been around for a long time and offers an opportunity to consider a situation, individual, event, group, organisation, or whatever is appropriate as the object of study, and perhaps to look at several cases, all of which represent variations on examples of the issues in question under research. Some of the origins of case study methods lie in health, others in social work or in the law.

One of the pluses of using case study methodology and methods is that an in-depth situation/individual can be explored fully. One of the issues is that you cannot easily generalise from one case. Either the case needs to be contextualised and carefully described so that others can consider its usefulness in other contexts and examples, or it is better to take a few cases from which to establish a range of examples and interpretations of a situation, event or development. It is essential throughout the use of a case study method (as with any other research method) that you insist on rigour in the methods of data collection and analysis, acknowledging the subjectivity of the researcher and the limitations of generalising from individual cases. You also need to defend the kinds of implications and shapes of the cases chosen. Robson defines case study methodology as follows: 'case study is a strategy for doing research which involves an empirical investigation of a particular contemporary phenomenon in its real life context using multiple sources of evidence' (1993: 52). It is a research strategy based in empirical research that focuses on the particular in context and, like action research, involves using a variety of methods of data collection. If you use case studies you will only use a few cases and they will be selected from many examples of a behaviour type, situation, development or whatever is your focus, each selected because it represents a version of variation. In the case study method you do not select large numbers of cases, because they tend to repeat. Instead, if you can perceive patterns, select a case from each of the major trends or patterns that emerge when scrutinising your data, and flesh out the case study with details, make it come to life, and involve readers in the narrative you tell about it.

Things to do

Consider:

- Why might you choose to use a case study method?
- What could you use as a case?
- Could you use several cases?
- Could you generalise for your case(s) (you do not need to)?

Often consultants are used to using case study methods to find out about a development, a problem, or an interaction within an organisation, and to point out difficulties and/or suggest changes.

When you have gained your evidence and explored, discussed, problematised and written it up, your case study could be useful as:

- an example of or for a consultancy
- an example of particular practices in operation from the point of view of a single set of issues in practice
- an example that others can use to transfer/translate into their own context.

See case studies 1 and 2 (pp. 218–19) for examples of situations in which the case study method is appropriate:

Some researchers will find it useful to work with the single case study, and others to select several cases, the commonality or variety of interpretations that they produce providing a greater claim for generalisability, and perhaps setting a range of versions and interpretations that others would find it useful to explore. This could be interpreting a set of examples, instances, events, behaviours, roles or whatever is relevant to the subject of their own case study. The use of multiple cases helps to establish a range and to increase the likelihood of generalisability. However, it must always be recognised that any experiment or survey, any study, takes place in the context of a specific time and place, with specific events, individuals or groups involved, and also taking you as the researcher into the equation. As such, then, anyone seeking to generalise from or replicate your work who used case study methods (and, actually, any other methods, however scientific they seem), would need to take such differences into consideration and acknowledge their potential effects. Using action research, which involves a variety of research methods and bases itself on changing the research with the participants/those researched in a collaborative manner (see Chapter 14), you might use case study method to explore behaviours in an organisation, for example. In such a situation you would need to:

- establish the aims and outcomes of the research
- establish the context
- probably set the scene of the issue in hand with the use of documentary evidence – so you need to carry out both exploratory and descriptive research using documents
- set the scene through asking insiders and outsiders for their views and experiences

Case study 1 – Alan and the external examiner system

In his work on the use of the external examiner system, Alan focused on the practices, problems, benefits and limitations of quality assurance of the system as it operated in his own college, taking that college as a case study. A simple description of activities would not have been appropriate, although description formed part of his case.

Description and documentary evidence

He described the system of use of the external examiner within his college, set this in the context of the external examiner system (a system where an examiner from another institution works with your own examiners and moderates or agrees/queries the way assessment works, and assures the justice of the marks awarded to students). He also set these practices against documentary evidence, provided by his college, about the way the system was meant to work there, as part of the overall quality assurance.

Use of observation and interview

As a field researcher, Alan established how the system was working through observation of external examiners in practice at award boards and through interviews with both examiners internal to the college and the external examiners. He asked both groups some overlapping questions and also some questions that were specific to the two different groups. The questions covered how the role, in practice, was seen to help quality assurance and ensure justice to students, and how it helped assure the appropriateness of the teaching, the assessment and the version of the subject taught. Finally, he asked how the various systems and practices of meetings, papers exchanged, results, consultation and so on actually operated.

He was using multiple methods of enquiry to establish a single case and to fit that case into an overall context, asking questions about the situation and practices that could be used by/transferred to others in similar situations. But, since he was looking at a single case, he expressed the note of caution that not all would be transferable, and that others using his methods or seeking similar outcomes would need to take into consideration their own context and position, as well as their aims and outcomes. As an insider of the college, Alan was aware that his role might affect what he asked, what he saw, how he was treated, the answers given, and his interpretations of all of this evidence, and so he described his own role, and explored and expressed his position and concerns about that position. This element of self or subjectivity does not invalidate the case study – researchers are always involved in their research to some greater or lesser extent – but did need to be taken into consideration because it would certainly affect what was recorded, how it was interpreted and presented, and the generalisability or transferability of what was found to other instances.

- decide on a sample – who will act as your case studies
- set up a research schedule that enables you to collect data from a variety of appropriate research methods – such as observation, focus groups, interviews and so on
- possibly ask those who form your case study to carry out enquiries with others, and become field researchers carrying out what can be called 'appreciative enquiry' (Cooperrider and Srivastra, 1987)
- involve those with whom you are collaborating in this research in interviews, observations, focus groups or whatever is appropriate.

In some instances, the researcher can be used as a single case study, if the researcher's own situation and experiences are an example of what is being studied. Clearly, in this instance, the context, the description of self as set against other cases, and the particular issue of unavoidable subjectivity will need to be considered. But using the self as a case can be a very rich source of insider information. The case of the individual self as subject can be set alongside other cases, but should not really be included as just another of the samples. It provides 'a chance of an insightful source for a case study.

Case study 2 – Florence and women working in the Chinese takeaway industry

Florence was a Women's Studies Master's student who used the case study method for the MA Women's Studies dissertation. Florence, working on the experiences of immigrated Chinese women (her term) in the Chinese take-away industry in the UK, decided, on advice from her supervisor, to use herself as one of the case studies. She also worked with three other women who provided other examples of case studies. In the use of herself as a case study she recorded her own experience and her reflections, and systemati-cally addressed the questions about isolation, amount of work, social interac-tion, rewards, and so on, which were the same questioning areas she applied to the other women. The example of her own experience used a storytelling format, set alongside the more formal self-interview and written questions. With the other women she asked for an oral storytelling response and the answers to the same set of questions. In this instance, she was able to both expertly use the richness of her own experience (which would have looked costly otherwise) and base her interactive insights and her rapport with her subjects partly on this experience, and also to collect information in a very systematic way.

Things to do

Consider:

Think of a problem, development, experience or situation you would like to explore as part of your research or, separate from your research, another interest and set of questions. Decide on using either yourself or someone with whom you work/a friend/a relative to act as a case study sample for you. Can you develop a brief case study outline that will enable you to use the person as a case study, in context?

Ask yourself:

- What? How? What are my aims and questions? What am I trying to find out?
- Who might benefit from this case study? What fund of knowledge and understanding, problematising arguments/debates might it contribute to?
- Who else has written in this area? Can I use them/what they have written, as part of my theoretical context?
- Whom am I using as a case study/in my case study? You need to develop a short rationale about why this is the appropriate method to use.
- What else do I need to set up as the context? What is the specific context of the research (location, people and so on, rather than theory)? Can I describe it from observation, or do I need to use documentary evidence of a recorded/written form as background and context?
- What research techniques can I use to enable me to gain the information I need from this person? For example: questionnaires, interviews, storytelling, a written account, an observation schedule or a mixture of these.
- When could I have access to the subject of my case study?
- What barriers and difficulties could there be to prevent me from finding out what I need to find out (for example, attitude, access, prior experiences, wrong questions, and so on)?
- How might I overcome these barriers?
- Carry out your first case study – sketch in the background and context, interview/observe/use questionnaires/ask for all story-telling evidence and so on.

Writing up case studies

Now you have your material – how can you write it up as a case study?

As with writing up any piece of research, a standard format can be adhered to that resembles a scientific report. However, at the other end of the spectrum, case studies can be more descriptive, and can follow the discourse and development of those observed or interviewed. For further details of different ways of writing up case studies, see Robson (1993: 415).

Lincoln and Guba (1985: 3, 62, cited in Robson 1993: 416) suggest that bringing the more technical and scientific report format into the qualitative method of a case study helps to mitigate against any questions over rigorous subjectivity and focus. Robson lists the following formats:

- **scientific journal** – focus, context for enquiry, description and analysis for data, discussion of outcomes
- **suspense structure** – findings, faults and reports on investigation and context flows afterwards
- **narrative** – a story told in continuous prose, or following question-and-answer sequence
- **comparative** – two or more examples compared throughout
- **chronological** – evidence presented in a chronological sequence – useful to show cause and effect
- **theory-generating** – sections establishing further elements feeding into the support (or underpinning of a theory)
- **unsequenced** – descriptive, but sometimes it is difficult to see what has been missed out and what is important.

When you write up your case study, you will have to decide what goes in the body of the text and what goes in the appendices, and whether tables and so on (in an appendix) actually serve any purpose. You also need to decide whether a descriptive narrative gives a flavour of the response in a more sensitive manner – each case will be different, and the reason for developing the case study will also contribute to the choice of the appropriate format for writing it up.

● Journals

Journals are a very useful way of capturing the changing decisions and reflections involved in carrying out research. They can help to capture things that would otherwise disappear from memory or, because they are not committed to paper or tape, might fail to be clearly articulated. They can capture:

- moments when you are asking questions
- showing engagement with problems and issues
- developing solutions

- showing moments of decision about research design or analysis, and so on
- developing reflections about experiences.

They tend to be used in two ways: (i) For the researcher to develop and keep a reflective account of the research; and (ii) as part of the research itself, when the subjects of the research keep journals – which can be used as documentary evidence; back up for interviews and observations; examples of their experiences, analyses and reflections on these and so on. If you, the researcher, are part of, or all of, the research sample itself, then your own journal can form part of the material for the research, rather than simply being a reflective journal kept alongside the research to help you articulate, clarify, reflect and record.

You could ask your subjects to keep journals as part of the research matter, the material you use. If you do this, you will need to ensure that they are aware of what kind of journals are needed, that is, not merely a diary record of what is done, unless that is the kind you seek (a blow-by-blow account), but a reflective and analytical piece, completed regularly, that enables engagement with issues and decisions. They also need to know that your sampling of the journal will not infringe their confidentiality or their liberties, and they will need to 'clear' with you which elements of the journal you use on the research.

Things to do

Consider:

- Could you use a journal yourself?
- What could it help you achieve?
- Could you use journals with your subjects?
- What would it help you and them to achieve?

● Synectics

Synectics are creative metaphors that enable the opening up of creative and imaginative comparisons from which decisions and arguments can then be created and developed. They can be used either as ways of gaining information, getting close to the subject of study, and opening it up and out for rich responses and subjective understandings. For yourself, they can open up your own creativity and/or serve as a method or vehicle to engage your subjects of study, in order to enable them to be creative, imaginative, sensitive and responsive, and to respond to the metaphor, opening up as a result.

- For yourself: As you start to develop research questions and areas of study, the creative technique of synectics can sometimes help you to visualise the area of study more fully and imaginatively, so that you can then consider how to approach it more fully.
- People: Clients, practitioners, students, colleagues, whoever is the focus of the research, frequently find it difficult to engage with problems, cases or issues that require creative thinking when they are in classroom situations. Synectics involves the use of creative metaphors with which students can engage. They might be asked, for example, to compare a particular problem position to a fruit, flower or supermarket – and the elements of the comparison free up their thoughts. Similarities and differences between each half of the comparison can be collected and problems or issues addressed.

For example:

- If I wished to research how, why and in what ways the organisa-tion and practices of educational development had changed over a period of time within a university, I might find it useful to compare the situation and practices of staff development at the beginning of the researched period with that at the end, and to use the creative metaphor of a garden to do so.

As those involved in the research engage in the comparison, they start to tease out different elements, sort problems, see trends and decisions, clarify their thoughts and make the change to causes and effects and its potential opportunities and problems in focus. They could use a SWOT analysis on the overall situation when they have identified, defined and clarified these elements in comparison with the metaphor (identifying strengths, weak-nesses, opportunities and threats). In this way, the creative metaphor releases energy.

Synectic tactics enable articulation of issues, practices and problems through the comparison. Other synectic tactics involve separating approaches and issues out by listing them under different headings on a flip chart and asking for different kinds of comment, information and contribu-tions under each heading. People involved in the synectics exercise can be asked to give information, and suggest areas in which they need help, under separate headings on the flip chart. The main group is then enabled to offer

An example of the use of synectics

- Educational development is the focus of this study. Educational development is a system of development, support and training in universities that helps and enables lecturers and/or administrative staff to engage with professional practice issues, and develop their skills and knowledge in these. It involves formal training activities and courses, less formal individual support or workshop activities and, sometimes, consultation with departments, heads or other university staff.

- In using synectics, you need to define the metaphor or comparison (or request the subjects to define it) and pose the comparative question, for example:

  (a) Start with an analogy: 'Five years ago, educational development was like a cottage garden – in what ways?'

  (b) Creative brainstorming and thinking then follows, and individuals or groups can start to engage with the comparison. They might think it through like this: 'Well, there would be a single developer like an individual gardener, operating in a small patch, weeding out the problem weeds and tending the growing plants, but the effect would be limited, it would not grow much. What it could grow could be a hardy annual, some solid crops (vegetables?) and the odd rare plant, maybe in a greenhouse. It could be killed off by freak weather or lack of care, and maybe no one would notice? They could set up another garden – although much of value would be lost. It could also be a focus for pride and joy, like the gardener who grows huge vegetables or wonderful strains of flowers and wins prizes for them.'

- Why is this like educational development?

  (a) Because often there is a lone developer or small unit without much support from the university, which works with individuals or small groups and nurtures innovations, enables people to tackle some of the problems of their work, helps to develop and train in a regular way – but is also rather vulnerable or overlooked.

- Now – since educational development has institutional support and national funding – what is it like? What can it be compared to in terms of gardens and growing things?

information or help and offers or points are collected on the flip chart. By dividing up elements of interest and information, synectics acts as an enabling device.

When the strengths, weaknesses, opportunities and threats have been clarified, those involved can look at how to overcome or avoid potential problems, and how to capitalise on and benefit from potential or real opportunities and strengths. Furthermore, they need to draw up a point-by-point development plan to do so. In this way, the creativity moves you on to planning and action.

This can be used to help you, as the researcher, to focus on problems in research, and can also help you to express your ideas and the shape of the work when you write it up. If, for example, your research is into how people process ideas, deal with issues and problems, and plan, being involved in a problem-solving exercise with your subjects – the people – can provide you with information on how they deal with problems, and so on.

Things to do

Take a problem situation or issue either in your professional/personal life or in your research. Can you compare this to a food or a holiday?

- How does the comparison tease out different elements?
- How do the different elements compare?
- How do they enable you to focus on the specifics of the problem when you look clearly at them?

Now do a SWOT (Strengths, Weaknesses, Opportunities, Threats) analysis and decide what to do work on, how to sort out the problem areas, how to avoid problems by prior planning and action, and how to capitalise on the opportunities.

Conclusion

We have looked at:

- [ ] Grounded theory, what it is and why and when to use it – fieldwork, development and so on

- [ ] Case studies – shaping them and using them

- [ ] Journals – for you as a researcher and for the subjects of your research

- [ ] Synectics – to enable you to clarify and focus on issues and problems in the research, or as a vehicle to enable your subjects for research to engage.

● **Further reading**

Cooperrider, D.L. and Srivastra, S. (1987) 'Appreciative Inquiry into Organizational Life', in W.A. Pasmore and R.W. Woodman (eds), *Research into Organizational Change and Development*, vol. 1 (Greenwich, CT: JAI).

Denscombe, M. (1998) *The Good Research Guide* (Buckingham: Open University Press).

Glaser, B. and Strauss, A. (1967) *The Discovery of Grounded Theory* (Chicago: Aldine).

Robson, C. (1993) *Real World Research* (Oxford: Blackwell).

Strauss, A. (1987) *Qualitative Analysis for Social Scientists* (Cambridge: Cambridge University Press).

Strauss, A. and Corbin, J. (1990) *Basics of Qualitative Research: Grounded Theory Procedures and Techniques* (London: Sage).

18 Action Research and Practitioner-based Research

This chapter looks at:

▶ Why undertake practitioner-based research?
▶ Why undertake action research?
▶ Action research – processes, cycles, collaboration
▶ Phenomenography – an introduction

Practitioner-based research enables us to research our own practice with those with whom we work – clients, customers, students, colleagues, and so on. For mid-career professionals and those whose organisations would like them to undertake work-related research, practitioner-based research is especially appropriate and popular. It carries with it particular issues to do with the support of the organisation – the alignment of our own interests with those of the workplace and the organisation, confidentiality and ethics – because the research is with those with whom you are working. You also need to take care over the balancing of work with research on a daily basis. Practitioner-based research can take many forms and is not a methodology but a focus. You might well carry out some practitioner-based research that is positivist, deductive and uses quantitative methods (such as testing of a particular practice), which is more effective than another practice, through pre- and post-test experiments, or with pre- and post-test questionnaires with colleagues/students/customers – with whomsoever you are working.

For an introduction to the range of methods you might use, look at the previous and forthcoming chapters on quantitative and qualitative methods of varying kinds. The issue is the focus – so, for practitioner-based research, you can construct a research design that suits your question or hypothesis, much as you would for any other research project.

● Benefits of practitioner-based research

You can focus on your own organisation, your own practice and find out what works, what changes, what might be improved, how you might solve problems, how something works, and so on.

Because the research runs parallel to work, your organisation might well fund it and should be very interested in what you find out. However, they also might want to direct and to own it, and this could compromise the objectivity of your work.

You can usually carry out practitioner-based research alongside your work so that you are not totally dividing your energies between work and research (but beware of conflicts of interest – see below).

Your organisation might well be so interested in what you find out that they promote you, recognise you, and even invite your strategic input.

● Possible pitfalls or problems

You cannot get away from work into research – they are closely intertwined.

You might not be able to research what really interests you because the organisation may wish you to research what they want to know about. The organisation might not want you to publish or share your findings should you start to discover awkward or confidential things. This could be difficult if it is a dissertation or thesis – which, of course, requires some dissemination. If there are related problems over this, you might wish to change your project instead. Alternatively, you could impose a restriction on who reads the thesis once completed, and avoid presenting except in selective and extremely sensitive ways.

Ethics and confidentiality could be an issue because people might not want you to reveal information about their practices to the rest of the organisation and might not trust you as a colleague should you have information that is problematic for them or the organisation. So, treading very carefully, checking everything out, ensuring that you are not compromising other people's secrets and peace of mind and not just being a 'management lackey' are all very important here.

One of the real benefits of practitioner-based research, however, is that you can often cause lasting and useful change in practice and in your workplace. Research is not just something to leave on a shelf: it can have impact and lead to change. In practitioner-based research of any design, you can have real impact and ensure sustainable development. It is potentially powerful and fascinating.

Since you can carry it out using any of the methods identified in the other chapters, we will now proceed and look at one particular methodology that is frequently used in practitioner-based research: action research. It is a methodology because it is based on a way of seeing the world that invests in practice, engagement, change, collaboration, ongoing development and ownership. The effectiveness, satisfaction, work-life balancing and the difficulties of practitioner action research are much the same as for practitioner research of any form, so do consider these elements in the lengthier discussion about action research below.

● Action research

What's so different about action research?

Action research aims to effect change, often in one's practice, and involves the commitment of whole groups to ensure the agreed change take place. Many of us who do so, choose action research because it enables us to work in partnership with the people with whom we are carrying out the research. It enables our participants to acquire full ownership of the processes of the research as it proceeds, and then to put in place the kinds of change that result during and after the research. It is particularly useful in practitioner-based research, has a history in education, business organisations and health contexts in particular, and is likely to combine quantitative with qualitative methods.

Is action research for you?

Please consider:

1   Do you wish to research your own practice or to enable others to research their practice and experiences, over time?
2   Would you like to find out how effective a practice or programme you run, or are involved with, actually is?
3   Would you like to try out an innovation, try and solve a problem, find out the experience and effectiveness of a developing or changing practice?
4   Do you want to enable positive change in practices at work, in your work, with others in relation to their work?
5   Are you committed to involving those who are the subjects of your research as full participants in the research?

If you have answered 'yes' to any of these from 1–4 and number 5, too, then action research might well be the right methodology to choose.

Many of us have been engaged in effective practice or changes in our practice and/or encouraging changes in others' practice and yet may not have rigorously researched those activities. Action research is an opportunity to capture and develop such experience with the participants over time. It has been most effective where those involved in making decisions in running an organisation are also committed to implementing the kinds of developments and suggestions that arise from it. This is, after all, action research – it involves action during and after the research.

Here are a few more prompt questions. Please consider:

1 What is action research?
2 Have you carried out any action research?
3 Do you intend to carry out any?
4 Have you read or heard of any?
5 If so, what are the characteristics of action research projects, as you understand them?
6 What is action research?
7 What are the advantages of practitioner action research?
8 Setting up and running action research in your own work.

Action research

Action research is research that we carry out with our clients/customers/ students/colleagues – those with whom we work or have been brought in to work with – in order to: find out if, how and why a developmental programme or activity is effective and in what ways; try out an idea or an innovation; try out an idea or plan about learning or practices; solve a problem; cause change; see what would happen if ... . However, the process is actually more rigorous than these objectives, which are merely descriptions of the ordinary kinds of innovations we carry out as practitioners. Using the principles and practices of action research, we can try out an innovation with our participants (students, colleagues, clients, and so on) and assess and evaluate its effects, then move on to apply it further. We need to have an initial question, problem, interest in the effectiveness of a practice, a plan, and a desire to enable effective, owned change. Those who are participants need to be fully involved in the development at each stage, so they need to discuss it, think about their involvement, and agree. The organisation in which the planned action research is taking place needs to be supportive and willing to take on board the ideas, information and suggestions that it will produce. Since action research is very often a stage in enabling change in practice in organisations such as businesses, schools, therapeutic practices, health and other practices, those who have the power need to be behind the research and willing to consider what it discovers and suggests. Unlike much other research, action research might well make some suggestions or recommendations at the end as well as during the research, because it is research that accompanies development and change in a continuous spiral.

Once the action research is agreed and set up, then you and your participants – and preferably other colleagues, too – would need to try out this innovation, experience the programme, work on solving the problem, carefully observing, discussing and reflecting on and sharing responses to its effects. As much of the research is likely to be interpretative, constructivist, and using qualitative rather than quantitative methods, you will probably be involved in working with the changes, then researching them using interviews, focus groups, observation, and so on, instead of, or in addition to, the more quantitative methods, for example questionnaires.

When we, and our participants, feel we have come to some insights or conclusions, we need to try these out and discuss them.

Action research fully involves participants, researchers and the organisation, but it is not the only form of practitioner-based research. Other forms of practitioner-based research might look at a practice, problem or development over a shorter time span and not need to involve the participants in owning each step of the process so fully. It is essential that it is practice-based and aims to enhance the learning of our students, rather than merely to collect information. Action research depends on working with other people to discuss, plan, test, retry, ensure validity, and so on. It is research related to our teaching and to our students.

Key features

- The researcher and those being researched are in partnership. The aims, practices, strategies and findings of the research are shared at each stage.
- The research often aims to develop those researched through their involvement and through their subsequent reflection.

Action research

- uses triangulation. This means that it uses at least two, and preferably three, methods to gather data. In this way, the analysis of results and findings can be drawn from several sources through the vehicle of several methods, ensuring increased validity, developing patterns of data. Because action research is not seeking to prove or measure, experiment and ascertain facts, it interprets findings from its various research vehicles and methods, bringing these together and ensuring results are as rich and rigorous as possible. Information from the different research methods backs up or casts new light, each on the other
- shares the research and findings with colleagues, as well as with participants who were helpful or made formative comments

- lends itself to reflection by the researcher and the researched
- feeds into change.

Advantages

Action research:

- is based in practice and thus avoids the problem of needing to be 'implemented' later somewhere else – it is causing the changes and reflecting on the experiences as part of the actual research
- enhances morale (individual and collective) because it encourages practitioners to develop, reflect on and use their strengths
- uses validity criteria and validation processes based on involvement in the practice situation, so it is rigorous and internally valid (but cannot be argued to be reliable or generalised, as each situation and context in which you carry it out is necessarily different).

Many MAs, MPhils and PhDs use action research strategies or are totally action research-based. If you want to be involved with your students, clients, customers or patients, and to make changes, try out models and programmes, and trial developments, you are probably going to be involved in action research.

The action research process

Experience – reflect and evaluate – PLAN → ACT → OBSERVE → REFLECT → REVISED PLAN → ACT – OBSERVE → and so on.

How is this different from practice? Essentially, it isn't, it is based in practice but it is research into, on and through that practice, and so requires and establishes a more sustained and explicit examination of:

- decisions
- relationships
- the knowledge base for decisions
- the critical interpretation of evidence/data
- the learning that can be derived from practice.

Resources for 'reflection' within practitioner-action research

- *collaborative* working with clients (challenging power relationships) and colleagues (challenging personal assumptions)
- awareness of emotions – one's own and others'
- evaluation of dilemmas within values and commitments

- drawing together the implications of *varied* bodies of knowledge (for example, theory, research, law and regulations, experience, feelings)
- comparison between current and previous experience.

In other words, it involves ongoing **critical analysis** – that is, awareness of a varied *context* and its *contradictions, the experiences of this and the experiences of people involved in it* leading to a sense of *alternative possibilities*, both in practice and in one's understanding of practice.

In this sense, the basis for action research is similar to the basis for the role of the 'reflective' professional practitioner – someone who thinks about, wonders about the effectiveness and development opportunities for their own practice. However, action research might not be just about your own practice; it can be about the workings of an organisation as perceived through its members, it can be carried out in partnerships with business, health, education and other practitioners to help them reflect on their practice and move forward with changes.

This in turn suggests a form of 'research' that is best undertaken by the practitioners themselves.

Action research plans

> **Things to do**
>
> Consider:
>
> - What parts of the work, if any, that you do with students/clients/customers/patients and so on would be appropriate for action research?
> - Why would you want to carry out action research on these concerns, developments and issues?
> - What would you hope to find out?
> - What are your research questions?
> - What kinds of methods could you use?
> - What might the perils and pitfalls be?

Considering action research as a popular process in researching practices in higher education, one of the key names in action research notes:

> Action research is not only a possible alternative to advancing knowledge in higher education; it is also a more effective and immediate way of improving learning and teaching practice (Zuber-Skerritt 1992).

Action and research are two sides of the same coin.

Let us consider action research in higher education as a case in a little more depth – you can then consider transferring the benefits and pitfalls of this case to other contexts with which you might be involved and in which you might want to use action research (in business, health and other contexts or instances).

Higher education and action research – Academics are in an ideal position to carry out action research: on the one hand, they can create and advance knowledge in higher education on the basis of their concrete, practical experience; on the other hand, they can actively improve practice on the basis of their 'grounded theory'.

The ultimate aim should be to improve practice in a systematic way and, if warranted, to suggest and make changes to the environment, context or conditions in which that practice takes place. The assumptions are that people can learn and create knowledge on the basis of their concrete experience through:

- observing and reflecting on that experience by forming abstract concepts and generalizations; and
- by testing the implications of these concepts, in new situations, which will lead to new concrete experience and hence to the beginning of a new cycle.

For academics, the processes of learning are a key to their practice, so researching and embedding the learning about learning not only can cause and enable positive change, but also can add to and enhance understanding about their own learning practices for communities of students and colleagues.

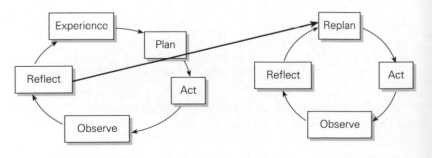

Figure 18.1 A spiral of cycles of action and research

What might the benefits be for organisations, health contexts, social work, or any other work activity that involves people?

Action research is an alternative approach to traditional research. It is:

- practical
- participative
- emancipatory
- interpretative
- critical.

It operates using:

- a critical attitude
- research into practice
- accountability
- self-evaluation
- professionalism;

and it entails:

- critical and self-critical collaborative enquiry by reflective practitioners
- being accountable and making the results of their enquiry public
- self-evaluating their practice and being engaged in participative problem-solving and continuing professional development.

Steps in action research

The steps in action research require:

- experience
- focus on the problem
- production of a general plan of action
- the building of ways of working together with the participant and collaborator group, organisation, colleagues
- taking an action step
- monitoring the effects of the step
- collecting the data
- reflecting on, discussing and evaluating the results
- reformulation of plans
- taking another step ...
- and so on.

A few tips

- For action research, we have to have outcomes and criteria against which to measure plans and actions, developments and results.
- You do not undertake action research alone. It is collaborative and involves testing your ideas and results in relation to those of others and in relation to the data and findings produced by several methods: triangulation – that is, the relating of the results produced from several methods in a balanced discussion – helps enrich results, and back them up or modify them.
- Rigour is immensely important.
- You can use both quantitative data gathering methods and qualitative methods in action research – you need to be aware of the benefits and limitations of each of these, and then pull together the different kind of data they prove in a discussion.
- Action research involves researcher and researched in a shared activity that usually leads to change.
- Ideally that change is in a context where those in power will support it and embrace the findings and suggestions arising from the research.

Another of the action research experts, Bridget Somekh, outlines eight methodological principles, namely, that action research:

- integrates research and action in a series of reflexive cycles, holistically;
- is united by a collaborative partnership of participants and researchers;
- involves the development of knowledge and understanding;
- springs from a version of social transformation for greater justice for all – emphasizing that it is not value-neutral;
- involves a high level of reflexivity and sensitivity to the role of the self in research;
- involves exploratory engagement with a wide range of existing knowledge;
- involves powerful learning for participants through combining research with reflections on practice;
- locates the enquiry in an understanding of broader historical, political and ideological contexts. (Bridget Somekh 2006).

Somekh's own research examples take power relations into account and are located in a variety of contexts in health organisations and education.

An example of action research

While writing the first edition of this book and in between the first and second editions, together with colleagues, I have been involved in working with a large cohort-based, international, distance PhD programme. Three of us began to research the experiences and practice we developed in the programme, the students' and supervisors' learning experiences and the effects of the various developments we introduced as a result of the ongoing research. As a piece of action research, it provided a perfect opportunity to involve the students as participants in the research. At each stage of their programme we discussed the research involvement with them, and used what we were finding to feed back in two ways:

1   as models of the ways in which research methods worked in practice (for example, trying out a questionnaire, reflecting on its effectiveness, looking at the data it produced in a 'what do I do with all of this data?' session in analysis); and

2   to enhance the programme by feeding the information back into developments. In this respect, it was a most effective piece of ongoing action research and can be expressed as a series of cycles or a spiral, where the programme ran alongside, fed in and out of the research and vice versa. As a result of the research, we enhanced research materials, developed different and more effective workshops, added two stages to the programme, and grew the research and teaching team to incorporate three of its graduates as full collaborators in the research. As a group, and in pairs and threes, we have disseminated internationally at conferences and in publications. For us, conflicts between the practice and the research were never an issue because it was practitioner-based action research. This second edition is one product, but for others see Wisker, Robinson and Trafford (2003).

Our research discovered and engaged in:

- a real, complex problem
- true participation and collaboration
- clear projection of reflective processes
- research needing to enable action
- the importance of being critical and self-critical
- argument (the 'golden thread' running throughout the thesis)
- evidence/proof for all claims
- contribution to knowledge in practice and theory

- originality
- ethical behaviour
- producing work of publishable standard
- emphasis on quality, rather than quantity (conciseness)
- the value and importance of being flawless in style, structure and presentation.

Much action research takes place within the methodological framework of phenomenography, which recognises an overall picture of expectations and behaviour in context (see Zuber-Skerritt 1992, 2004).

● Phenomenography

Phenomenography is a theoretical framework that relates to being in the world (phenomenology) and so, in terms of research, enables us to focus our feelings, interactions and experiences of our subjects in context. This sounds both highly subjective and very broad. In fact, phenomenography – by encouraging us to track, focus and capture experience, between people and people, people and things, and people in events in context – enables us to recognise more clearly all the influences and interpretations that affect our research. We also become aware of the need to concentrate on one small segment of interactions in context, rather than trying to capture the whole.

Phenomenography began as a theory that focused on student learning.

> Phenomenography is a research method adapted for mapping the qualitatively different ways in which people experience, conceptualise, perceive, understand various aspects of and phenomena in, the world around them (Biggs 1999; Marton 1986: 31; Säljö 1994).

Phenomenography derives from the philosophical system of phenomenology, which looks at ontology. Phenomenology, then, begins by considering being in the world (ontology). Phenomenography is a research method that explores experience and interactions in the world. It considers:

- being, preconceptions, perceptions, experience, feelings and attitudes
- situations in the world, in context
- focusing on interactions in this space/activities/context between these people

- a preference to focus at the level of the group, not individual
- using a variety of methods to look at some of the interactions

An example of phenomenography might be the interaction between the effect of student preconceptions and learning styles, and the learning and teaching processes, and curriculum; teacher preconceptions; and the assessment.

In this model (see Figure 18.2) we recognise that we can say something about how student learning takes place by looking at the interaction between student conceptions of learning, students' learning styles, learning approaches, strategies, the object of study (learning outcome in the subject) and the way it is being taught and assessed. It also enables us to consider these interactions more broadly in context. For example, the learning experience of a group of Israeli PhD students working intensively in a badly

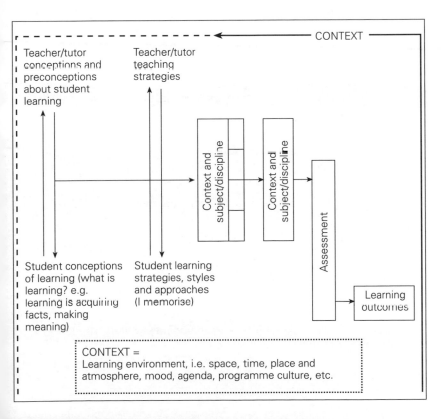

Figure 18.2 Phenomenographical model of student learning

ventilated room on a cold day, in a summer school in the UK, would be recognised as quite a different learning experience from that experienced by a small group of UK managers in a plush conference suite on a weekend residential course, or in an adult evening class in a schoolroom in Norfolk in November, studying for 'pleasure'.

Should a researcher be trying to *study* any of these situational interactions and experiences, he or she would need to take a number of the factors into account, and focus in their study on an *element* of the whole field of study. This is, of course, true of all research to some extent, for we only ever take a focused 'slice' of the whole field. Phenomenography looks at being in a context and at interactions between some elements of that context and being.

Interviews and observations, among other methods, can be vehicles for phenomenographical research, and phenomenography often operates by inviting researchers to combine quantitative and qualitative methods.

The next chapter focuses more specifically on both interviews and observations.

Conclusion

We have looked at:

☐ Practitioner-based research

☐ Action research – practices and planning

☐ Advantages, resources and outcomes of practitioner action research

☐ Phenomenography – a study of interactions in context

How might any of these ideas and practices fit in with your own research?

● Further reading

Biggs, J.B. (1999) *Teaching for Quality Learning at University: What the Student Does* (Buckingham: Open University Press).

Marton, F. (1986) 'Some Reflections on the Improvement of Learning', in J.A. Bowden (ed.), 'Student Learning: The Marysville Symposium', (University of Melbourne: Center for the Study of Higher Education): 31.

Prosser, M. and Trigwell, K. (eds) (1999) *Understanding Learning and Teaching: The Experience in Higher Education* (Buckingham: Open University Press).

Säljö, R. (1994) 'Minding Action – Conceiving of the World versus Participating in Cultural Practices', *Nordisk Peadagogik*, 14 (4): 71–80.

Somekh, B. (2006) *Action Research: A Methodology for Change and Development* (Oxford: Oxford University Press).

Wisker, G. (1999) 'Learning Conceptions and Strategies of Postgraduate Students (Israeli PhD Students) and Some Steps Towards Encouraging and Enabling their Learning', Paper presented to the Quality in Postgraduate Research Conference, Adelaide.

Wisker, G. and Sutcliffe, N. (eds) (1999) 'Good Practice in Postgraduate Supervision', SEDA Occasional Paper 106 (Birmingham: SEDA).

Wisker, G., Robinson, G. and Trafford, V. (2003) HERDSA Conference.

Zuber-Skerritt, O. (1992) *Action Research in Higher Education* (London: Kogan Page).

Zuber-Skerritt, O. (2004) 'Quality in AR Research' conference, DBA Associates in the Business School Netherlands, Johannesburg.

19 Problem-based or Enquiry-based Research and Problem Solving

Problem-based learning places the student at the centre of the learning process and is aimed at integrating learning with practice (Ross, in Alavi 1995). Maggi Savin-Baden has done a great deal of useful work on problem-based learning and its research (Savin-Baden 2003; Savin-Baden and Howell 2004; Savin-Baden and Wilkie 2004).

Many dissertations and theses develop out of a concern with real-life problems, which spring from practice. This is particularly so in the area of health, business and social sciences. There is an increasing number of practice-related, problem-based or enquiry-based research projects and products, and, if you are considering embarking on one of these, it is useful to look at some of the strategies and stages involved. See Chapter 3, which mentions practice-based research degrees, and Chapter 18, which describes action research. For students involved in an MA, MPhil, PhD or an EdD (the education doctorate), often a practice-based problem-oriented piece of research that will contribute to your professional practice is the best choice. Sometimes, it is even possible to obtain employer funding for such research.

All research involves the posing of problems or the positioning of ideas, innovations or questions of some form or another. This happens at the start of the research, and often during it at different stages, sometimes following revelations or disappointments, successes and failures, and at the necessary stages of different elements of the research. Problem-based learning (or enquiry-based learning) is the basis for whole curricula in health subjects in particular. We are considering it here as a structural element at key moments in the research, *one that promotes use of some of the creative energising practices of problem-based learning and problem solving.*

Essentially, problem-based or enquiry-based learning – or research, in this case – involves the researcher conceptualising the problem or underpinning question. Everything that you set out to discover springs from the problem or question posed. Some of the strategies of problem-based learning that release creative energy in the learner can usefully be transferred to and engaged with in research. Indeed, if they are not used, often the research itself becomes quite dull and merely descriptive, rather than exploratory in even the most basic way. It can be argued that problem-based research is the stimulus for creative research, and a strategy for going about that lively and necessary release of creative energy that makes for a quality piece of research.

Some of the key features of problem-based or enquiry-based research at any level are that it starts with the needs, interests and goals:

- of the researcher
- of the work team/research group.

Also:

- it is centred around a real concern, development, problem or issue in relation to the research/the real world/the context of the research
- it is both sufficiently challenging and realistically solvable/achievable
- it encourages the acquisition and organisation of information
- it encourages the development of appropriate skills and behaviours/attitudes
- it helps develop transferable skills useful in the thesis, further research, the workplace and in the future (and in the learner's work/life)
- it helps to encourage individual skills and teamwork skills.

● Stages of problem-based or enquiry-based research

Problem focus

A problem/development/innovation/issue lies at the centre of all the learning and research that takes place. It sparks off the learning that is necessary to tackle the problem/issue.

All teaching and learning sessions or activities relate to the problem or project, and spring from the kinds of questions and needs you have to help you to solve it.

Case study

How to overcome non-compliance with procedures for ensuring precautions are taken by nurses for health reasons.

This problem is central to a thesis and needs approaching with the nurses and the researcher (and access to the nurses and the problem) in mind.

Initial enquiry

Initial enquiry into the nature and scope of the problem/issue/innovation is undertaken by the researcher, eventually involving all the stakeholders, that is, all those involved in the actual situation who stand to be related to it or to gain by its solution. There might be a problem in carrying out your research – you have hit a block, for instance – and you and the rest of any research group could benefit by solving it. Or you could identify one of the essential issues or problems you are researching, as you see it, and as you research, you could share this with those involved. The problem is contextualised as a question, which is then structured into a project to be tackled. Sharing essential enquiries and ongoing problems often leads to a group employing problem solving strategies to help tackle the problem, and so solve it.

Planning a course of action

- The problem/enquiry is identified and broken down. Using problem solving strategies (force-field analysis), the various elements – people, context and resources – involved in the problem are discussed and analysed, objectified on a diagram and then broken down and considered, which makes each element manageable.
- The outcomes sought are identified and when planning and actions are considered, they are checked against the sought-for outcomes. Will research activities, vehicles and strategies really help achieve these outcomes?
- Strategies, people, resources and so on, and plans of action are discussed in relation to each aspect of the problem/project defined, and a list of action points drawn up to help tackle the problem/engage with the project.

Next, you will need to ask what you can actually do to engage the nurses in following established compliance behaviours and in overturning bad practices. You look back at people, practices and policies that cause problems and consider strategies to cause change together with strategies to encourage and enable that help.

Case study

If nurses seem to be non-compliant with procedures for precautions and you want them to *be* compliant, you first need to identify:

- who is involved (nurses, doctors, patients)
- what is going wrong – for example, precautions not taken
- what results (or might result) in reality or possibly from not taking precautions (illness, health hazards or danger, spreading bad practice)
- what is blocking the taking of precautions:

  > attitudes
  > analysis
  > time
  > experience
  > fears

- what is working against your success in persuading nurses to take precautions:

  > attitudes
  > power
  > time
  > access
  > your position

Are there any hidden areas of nurses' responses or reasons that could be a problem? Consider these, then look at what could be used to help or cause change:

- who or what could help you change the nurses' behaviours: – people:
  > immediate managers
  > nurses themselves
  > top managers
  > patients
  > doctors

- practices:

  > developing good practice through modelling
  > developing good practice through training
  > visible and discussed policies for compliance.

Then turn the strategies into an action plan with outcomes and a timeline to help you see what needs to happen first, and when, and what needs to happen next.

The actions and strategies need to be identified and costed in terms of time. Plan the time to fit in each stage of the research, activities, reflection/evaluation, replanning, and so on, to include conclusion and the writing up/presentation of results (a critical path/time planning exercise is often carried out here).

Consulting resources

Identifications of resources and skills, strengths and needs are established to carry out a project that is based on problem solving. If you are engaged in your own individual research, you will need to look at how you fit into the research groups/company/team/situations appropriate to the kind of research in which you are involved, and in relation to the knowledge base and conceptual structures of the subject/discipline.

- You need to decide what skills you have, what skills you need, what knowledge you have, what knowledge you need to acquire and what kinds of energies, people, powers, practices and policies are there to help you with your work, or seem to hinder you or simply do not relate. You will need to identify the problem and project, those things that can help you, how to overcome contradictions and problems and negative responses. Then consider tackling the problem. You will also need to consider acquiring the skills and knowledge to tackle it (and to determine if you need new skills and knowledge).
- How are you going to write the problem up? Is it a whole process or element of your research, or will it be one that has invisibly been solved so that your research can proceed – in this case, it might only appear in your journal.

Do not forget that you are working on two different activities at least here, depending on how many different problem stages you find in the research: (i) the problem, (ii) the thesis. When the problem is solved or the project completed, the thesis still needs writing.

Your whole thesis might concentrate on solving a problem, or part of one. A thesis, dissertation or a write-up are a snapshot in the life of some ongoing projects or problems. They are not merely self-indulgent activities because of this, however. They help capture the difficulties, and the energies and activities spent engaging actively with these difficulties to achieve a positive solution, so they form a kind of interim report. An interim report is not enough for a PhD, however. If your work merely reports rather than engages with the concepts and the literature, it will not be of a sufficient standard to gain a PhD – and this could be of concern if that is the level of award you are seeking. So, ensure you have a sufficiently important issue or enquiry problem to solve or enquiry to pursue (if it is your main research area), and ensure you engage with the necessary theory, literature and concepts as you tackle it.

Putting resources into action

Once you have identified, clarified and strategically planned to solve your problem or carry over or pursue your enquiry, you need to set about acquiring the information, using the resources and seeking help from people, carrying out experiments and assessing results, collating data, interacting with samples or materials and transferring information to presentational formats (as appropriate to the problem solving activity).

Examples of problem solving activities and strategies: force-field analysis

Consult Maggi Savin-Baden and others for a fuller, thoroughgoing exploration of problem-based research. However, you might find it useful to carry out a brief problem solving exercise to solve a problem in any research.

- Identify the problem/enquiry issue as you see it, and think carefully about the preferred outcome(s). What do you ideally want to happen – or to avoid? For example, what kind of action needs to take place for the variety of people involved?
- Next, identify the various forces (people, practices, policies, contexts, resources, rules, crises, and so on) that are causing the problem or are working *against* you and which could cause problems in a development or changes. Fill these in on the diagram in Figure 19.1.
- The object of the exercise is to *objectify* and to *visualise in a diagram* these various forces, and then to look at what forces (people, contexts, policies, decisions and so on) you have working *for* you in your planned change/development/problem solving.

Weigh up precisely what could be difficult for you and consider the worst that could happen.

Now consider:

- systems, plans and actions that need putting in place
- what actions you need to take, the research needed – how and where to go about it
- who you can work with, tasks to be started, actioned and completed
- who can help you in your work, people to be persuaded and negotiated with

- what policies, resources and practices can help, working systems to be set up with the team at your disposal in order to achieve your outcomes, team roles and responsibilities negotiated
- plan the activities on a timescale related to your plans:
  ANALYSE → PLAN → ACT → EVALUATE AND REFLECT → REPLAN

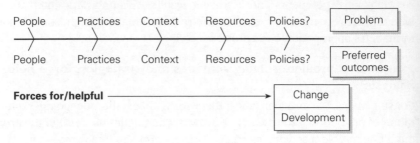

Figure 19.1 Problem solving

Reflection, refinement and development

As a researcher, you will probably find it useful to keep a journal or learning log of the plans, thoughts and learning activities you undertake in relation to the problem. Reflection on your observations, ideas, and so on, will reinforce your sense that you are learning as you go along. This is particularly necessary if the problem forms the bulk of your research. It is also necessary if it is a small problem you have overcome or faced along the way. Record the stages. You will need to note other skills and knowledge that you acquire as the result of more conventional training and development activities (for example, you might find that, in order to tackle the problem, you will need to update your Information Technology (IT) skills or undertake other research methods courses).

Findings and analysis

At different stages in the problem solving work/the project/the research you will need to sum up, review and assess your findings, and decide whether you have achieved your intended outcomes – and, if not, what to do next to further your work. If you are reviewing stages of problem solving/projects as parts of the research, you will need to review what these findings mean and how you can refocus and structure your future work.

Project conclusion

Depending on what was being studied and the nature of the problem, this is the moment to review what has been achieved and what has been learned. For example, in health subjects, an appropriate solution might be the diagnosis of a problem situation, a plan of action to deal with it and a specified means of evaluating whether the plan of action was successful, how far it was successful and how it might have been improved.

Some points concerning problem-based or enquiry-based research for practice-based doctorates

Problem-based research and learning are action learning-based and often, therefore, related to the workplace. They:

- enable continuous engagement and improvement
- encourage self-reflective researchers/learners who can continue to learn
- encourage learners to transfer the learning from the problem-based project/case to their work with the organisation and the various problems and projects that emerge during the course of this work – that is, the learning is transferable and practice-based
- encourage teamwork, goal analysis, action planning, time management, evaluation and presentation of results to others.

This is why students studying for EdD programmes or for MPhils and PhDs related to their practice frequently adopt a problem- or enquiry-based approach.

Solving individual problems in any research using problem solving strategies – after the individual problem

If and when the problem is solved, ask:

1   If it is a problem about the process, can you now carry on with your research? For example, if you were trying to gain access to some sample, what do you do if you are unable to gain that access? Implement changes, develop, change direction ...
2   If the problem is the core of your research, will you be able to take forward any insights or changes your research has produced? What needs to be done beyond the thesis?

Conclusion

We have looked at:

- ☐ Carrying out problem-based or enquiry-based research

- ☐ Solving problems that form the main question or focus of your thesis or dissertation

- ☐ Solving problems that provide difficulties along the way, as part of the research process

- ☐ How you might identify, tackle and action problem solving, and record your activities

- ☐ What you might do to ensure appropriate change after you have solved the problem and even after you have written up the dissertation/thesis.

● **Further reading**

Alavi, C. (1995) *Problem Based Learning in a Health Sciences Curriculum* (London: Routledge)

Savin-Baden, Maggi (2003) *Facilitating Problem-based Learning* (Maidenhead: Open University Press).

Savin-Baden, Maggi and Major, Claire Howell (2004) *Foundations of Problem-based Learning* (Maidenhead: Open University Press).

Savin-Baden, Maggi and Wilkie, K. (2004) *Challenging Research in Problem-based Learning* (Maidenhead: McGraw-Hill and SRHE).

20 Research Methods for the Arts and Humanities

This chapter looks at:

- ► Strategies for arts and humanities research
- ► Conceptual framework and research methods
- ► Self-reflection, linking theory and practice, relating the creative to the analytical

Some arts and humanities research uses social science strategies, particularly in subjects close to the social sciences – such as history, and cultural studies. However, much of the research in the arts and humanities uses quite different strategies and, when presented, the thesis can be of quite a different shape to that of a social science thesis. In terms of both research methods and overall final shape, some arts and humanities research can – to the reader, the non-artist or the researcher – tend to seem amorphous, or even highly subjective, when it needs to be just as conceptually clearly organised and managed as any other research in any other field.

There are serious debates about the kind of research that arts and humanities students undertake. It can be seen to range from a focus on the discovery, collection, analysis of and critical commentary upon data – much as would a piece of social science research or even a piece of scientific research – to highly creative and reflective, even personal, work. In the former instances, it might be based on archival research exploring, for example, primary sources about a historical event, a group of people, a trend; identifying and tracing the origins and provenance of rare books; or using the papers of a living (or dead) writer or other artist as part of the source material. Much arts and humanities research is based on and forms largely critical and analytical work that explores and traces, for example, themes and patterns in text, image, historical documents and events; asking questions about what they represent, as well as – or instead of – why and how they were produced; and to what ends they were used.   At the other end of the spectrum are instances where the research process itself enables the creative process – or, indeed, is the research process, where appropriate – instead of standing in for it, or being irrelevant to it.

To the uninitiated, and particularly to the highly structured social scientist, research in the arts and humanities often seems (erroneously) to be simply a matter of reading and responding, even responding from a subjective and personal point of view alone. This is because the object of study is itself likely to be imaginative, creative, reflective, not as tangible and situated or grounded in the real world as the objects of social science or health practice research. We might ask several questions about the effectiveness and rigour of arts and humanities research such as:

- What kind of change can analysis of literary texts possibly produce? Why does it matter?
- What does it contribute?
- How does this relate to the real world, if at all?
- Is it merely self-indulgence, or is there rigour involved in this kind of research also?

Actually, much literary and arts research is concerned with exploring critical questions in the material, in the same way as social science and health-related research. It can be more overtly engaged with the researcher, perhaps, than some social science research. For example, the researcher could even be the producer of what is being researched – as is the case with creative writing PhDs – or could be what/who is being researched, where the researcher might be a case study or his or her reflections on producing an artwork might be part of the subject of the research. In arts and humanities research, a personal connection between an author, a performance artist, or an oral history context is not necessarily part of the research, and most arts and humanities work does not directly involve the researcher reporting in person, except critically and analytically. Whether the researcher is or is not personally part of what is being researched, the research process is still rigorous. What is rarely expected in arts and humanities research is the personal emotional response alone; instead, a critical and analytical response is expected.

Arts and humanities researchers acknowledge their own directness and involvement in the work, as do social scientists involved, for example, in participant observation, or in selecting and gathering data using the constructivist or interpretivist paradigms where it is clear the researcher is involved in the production of interpretation and knowledge, and acknowledges this as being the case.

● The documenting, critiquing and creative continuum

We might consider arts and humanities research along a continuum from, at one end, a literature researcher who, for example, might be relating personal critical responses to a group of writers, a writer, a group of texts, or a phenomenon, theme, or issue in texts, to those of established critics, and weaving something new out of this mixture of the personal and the established. Or the researcher might be writing a creative piece, a novel or poem sequence, and accompanying that with analytical, critical and reflective versions, and with commentary. A creative artist might be carrying out visual research using sketchbooks, to build up a creative response, keep notes, work at ways of creating something out of a situation or feeling; or he or she could produce an installation, a set of paintings, sculptures, or chairs or other functional objects designed by him- or herself, and the research explains how, for example, the artist has been able to produce and express his or her own work based on research into collections by others, into interactions between materials and the creative self, in reaction and response to an idea or argument he or she wishes to put forward where the artwork is an articulated expression of that.

Or, at the other end of the continuum, arts and humanities research can be much less personal, much less creative, and far more analytical.

What are the objects of study? And how might the research be carried out?

Arts and humanities researchers focus on a range of products and issues, their production, the ways in which they construct and represent, and their reception.

Documentary analysis

Much arts and humanities research relies upon the analysis of documents, both primary and secondary sources (primary sources are those produced at the time, and by the originator; secondary sources are works about the sources, about the time or the originator, written from the perspective of an analyst, a critic, someone commenting on the source rather than being the source). It is not merely a personal response, and it is not merely documents that you read or see. Such a simplifying of the arts and humanities research processes could lead to a sense of amorphousness and a lack of direction.

Primary sources and archival research

Researchers might well be asking questions about, and looking at, primary sources, that is, those produced at the time of study rather than commentaries and critical views upon such sources. Primary sources are often the object of study for historical and cultural researchers. The researcher might be tracking down and classifying primary sources in order to develop an argument about their original meaning, intention or some other issue. The researcher might be using primary archival sources – for example, an author's papers – to identify how and in what ways the author has been using primary material in order to influence his or her own writing, and to what effects. The researcher might be looking at the production and publication of, or the reception of, primary sources or products in order that he or she might focus, for instance, on the cultural reception of films or texts, or looking at audiences and audience response in order to identify who responded to what and in what ways and why. One researcher looking at books as primary sources, their production, use and intention might, for example, be identifying instances of armorial stamps (usually gold family arms resembling heraldic crests placed on the front cover of a book to indicate who owns the book – many of which date from medieval and renaissance times), thereby exploring the provenance of books, who produced them, published them, owned them, and passed or gave them to whom (or had them stolen by whom) and what that says about habits of book ownership and reading through the ages. This is both archival research (looking through old collections and lists, through databases) and also very 'hands on' (involving visiting book collections in the more ancient parts of ancient libraries, or public schools, or ancient universities round the world). Another researcher might be looking at how primary sources on scientific disasters and genetic modification influenced an author – Margaret Atwood, for instance, in her writing of a work of fiction (*Oryx* and *Crake*) – the development of an argument within the book, and the critical reception of these ideas from readers.

Charting and recording

Charting and recording what exists in itself is not usually adequately complex and conceptualised enough for a postgraduate piece of research, although both charting and recording are necessary steps in such research. Charting, recording and narrating what is there, or is being developed, can form part of many kinds of research project. For example, the researcher might chart and record instances of an artist, photographer, dance specialist, or dramatist's work in response to certain issues, over time. The researcher might equally, if engaged in a historical piece of research, be charting instances of behaviour in, for example, family history, the history of house decoration, and so on. The researcher asks questions about patterns of behaviour, their relationship to historical or cultural context and change, what they can tell us about behaviour, ways of expressing ideas and views, and ways of receiving and responding to the behaviour or creative work. The researcher might well concentrate, for instance, not merely on instances of the response and product but also on the ways in which the form an artist or dance specialist has chosen can articulate any message, make a major comment on some cultural issue, or a major contribution to a cultural issue. Provided there is an underlying research question and a conceptual engagement, then it is possible to make a recognisable research-oriented contribution. The researcher might also delve into the personal or the creative context and expression or reception of the artist, dance specialist, or other.

These definitions and descriptions of research in the arts and humanities begin to pinpoint not only the crucial elements, but also the elements about which there is the greatest dispute, that is, relationships between collation of instances and patterns, conceptual frameworks and conceptualisation, and then of personal response.

Engaging with theory

All research needs to be underpinned and informed by theoretical or conceptual frameworks otherwise it is in danger of being merely descriptive, rather than theorised and analytical.

Arts and humanities research needs to ask questions of its subject matter as does any other research area; just like the scientist, the artist cannot afford to be merely descriptive or narrative in his or her research recording mode.

Much arts and humanities research can be carried out in a manner focused more on theory than product and reception, such as when engaging with the debates between schools of critical thought in terms of the interpretation of historical movements, of artistic products, or literary pieces. This kind of research is carried out in similar ways to those produced by a scientific or social science researcher who would measure different theories and theoretical or conceptual frameworks against their objects of study in order to evaluate the appropriateness and validity of the interpretations these frameworks offer.

Integrating theory and practice

Arts and humanities research often integrates theory and practice, as does much social science research. For example, a performance artist might be researching his or her own or others' individual relationship to, and interpretation of, the world in the context of the underpinning theories. The artist would probably ask him- or herself to what extent, and in what ways, at what times, do theories underpin the personal and professional practices? And how do these practices engage with, contribute to and further the development of theory? How does the artist reflect on the development of the project using theories – as well as personal responses? Literature theses have underpinning theories, just as any others, and many arts and humanities research areas are interdisciplinary by the time they get to Master's or doctoral research stage.

What are the major paradigms and perspectives driving the research?

A particularly lucid explanation of different research paradigms is offered by Denzin and Lincoln (1998: 185–93), and was referred to in Chapter 7 of this book, where we looked at the positivist and postpositivist paradigms, for example. These focus on internal validity, external validity, reliability and objectivity, and cannot fully take account of the ways in which enquiry is interactive. Sets of facts can be read in different ways, and are value-laden, not value-free. Constructivism and critical theory rely on relations between people and ideas, things and events, for instance, on argument and dialogue and the construction of knowledge, rather than its recording and re-creation.

Such interpretative perspectives enable an examination of relationships and values in context, and also have some room, where appropriate, for the arts and humanities researcher to reflect on his or her own responses, processes and creative or other decisions. While these research paradigms and strategies are oriented to applied/social science and cultural studies, they can also be widely used by arts and humanities researchers who examine texts of whatever kind – literary, popular, film, media, documents, diaries or the personal record – and they can also be used when researching, for instance, the relationships between design objects and their culture, their context, their development in context, their reception and use. The strategies can also enable the researcher to look at other sites for the dialogic and interactive – such as the individual in a performative space, in a cultural context, the literary text in a cultural and critical context, or making a variety of cases about a cultural phenomenon.

For example, Norman Mailer's semi-fictionalised autobiographical text *Why Are We in Vietnam?* can be seen as a personal, informed, creative but historically contextualised response to a real event, understanding the importance of interpreting real events and how interpretations and people make meanings. The novel questions the political positioning and actions of others during the historical moment of the Vietnam War through a personal, critical and semi-fictional response. It sets up a dialogue that researchers can use to focus on how individuals construct meaning in a context.

Many texts, artworks and performances themselves question such inter-actions, set up such a dialectic, and encourage a post-modern approach, that is, one that does not accept there is a fixed meaning and interpretation but recognises that meaning and interpretation are constructed in dialogue between people, events, space, time and so on. Researchers such as artists, writers and critics can use all texts and performances as examples of contextualised products that say something about their times, origins and construction as part of a cultural discussion. Within this research paradigm, some research is driven by investigation into interactions and cultural and social reproduction of meaning in and through texts, projects or performances and their readership, audiences, performers, producers. Much feminist research, as well as ethnic and cultural research, is informed by these paradigms.

Example

Arts: women's writing

A student engaged in exploring the development of women's writing since the second wave of feminism, for example, would need to involve research methods more usually found in research focused on history, culture and society, as well as literature. They would also have to engage with some key questions in their exploration rather than merely delineating an area. The exploration is likely to be dialogic and interpretative, looking at how at different points in time, different constructions and representations have been produced and why, and why and how these might be critiques, and might change. Some underpinning questions might, for example, include: In what ways do women authors of the period engage with the developing issues of feminism? How do they challenge representations of women and their role? What kinds of writing strategies, themes, characterisation, style and so on do they use to help them in this engagement?

The development of these questions has already teased out a range of issues from the bald statement of the period and the area of study – and this suggests some underlying assumptions that will need establishing, checking out and exploring through the object of study: the texts themselves in context. Assumptions include the thought that women's writing in this period will involve itself with issues to do with the representation of women's roles, and so be aware of and, to some extent, enact or mediate feminist criticisms and feminist theory as it develops.

Methods used would spring from these questions. Some would need to be largely documentary and to include analysis of the kinds of themes and variation of the arguments in these themes in the texts, which deal with representations of women, and comments that critique the established versions of women. Some researchers have chosen to count the times that such themes emerge and so to indicate patterns and frequencies. This rather scientific approach is not so popular at the end of the twentieth and beginning of the twenty-first century. Equally unpopular is the merely personal response of enjoyment or empathy. There needs to be a middle way between recognising and characterising themes, patterns and language, and indicating how these serve as vehicles for argument, how language affects emotions and responses, as well as how the text is structured. The personal integrates with the analytical at every stage, but both are clearly defined. And the dialogic is a key here – meanings, representations and interpretations are relative, are produced through interactions between people, events, events and people, and so on, and they change as they interact with each other. This is explored in such research even when it captures a very narrowly defined moment and set of texts or text, because it situates such moments and such expressions and texts within a constructed and interpreted frame. The researcher is always part of the research project, though not necessarily its focus.

The same researcher, though, might want to use her research project as an opportunity to create and express, then reflect on and analyse her product, which is a response to and an exploration and expression of the research. She might, for instance, want to produce a quilt that reflects her responses to a novel – for example, Toni Morrison's novel about slave history being present in the lived experience of African Americans, in particular, *Beloved* (1987) – and to do this research she:

- wants to reflect, to discover about slavery and the working of this novel in critical, cultural and historical contexts
- to provide a quilt that is a response to her research findings and feelings.

So, she researches quilting for the time of the slave crossing, the time in which the novel is set. She also produces quilt patterns that reflect her own responses, and puts the whole together into a wonderful artistic product, accompanied by analytical, critical, theorised text that explains her working research and artistic processes as well as answering a question and responding. She might accompany this with a log or reflective diary that charts her responses, decisions about the research and the creative piece, and a sense of how the whole comes together. Such a project spans the archival kind of research right through the theorising and critical, to the personal, reflective and creative.

Example

Literature research: representations and debates in context
It is important to take a critical and analytical approach to reading and artistic practices. A typical literature research project would set out to critique, explore, analyse and evaluate a body of work – that of one author or of several authors, of several texts on a specific theme or issue, texts in context in relation to the cultural and historical context, texts in a theoretical framework, and so on. It would bring to bear specified theoretical and critical frameworks – such as historical/Marxist, psychological, linguistic, biographical, feminist, structuralist, deconstructionist, poststructuralist, postmodernist and so on. It would need to define and defend the theoretical frameworks and the bodies of knowledge/approaches, and to situate the investigation in the

context of their work and other writing with similar and opposing frames and views, so that this new piece of research contributes to a debate. The 'variables', as such, to use the social science terminology, are likely to be relationships between, for example, the author in historical context and his or her work – for example, how Thomas Hardy's novels engage with explorations of the changing experiences of families in the nineteenth century. This is a historical, literary perspective.

Another thesis might look at the works of African women writers' representation of women's lives in Africa and the UK. So, they might compare, contrast and explore representations of women's lives in Africa and in Britain, establishing and relating with contexts of everyday life, cultural practices, and practices of literary or artistic expression, defining the particular version of these that their chosen authors develop. This latter would involve cultural context; the texts; the writers; feminist criticism; awareness of debates about culture, gender and ethnicity; and also an exploration of the literary in that the work would involve the imagery, characters, themes, language and shape of the novels themselves. The 'what' of the text is added to by 'in what way?' and 'how?', as well as 'in what theoretical and cultural context?' and 'through what approaches?'

The 'approaches' question is one that substitutes for questions about qualitative and quantitative methods, although literary research can use the social science strategies when it is interdisciplinary in nature, and could, for example, in one version, look as much at audience response (using statistics, as in the way in which texts and writers represented things and events and people), as at the texts themselves.

Examples of titles:

1 The treatment of relationships as an index of cultural change in the fictional work of Elaine Feinstein

2 Kennedy's political strategies and the Cuban crisis: A turning point of American political response to Communism

3 Techniques of confessional poetry and the explorations of self and the body in the work of Sylvia Plath and Robert Lowell

4 Star Trek and beyond: How TV science fiction negotiates and represents versions of cultural imperialism

5 Bodies in space – A creative exploration of the lived self in cultural spaces

6 Thomas Hardy's dysfunctional families as an index of historical change in the nineteenth century

Let us look in depth at title 6. What follows are some of the questions to ask in order to start to research and to answer the research questions.

Things to do

Choose one or more of the humanities and/or arts titles (below) that could underpin a dissertation or thesis and consider:

- What mini-questions and subsidiary questions are involved in approaching this title?
- What theoretical frameworks and theories could you use to help you to approach the asking of these questions?
- What material could you use to drive the asking of the questions? For example, what literary texts, artistic products, mixture of documents from different sources – historical, diary, and so on – could you use? Could you use media texts? Would you need to use social, cultural and historical information, and where might you get this from?
- Which theories are you using to develop and underpin your own? What critical, contextual, interactive and personal elements are involved in your research, and how do these all fit together in your work? How can you argue that the mixture of theories and other elements fit into a cohesive, directed, whole piece of research?
- Why do your questions matter, and are you sure/how could you argue that your explorations and theories underpinning and driving these can really help you answer your questions? What are the tasks involved here?
- Why does your research matter? Will it affect others? Cause change? Contribute to knowledge and argument? What will it do?

NB These are the questions you will need to ask and answer of your own arts or humanities research.

Questions to ask:

- How can texts represent versions of historical change?
- What were the historical changes to the family and to people's lives as a whole – key points – during Hardy's period?
- What specific texts act as examples of representations of historical change in the family in the period?
- What kinds of families does Hardy deal with? What might they represent? Is there any argument developing over time in his work in relation to dealing with the changing family in history?

The critical approaches

This work integrates the historical, the cultural and the political as well as the textual area or materials, and it also asks for a dialogue and interpretations – a dialogue between the historical change and the texts that represent it through the fictional families, and which charts events, images and so on. How can you defend the work at the intersection of these different theoretical approaches? This would be a key question here.

Some critical approaches and theories we will need:

- Marxist historical criticism – this enables us to look at the relationship between textual examples, their production and the historical moments in a politically aware sense; seeing the people's lives as produced by the political and historical moment, and seeing textual representations as ways of exploring, arguing and debating things about how people lived
- Literary critical analysis of language, image, symbol, characterisation, the narrative and so on
- Some historical approaches to document analysis, acquisition of historical data through other means (archives? testimony?)
- Some feminist critical approaches – because this deals with families, it will be saying something about women's roles and mothering, motherhood and the upbringing of children. This will be usefully interpreted through feminist critical approaches since that will allow for the recognition of stereotyping, impression, originality, argument, interactions between representations of women, children and families and the questions of role and opportunities for women at this time – especially as represented by a male author.

How would you write up your methods?

You would not necessarily detail what you did step-by-step, as you would in social science methods. Having set out the theories that underpin your exploration, you would then engage in exploring and pulling together the context and the material, and using the secondary critical theoretical material (the Marxist or feminist critics, for example) to bounce off/underpin/inform/guide your analyses of the texts. In a theoretical context, you would be establishing and developing your own readings, but using the critics to establish, back up or disagree with you – so your own contribution is engaged in an informed dialogue with them. If there are critics with whom you disagree, have a dialogue with them. It is also important that you do not spend all your time arguing with them. You have your own case to establish and critics to use to back this up and inform it. You would use evidence from the texts and other appropriate documents, quoting and analysing, synthesising from different parts of the texts and different critical or theoretical areas and comments. This is so that your synthesis and analysis are your own, your choice of quotation is your own and used at different times in different places in different ways to variously illustrate, exemplify and explore the arguments (through close critical analysis of the images and language, and so on).

Different chapters could segment the material and the approaches to the questions differently, depending upon your choice:

- You could deal with an underlying set of questions as explored systematically through different texts and cover one per chapter, possibly in chronological order, possibly as they exemplify different angles or answers to the questions.
- You could scrutinise your area of questions further. Are there themes emerging? For example, in Hardy's work: names, titles and events or elements set up an argument that, because of the changing employment conditions and economic situation of the rural poor, families were less likely to be cohesive and able, caring and nurturing, and so there were many broken families and feckless fathers, who sacrificed, harmed or abandoned children.
- Hardy explores the ways in which the middle classes started to develop, with education and economic growth, and he worries that this could be a problem. Some novels reflect on the many scenarios in families where education was sought, but leads to suffering and lack of economic growth, broken families and unhappiness.

Either the themes or the critical arguments could head the chapters – the choice is yours and depends on the overall direction of the research.

● The form and shape of arts and humanities theses

Students undertaking literary and arts research need to discover and defend their critical approaches and frameworks probably rather more than defending their research methods, unless these are unusual. The theoretical frameworks and literature review chapter will explore the critical and theoretical approaches used, while a methods chapter will possibly not be part of the thesis. It would also be unusual to describe the research activities and analysis. The findings of literary research theses are more likely to contain chapters on exploring themes, angles and arguments through contexts, and interweaving the debates by leading from one chapter to another and referring back and forth. They do not necessarily move in a chronological sequence through one piece of research, followed by another, followed by findings – the 'findings' or point of argument, as such, is led into at the beginning of the chapter, and the exploration flows on within the chapter. This is more of a journalistic than a scientific report-writing method (see Chapter 27 on writing up). Chapters might follow developments within research, deal with periods of change, or deal with grouped themes in an author's work.

The thesis – its possible shape

Abstract

Laying out the questions that underpin the thesis, the conceptual framework that allows the questions to be asked and tracking through the different kinds, stages or focal points of the different chapters that are asking and addressing the questions through the material.

Introduction

This incorporates the theoretical perspectives chapter – although there is sometimes a separate theory chapter.

This acts as a chapter to both situate the enquiry, and its theoretical and conceptual location and framework. Unlike a social science thesis, there is not usually a separate theoretical chapter, although there could be. It should be written in the third person, and in the past tense.

The Introduction concentrates on situating the arguments and questions in theories, context and background; the work of those interested in and working in the context of the questions and ideas, even one's own practices; and establishes a critical, theoretic frame and focus for the work. Here, the researcher is explicit about the research paradigms and key theories, and the researchers whose views and approaches are being used and why. If it is an interdisciplinary research work, the integration of, relations between, and use of different theoretical and conceptual approaches and contexts would be outlined, and an argument put forward for integrating them into or relating them to the inquiry.

Body of the thesis – discussion chapters

Several chapters would then follow, analysing and discussing primary source material as data. These could include instances of representations of dysfunctional families in Hardy's novels as they develop an argument about, and a representation of trends in social change of families at the time. The data in these chapters are quotation, images, recordings, constructions and products – as appropriate for the subject.

Conclusions

All theses and dissertations have a conclusions chapter. See Chapter 28 for the discussion of what to expect from a conclusions chapter. This would contain: (i) a synthesis and summary of the main factual findings, what has been discovered, its patterns, why this matters; and (ii) a conceptualised level of discussion of how and what the research has added to our understanding of the topic, to its meaning.

Bibliography

Here are two case studies as examples of how to pull your thesis together:

Case study 1

In a performance arts PhD, MPhil or MA, which includes the self as an artist, a researcher might:

- establish the theories of the key performance arts, arts critics and theorists, and stake a position in relation to them
- set up a position for integrating his or her own performance work in this critical and theoretical context, reading it through the theory, and reading the practice through the theory
- establish the critical distance and objectivity, and the issue of subjectivity because of personal invention – using the self as the case study. This is really very similar to many other dissertations or theses, which would here establish the position of the researcher involved in addressing these specific questions. A separate theory or methodology chapter would be unlikely, but possible.
- Meanwhile, the non-thesis elements of the research products could be a CD-ROM of the artistic work in practice, performing, or, in another instance, a set of artworks.

Case study 2

A researcher writing on gay male writing since Stonewall, charting the different themes that run through this writing, its relationship to the cultural and historical contexts of the times, and its historical development for a few key writers would need to:

- define the underlying questions and make some assertions about the field of study
- clarify the theories and critical approaches being used in the context of 'queer theory' (which would need explaining): a cultural theory 'take' on this would need to be established, as well as a discourse analysis-based critical way through

● establish the reasons for the choice of themes and texts. This would form the focus of the beginning of each of the chapters. Establishing themes, clear approaches and text choices would provide a good lead-in paragraph or two to direct the reader in each chapter.

For both theses:

The ensuing chapters would focus upon the themes and the source material (texts, artists, performances, artworks, cultural products) and interactions with self, in context (as appropriate to the dissertation or thesis), and choices, developing the arguments through each chapter, linking the chapters. There could be a dialogue between the texts and the researcher, especially if the researcher is using him-/herself as a case study. There could also be a dialogue between different interpretations offered by different critics or by the writers/artists and their works and the critics, so that meaning is made through a dialogue, a dialectical approach, and the argument is seen as an interpretation that is situated.

The conclusion would establish the overall significance for the arguments, explorations and discussions as developed through the dissertation or thesis, and could point towards cultural or social change. It could establish a new take on the theory/ies that have been underpinning the work; or it could bring opposing views together into a new synthesis through the interpretations of the texts/artefacts/actions, as appropriate.

● **Researching your own creative work/using the creative in your research work**

Many students are involved in the kinds of critical approach we have discussed, at all levels. However, many engage in literary, artistic, musical or performance work directly, rather than through the lens of a critic as such. So, their research is not merely in the arts and humanities but also in relating their own performance and production, their own creative practices, to these areas, seeing their creative work as a product of the theories and critical contexts, and being fed by them. Technically, they are therefore exploring their own work as if it were a large-scale case study in the social science sense, analysed critically and contextualised. They could study their own experience, as well as the product itself. At undergraduate level, those who have already been involved in creative work – art, creative writing, video production and so on – will be familiar with the issues of relating the actual texts, artworks or creative products and activities to an analytical framework. There is a set of theories that help engage the work with concepts and argument, and which enable a link between the theory and practice to be established.

Critical approaches and theoretical frameworks, as well as the basis of the dissertation or thesis, can be very much the same as those already discussed. Much creative work takes place in the intersection of critical perspectives, cultural contexts and the personal. Its main difference from more standard arts and humanities research is the inclusion of the creative work as part of the research object explored by the theories and critical perspectives, and the involvement (here, appropriate) of the self as a research object, because the self is a vehicle for the creative work if it is a performance, or if the self is partly the topic of the research.

Some students choose to carry out this kind of research through the use of artwork itself. Where does the personal and developmental work go? Some work needs to capture the personal as part of the critical element of the thesis, focusing on the personal/critical/developmental choices and responses, the critical decisions made in the performance or artwork and integrating theses, and what were the theoretical and critical perspectives and arguments in the context of which other work has developed. One student involved in a piece of performance art developed her performance work out of her own theories – about the relationships between the virtual (technology, media representations) and the visceral (the real person, the body in the space). This student then acted out the performance, which she had videoed and included on CD-ROM, as well as videoing each element in the appropriate technological format. She then accompanied the work with a standard thesis, which explores decisions made about, and the theoretical underpinnings to the performance, and the ways in which it acts as a vehicle for explorations and discussions about the critical theories between them. She comments on the way it contributes to the thesis, using both personal comment, critical comment on personal performance work – which has been made objective because it has been shared with an audience – and the comments from the theorists, moving in a dialogue between them. Programme notes linking the performances themselves with the thesis are a great help here, as readers are not so used to making the links between performance in space and its theoretical explanations.

Another student, now that she has moved to live in the UK, chose to explore her own relationship with her own history of artistic and personal response to her memory of life in South Africa as a woman in her family. She is a visual artist working in installations, and she videoed and produced several linked pieces:

- A thesis that set out the drift and theoretical frameworks, and explored and explained the video and all her critical points about self, memory, place and artistic response
- A log or journal of her developing personal explorations and critical choices about the thesis – issues to do with the difficulty of capturing the feelings and experiences about decisions concerning visual representation. This includes questions about actual videoing, problems such as fading, using sound on, over or off. It also involves looking at the visit back to South Africa, the shooting and the planning or accident involved in this. It notes what could or could not be caught on film and how
- The video itself and accompanying notes, explaining and exploring its links with the arguments of the thesis and explaining, also, how its shape and form enable the arguments to be developed.

These examples of creative products, including videos, have involved the construction of sculptures, a dress, objects in installation and creative pieces of writing. They need also some form of accompanying work for an exploration of the critical and theoretical engagement. This should lead to, and enable the production of comment and analysis of themes and issues of the work itself. A log and analytical, critical piece are the natural accompanying pieces of work.

A more standard thesis piece that uses the theoretical and critical to establish arguments and explorations, and place this work within the context is additional. This serves to establish its contribution to critical debates in which it is placed.

Conclusion

We have looked at:

- ☐ Arts and humanities research integrating the critical and the creative, interdisciplinary approaches

- ☐ Creative performance and critical work using the creative and the personal

- ☐ The specific form and shape appropriate for arts and humanities research and the thesis itself.

● Further reading

Atkinson, P., Delamont, S. and Hammersley, M. (1988) 'Qualitative Research Traditions: A British Response to Jacob', *Review of Educational Research*, 58 (2) (Summer): 231–50.

Creswell, J.W. (2002) *Research Design: Qualitative, Quantitative, and Mixed Methods Approaches* (2nd edn) (Thousand Oaks, CA: Sage).

Denzin, N.K. and Lincoln, Y.S. (1998) *The Landscape of Qualitative Research, Theories and Issues* (Thousand Oaks, CA: Sage).

Websites accessed

http://carbon.cudenver.edu/~mryder/ltc_data/pract_res.html
http://qualitativeresearch.uga.edu/QualPage
http://www.qualitative-research.net/

Part Four

Support, Progress, Analysis, Writing Up, the Viva, Presentations and Afterwards

21 Being Organised, Keeping Records, Writing up, Stage-by-Stage

This chapter looks at:

- ▶ Planning your study – time plans and critical path analysis revisited
- ▶ Planning the stages of the thesis and the chapters
- ▶ Getting into good habits – recording references, colour coding, keeping files and cataloguing research activities and results
- ▶ Organising your findings and your draft, writing up

Here, we consider writing up as an ongoing activity rather than something that happens in a rush at the end of the thesis or dissertation. You should find it useful throughout your MA, MPhil, EdD or PhD, and particularly useful as you start to produce drafts, then final versions of your dissertation or thesis. Read it as you start to work and as you continue.

It is important to get into good habits in your research, using your time fruitfully in a planned way, and to get into good habits in writing up. Do look back at the section on managing your time. This will be particularly important for you if you are also balancing paid or unpaid work and domestic responsibilities, but strangely (perhaps), it is often those engaged only in full-time research who might lose track of their time in relation to their research plan and possibly even fail to complete. They might have become overwhelmed with other activities, or have lost their way in the research and the thesis. Do be careful to keep a clear idea of your way through your developing research, and your writing about your research. This is not a blueprint for rigidity and being closed to new ideas: being open to surprises and needing to change as a result of findings as you go is not the same thing as having no real plan in the first place. It is often the case that, as you begin to write, your ideas become more complex, clearer, and you can work your way through various problems through writing about your work, and about your processes and discoveries: use writing as a way of managing your workload and working out ideas.

Look at Chapter 12 on time management, consider the example of a time plan or critical path analysis and map your own plan of study in a similar way, or in overlapping lines, to indicate different coincidental elements of your work as you have proceeded. Right now, as you are proceeding with

Things to do

Look back at your draft plan of the study.

- Have you clearly and carefully plotted each stage of the research?
- Have you ensured that some activities, such as the literature searching, continue alongside other research activities all the way through your research?
- Have you written in enough time for each stage of the activity?
- Have you considered what (technology, equipment, and so on) and who (subjects, helpers and advisers) can help you at which points in the research? Where, when and why might you meet difficulties?
- How can you overcome these difficulties with good practice, rescheduling and the help of others?
- Do you intend to give presentations, work-in-progress seminars, conference presentations, or write papers along the way? If so, when might you plan these in?

parts of your work, consider and review in brief the whole process for the next few years. Use the space below to map out your time and task plan of study, briefly identifying difficulties. You will need to add in the dates against which you are plotting your work and you will also need to add in the clashes and difficulties that emerge in your other life – that is, work and home.

Discuss the plan with a colleague. Can you detect any difficulties? Explain how it will work, how it has worked *so far* and where there might have been stressful moments, clashes of work and other interests, a need to rely on others, possible delays and so on.

Look back at Chapter 12 to consider how you have been successful with these planned stages and some planned and unplanned incidents.

● Time and task plan – key stages and obvious potentially difficult moments

How have you managed any of these so far?
What might be coming up in the future?
What would you do if some of the demands on your time clashed?

1 Research question, choosing your university and supervisor. Interviews and house moves? Job changes?;

2 Refining questions and sub-questions, defining methodology and methods. Meeting supervisor to clarify;

3 Ongoing literature searching, craft submission – meet supervisor;

4 Submit/revise/meet supervisor – resubmit. Carry on with the research;

5 The business of the research – using pilots, refining methods, gathering data, continuing to read, *starting to write up each tentative part of the work*, meeting supervisor to check ideas, arguments and findings;

6 Carry on as above, for the bulk of the time, and continue to write up drafts and discuss with supervisor;

7 Progress reports/transfer documents;

8 Work-in-progress presentations with other researchers, some publications, continue to work as above – drafting and redrafting as you go and seeing supervisor;

9 Organise charts, diagrams, produce them, refine write-ups, produce final versions and discuss them;

10 Edit and re-edit, check rules for layout and presentation again, ensure bibliographies are in correct format and that nothing is missing;

11 Submit (unbound, in case of revisions);

12 Viva and success or viva, some rewriting, resubmission/sending in of rewrites and success;

13 Celebrations, conferment of degree, publications and different work.

These are the expected stages of your progress. There might have been some problems, both professional and personal, along the way, that have held up some parts of it – do not worry, this is normal. You need to recognise the drain on your energy that such problems present and then reorganise your time plan, reschedule your work, and get on with it. Often, knowing you have the thesis or dissertation there to be done can take your mind off other problems – do try not to let it be the problem. If it makes you too stressed, take a break, even to the point of taking time out and intermitting, returning with renewed energies.

Research as a journey and the thesis as a piece of architecture – a building

Over the years, when I have worked with students individually – and more so, when working with research development programme groups – I have found that being able to separate the research process itself from the finished thesis, in terms of shape, trajectory and development, can be very helpful. When you read someone else's thesis it seems a perfect piece, coherent from start to finish. All those aspects (look ahead to Chapter 22) of a typical, or even an unusual, completed thesis seem perfectly placed to develop an argument, prove a case. Each bit is coherently linked to the whole, there are themes and theories running throughout and the whole thesis has a main argument. When it makes claims it has evidence to back them up and there is no extra evidence hanging about without being linked to a claim and the argument. It is a model of building an argument with reading, theories and evidence to help the argument, and it is also flawlessly written.

This is the finished thesis. If you can, do look at a few rather than taking a single thesis as the perfect and only model. They should all be similar in terms of the quality and coherence I have just described, but they have not been written by superman or superwoman. Behind this perfect piece lies a research journey, with many difficulties and false leads, writing blocks and so on – many struggles and moments before finally the ideas, arguments, evidence and conceptual level of work all started to fit into place and then be expressed clearly in order to enable the reader to engage with the importance of the achievements of the research. If you keep a log of your research process and progress, you can yourself both record and then revisit what those lived stages of your research journey have been like. This is useful to remind yourself of the pleasures and difficulties, and also useful when you review why you made certain decisions for the final version of the thesis and for your viva, if you have one, when you might well be asked to explain why you chose this method, changed that sample, worked on these books or that documentary evidence in those ways, carried out those procedures only so far. Examiners like to hear about the research journey and recording it will actually also give you something to keep writing about, even when the data gathering is going slowly or your work is remaining only at the 'busy' level, largely collecting and descriptive, not really conceptual yet.

See Figure 21.1 for a useful comparison between research as a journey and the thesis as a building.

Although the research is planned and organised, through the research proposal, there are many exciting moments when you discover things you did not expect. There will also be moments when your plans are blocked, the sparkle is not there, the experiment goes wrong, the interpretation of the data does not give you the answers you expected, people behave in an unusual way, you cannot find the books, and so on. Your research is a long journey of surprises, blocks, problems and revelations. Eventually you finish and you have been writing about what you are doing all along: the arguments, the theories, the themes, the decisions, the data, and the gradual

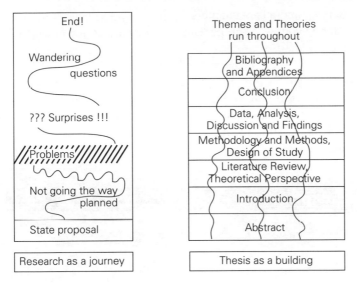

Figure 21.1

level of the writing will have been raised. As the level of your thinking rises, you start to think about meaning, contributing to understanding, to think conceptually, in other words, other than merely in terms of description and data gathering.

As you have been writing all the time, the thesis has been growing, but it has not necessarily (in fact, rarely has it) been growing in stages from the abstract through to the conclusions. In reality, the writing moves on at different paces and stages. You can, for instance, keep adding to the literature review/theoretical perspectives chapter right through to the end of the thesis; you will be writing the abstract and the introduction at much the same time as you finalise the conclusions chapter – because they position the work and emphasise its overall shape, intent, achievement and meaning and so cannot really be written until the research journey itself is complete, for the moment. There is always more work you could do – but remember your slice of the cake. It is important to stop at some point, capture the work, write about it and then move on.

What follows are some thoughts about the processes and details of the research in terms of your writing part of it as you go along, and then finally writing drafts in the appropriate thesis or dissertation shape. It looks at:

- keeping good notes of sources, methods, results and data
- talking and thinking through drafts of chapters

- writing up drafts of chapters
- altering your work in the light of comments from your supervisor(s)
- more editing.

Have you had any difficulties in writing up, in keeping good records? As you start to write up your final version of the thesis or dissertation or, for EdD, your final progress report/thesis, you will start to revise your record keeping and update it, and start to rewrite previous chapters to make them fit into an overall cohesive work.

Conclusion

In this chapter we have looked at:

☐ Planning your study

☐ Organising your work habits

☐ Keeping records

☐ The research as a journey and the thesis or dissertation as a building

☐ Starting to write up stage by stage

The next chapter looks in more detail at what is expected of a thesis or a dissertation, and how to maintain momentum through the writing process. Chapter 23 focuses on the writing process and overcoming writing blocks, editing and fluent writing of a completed thesis or dissertation.

● Further reading

Dunleavy, P. (2003) *Authoring a PhD* (Basingstoke: Palgrave Macmillan).
Murray, R. (2000) *Writing a Thesis* (Buckingham: Oxford University Press).
Murray, R. (2004) *Writing for Academic Journals* (Buckingham: Oxford University Press).

Murray, R. and Moore, S. (2006) *The Handbook of Academic Writing* (Buckingham: Oxford University Press).

Winter, R. (1993) 'Continuity and Progression: Assessment Vocabularies for Higher Education', Unpublished research report data, Anglia Ruskin University, Faculty of Health and Social Work, Chelmsford.

22 Writing the Thesis or Dissertation

This chapter considers:

► Writing each chapter what each can contai coherence
► Developing the frame work of different chapters
► Structure of a chapte
► Language – 'fog', technical terms and accessibility

● **Developing the framework of different chapters**

Areas you will have considered when writing your proposal provide a key to the main areas of the developing thesis. Look at these again now, and ensure that your proposal is aligned with the developing work. Ask yourself whether it really addresses each of these areas. You will find that the areas of the proposal that you address will form important beginnings for your chapters. However, do remember that the research journey will have changed some elements of the proposal. A proposal is often written in the future tense – and you are now writing about something which is complete – so do not just copy it over without correcting these issues.

In your proposal you will have thought of (a reminder):

1   **Indicative title** – What will you call the dissertation/thesis? It is better to pose a question and to make a suggestion about links in argument rather than to give a single word or area of study.

2   **Aim and focus of the study** – This should suggest the underlying research area and your main question and sub-questions. Eventually, it helps to form the abstract of your thesis, so think about it carefully. What are you really exploring, arguing or trying to find out, hoping to find out, and then suggest? What links with what in your mind?

3   **Context for the research** – What issues, problems, history, background and others' questions provide a context, an academic culture and ongoing set of questions, thoughts and discoveries for your own work? How is it contributing to academic work in this area? How well are you placed to undertake the research and write the thesis? *As you start to write up elements 2 and 3, these form part*

of your Introduction, where you lay out your main arguments driving the thesis. It is also important as, in a viva – if you are working for a PhD or EdD – you will be asked about your own reason for the research and its relation to your work and life (if that is relevant).

4 **Theoretical perspectives and interpretations** – Where have you taken your theories from – what kind of framework? What are the underpinning theoretical perspectives informing your ideas, for example, feminist theory or Marxist theory? These elements will have developed from the literature you have been reading, your own development of a dialogue and debate with the theorists, critics and the other experts in the literature, also you are clarifying the main theories that help you ask your question and underpin your interpretation of data and findings. *As you start to write up 4, this will go into your Introduction and into your literature review chapter, if you have one, or probably into your theory chapter.*

5 **Research design** – How will you go about collecting information, carrying out literature searches, and so on? Provide an outline of the different activities you will undertake, at what points in your research and perform a critical path analysis of this. *When you write up, the design is explained in the methodology and methods chapter, and reappears as you explore and develop your argument through your data analysis and discussion chapters. You mention it in brief in the abstract because it is the shape your work has taken to help you ask the question or address the issues.*

6 **Research methodology and methods** – What is the research methodology underpinning your research, and what methods or vehicles and strategies are you going to use? Why? How do they link with and help inform and develop each other? *This is a whole chapter in the thesis. It also involves you entering into a dialogue with experts in the field of methodology and of methods, so that you debate why you chose the methodology you are using and why you have selected which methods, and use the theorists and practitioners to back up your choice.*

7 **Ethical considerations** – Most dissertations and theses have ethical considerations, and these will be particularly complex when you are using human subjects. Obviously, if you are involved in medical research this would be so the case. However, it is also true of protecting the identities of those who give you information through questionnaires, focus groups or interviews. You will need to take care when asking certain sorts of personal questions or using documents that refer to people alive or dead – and so on.

Items 5, 6 and 7 form the basis of your methodology and methods chapter.

8   **Outline plan of study** – This part of the proposal asks you to indicate what you thought would be the main features of each of your chapters. It would be useful to revisit this at different points in your ongoing research and consider how they are developing, whether any early findings are changing these.

9   **Justification for level of award** – An MPhil, EdD or PhD usually involves answering this question – you will need to describe and discuss what you feel your research will contribute to the field of knowledge, the development of arguments, and the research culture. What kinds of practices, thoughts and arguments cannot move forward? How can it make a difference? Why does it matter? And why is it obviously at this level? Is it serious, broad, deep questioning and sufficiently original? Primary references – there should be 10 or 12 of these in your submission. *Item 9 partly ends up in your abstract and also appears in your concluding chapter, where you are arguing about the conceptual level of your work, and its contribution to knowledge and meaning in the field.*

Of course, much of your thesis goes way beyond the original proposal because it is all about *what* you find and how you place it in your conceptual framework, what it means and what sorts of analyses are made. The conclusions will be what you draw from what you find.

● The shape of the thesis as it develops

When you come to think about the actual shape of your thesis, you can bear several models in mind. A thesis often has a narrative or storyline running through it together with some secondary storylines – these are the trains of thought or argument in which your investigations, readings and findings all fit. Start by thinking what case or major argument you want to make and then consider the questions you need to ask, where and how you might ask them, the research methods and vehicles you will use, and the way the main reading and theories informing your work all fit together. Broadly speaking, you are considering:

1   your research area and how you have defined your topic and your questions – and how you are defining these;

2   your thoughts and arguments exploring why you are asking certain

questions using certain methods and vehicles in certain ways to help you explore your research area;

3   discussion, analyses and reports on the work you have done, your discoveries and arguments, the way some information leads to other thoughts and links to other information and ideas and helps develop arguments further. This involves looking at the data that you are producing and analysing it, asking it further questions, speculating, making creative leaps with ideas, and pulling ideas and findings together;

4   some of your solutions and conclusions, and further thoughts on future work – recommendations for developments, actions and explorations beyond the scope of your thesis here.

There are differences between theses in different fields of study. Arts and humanities theses tend to concentrate on exploration of arguments in a storyline throughout the thesis, rather than in methods sections, findings and conclusions (often there are no conclusions as such, instead, there are arguments that seem, now, to be proven and well founded in the reading). Social science and health-related theses tend to have more explicit characteristics. They usually analyse and interpret the information and data, and move conclusions forward to new stages of investigation, then come to some proven conclusions and suggest further work.

● Models

It will certainly benefit you to look at other people's theses in similar areas, and these can probably be found in your local university library. Do not get too embroiled in the arguments. Look at them for their shape – their abstracts and so on – and look at more than one, so you are able to see that there is a variety and do not copy the shape of the only one you have read. Do not read for sense, but rather for the shape.

A typical plan of a thesis is frequently as follows:

- title
- abstract
- preface/acknowledgements
- introduction
- literature review/theoretical perspectives chapter
- methodology and methods explored and explained, including the design of the study

- presentation of findings and results (a separate chapter for scientists only): for social scientists, arts and humanities students, the results, or data, are seen as evidence for the argument, findings and claims based on the research, and they appear in a dialogue with such claims, that is, presentation and discussion of results, analysis, arguments, development of ideas based on results – interpretation of findings
- conclusion: both factual (what was found) and conceptual (what does it mean? what does it add to meaning and understanding about the area/field/issue?)
- appendices/statistical tables and illustrations
- bibliography.

Throughout the thesis there is an argument, a narrative/storyline that develops by linking your underpinning reading, themes, theories, ideas, methods, findings and arguments together. Go back and forth through the thesis as you start to write it up and edit it to ensure that this coherence develops – taking a reader clearly and logically through your work.

Your plan of the thesis – what chapters and their main points/arguments/role?

Complete the plan chart below, planning the stages and elements of your own thesis. This will help you think through your work to come, and see how ideas and arguments develop from each other, interweave and lead to each other.

Your plan of the thesis

1

2

3

4

5

6

7

8

9

● **Elements of the structure of the thesis explained – and variants discussed**

Title

Put your title on a separate title-page, try to keep this to one or two lines, and develop a title that is clear, suggesting the questions you are posing and assertions you are making rather than just the field of study.

Abstract

An abstract is usually about 500 words and answers the questions: (i) What is this thesis about?; (ii) What does it argue/prove/contend?; (iii) How did the research design enable it to ask these questions and gain answers?; (iv) What does this work/what has been found contribute to knowledge and meaning?; (v) Why does it matter?, and so on. It should use the third person and passive verbs, for example, 'it is argued that ... in discussing ... using ... evidence is presented which suggests that ...'.

Preface and acknowledgements

Introduction

This lays out the:

- background to the thesis
- brief introduction to other work in the area
- general ideas and developments related to the thesis
- your context – why you are the right person, in the right place, to write this
- topicality and context of the research itself.

Usually the introduction tends to be written last – it provides a coherent introduction to themes, arguments and findings: this is difficult to do until the whole anatomy of the thesis has actually been constructed and flesh put on the bones of each chapter.

Review of the literature/theoretical perspectives chapter

Not all theses have a separate literature review chapter, but all do have a chapter where they use the literature they have read, the theorists, critics and the experts to set up debates and dialogues. This chapter also indicates how their own work contributes to the debates and enters into an academic dialogue with previous and current work. If all your work develops logically and smoothly from the reading you have done, and your research and findings follow on from a coherent body of established work in the field and established informing theories, you will develop a literature review or theoretical perspectives chapter at this point. The theoretical perspectives chapter will: (i) establish the main underlying and informing theories and arguments; and (ii) discuss the main debates, research and authors who contribute to the field. In this chapter you need to contextualise your own work and enter into a dialogue with the work of others.

This is not the last time you will be discussing the literature and the work of theorists and experts. You will be moving stage by stage and, at different stages, need to introduce and develop theories and reading, so you should find all your chapters use and interleave the literature, theory and arguments. Do remember that the literature review or survey/theoretical perspectives chapter is not just a collection of all you have read. You need to weave the reading and main points and arguments made into your own discussion, using it to back up or counteract some of your arguments. If you have found a few main themes developing logically and coherently through your reading, these can help form the basis of your main chapters.

Methodology and methods including design of the study

For the social sciences, education and related research, this is as crucial as it is for scientific research. You need to explore the methodology that underpins and informs your research. Have you chosen to set out to prove something, measure it, experiment and discover factual answers, in a piece that is positivistic, deductive (theory testing), using quantitative methods? Or have you set out to explore interactions, constructions, versions, interpretations, feelings and things that are not measurable but, rather, interpreted? This would be a postpositivistic research study that was inductive (theory making), using qualitative research methods. It is possible your research is a combination of both, that you set out to explore if, how and why (inductive) and then, having made your discoveries, you built, tested and measured (deductive), or the other way round. Explain your methodology and defend it, explain your methods and defend them, and clarify the design of your study. Here, you also use some of the literature and theories you have been reading, this time of those who are experts in methodology, so that you defend your choices of methods – questionnaires, for instance – and explain whose theories and practice underlie their usage here.

Explain why and how you designed your studies – mentioning the pilot stage if there is one, decisions taken about interviews, focus groups, questionnaires, samples and so on.

If your research is more humanities- or literature-based, you might well find that you have already described what your research questions are along with your main ideas and arguments in the preceding chapters. In this case, there is no specific study in logical stages, each depending on the data from previous stages, as such; instead, each chapter takes a different theme, critical approach or point of view, or different author or book, and so on. There might well be a methodology and methods you can describe and defend; however, since you could be using documentary analysis, autobiography, storytelling, the self as a case study, archival research and interviews with text analysis, all of these need discussing and defending.

Presentation of results, discussion and analysis

For the scientific thesis, there is a chapter that can be just a clear, annotated record of what has been discovered. However, you are unlikely to have a chapter that just presents results if your work is in social sciences, education, health, literature or cultural studies, the humanities, or the arts. In this case, your 'results' or discoveries and arguments will form part of the discussions in separate chapters.

Presentation/discussion of results

While in science theses there is a chapter or more to discuss the results, in the social sciences, arts, humanities and business theses, the presentation of results or data and their discussion are always interwoven: no evidence (data) without a claim and no claim without the data to accompany it. I always suggest no extract of data, whether it is a table or a quotation, should be any longer than a short paragraph, before you discuss it in terms of the theories informing your understanding of it, the themes that are emerging and the ways in which it relates to your question and your argument. For a social sciences, health or education thesis, this is a logical place for working through different results, putting tables, statistics and bar charts – either in the main text or, if you do want to include large tables and charts, and so on – referring to them in the appendices, and conducting a narrative that explores and brings in different results to develop arguments and present your coherent points and findings.

For a humanities- or literature-based thesis, and also often for one in the social sciences, health or education, there are often *several chapters* exploring different themes and issues in a linked discussion. The results, as such, will be your critically informed comments and arguments on the texts, images, your readings and so on. You are analysing the data and interpreting the findings in the light of your question. You might find that the main themes identified in the literature review appear here as main topics in each of your chapters.

In a humanities- or literature-based thesis, there might well be a more *organic* structure of chapters focusing on different themes, developing issues and authors.

Conclusion

All theses have a conclusion; however, many students – exhausted – run out of steam by the time they get to the conclusions and just sum up what they said already and the facts they have discovered. This is not satisfactory for a conclusion! The conclusions establish the importance of your work; state its contribution clearly; and summarise the main points you have made – where, when and how. It rounds off your arguments, even if there are still points open for further work and questioning.

You will have factual conclusions: what facts or evidence have you discovered? How have you added your knowledge about the issue you researched? Conceptual conclusions: how does what you have found and argued help to develop meaning and understanding – perhaps of the data, the complexities, the paradoxes, as much as the particular version of understanding of the field that your work has revealed and established with its evidence? Usually, these do not contain recommendations; they sit better in a report. However, at this point – in theses that seek to suggest change or development, or to contribute new ideas and strategies and so cause development and change – there could well be a section for suggestions for further work and perhaps for others to take ideas into practice. If your work does indeed seek change, then it is essential that you think throughout the research how you are going to make constructive and realistic suggestions here based on your findings. But most theses DO NOT make recommendations.

Appendices, statistical tables and illustrations

These might appear in the main text, with the argumentation that refers to them. Ensure each item is clearly labelled and referenced as to where it is used in the thesis. If they are not explained in the body of the thesis, explain them fully here.

Most theses tend to use a bibliography that sums up, in alphabetical order, the texts used in the thesis itself. However, some theses cut this into both references and a bibliography.

References

If you are using footnotes, they usually appear at the foot of each page, and endnotes appear at the end of each chapter. Some writers leave all the endnotes to the end of the thesis, collected chapter by chapter at that point and integrated with the references. References in the text appear in the bibliography. For example, 'Estelle M. Phillips and D.S. Pugh (1994) *How to Get a PhD: A Handbook for Students and their Supervisors*, 2nd edn

(Buckingham: Open University Press)' placed at the end, in the references, can be signalled in your actual text as '(Phillips and Pugh 1994)'. Consider the referencing format for your discipline and your university, as there are many variants. The most important rule is to stick to the same method throughout.

Writing chapters

Each chapter is like an essay in that it has a focus, and a linked, developed narrative and argument, which is a subset of that of the thesis as a whole. As such, then, you will probably begin by *planning* it using diagrams, mind-mapping, brainstorming and the development of key points, followed by notes to illustrate and fill these out.

State the main argument of the chapter in an introductory paragraph or two. If you have several main arguments, suggest here how they are linked, for example:

Example

In this chapter the arguments for developing regional colleges are made clearly. Regional colleges provide a valuable service for students who cannot attend the main sites of universities owing to distance or other commitments, and their usefulness should be valued politically as well as pedagogically.

You need to remember that you are writing to make a case that is backed up by evidence, and underpinned by theorists and experts whose work is referenced – a mix of your own work and that of others. You also need to think clearly about which chapter it is you are writing, because each has a special focus and concern (see above).

Developing notes

Under key headings for each element of the chapter – for example, 'regional colleges' – explore the information you are going to provide and the examples, references and theories to which you will refer. For instance, in this subject area you might include an introductory chapter that begins the thesis and moves on to set up the research theories, methodology and methods, and the design of the study to show:

- their role geographically
- their role as access providers for the region
- their political role – enabling disadvantaged or distant students to gain university/college qualifications

- the franchises and mechanisms for linking regional colleges to universities, or enabling them to remain separate – the pros and cons.

This is an introductory chapter; much of it is initially descriptive. You should also outline the issues that you are going to research, questions to ask and your own context and role, as well as why it is important to ask these questions now. Move through the argument and the narrative of your chapter, ensuring that (i) there is coherence between the different elements and examples discussed within the chapter; and (ii) that each of the chapter's streams of argument are related to the thesis arguments and themes as a whole.

You will need to ensure that there are links between arguments and examples or illustrative material, theories and abstract ideas and concepts, generalised comments, and specific, worked-through examples. Do not be afraid to introduce major arguments that contradict your own – you need to argue with these in order to show you have taken other points on board and understand their relevance. Do not just include other people's work to show you have read it, but use it in a discussion/argument. Using the work of others in such a discussion also appears in the theoretical perspectives chapter, where it establishes: (i) the theory and major work in the field; (ii) major debates into which your work will fit in the methodology chapter where you are also placing your methodology and methods choices in the context of work done by others, which can be used to argue for the methodology and methods you have chosen; and in the thematic data analysis and discussion chapters, where the experts are also there to remind the reader of what you are interpreting from your data and arguing about, and that what you are turning into findings is underpinned by theory and debate in the subject.

Using quotations

If you are quoting, try to break up long quotations with discussion. This is true both for the quotations you use in a theoretical perspectives, methodology or discussion chapter, where you take from someone else's work to engage in a dialogue with your own, and from your own research, when you are discussing and interpreting your data. Do not depend on the plan and construction of the other author's work for your argument – make those elements of his or her arguments you use fit in with your plan of argument. Use his or her arguments as illustrations, or points to argue with or against – setting up and pulling down points, and so on. Do not simply fall into re-describing and paraphrasing: make it your own and, of course, reference it fully and carefully. Disputing and arguing with authorities is all part of developing your own contributions and ideas, as is agreeing with them. Do be careful to reference fully and so avoid any accusations of plagiarism. For students from outside Britain, the USA and Australia, where English is not the first language, different conventions often operate in relation to the use of authorities. However, if this is a thesis in English for an English/US/Australian university, you will need to follow conventions of arguing with and carefully referencing any authorities, quotations, and so on that you use. Check conventions with the university authorities and guidebooks for good practice in writing.

When you reach the end of each chapter, just as in the whole thesis, summarise what you have argued and 'proved'. At this point you are summing up the chapter, indicating where it fits in your overall argument and in the thesis, reminding us as readers of the facts you have mentioned, and also writing at a conceptual level, indicating to readers what this has contributed to enhance our understanding of the meaning, the importance and the contribution of the work to this field of study, these arguments, these beliefs and so on. For example:

Example

This chapter has suggested that the development of regional colleges should be supported because of the specific access provision they present. The chapter has argued for several models of linking with universities, emphasising the importance of some autonomy in this relationship. A number of examples have been considered and their position and value explored. Issues of the assessment relationships are explored in Chapter 5 and issues of overseas 'regional' colleges in Chapter 6.

These final points link your chapter to the rest of the thesis and show that there is a coherent argument throughout.

Language

Think of your audience's needs. Check conventions. Many university departments do not like the use of 'I' or 'we'; however, others recognise that the research has been carried out by you (or you and others), and that you wish to place your own views and arguments in your work, and so to signal them with the first person. Feminist research and action research, for example, quite often prefer the use of 'I' because it acknowledges engagement of the researcher with the research. If, for instance, you are using yourself as a case study in a social science, business or health context, you should also use 'I', but only for those parts. Be careful, above all, to be readable. Adopting distanced and stilted language can be off-putting for readers.

If you are using technical language, of whatever sort, explain acronyms on their first use and explain complex technical terms (unless they are clearly in everyday use among specialists such as yourself and the readership you expect). When in doubt, explain terms on first use and, if there are numerous unusual terms, include them in a glossary in an appendix.

Avoid 'fog', which is very (unnecessarily) dense language. This is common, especially in scientific writing, and even in the social sciences and literary criticism. Those who write theses are sometimes as guilty as anyone else in 'fogging up' their expression with too many unnecessarily long and complex words when a straightforward word would do just as well. Do not sacrifice technical terms, but do ensure that there are limited numbers of words of several syllables explaining the most straightforward elements of your argument, especially when they are all gathered in a sentence that includes technical terms. If too many long, complex, unusually specialist words and technical terms come together, the reader will experience 'fog'. They will not be able to get through the density of your prose to your argument. It is not impressive; it is confusing.

Try out early parts of early chapters on colleagues who are semi-expert in your field – if they are entirely happy, then it is probably readable prose.

Things to do

Expression

Look back over the research questions you have formulated and the brief outline of what you feel your thesis will be about, or at your developed proposal, especially the theoretical perspectives element.

- How clear is this?
- How logical?
- Is the language unnecessarily filled with long words in addition to technical terms?
- See if you or a colleague can summarise your arguments easily.

Consider what it tells you about readable prose that is, nonetheless, working at a high level and making a complex argument.

Submitting the thesis – forewarning for good practice (see final chapters for further discussion)

Drafting, redrafting, changing, editing and so on take a long time – do allow for this. Various things can go wrong with your data collection and analysis, and even with your hypothesis and the arguments you were exploring. You will need to discuss why and how you changed your mind and some elements of your focus, and you will also need to reschedule if this happens. Try out drafts of your work on your peers, a family member, on a critical friend. You need supportive development and advice rather than destructive criticism or empty praise! Of course, you are also sending drafts to your supervisor and working with his or her comments.

Finally, once your thesis has been edited and re-edited, and reads coherently and well, and really makes a powerful case for your research, you can proceed to submission.

Conclusion

To sum up, a few points to bear in mind as you are working:

☐ Your supervisor should have read all of your work before submission and can advise on layout, as well as more complex arguments, and so on.

☐ Ensure you have read the university guidelines about layout, typeface, presentation, binding (or not, until after the viva) and references, and that your work conforms to all of these. Many theses have difficulties simply because of their presentation – which is a waste if the hard work has been done and the presentation quality lets this down.

● Further reading

Dunleavy, P. (2003) *Authoring a PhD* (Basingstoke: Palgrave Macmillan).

Murray, R. (2002) *How to Write a Thesis* (Buckingham: Open University Press).

Phillips, E.M. and Pugh, D.S. (1994) *How to Get a PhD: A Handbook for Students and Their Supervisors* (2nd edn) (Buckingham: Open University Press).

Wisker, G. (2005) *The Good Supervisor* (Basingstoke: Palgrave Macmillan).

23 Overcoming Writing Blocks and Learning from Feedback

This chapter considers:

▶ Writing – conceptualisation and critical thinking, style and choices, and presentation
▶ Ways in which you can overcome writing blocks
▶ Maintaining the momentum with your writing (keeping going whatever happens)
▶ How to use your reading and your data effectively in your writing

This chapter looks at writing and overcoming writing blocks. The next chapter continues the discussion, and concentrates specifically on learning from feedback, an issue introduced here.

● Writing

Conceptualisation and critical thinking, style and choices, presentation

It is important in writing your dissertation or thesis that you write in an organised, fluent, coherent fashion; it is also important that your writing is at a conceptual level (engages with ideas, uses underpinning theories to explore questions and findings, interprets data and contributes to meaning) as well as being detailed.

Let us begin by looking at what is expected in terms of the level and content of a dissertation or thesis.

Dissertation or thesis writing – A sound dissertation or thesis:

- has question(s) underpinning the whole
- has a conceptual framework identifying key concepts to be problematised, which causes a problematising, critical attitude and hopefully prevents the thesis being composed with merely straightforward/descriptive statements
- is written in such as way as to ensure that all you say is underpinned by the research question(s), appropriately asked through the appropriate methods and research vehicles

● ensures that all claims about importance, meaning and the interpretation of data and reading are backed by appropriate evidence
and engagement with theories and experts in a critical dialogue to
which your work contributes.

Some of the phrasing you might use to develop such a dialogue includes:

'Previous work by ... indicates ... while the findings of ... seem to
suggest that ...
My work with ... argues that ... and in so doing refutes ...'.

Your voice and contribution

You need to 'find your voice' among the others, the experts. Initially, you
might feel the experts have said it all and you have nothing to add: this is not
true. Find how your work fits into the ongoing debates with their work, get
into a dialogue with the work, comment, critique, add what your work will
show or hopes to show or has found, how you are moving the field and the
debates on. You might not have much to say at first because you are reading
and thinking yourself into the field, especially if your work is now in a different field from undergraduate work you have carried out, but, once you have
read, debated and carried out some research, you need the courage of your
own convictions, and faith in what you are thinking and have found, to
engage in the debate with others.

Finding your own voice, then, comes gradually. You might want to shape
the thesis accordingly, so that what starts out in your writing to be an exploration, a 'Who dunnit?', ends up in the final draft as you leading the reader by
the hand and revealing the reading and developing arguments; the ways in
which the theorists back up and underpin the questions you are addressing;
how the methodology and methods enable you to access your subject matter,
population, reading, sample data – and to question it all and interpret what
you are finding; and how they reveal an argument about what this all means
in the end – and how that contributes to meaning. We explore some of this
writing in Chapter 22. Much of your comfort and satisfaction with the tone and
certainty of your own expression will emerge as you write and then refine
what you have written following re-reading it and taking into consideration
what critical friends and your supervisor provides as constructive criticism.
There is a similarity between your own debates with the established field and
your supervisor's developmental discussion with your own work provided in
feedback. For more on feedback see Chapter 24.

Major issues for your supervisors and anyone reading your work are listed
on p. 294; so, ask yourself these questions as your work proceeds, and at

several stages in your writing, then finally when you hand in drafts and the final thesis.

Are you working at a critical level?

- How does this show in your expression? Are you sure it is not merely descriptive?
- Is it theorised – or merely stated?
- Are you working at a conceptual level – showing the contribution to knowledge, new ideas, new meaning and understanding of meaning? Or are you only telling the story and identifying the fact? Only making judgements and stating opinions?
- How is this indicated in the choice of words, shape, links, claims?

We will look below at staging and structuring your writing, overcoming writing blocks, developing writing and, in Chapter 24, responding to feedback.

Writing in stages

Much of what you introduce in your theoretical perspectives/literature review chapter and your methodology chapter – that is, the theories behind your argument and your methodology and methods choices – will reappear when you analyse your data, and need the theory and expert comment to underpin and back up your analysis and discussion. In this respect, you might well find yourself writing at length in an introductory fashion and referring to it later.

● Analysis of narratives, interviews, interactions, cases

- You might want to include all the data and text, but you need to be selective in order to back up your argument, rather than include it all and expect the reader to select.
- Identify the categories and themes, select in order to argue the case, include primary sources and examples. You could, if you wish, put some full text in appendices – perhaps an example of a transcript of an interview and a completed questionnaire. If your work is based on small numbers of in-depth interviews, you might want to include their full texts in the appendix.
- Select typical examples and discuss them, commenting and analysing. Look, for instance, at the whole shape of an interaction in an interview, at a case, a narrative, a dialogue, a set of statistics related to a single question, or to comparing a couple of issues and

areas – depending on what you are looking for, what you have asked in your research. You could mark the categories you are looking for visually onto the text as you sort out the sections of text, examples and data you are going to use, then sum it up and argue about it beneath the extract.

In your writing, you need to move through several stages or levels of dealing with theories, arguments, analyses of data: all of these stages will probably be present in your final thesis, each in the right place. If your work remains at the level of description, narrative and summarising, then it will need to be moved onwards and upwards to reach conceptual, critical, evaluative and more creative levels, or it will not be sufficient for a PhD or a good MPhil or Master's dissertation. The stages of your work, arguing and writing are: descriptive and detailing, narrative, summarising, synthesising, contrasting and comparing, analysing, criticising, conceptualising, evaluating and reflecting, creating.

Descriptive and detailing – Early work is often only descriptive. When you finish your thesis, you will find that you are descriptive in some places in most of your chapters – about context, previous work, the data collected and so on – but you also need to be analytical and to work at a conceptual level and add new meaning.

Narrative – Telling the story of your research is necessary in the Introduction in places, when you discuss your methodology, methods, choices, and detail the story of the way you analysed your data. It needs to be augmented by conceptual and critical work.

Summarising – At the start and end of chapters, you will need to summarise what you are going to say/have said, and what points you have just made and where the discussion will develop in the next chapter. You also summarise the arguments of others, but you will need, in this second instance, to then move on and make links to the conceptual and critical use of their work in relation to your own, so that you can say how your work fits into a dialogue with the experts and others working in the field. The final chapter, the Conclusion, contains some summarising of your work, but also involves conceptual conclusions – answering the 'so what?', 'why does that matter?' questions.

Synthesising – A higher level kind of response and writing, this involves not only a summarising of what you have read, done or written, but also identifies the key arguments and themes, the key points, pulling them together. This requires writing a little more abstractly, indicating the essence and importance of what has been said or found through turning it into something more than the sum of the essays read, data collected and your own comments made. Here, in synthesising, you are answering the 'so how does this all relate?', 'taken together, what might it suggest overall?' questions.

Contrasting and comparing – When reading the work of others in the literature review/theoretical perspectives chapter or the methodology and methods chapter, by recognising contrastive and comparative views, you can start to see what is unique and what contributes to the developing dialogues and arguments as these emerge from each of the different writers' arguments and work. Similarly, when you look at your own debate from a number of sources – such as interviews and questionnaires; or initial stories that, when analysed, lead to cases; from different texts or documents you have analysed; from observations, activities and programmes that you have monitored – you can see patterns and differences emerging. These variations and patterns help to suggest ways of understanding the information, ideas and data; and your understanding leads towards your contribution to the debate when you can add something that shows these differences and adds another level to them. You can add your own comparison and contrasting comments in relation to the work of other people that you have understood and mentioned, and then you can add your own work, indicating how it fits with the patterns and the differences of the ongoing debate about the subject and question on which you and others have been working.

Analysing – When reading others' work, considering our own data and reflecting on our own research and writing, we do not do so merely passively, but analytically. We ask questions: 'How does this work?', 'What was the question underlying this?', 'How do these parts fit together?', 'How do they lead one from the other?', 'How do they add to/alter/develop each other?', 'How does this element, this piece of data, quotation or argument fit into the pattern of these several arguments or data?', 'What does not fit in here?', 'What is different?', 'Is this a mistake? Or is the difference really interesting and can tell us something about the ways in which we have determined what matters and what patterns there are?' and 'What does this all mean?'. Here, you are questioning, interpreting and analysing, and developing some of the answers to these questions, all of which helps you to comment on, analyse and draw some findings from the work of others, and your own work, in a debate.

Criticising – This can take two forms: a disagreement that fundamentally undercuts someone else's work (or your own) and indicates where it has flaws, shortcomings, problems, or else is more of a critique, which is an analysis that makes some comments about how effective the data, piece of work or argument is, and makes some suggestions often for improvement or development. You might well write in this way when looking at others' work and arguments in the theoretical perspectives chapter, and again when looking at the ways your own work has developed and what your data seems to be saying later in the discussion chapters and the conclusions.

Conceptualising – Current learning theorists have made us all even more aware that working at a conceptual level in our thinking and writing is the real key to postgraduate work, research and the contribution to knowledge and meaning. You deal with ideas and theories; you initially take nothing for granted but instead ask questions of what seem to be established beliefs, ideas, theories and terms – even terms such as 'youth culture', 'homelessness', 'identity', 'book', 'creativity', 'damage' – problematise what seems straightforward, in order to clarify the terms of a particular topic or question upon which your work is based. Concepts in your research topic and question are questioned or problematised, and so are the concepts used by theorists and experts whose work you are dealing with in order to develop your own. Conceptualising means you move beyond descriptive summarising and analysing, and start to identify the ideas and the theories more clearly, add something new. Working and writing at a conceptual level means that you are aware of the thoughts and findings, theories and data coming together in your work to make new meaning. Working conceptually has been compared to going through a doorway into another level of thinking, writing and working. It is certainly a change in thinking and expression and, once you have made this 'learning leap', gone through this doorway into another level of thinking, you will never again suddenly revert to descriptive thinking, writing and work, unless you know that you have to put in some background or informational details in a particular place in your writing.

The sorts of comments you make and questions you ask when conceptualising include: 'I'd like to ask you what you mean about that?' 'What are the key ideas here?' 'I understand, my work contributes to our understanding of ... by arguing and showing that ...'.

Evaluating and reflecting – This is also work at a higher level than merely descriptive comment. It involves evaluation of others' work and your own, reflecting on how well a piece of work, a piece of research, some findings, a task, has worked, how clear it is, how effective a part of it has been. These are all-important elements of the thinking and writing in your thesis, and appear throughout. Reflection appears more in your log or journal, where you look at why you did things, what has been read and what it might lead to, how it moves you on. Then you take elements of this reflective writing through into where you are commenting on the implications of others' pieces, writing and work for your own arguments (the theoretical perspective chapter, and the methodology and methods chapter). Elements of reflection also contribute to the sections where you look at what has worked or not (comments on the data analysis and findings) and what to do next in terms of your own reading and data gathering and analysis. Finally, you also write reflectively in your final chapter – the Conclusion, where you consider what you set out to look for or question, how well what you have done has contributed to addressing your question and expanding our understanding, the contribution your work has made to meaning, and what you might do next.

Creating – If you are writing a creative Master's or PhD, then you are writing creatively for much of the time, although you will still be writing analytically and descriptively, and so on – and certainly also conceptually and reflectively. Many students are worried about whether they are actually being creative and original in their work. Being original means you contribute something new, and perhaps it is mostly a synthesis of work that has been done before, adding a new element, a new perspective, a new context. Being creative means producing something new, a new thought or theory – expression, interpretation, moving the field on, knowing that no one has made this before or written this before because it came from you in relation to the

Things to do

You might find it useful to review the kinds of reading, thinking, researching and writing you are doing currently.

- Are you moving beyond the descriptive stage?
- How conceptual is it?
- Are you asking yourself those questions embedded in the terms when they are explained?
- And, if you can ask yourself those questions, question your own writing, how can you move on?
- When will you know your work is the right mixture of descriptive, synthesising, analysing, conceptual work and writing?
- Now – can you look at a journal essay that is important for your work and identify the different stages of work and writing within it? Is anything missing?

things you have done and read. Since dissertations and theses contribute something new to understanding and knowledge, even if they do not produce something absolutely new and original, all dissertations and theses are a little bit creative, at least. Some work is a creative product – such as an artwork, video, poem sequence, invention, patent. With such creative work, it is necessary to produce an analytical commentary that explains how the creative work engages with theories, and addresses questions.

● Some ideas about the writing habit

Good writing develops as a habit on which you focus. There are many ways in which you can develop your thoughts and writing skills. These include:

- Writing regularly - keeping a journal of research processes, choices, successes and failures - (a) to draw from explaining research processes, (b) to keep developing your writing habit
- Writing up notes, experiments, comments on interviews, early jotted thoughts about transcripts, analysed questionnaires, and focus groups helps break barriers of data analysis, excerpting of evidence and developing discussion and dialogue.

Breaking blocks
Writing blocks

We all have writing blocks, no matter how much successful writing we have ever done. This is normal. There are moments where the level of one's thinking is really stuck, and you cannot find ways of working through a problem of expression. There are moments where you are bored and going round in circles, or just feel you have nothing new to say. And there are moments where it is so long since you entered into the argument of your work, that you have a great deal of reading and thinking to do before you can write again. The point is, whatever the block that is preventing you from writing, you need to relax; remind yourself that you have a lot to say, plan your way out of the block, try writing through a variety of tricks and get on with it. There is no substitute for writing through, anticipating your problems, tackling them and trying to express yourself – then refining it so that it reads better and your work can move on: without this, your thoughts remain just a whim or a fancy. They need to be written out.

Here are some suggestions:

You could break writing blocks by continuing writing in your log or journal, or employing a series of other tricks to free up thinking and initiate writing.

- Start writing in the middle of something: a chapter, an argument, a dialogue with an expert. Just begin where you feel comfortable to write. Step back and produce a brief diagram of where this could fit in your chapter, so you can jigsaw it in when you have written other parts.
- Remember it is only a draft! – Write fast as it comes to you and then return to edit for:
  - Conceptual level – ideas, theories, themes, as well as concepts
  - Expression – does it say what you want it to?
  - Clarity of expression – deal with grammar and punctuation, inexplicit words and expressions.

Practise 'free writing' to loosen up thought processes and creativity. In my own work, I call it 'splurge' and write fast (and inaccurately). Then I go back over it and give it form, find the right words, and turn the sentences the right way round.

> The most effective way I know to improve your writing is to do free-writing exercises regularly. At least three times a week ... simply write for ten minutes (later on, perhaps fifteen or twenty). Don't stop for anything. Go quickly without rushing. Never stop to look back, to cross something out ... If you get stuck it's fine to write, 'I can't think what to say, I can't think what to say' as many times as you want ... The only requirement is that you never stop. (Elbow 1973: 3)

Murray (2002) comments, 'This is the opposite of knowing what you want to say first, and writing about it second' (p. 78).

Of course, you need then to change it into something coherent and eloquent. If you cannot do this, then avoid the exercise of 'splurge' or 'free writing'. However, for many, 'getting it down' then dealing with the appropriate expression is a way through writing blocks.

I explore this further in *The Good Supervisor* (2005), from which the following is adapted.

Try to:

- brainstorm initial ideas without having to express them perfectly
- get out of a writer's block by doing some writing – the physical act

- work through psychological, intellectual or emotional responses
- open up ideas by writing them down a little
- get ideas and expressions circulating in your head down on paper so that you move on
- gain confidence by writing – producing an *amount* to be edited later by articulating ideas and arguments in your head, however (initially) poorly
- avoid using halting, formalised phrases and getting tied up in them, thereby *saying* nothing.

Visualise

Using diagrams and visualisation is another way of starting to write freely. You could try:

- Expressing contradictions through writing about both or more sides of an issue, separating, then linking them. See Figure 23.1 for a topical issue in the UK.

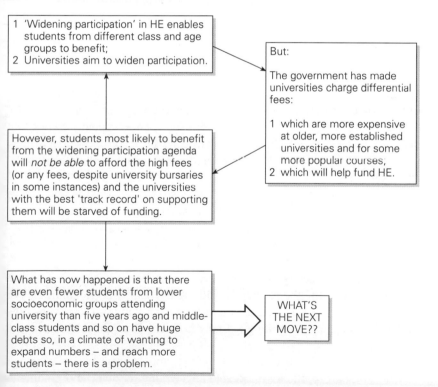

Figure 23.1 Visualising a research topic to aid in writing your thesis

Expressing different strategies and paradoxes, then indicating contradictions, can help clarify an argument, making the problems more explicit, and identifying the underlying concepts – in this case, definitions of equality, accessibility and the relationships between economic situation and a kind of cost benefit analysis (on the part of the student and the university). You can next suggest prompt questions to yourself: how and where you can add information, activities, references, quotations, other reading and data to the different bubbles or boxes of the arguments, starting to express the contradiction clearly and build a case.

Visualising complex or contradictory ideas can help to build up elements of an argument, subsequently underpinned and informed by theorists, critics and primary sources. Like free writing, visualisation helps express the kinds of complications and paradoxes inherent in research.

The advice given by Elbow (1973) and Murray (2002) is useful for free writing. Diagrams or visualisation (see Wisker 2005) can also help by opening up writing, and what Boice (1990) calls generative writing is also useful.

Generative writing involves the following:

- Write for five minutes without stopping
- Go back and reshape it.

Reflect back on the writing, using it as a prompt for discussion and future writing. Take a different coloured pen and annotate or correct it.

Cut it into bullet points, writing more for each key point, cutting out elements that now seem irrelevant, clarifying the hazy ones, adding new ideas, expanding or enhancing contradictory arguments, seeking exactly the right expression.

You can do this alone; share with another student, critical friend or family member with writing skills; or as part of a supervision.

Murray identifies 'binge' and 'snack' writing, using experiences including free writing or short sharp pieces of writing on specific topics. This is helpful at different points: all methods need 'tidying up' (Murray 2000: 170). Murray also discusses 'generative' writing – a focused follow up to free writing, shared with others. Sharing with others acting as critical friends or peer assessors gives you your first real readership, and also indicates how readable and clear your writing actually is – and what you might do about it.

On his creative writing course at Ruskin, Oxford, Alistair Wisker used two students to share portfolios of developing writing, critique and comment, and then reflect on how this peer exchange informed their writing.

We have explored:

- Free writing – limited time, without stopping, loosely round topic – frees up your writing energies, then you can work further on it and ensure it sounds better, reads well, really says what you intended
- 'Splurge' writing about the topic – put down your first thoughts: it does not matter if it is ungrammatical/badly punctuated/has poor wording. Then, you think about it, develop your ideas, return to the writing and shape, discard, rephrase, clarify
- Start where you feel you have something to say – in the middle, in a section – you do not have to write a whole thesis from beginning to end. Pick bits of chapters and work on them as you feel you have something to say. Sometimes when you are stuck in a particularly difficult chapter, to free yourself up you can write a part of the thesis about which you feel comfortable – maybe an addition to the theoretical perspectives/literature review chapter, which is ongoing; perhaps tidying up and discussing a section of that. Think of the thesis not as a set of blocks to be completed, but as a patchwork quilt where you can work on one square at a time, but can also move to work on different squares to relieve the tension, change the pace, break a block, capture a moment. Later on, of course, it will be sewn together into a wonderful pattern – whole
- When you get data back, your first thoughts are often really rich and useful, and you will refine them later but, for now, annotate with scrawl – type up later and refine your comments
- Write with a partner or colleague or in a writing group – share, discuss, shape, share others' work and ask critical friends; articulating in front of others and commenting on each others' writing moves you on a few stages and, sometimes, they can ask questions or suggest really clear expressions where you have become stuck
- Co-referee, then co-edit each other's work – but do stick to the ground rules – constructive criticism and positive advice
- Produce some staged work that you can add to in the future. In this respect, the development of an annotated bibliography is useful as you build the theoretical perspectives chapter – here, you can explore key points of key texts, indicating dialogue between them and with your own work, then expand this into the full chapter later
- In order to remind yourself about the shape of a good piece of writing (should you become stuck in description or one part of the

thesis and cannot see the whole), read through and critically evaluate a key essay in the field to determine the ways in which it is fulfilling the essentials for good writing – the objectivity you need to use will act as good advice for yourself. Note how the author is establishing the research question/main points, argument, intellectual rigour, engagement in dialogue with the literature and theories/theorists, themes, evidence to back up claims, both conceptual and factual conclusions

● Coherence and organisation are important, so start writing like this early on. In the thesis, the clear abstract indicates what the research set out to look for, questions, and so on; why you went about the research in the way you did (but do not use 'I', at all, to discuss this); and why what you have found matters – what it contributes to meaning and knowledge. The introduction sets context. See comments in Chapter 22 about the contents and kinds of writing in the different chapters. Coherence is important throughout the thesis – at the level of chapters, paragraphs and sentences, it shows your ability to sequence and hierarchise ideas and arguments – links between paragraphs and sections indicate how you are developing an argument, and using what you have read and found in that argument. Referencing shows where and how you are using what you have read in this argument, and where a reader can go to find more of the work of those authors you refer to

● If you are working with someone else's text, as a critical friend:
  - use prompts, problematising questions and suggestions in margins
  - use counselling expressions – 'someone else would argue that, suggest that, put it this way ...', which can help move ideas on and are not either critical or demanding
  - then 'mark' or provide feedback on your *own* expression using the characteristics of writing a successful thesis
  - alter some elements of your colleague's expression at the level of a specific reference, sentence, example of analysed discussed data, or paragraph *as an example* for him or her to take its characteristics throughout the text
  - use 'track changes' to show changes, and ask your colleague to do the same on work returned to you, labelling versions, plus cover sheet listing changes and responses to your comments
  - tell one of your peer group (orally or in an e-mail unconnected to the actual text so far) what he or she has found, what the arguments are

- explain it all to someone else, each report back/rephrase content and comment.

This work with others can then be carried out by the others on YOUR work or by yourself on your own work (talking to yourself about improvement is allowed here!).

● Developing writing

Below is an example of building up writing from initially descriptive detailed summaries of research carried out by others and research into government statistics into an argument that analyses; works contrastively, with imagination and a critical eye, drawing out themes, theorising the findings of the research; and reports on and conceptualises the whole. The subject is the lack of involvement of young men or 'boys' (young adult males) in further education and higher education.

You could 'mark' the pieces, looking for (1) coherence; (2) clarity of expression; (3) level of conceptualisation; (4) theorising; (5) argument and see where and how the first piece, largely descriptive, can be developed, so that it becomes a first very useful step to the whole piece; that is, pieces 1 and 2 together, where evidence, claims, reading, theorising and conceptualising, and arguing are all present.

Note how pieces reference:

1 Facts written about other researchers that have been collected as notes. These are:

- UK has high drop out among post-16s, especially young men
- means test affects participation and drop out, especially for young men in low socioeconomic groups
- socioeconomic status, poverty, truancy, having a special educational need, membership of some ME groups, poor performance at 16, mental health problems for girls, teenage pregnancy affect participation
- availability of training for rural boys
- young men at university distracted by social activity and do not seek support
- perceive drop out as failure;

2 Notes are turned into discursive paragraphs that link ideas and facts together, compare and contrast, synthesise different reports into themes:

(a) The Education Maintenance Allowance, introduced in 2004, to tackle what Education Secretary Charles Clarke said: 'the UK has one of the highest post-16 drop out rates in the western world'. A major impact evaluation of the means tested, and performance driven schemes, found that whilst 16-year-old participation increased by 5.9 per cent among the eligible cohort, it had a bigger impact on 16-year-old boys – 6.9 per cent of the eligible cohort. The staying on rate of the lowest socioeconomic groups increased by around 10 per cent (Article (2004), t magazine online, http://www.tmag.co.uk/articles/July04Pg20.html, 26 January 2006);

(b) A report by Renewal.net identified socioeconomic status, poverty, truancy, having a special educational need, membership of some ME groups, poor performance at 16, mental health problems and – for girls – teenage pregnancy, as indicative factors when predicting teenage drop out from education. The availability of appropriate training opportunities – particularly for boys – was also an issue for rural students who had been used to going to school nearby their homes. (Renewal.net (2006), Increasing Participation in Education and Training, http://www.renewal.net/Documents/RNET/Overview/Education/Increasingparticipationedcation.doc, January 2006);

(c) Quinn *et al.* (2005), in an investigation into drop out from higher education, report that fewer young men than women participate in university, and men are more likely to drop out. Interviews with 40 young male ex-students revealed that they were more likely to be distracted by social opportunities than women, and less likely to admit to difficulties with their work. They were also reluctant to seek student support, and felt that they would be earning good money if they were not at university. Most had made the decision to leave rationally, but had felt disempowered because of the external perception of drop out as 'failure'. (Quinn *et al.* (2005), 'From Life Crisis to Lifelong Learning: Rethinking Working-Class 'Drop Out' from Higher Education, Rethinking Working-Class 'Drop Out' from University', Joseph Rowntree Foundation, (http://www.jrf.org.uk/bookshop/eBooks/1859354130.pdf, 25 January 2006);

Conceptual, critical work, developing an argument, theorising and adding to discussions producing – new interactions, new debates, new meaning

3   At each age stage, drop out and poor performance appear to be more closely associated with socioeconomic factors – including income, parental education, home circumstances, and so on – than with gender. At mid-teens, however, teenage pregnancy is a key factor for girls. There is very little literature on gender aspects of higher education drop out; however, intuitively, you might expect that the introduction of fees might – once again – disproportionately affect those from poorer socioeconomic backgrounds. In light of this, Scotland has abandoned higher education fees and top-up fees.

It should also be realised that a decision to 'drop out' may indicate the failure of government policy or university retention policy, but does not necessarily represent the failure of the individual student (although the student may feel it to be so). It appears that higher education drop out decisions are made rationally, by adult students, and do not necessarily disadvantage the individual in the long term.

Look carefully at how the information is developed from notes through to discussion and synthesis and then to conceptual work involved in an argument that adds to meaning. You could choose or write some staged examples from your own subject to work on. This will enable you to focus on what constitutes good writing or sufficiently good writing at the conceptual/critical level and the level of expression, it will also help you to identify how you can move on from stage 1 of the collection of the facts in notes, through to stage 3, where you have used the information and arguments of others in a discussion and added new argument, thoughts and meaning.

What follows has been developed from *The Good Supervisor* (Wisker 2005), where it appears in a slightly different form, as advice and suggestions to supervisors for working with students.

Reading, thinking, using your reading in your writing and asking questions

One way of encouraging critical and conceptual work – analytical rather than descriptive and factual – is to set up good reading practices, and supervisor/student interactions that draw on these to develop thinking and writing. Delamont *et al.* (1997) mention three kinds of reading needed for carrying out research. You might find it useful to think about levels of response and conceptualisation that you can employ in their work. 'For arts and social science students there are three types of reading to be done: reading on the topic, contrastive reading and analytical reading' (p. 57). They offer worked examples of the three kinds of reading. Your thinking also needs to be at three levels, which encourages reading and involvement in your area of work. Do be careful about engagement at the more than descriptive level; engage also in the conceptual, critical and analytical levels so that your writing, building on your reading and thinking, shows the development of conceptual, critical and coherent argument, and eventually really clear expression. Consider the examples (below) and ask critical prompt questions, helping you to develop conceptually, critically and expressively.

Let's look at an example of:

(i)   a topic area developed into a question, which prompts;
(ii) thoughts about reading to be undertaken; and
(iii) the beginning of conceptualising, rather than describing and detailing.

Topic area – changing nursing students: the development of autonomous, reflective and active nursing students as researchers and problem solvers.

Title – the autonomous nurse: developing nursing students as researchers, problem-solvers and reflective practitioners.

Research question:

- In what ways can the changing nursing curriculum help to develop nursing students as autonomous, active researchers, problem-solvers and reflective practitioners?
- Why might nurses be expected to change their behaviours to become more autonomous, active, problem-solving and reflective practitioners?
- How has nursing changed since ... ?
- What have been the shape, content and outcomes of the nursing curriculum and how has it changed? When, why, through what reports, bills, and so on?
- What learning theories underpin the changes, and how to do they relate to the development of a more autonomous nurse?
- How effective have these changes been in developing the more autonomous, active, problem-solving reflective practitioner nurse?

Theory

To ask this question and its sub-questions in terms of my reading and theorists, I will need to use and explore a variety of areas including:

- Autonomy – how students are encouraged to learn from themselves and own the learning, then be able to make decisions without concentrated supervision at every turn
- Reflective practice – what is meant by being reflective as a practitioner, in this case in nursing? – thinking about what you do and why you do it in a variety of instances
- Curriculum theory and practice – work on the construction of curricula, learning outcomes, links between teaching, learning and assessment and achievement of learning outcomes
- Changing roles of nurses.

Working at a merely descriptive and factual level a student might produce the following:

> Nursing curricula have changed over the past five years and now contain many modules and courses which encourage students to engage in reflective practice and to take responsibility for their own decisions, as well as the courses and practices which expect nurses to be well trained and to know the right decisions almost mechanically in specific situations.

Working at a more conceptual, analytical, critical level the student might produce the following:

Example

In the twenty-first century, nurses are faced with an array of new problems and problem-solving opportunities, where the mechanical, trained response to a specific situation is not on offer. They need to be more autonomous and reflective as practitioners and to be aware of the range of options open to them in any decisions regarding patient care and health practice, to understand the pros and cons, and to be able to use their knowledge and problem-solving skills to make the right decisions for the context and moment, in other words, to act autonomously using their knowledge as effective practitioners and then to reflect on and learn from this experience. Their roles have changed to become more a matter of informed decision-making than mechanical responses to a known situation. This change, in effect, if handled appropriately at curriculum, learning, teaching and assessment levels, encourages nurses to not only learn the details and facts and the range of strategies involved in a typical range of decision-making situations, but to also theorise, step back and address specific and different problems, taking responsibility for their informed, imaginative decision making.

Supervisors might well give feedback on the different responses you produce – as shown in the case above, some responses are at a descriptive level and some at a more conceptual level. It is to be expected that they will comment on your work verbally or using 'track changes' in the text. However they do it, they will be engaging in a developmental discussion with you using prompts, the language of counselling, suggestions and questions, each of which on its own is meant to prompt you to think about the effects, effectiveness, range and possible development of the work you have produced. Even if your supervisors seem harsh and critical, they are actually trying to prompt you to develop further. Not everyone knows how to communicate in the carefully toned responses that clarify any problems, congratulate on any successes and nudge you into moving further in your work, perhaps into a conceptual level of which you are not yet aware.

They might say of the first piece:

> This is an interesting and informative piece about the changes and demands on practising nurses. What might changes in curricula suggest about how nurses could be prompted towards more problem-solving, reflective and autonomous decision-making? How might this happen; what evidence and examples are there of it? What kind of theory (look at learning theory) might underpin such a development?

The reason for this kind of questioning or feedback is to encourage critical and conceptual, analytical thinking. Considering an example of such feedback should help you to problematise and conceptualise. We explore learning from feedback more directly in the next chapter.

Things to do

Problems you may meet

Please consider how you would deal with these scenarios about ongoing writing, suffered by other students. Thinking about how to help them in their work might help unblock you in yours, should you meet similar difficulties:

1 John has accumulated large amounts of data and seems unable to analyse, interpret and draw or express findings from it. There seems to be little connection to the question or theories;
2 Mira has produced several chapters at a descriptive not conceptual level;
3 There seems to be little argument running through Oonseng's work so far;

4 Little has been written by Ruth, or what is written is fragmented, not linked to other writing;

5 Midway into research, Alan has made little progress and now wants to change the question;

6 So many personal and family/work/money crises and pressures have left Mohamed unable to complete anything or develop work coherently;

7 Dalia cannot move beyond notes – she feels removed from her work;

8 Meiko writes in a mixture of colloquial and stumbling/simplistic, descriptive, narrative and elevated, unnecessarily complex 'fog' and jargon without clarification/someone else's phrasing.

   Is there any plagiarism? Can they find 'their voice'?

9 Ali has written down all he has read, done and found but does not seem to:
   - develop it into a dialogue between experts and theorists, fitting in his own contribution
   - select, manage and clarify the contribution of evidence and data – interpreting in relation to themes, theories and arguments
   - be able to indicate what contribution his work makes to answering any research question, moving on our understanding and knowledge in the field.

Having thought through how to help these other students – finally:

- What issues about your writing really concern you?
- What could the university/college/others/your peer group do to better support your writing?
- What can you/will you do to encourage, enable and empower yourself and others to develop good writing practices, and proceed through to a sound piece of well written up research in a thesis of merit? (and beyond to publishing?).

● Further reading

Boice, R. (1990) *Professors as Writers: A Self-Help Guide to Productive Writing* (Stillwater, OK: New Forums).

Dunleavy, P. (2003) *Authoring a PhD* (Basingstoke: Palgrave Macmillan).

Elbow, P. (1973) *Writing Without Teachers* (Oxford: Oxford University Press): 3.

Murray, R. (2002) *How to Write a Thesis* (Buckingham: Open University Press): 78.

Quinn, J., Thomas, E., Slack, K., Casey, L., Thexton, W. and Noble, J. (2005) 'From Life Crisis to Lifelong Learning: Rethinking Working-class "Drop Out" from Higher Education, Rethinking Working-class "Drop Out" from University', Joseph Rowntree Foundation, (http://www.jrf.org.uk/bookshop/eBooks/1859354130.pdf, accessed 25 January 2006).

Wisker, G. (2005) *The Good Supervisor* (Basingstoke: Palgrave Macmillan).

Websites accessed

Article (2004), t magazine online, http://www.tmag.co.uk/articles/July04 Pg20.html, 26 January 2006.

Renewal.net (2006), 'Increasing Participation in Education and Training' (http://www.renewal.net/Documents/RNET/Overview/Education/Increasingparticipationedcation.doc, accessed January 2006).

24 Analysing Data and Thinking about Findings

This chapter looks at:

▶ I wouldn't start from here ...
▶ Organising your data – quantitative and quali- tative
▶ Recognising how the data collected relates to the questions asked and the conceptual framework of the research
▶ Methods of data analy- sis
▶ Deducing findings from analyses
▶ Where to end?

There is no substitute for having a clear idea of what you are looking for – your research question(s) – and continuing to stay as close as possible to the data as it emerges raw from the participants, the texts, the docu- ments and so on, so that you can get a 'feel' for what is emerging. Then you stand back; clarify the areas of questions, the theories and the conceptual framework; and start to put it all into some kind of order, so that your data can genuinely be analysed, and findings drawn from the analysis that relate to your original questions and conceptual framework.

In my work with colleagues on a postgraduate development programme for cohorts of PhD students, mostly from Israel, we run a session called 'What do I do with all this data?' This session mimics how I, and so many others, felt when faced with the over-rich results of our hours of carefully planned research method application fieldwork, the collection and ultimate stockpiling of material – both quantitative (largely numbers) and qualitative (largely words) – arising from research. Of course, you would not start from here. The data that you have collected, which probably looms up in what Miles and Huberman (1994) have described as an alpine shape – that is, in a large mountain (probably about to become an avalanche) – is a product of your research design.

Your research questions are clarified and organised by your conceptual framework, which is actioned and enabled by your research methods and your data, once collected.

But you will probably have far too much data to incorporate fully into your thesis, and could ask questions of it for several years to come. At this stage, remember the initial comparison of your research to a slice of cake. There is more cake there; and other people can take slices and find out, analyse, make deductions, carry on with the work and eat them later. You need to focus on your slice of the cake and make sure it is neat, clear, clean, tasty and wholesome, and satisfies the needs you set about satisfying in the first place. Do not use everything. Do be selective and focused in your analyses.

So, you need to manage (organise) what data you have to date, be ruthlessly selective in considering what is really relevant, and clearly focused on finding out what it all really 'means', that is, what the findings are and how they relate to your questions and outcomes.

One important thing to remember during your research is to ensure that you have your data analysed as far as possible when it is available – in batches. This enables you to integrate it and see whether you need to change your work direction; it also indicates what kinds of findings are emerging. This can be a useful and comforting guide when you are faced with the avalanche of data.

You will probably have a great deal of raw data, but these – questionnaires, transcribed interviews, transcribed focus group interviews, completed observation schedules, and so on – are not findings. Findings need to be derived from the analysis of this data, which means:

- managing the data – reduce its size and scope, find the 'slice of cake' that fits your own enquiries so you can report on this usefully.
- analysing the managed data – ask analytical questions, abstract and generalise from them, use them to back up the arguments and indications they seem to present. You need to integrate them in order to analyse them.

You may also find that much of the analysis and interpretation of your data is a repetitive (and even monotonous) activity because you are very carefully labelling, counting and charting data, and carrying out analytical activities over and over, meticulously categorising and recording what you find. Remember, if you are not careful and meticulous, your findings might be questionable. If you are slipshod and your findings unreliable, there is nothing worse when giving a presentation on your findings to have a query from the audience that picks a huge hole in your analysis and the figures you have presented – just because of a few mistakes or lack of concentration at this stage.

● Making sense of your data – interpretation and findings

Many research students work busily at collecting and categorising their data, but find the problem of making sense of it almost overwhelming.

Anecdotal evidence might be reassuring for you here. One of my EdD students rang me up. She has spent the summer reading and reading, writing and writing, transcribing her interview tapes and taking notes. She confides that she is exhausted and overwhelmed by all the data, and has no idea what to do next.

I sympathise, I have been there; this is how I work, too: it is a way of labouring through hard work only to lose sight of the 'wood for the trees'. Researchers are hard workers. This is a normal situation. We discuss what to do next.

I put it to her: 'What were you asking and looking for when you developed the questionnaire/interviews/focus groups/discussion schedule/action research set of cycles/documentary analysis questions?'

'As you read through and wrote up your data, what thoughts did you have about how it related to those questions and concerns, and what the theorists said about what you could turn up in such information and responses – about some of those major ideas suddenly seen in the comments our respondents produced, also the things you read and started to take notes about? What was confirmed and expected? What seemed contradictory and surprising?'

● Managing data, both quantitative and qualitative

You need to code the data – preferably, this should be done as the data are collected. Indicate the date of the questionnaires, who they were completed by, and the number of returns. You need to categorise your data at this stage, too, for example, in relation to gender: female (1) and male (2), or origin: Malaysian (1), European (2), African (3). Ages are commonly expressed in ranges, for example, 21–30. Much of this kind of categorising should have been done on the original questionnaire but, if not, it needs coding for consistency now you have the data.

For more open-ended questionnaires or semi-structured, open-ended interviews, you will need to read them through carefully and code them after the event, that is, code in relation to the kinds of answers, themes and issues, and categories of response (keeping a note of what the codes refer to). When you are collecting data concerning people you also need to be careful about the Data Protection Act. You are not allowed to keep the names of your respondents in sufficiently close proximity to their responses for them to be attributed, and you must find a way of coding names against numbers and numbering responses, then keeping the list relating the two in an entirely safe place. Do check with university regulations and the details of the Data Protection Act.

● Annotating

This is a process of managing some of your data. If you are collecting documentary evidence or taking notes from books, and so on, you will need to develop a process for keeping marginal notes, taking notes from sources (see Chapter 27) and then pulling these items of information together.

You will also find it useful to annotate thematically in the margins of transcribed interviews. Labelling the important themes or issues as they appear helps you to draw different responses together, and to draw together responses from the different sources, for example, documents, interviews and texts that relate to the same areas or themes of your enquiry when you write them all up. You might well find your first thoughts – as you look at your field notes, notes from texts, transcribed interviews, analysed statistics – are really rich and need to be used to help you to make more conceptual complex comments later – do not lose those first thoughts. Annotate data with notes and questions – and return to them later.

● Summarising and generalising

From the whole range of your data, you need to draw some relative generalisations (rather than conclusions). Ask: What kinds of responses keep recurring? What are the deviations from these? Are there themes emerging? Patterns? Contradictions?

Summarise and generalise, using figures and quotations to illustrate your summaries and generalisations. The use of examples is a product of selection and you need to focus on a few cases or examples that illustrate the points you are making. As a result of analysing your findings more broadly, you may find someone whose behaviour is typical, or a new person whose work and behaviour fall into a set of extremes or contrasts. Then you could take this person or persons as cases or samples to select and emphasise (keeping the selection of individual cases anonymous, for confidentiality). This helps to illustrate and highlight your findings, because, as with journalism, others reading your work respond well to the individual case, which represents an example of the argument.

Example

Much research combines a range of methods to approach research questions, and often begins with a broad survey, perhaps by questionnaire, narrowing down to individual cases for a more in-depth enquiry.

For example, in a piece of research on the learning of postgraduate students it was discovered that there was a set of significant responses. A significant number of students tended to be taking accumulation or surface learning approaches but seeking transformational outcomes. While this was true to a lesser extent for most of the students surveyed, it was true to a significant degree for 6 individuals out of 50 surveyed. These six students were then selected for further closer scrutiny in order to illustrate the problem, define it, and start to share it with the students so that they could deal with its implications in relation to their own learning. The analysis was carried out by categorising numbers of questions, in relation to certain categories of which accumulation approaches, meaningful learning approaches and transformational outcomes were the main areas of focus. Questions in these categories were then scrutinised in relation to the initial overall frequency analysis of all responses to all questions.

For a broad-brush response, categories of questions could be grouped together to indicate patterns of response – showing up those proportions and percentages of students taking accumulative approaches, meaningful approaches and transformational outcomes. However, it was important to place these three items in relation with each other. Some cross-tabulation was necessary to indicate where the students taking an accumulation approach were also stating a transformational outcome. We needed to add to these certain rigorous questions, directed to the students themselves, in discussion (in focus groups). Their responses were collected together and scrutinised. The individual students taking these 'problematic' approaches in relation to transformational outcomes could then be alerted to the potential problems arising from their approaches, and supported in developing learning behaviours that could help them avoid the potential problems.

The potential *problem* was that if you accumulate large amounts of data as your main approach, you could find it difficult to make the transitional leap to the conclusions that suggest a change, or transfiguration – the hoped for outcomes of the research aims of these students. Various strategies could help overcome the problem: different methods, links between collection and analysis; and analysis in the drawing of findings, in the research design, are two very *obvious* strategies here.

Here are some rules for coding up your data so that you can use and interpret the information. Fielding insists:

- codes must be mutually exclusive
- codes must be exhaustive
- codes must be applied consistently throughout.

Also, he identifies five stages in the coding process:

- developing the coding frame for both pre-coded and open questions
- creating the code book and coding instructions
- coding the questionnaires
- transferring the values to a computer
- checking and cleaning the data. (Fielding 1993: 220, 225, in Denscombe, 1998: 194).

If yours is quite a small-scale study you will probably not need to go beyond the description of your statistics and the relation between a few variables. These variables might include, for example, the age of respondents and their likelihood of saying 'Yes' to certain questions about what they buy in a supermarket, or, say, the relation between the gender of respondents and their indication of how many hours they work each week. In all cases, you will need to contextualise what you find. It is probably the case when looking at the latter example (gender and hours of paid work) that women respondents might seek part-time work, or perhaps they are only able to take part-time work because of childcare responsibilities. You would need to have some idea of this (from interviews, from sociology, background information, and so on), in order to make sense of the statistics that show women in a certain group having part-time work and men having full-time work in greater proportions.

But the data that arise from a questionnaire are much richer than such a set of questions. We could scrutinise them again and ask – is there any pattern of approach and outcome that relates to gender? Or to ethnicity? Or context? Or age? If we have asked these questions in the first place and seek the answers because they seem to be meaningful when subjected to more complex statistical analyses, then diagrams can be produced that show overall norms and deviations from the norms, and patterns that indicate where individuals are very far outside the norms, when presenting your findings. If you wish to carry out such complex *statistical* analysis you will find it useful to consult such texts as Robson (1993), Blaxter, Hughes and Tight

(1993), and texts more directly engaged with statistical analysis, the detail and complexity of which lie outside the range of this book. Quantitative data analysis usually involves statistics because it uses numbers. But for those squeamish at the thought of number crunching, qualitative data analysis is not an easy option. This involves words, which are always produced in context, and then contrast affects their interpretation (even more so than questionnaires). Their interpretation is related to the intentions of the researchers as well as the relations between researcher and those interviewed/surveyed in a focus group (see Chapter 16).

● Qualitative data activity

Analysing qualitative data involves close and thorough reading and coding, as does quantitative data analysis. If you had a mountain of transcriptions from various interviews, one way of managing this data would be to read through most of them, referring back to the reasons behind the underpinning questions lying behind the questions you asked in the interview. Look for themes in the responses of the interviewees, and categorise the responses in relation to these themes.

You can do this logically:

- Read or look back at the underpinning questions
- Look back at specific questions
- Determine a range of those that relate to these questionnaires, the issues to which they relate
- Colour-code responses, for example, blue for one of them, green for another, and so on. Try blue with two stripes and green/red, and so on, if you have lots of themes – but do not let yourself become too overwhelmed with different categories or you will find it difficult to draw any conclusions or say anything about your data.
- What kinds of *patterns* of response are emerging? What kinds of *themes* are emerging?
- Could you look at those patterns and themes, and label them as categories and themes, so you can more easily spot the very regular recurrent ones and those that are different?

If you can put your qualitative data through computer programmes such as Nudist or NVivo, you will find that, guided by you, these programmes can help with the thematic analysis. You need to read carefully, first to determine categories and themes, and indicate to the programme key words and phrases that appear in these themes so that it can pick them out. It will then pull these together in a continuous run of labelled paragraphs so that you can both see the amount and type of responses in the thematic area and refer back to the whole transcript because it is coded into each of the quotations.

Robson has developed useful tactics for drawing conclusions from qualitative data, which I use here. You will need to count numbers and frequency of responses (for example, themes, issues); recognise and develop patterns, so that you can draw differing responses together because of their similarity and frequency; cluster them; and bring them together because of their relation to a limited number of factors. You will need to relate certain variables together to make sense of the data, and both build up networks of causal relations between items, and then, very carefully relate your findings to the theoretical frameworks from which they spring, into which they fit, and into which others can fit them. Robson suggests (1993: 401):

1   Counting and categorising data, and measuring the frequency of occurrence of the categories;
2   Patterning and noting recurring patterns or themes;
3   Clustering groups of objects, persons, activities, settings and so on, that have similar characteristics;
4   Factoring and grouping of variables into a small number of hypothetical factors;
5   Relating variables; discovery of the type of relationship, if any, between two or more variables;
6   Building of casual networks; development of chains or webs of linkages between variables;
7   Relating findings to general theoretical frameworks; attempting to find general propositions that account for the particular findings in this study.

● **Documentary analysis**

This is not merely reading and taking notes but, rather, the careful identification of key issues, labels and themes. One student working on internal organisational documents within a school to chart the decision-making processes and decisions made over a four-year period carefully:

●   read through every single one of the documents
●   read both quantitative and qualitative analysis

- labelled up the categories of response, was involved in discussion in committee meetings, decisions, themes, rules and those involved in the decision-making processes
- carefully analysed and labelled the themes in relation to the decisions made
- read through all of this again and came to some careful conclusions about the relationship of decisions made from committee discussion and the specific power relations of the head of the school and his or her close team.

Things to do

Documentary analysis

Find an internal document from your university, college, organisation, or local group, as appropriate:

- What would you need to know about its context?
- How could you both summarise the key points and recognise the themes and issues as they present themselves here?
- What other information would you need about timing, reason for the prediction of the document, audience and results, in order to make sense of it?
- How can it be labelled up in relation to a line of enquiry; for example, the decision-making processes or the frequency and kind of decision made regarding the use of school committees?

So what does all this mean?

● Findings

As you analyse your data and start to produce some findings that could be shared with others, you will need to think about the different parts of the findings and conclusions 'jigsaw'. As Judith Bell (2005) reminds us:

> Any conclusion which can justifiably be drawn from findings should be made. If you do not find what your research set out to seek, you will not be able to claim it – you could not back it up with the necessary analysed data. You might well find some very interesting and relevant things you did not set out to find.

For example, in analysing the data about the learning of a cohort of PhD students, I discovered (Wisker 1999) that some students were largely motivated not by the example set by parents, friends, or by religion and a sense of civic duty (as were younger students in the first instance and social workers in the final instance), but by beliefs that learning can advance you professionally, and that learning and research can effect important social change. Perhaps these are the kinds of motivations we would expect from more mature and established students.

In a sample of social work undergraduates, a surprising result was their lack of motivation in terms of duty to others. In spotting the low responses on questionnaire items related to duty, their tutor then began to focus on the issues of social duty with them in class – because one of the results of their involvement in studying learning approaches and motivation was to enable the curriculum to better suit both student and the learning outcomes of the subject area. Certainly, a lack of a motivation that involved duty was perceived as a problem (Wisker *et al.* 2000).

You need to consider:

The significance of your findings – In statistical terms, this means the likelihood that a result could have been discovered by chance or how statistically significant it is. If it is a result that represents a genuine occurrence discovered by the research, the term 'significance' means it has some meaning with some weight, with some importance in terms of your arguments, in terms of life.

Generalisability – One of the elements that makes a piece of research of high postgraduate level, particularly PhD research, is the generalisability of the research findings. You have discovered something interesting, but how can other people relate it to what they are finding or what they are doing? If you have carried out a very detailed study of a small-scale group (see the case study work in Chapter 16), for example, you would need to ensure that others could see your model and findings, and replicate your study or feed it into their own – build on it, develop it and generalise from it.

Reliability – Reliability relates to how well you have carried out your research. It is considered reliable if another researcher carrying out the same research activities with the same kind of group would be likely to replicate your findings – although their findings need not be identical.

Validity – This is absolutely central to the whole issue of the cohesion in your work between conceptual framework methods, questions and findings. If your methods, approaches and techniques really fit with and measure the issues you have been researching, then the findings are likely to be valid. If you have used inappropriate methods, you are likely to find they are less valid or totally invalid. For example, if you wished to chart behaviour and change in a volatile situation, it would be very inappropriate to do so with documentary analysis of some legal documents only loosely connected to the change, and then make a huge leap from these to statements about the change. Similarly, it would be inappropriate to rely on a poorly developed questionnaire that asks single 'Yes' or 'No' answers to decide complex and changing patterns of emotional response. Some of these more sensitive, human-orientated issues need capturing through a mixture of qualitative and quantitative data vehicles, or through qualitative analysis, in context.

Things to do

Look at the jigsaw diagram of these four elements of research conclusions and findings below. Can you briefly note responses about your research in each of the parts of the jigsaw? How is your research: valid, reliable, generalisable, significant? Provide a brief defence and some information. You are likely to find this very helpful in writing up, and in defending your thesis.

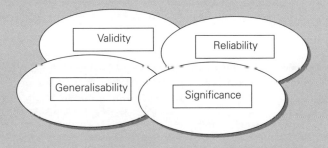

Write up your findings, indicating what your findings and evidence show and mean.

You now have an idea of how significant, generalisable and important your findings could be, and need to share these with your readers and examiners. Writing up is covered in the following chapters, but it is important at this stage to consider how you are going to organise your findings and evidence in order to be able to share it in a coherent fashion, and share your enthusiasm for it, too.

Things to do

Looking back now at what your findings have been so far, can you address these categories and see what kind of points you could make? Each category is followed by a prompt in italics.

- Link your findings together and show how they flow from the research questions. Indicate how your findings relate to the research questions – do ensure that your findings enable you to provide satisfactory answers to your questions and to engage with the questions. Indicate why some elements of the answers are satisfactory and others thwarted. *Are your findings linked to your questions? Do the findings provide satisfactory answers? If so, why, and if not, why not?*

- Ensure that your findings can be related back to your methods and your conceptual framework. *Make a brief argument about the coherence and link between your findings and the conceptual framework overall and questions of methodology/methods.*

- Explain how your findings exceed (carry on further) the research of others and can be carried on even further by others carrying out similar research activities later. *How does what you have found fit in with others' work? What else could other researchers take forward in relation to your work/areas to be developed?*

- Do not make unsubstantiated assertions and do illustrate and 'prove' all your assertions with reference to your findings. What assertions can you make? *Make a couple and indicate in note form which bits of data and findings you would use to prove them.*

- Acknowledge weaknesses in your findings and acknowledge ways in which the context, and so on, could have limited the findings in terms of reliability, scope and so on. *What are the limitations and weaknesses in your research? Why?*

- Make appropriate assertions of the importance and significance of what you have found. *Why is what you have found through your research important as a contribution to knowledge? And in furtherance of the field? And to other people?*

Answers to these questions about how your findings flow from your *questions, and the scope of your research and its significance, will all* feed into (i) your claims in the Abstract for your thesis or dissertation; and (ii) your conclusions, which emphasise the significance of your work and its contribution to the field of knowledge.

Conclusion

We have looked at:

- [ ] Some essential issues and questions in analysing your quantitative and qualitative data

- [ ] How you might pull together and defend your findings

- [ ] How to justify the importance of your findings in your research.

Further reading

Bell, J. (2005) *Doing your Research Project* (4th edn) (Buckingham: Open University Press)

Blaxter, L., Hughes, C. and Tight, M. (1993) *How to Research* (Buckingham: Open University Press).

Denscombe, M. (1998) *The Good Research Guide* (Buckingham: Open University Press).

Miles, M. and Huberman, M. (1994) *Qualitative Data Analysis* (London: Sage).

Robson, C. (1993) *Real World Research* (Oxford: Blackwell).

Wisker, G. (1999) 'Learning Conceptions and Strategies of Postgraduate Students (Israeli PhD Students) and Some Steps towards Encouraging and Enabling Their Learning', Paper presented to the Quality in Postgraduate Research Conference: Developing Research, Adelaide.

Wisker, G., Tiley, J., Watkins, M., Waller, S., Maclaughlin, J., Thomas, J. and Wisker, A. (eds) (2000) 'Discipline-based Research into Student Learning in English, Law, Social Work, Computer Skills for Linguists, Women's Studies, Creative Writing: How Can It Inform Our Teaching?', in C. Rust (ed.), *Improving Student Learning through the Disciplines* (Oxford: Oxford Brookes University): 377–97.

25 Learning from Feedback

This chapter considers:

▶ Responding positively to the feedback provided by your supervisors and any others
▶ Setting up situations where you can give feedback and receive it

This chapter follows on from Chapter 23 on encouraging and developing good writing, and considers ways in which you might learn from your supervisor's comments and the support of others.

● Working with supervisor and other feedback

Criticism is not the same as critique, and your critique of the work of others and your supervisor's critique of yours should be constructive, not destructive. You might like to begin by giving yourself some feedback.

Audit your own work – consult the experts

One exercise involves you in auditing and editing a piece of your own work, marking it up and giving yourself such feedback as we explored in Chapter 23, then improving on the work accordingly.

There are many books on academic writing that can aid you in expressing ideas succinctly and elegantly. You might find it useful to buy and consult these when producing early drafts, and particularly when writing up final drafts and editing (see Further reading). For international students, the issue of tertiary literacy is explored further in Chapter 15, but contributes considerably to your experience of translating the critical arguments you might wish to make into acceptable subject and research discourse. The language facility of both home-based and international students might hamper these arguments. See Chapter 28 for discussion of coherence in the finally submitted dissertation or thesis.

Supervisor and other feedback to encourage critical and creative thinking to improve writing

You need to work alone, or with your supervisor or critical friends, to set up working situations in which creative thinking and expression are released, in which you can approach issues and ideas in a number of ways – some imaginative, some more systematic, planned and finished – and then work to incorporate them into an organised, analytical answer, whether written or spoken. Harnessing diversity of thought, experiences and responses, and helping to shape them, is an enabling process. You could usefully prompt on each other's work, ask questions and respond orally, or brainstorm and work with colleagues on elements of the development of your thesis. Two or more heads are better than one – and you have looked at the difficulties of expression of what you want to say at this point in your work, and tried out several strategies. In Chapter 14, on communities of practice, we consider ways of setting up peer groups and work in progress sessions where you can share your developing work with your peers and provide constructive feedback on the full range of elements of each other's work – from methodology and the research question through to analysis and presentation. When you are working with peers, using and sharing feedback, it is important to ensure that there are ground rules about giving constructive criticism and feedback rather than merely being destructive. Later on in your career, when you present at conferences and write journal articles, you can hope that you will also receive positive constructive feedback (although referees for journal articles sometimes do not seem to have read the rules about constructive feedback, so beware and learn to benefit from what they do say, however negatively it might be phrased).

Feedback on drafts

Feedback to encourage writing that is critically informed, well argued and well expressed is essential for the development of a good thesis/dissertation. Beware. Some supervisors seem overly harsh and critical in their comments – sometimes these comments seem terse, a little vague, rather thin, or so excessive as to overwhelm you so that you are unaware of which aspect of the work to deal with first. Some students report confusion at being given a paragraph that is heavily corrected, a few guiding points and then being told to go on and take such a level of change through the whole chapter. This is, in fact, hard to handle the first time you are asked to do it, but it is an attempt to ensure that you understand and own the changes you are making and do not just copy what the supervisor says. The intention is that you take this kind of response and suggestion throughout your own workload so that you will understand, rather than just respond or copy.

Feedback on drafts of work can lead to miscommunication and confusion about direction, leading to extra unnecessary work, or writer's block. You might have some difficulties over comments that seem cryptic or confusing, for example:

- Please clarify
- Not sure what you mean here;

comments that suggest further work or reading but do not indicate how much:

- Say more
- Have you looked at Rogers and Brown?;

or that seem to contain veiled threats of failure:

- Conceptually weak
- No!
- Too many errors of expression here
- What do you mean?

Even those that generally suggest a satisfied response, but do not indicate what it is that they like, are confusing:

- Lots of interesting work here
- Yes!

If these rather vague 'phatic' comments are used, you might need to ask your supervisor for clarification and specific advice, including examples of good expression. Alternatively, you could just see them as the development of a dialogue between you both. More importantly, are there any comments that model ways of rewriting, that prompt thinking and examples of alternatives? These include phrases such as:

- Someone else might argue that ...
- Had you thought of asking whether/in what ways could this be said to be ...?
- If this is the case, what follows and what might this mean?

Strategies supporting good writing

There are many strategies supporting good writing. You could write early drafts so that you can share discussions about critical and conceptual levels, involving reading and theorists in a dialogue with your own work rather than merely summarising. This helps you develop a style of your own, suitable for the level of the work.

Some activities encourage the use of metalanguage of the subject, and others of developing your own voice. So, some questions could be 'How does this relate to the conceptual framework? What is the contribution to knowledge offered by these findings?'

These are metalearning, cognitively complex, conceptual questions. Although they might seem straightforward, they are asking for your engagement between what you have found, your theories and theorists, the arguments, the claims, the evidence and the importance of the contribution of the work to your understanding and the extension of knowledge and meaning in the subject area.

Treat them seriously and consider how you can genuinely develop your work in order to better answer these sorts of questions. This would help create a more conceptual, critical, problematising, meaningful approach to your work in its expression.

We have looked earlier at discussing questions, constructing conceptual frameworks, using prompts to help identify and suggest ways of dealing with problems, critique, critical evaluation and conceptualisation in thinking and writing.

Rowena Murray, concerned about explicit guidelines, asks questions about feedback that should give you some ideas of the range of comments you might receive from the large-scale to the local, the conceptual to the actual. She asks:

> Are the comments global or detailed or both? ... Do they want to make you focus on the 'big picture' of your whole argument, or a section of it? Or do they want you to tidy up the style? Is clarification of terms paramount? Given that these are all quite different questions, requiring different focus and action, the supervisors may recognize that one is more important, at this stage, than the others. For example, they may decide that the priority is to get you to define and use key terms with more clarity. There may be other aspects related to clarity that they want you to work on and this would make for an effective theme in their feedback (Murray 2002: 78).

She makes an interesting comment on your possible expectations that you might well expect more comment on the content but, unless you are really going in the wrong direction, many supervisors will comment on how you express what you are arguing, rather than the content of your work. They will not comment directly on the content of the data unless it clearly does not fit with your claims and will, instead, comment (maybe irritatingly) on how you have used too much and not said enough about it, rather than quoting it.

They are enabling you to make decisions about managing your arguments and using your data. Respect this, taking the level of their comments throughout your own rewriting. Murray comments:

You may have been expecting more feedback on what you think of as the 'content', but they see the use of terms – and assessing whether or not you can use them properly – as a priority. You can regard this as a tension between what you expect and what you get. Or you can accept that you have work to do – and who would not have – in clarifying what you have written. (Murray 2002: 78).

Selective feedback and hierarchies of feedback can enable you to focus on several issues at a time. Often supervisors write specific suggestions in margins, providing models of argument or expression, or extracts to analyse and consider – alone or as part of supervision. Models of writing required are very useful if you are going to write to a different level and in a different way. Look for successful theses or journal essays, and process them at the level of expression as well as of structure. Look at how they introduce their main points and theories, develop and link arguments, how they use their evidence and data selectively to argue their case, how they build on their arguments using comments that suggest links and developments, for example, they might use phrases such as:

- 'in this respect while ... '
- 'it could be argued that ...'
- 'although ... it can be suggested in the light of this evidence that ...'.

Preferably, look at least two examples for comparison so you do not rigidly follow one model. Produce short examples of writing, and ask your supervisor to work very closely on providing feedback on a single paragraph of your work in terms of expression, grammar and punctuation, asking you to take the changes in the text through the whole chapter, then return it to them for further assessment. This will enable you to try to write in the way they have suggested and to test it against their responses and move on.

Using supervisor feedback

Students have commented in interviews on being 'blocked' by supervisor feedback. Unblocking, the development of ownership, independence and reflective self-awareness of the needs of one's own writing practices and styles should feed into your writing improvement.

How can you work with constructive and developmental feedback?

Try not to be silenced by overly critical feedback – it would almost certainly not have been meant to silence you! But not everyone is sensitive to the tone of feedback, so we need to work with what we receive. Rowena Murray has developed a useful list of the intentions of critical comments for students' work (elaborated below). When annotating e-mail attachments between you and your supervisor, in an ongoing discussion about your developing work, it is useful to use the 'Track Changes' mode in 'Tools', and to alter text in a colour, making other marginal notes in another colour (not red! – this signals bad errors and looks patronising) and you can also use 'Comment' in the 'Insert' mode.

Rowena Murray's typology is very helpful. It recognises comments both at the conceptual critical level and that of presentation; that is:

- Argument
- Clarity
- Develop
- Discuss
- Distinguish
- Expand
- The mechanics, that is:
  - punctuation, and so on
  - praise
  - probe
  - prompt
  - role switch
  - style.

Murray proceeds to suggest how you can translate and act on supervisors' comments.

I have developed comments that attempt to encourage critical thinking and are derived from counselling. I have also developed some examples below, taken from *The Good Supervisor* (see the book for further work on this).

Examples of kinds of comments

- You need to ensure apostrophes are in the right place: It's = 'it is'; instead of saying 'people I worked with ...' try 'people with whom I worked...' (*punctuation, grammar, spelling, style*)

- Please comment on your table; discuss how the quotation exemplifies your theme (*argument, specific relevance*)
- What do you understand 'ontological insecurity' to mean in Plath's poetry? (*asks for conceptualisation and further discussion*)
- Tell me more about the link between the specific act and general trends (*expand, important point*)
- You say 'it was an age of great change', for whom? When? In what ways? (*clarity needed*)
- Why do you think Heads expressed role conflict? (*probing and prompting*)
- Another person might argue that ... (*changing perspectives to expand thinking*).

Issues of clarity, specificity, expansion, discussion, inclusion of data in a discussion to ensure it acts as evidence for claims, encouraging argument, conceptualisation, critical thinking *and* suggesting accurate, referred detail, and appropriate expression are all important in feedback. You might find it useful to consider different kinds of concerns from the conceptual/critical to the clarity, experiences and appropriation of argument, to use of data and to expression.

- You have obviously covered a great deal of reading here ...? (*comment on momentum*)
- Add a short paragraph about Bloom's main points here (*expanding the information in your points*)
- Do Bloom and Dewey really disagree about curriculum models? List them, expand where they argue and where they differ (*developing the complexity of student arguments with differentiation*)
- You have repeated various phrases here – can you find another word for 'focus' or 're-focus'? (*tidying up writing style*)
- Be more specific. This is a little generalised (focus, expression)
- How many exactly argued that the curriculum was too packed? (*accuracy*)
- What did they mean, and do you mean, by 'packed'? (*asking the student to be more specific, detailed, accurate, refined and discriminatory*)
- Were there any more differentiated points about the 'packed' curriculum made by the respondent? (*expand, open up*)
- Read more of Entwistle's (1998) points here (*guiding reading by being more specific*). See pages 34–8, 120–2. What does he argue about the changing purpose of the HE curriculum?

Here is a supervisor comment on the use of feedback to aid the quality of students' writing:

> I see a development of critical thinking, of rigorous examination of information, rigorous questioning of information in order to establish its validity, its relevance and so on and I think that process develops in practice.
>
> You ask questions. You say 'Why do you say that? What has it come from? What's the connection between this statement and anything that you have stated before as the material from which this statement, this conclusion, apparently derived?' and if there's a good answer to your question then there's a secondary question, 'Well, why doesn't it say that in your writing?' and, if there isn't a good answer, then it's an indication that the student needs to go away and think more carefully and not to present conclusions – even low level conclusions in the form of statements or assumptions – that don't arise from that evidence. As I say, I think that most students are quite receptive to that because they have begun their doctoral work with a higher than average acuity for critical examination of information – much higher than the general population.

Feedback: How would you respond to these comments from a supervisor on a literary thesis?

Example A

> Refocus the question. This is inevitable. It's particularly more so with literary theses, it seems to me. You propose and explore, actually, with a literary thesis. Further developmental questions can arise out of dealing with the facts. And then I'd bring in some critical focus on the way the texts develop. I think, I'm not being insulting by saying that, because you've got a lot of material now and you have to step back and say what is the question and what is the argument, because if you don't focus on how she does *this* this way because she's arguing *that*, you could end up having too much stuff, which is where we were occasionally last year. I think a lot of this is much more focused.
>
> Last year you were, and you still will be, because a lot of that work still exists, I think, probably in the same shape, you were focused on looking at single books. They will be your examples and the arguments will run through the comments on them, but don't just tell us about the events, story, characters – make sure that you use these parts of the books as part of your argument, so use them as evidence of, as examples of the development of the idea you are arguing about in the texts themselves ...

This piece of feedback is working at several levels:

- Structural
- Conceptual
- Expression.

How could you deal with it and improve the work?

Here are some more to consider:

Example B

It felt like a different kind of writing, it felt like your opinion here, and I think in a ... I don't have a problem with people having their opinions, not that, but it needs to be couched in a more scholarly way, see, there are several views about the representation of women and their feelings about their children, particularly a male child, ...

This piece concentrates on the voice being used, and on the kinds of comments we can make when writing – straightforward opinions are not really to be written through in a thesis, but you can develop an argument that expresses your views or opinions, through using critics, theorists and your evidence.

Example C

Sup. And, at the moment, each one of the chapters is a patchwork text of a lot of historical, real, in-depth scholarly historical detail and some more generalisations and not quite enough historicist or feminist theory writing through. Sometimes, that's used to start the chapter but then you get bogged down in the details and the theory then kind of disappears from your analysis.

Stu. I think part of the problem is because I'm looking at my details as speaking for themselves, as an exemplification of the theory.

Sup. For the reader, you have to make it really straightforward that that is what you're engaging with.

Stu. Then I get into the problem of repetition.

Sup. No, the repetition is within individual sentences, or between sentence and sentence, or where you haven't clearly said, at the beginning of the chapter or within a paragraph, you haven't clearly said once what you're going to say, you ramble round it a bit. That's the kind of repetition. So there are actually three sorts of writing going on: there's very dense, historically accurate, kind of sorted-out details about what happened here, what happened there and detail within the text of the same sort. There's also some theoretical writing which needs to be driven through that detail, and then there's some bits that need firming up and editing because they are a bit wobbly, a bit repetitive and you don't always use the right word.

This works at several levels too – it begins by looking at the appropriate use of theory to underpin argument and suggests that the theory disappears and the descriptive, factual details take over. The student feels he or she does not need to step back from the thesis, analyse, reflect, evaluate and point out how the details and the theory link together – the supervisor says it needs to be more straightforwardly written to guide the reader. When the supervisor suggests emphasising points and signposting, the student believes that this is repetition, but the supervisor clarifies the difference between repetition of points, and clarification and signposting. They end up with the supervisor suggesting there are several kinds of writing going on in the chapter.

Look back over some of the feedback you have received and decide what levels it is at. What is expected? What is there to do to improve your writing and thinking as a consequence of working with the feedback?

Conclusion

We have looked at ways in which you might audit your own work, seek feedback from peers and, most importantly, work with the feedback provided by your supervisor so that you learn constructively from it and improve your writing accordingly.

● Further reading

Dunleavy, P. (2003) *Authoring a PhD* (Basingstoke: Palgrave Macmillan).

Murray, R. (2002) *How to Write a Thesis* (Buckingham: Open University Press): 78.

Wisker, G. (2005) *The Good Supervisor* (Basingstoke: Palgrave Macmillan).

26 Writing Transfer Documents and Progress Reports for MPhil, EdD and PhD Theses

If you are undertaking an MPhil or a PhD, you will probably be expected to provide a programme report on your progress and, usually, you will need to write this after one year's study, if not more regularly. Students on EdD or professional – probably educational – doctorates are expected to provide a series of progress reports, culminating in a long report at the point of transfer to the second stage of the EdD, the writing of the actual final thesis. MA students tend to deliver oral reports on their progress.

This chapter describes a fairly large progress report undertaking that suits MPhil transfer, universities that require large reports to confirm candidature, and the final longer report for the EdD. At your own university, you might only be asked for a one-page summary, so do check on the breadth and scope of what is expected of you. EdD study is very structured and varies between universities, but the example of that of the Open University (UK), which follows, can serve as an illustration.

● Open University (OU) EdD

For the Open University (UK) EdD, Part A comprises an MA-level study, which potentially provides the appropriate level qualification for entry to Part B, as it does for entry to many PhD studies at other universities. A research proposal forms part of this entry to Part B, as does entry to a PhD or MPhil in other universities.

Part B comprises two stages: in Stage 1, the assessment is a series of progress reports, four in all, the first three at 3000–4000 words, the fourth at

12 000–15 000 words, a draft of which forms the Stage 1 final report. In Stage 2 Year 1, there are three progress reports of 4000–5000 words. Two in Year 2 are of the same length, and the tenth progress report at the end of Stage 2 is a final dissertation, the major assessment for Stage 2, at 40 000–50 000 words. This is comparable to the final thesis in a PhD. Note, however, that this chapter can help you to determine the structure of your progress reports throughout your EdD study, while further chapters will be more suitable for the final Stage 2 Year 2 dissertation for the OU EdD and any final thesis for other universities' EdD programmes.

This chapter looks at progress reports, and also looks at transfer documents. Transfer documents tend to contain the same elements as progress reports but, for those registered on an MPhil who wish to transfer to a PhD, they crucially act as proof or documentary evidence that you have been carrying out doctoral research. The reasons for each document remain basically the same, however: to report on progress to date, noting how far you have worked towards and achieved some of the underlying aims, answered the questions, and conducted the research, and met and dealt with problems of the research you have been undertaking. In the case of an oral report or a progress/transfer document backed up by discussion with a supervisor or peer session, you will need to take full note of the feedback given to you about developing your work further. The discussions below should help you to compile your report, whatever length or format is required.

The following areas of progress reports and transfer documents are covered:

- Reasons for transfer documents
- Reasons for progress reports
- Where they fit in the development of the higher degree thesis
- What should be reported and explored, and what should be evidenced and planned in a transfer document or a progress report
- Transfer document and progress report stages
- Models
- Submitting transfer documents and progress reports – the process, including referees and university research degree committees.

It is common practice in UK universities to expect:

- students registered for an **MPhil with the aim of transfer to a PhD** to complete and submit a transfer document to the research degrees committee, or equivalent, approximately one year after being registered for the research

- students registered for a **PhD** to complete and submit a progress report document to the research degrees committee, or equivalent, approximately one year after being registered for the research
- students registered for the **EdD** to complete several shorter, then longer progress reports during their three years of study, which then lead into the final dissertation.

The main aims of a transfer document or progress report are to ensure that:

- good progress has been made on the research
- the scope and range of the research have been appropriately shaped
- the work carried out to date is organised and has achieved some of the planned stages
- the work to date can be summed up
- where refocusing, extending or cutting back, reshaping the topic and its objects of study, changing or developing further the necessary methods, this is recognised, understood, explained and planned for in the future work
- the research student now focuses on the rest of their PhD research and effectively plans ahead to its completion.

The transfer document or progress report provides an excellent opportunity for taking stock of work to date and for the future. In it, the researcher can sum up their work to date, put a shape to it, and indicate what plans they have for the future to complete their research and to write up their thesis.

● Transfer to a PhD

In the past, many university postgraduate research students have registered for an MPhil with the possibility of transfer to a PhD and have usually exercised that option, making the transfer when they had completed enough work of the right quality to argue the case for a PhD level of work. Your supervisors will advise you on your readiness for transfer. When your supervisors are convinced that you are working at PhD level, an application to transfer can be submitted to the appropriate research degrees committee. The arrangements for the transfer of a candidate's registration from Master's to Doctor will appear in the university's information on research degrees.

Let us look at the similarities between transfer documents and progress reports, both of which enable you to take stock of work so far, write it up, refocus if necessary, plan ahead, and negotiate all of this with your supervisors. The supervisors then advise you to submit your work to the research degrees committee, and gain the support and agreement that you can proceed with your research as designed and defined in your transfer document/progress report in relation to your original PhD proposal.

If you do not have to write a transfer document, you will certainly have to produce progress reports, as everyone registered for postgraduate degrees usually has to do this. Let us look first at progress reports. Below is a typical progress report outline for a PhD, and probably also for an EdD – though these are of varying lengths for EdD (see above). Note also that length requirements for all progress reports vary from university to university, so do check the details.

Progress reports

With your supervisors' guidance, you should produce a progress report (of 3000–6000 words) consisting of:

- a critical review of the research so far
- a statement of intended further work for the PhD programme, including details of the original contribution to knowledge. Once the progress report *together with an ABSTRACT of not more than 500 words* are agreed by your supervisory team, you can apply to the appropriate research committee to transfer to the PhD by completing the appropriate form.
- The supervisory team must sign the form (giving the reasons why you are ready to transfer to the PhD). The *abstract* of the progress report must be included as part of the application.
- As before, details (name, address and telephone number) of an independent academic who is willing to complete a specialist report on the application must be provided with the application, which must be submitted *at least five weeks* before the appropriate committee meeting. The secretary of the research committee will send the external referee a copy of the application form, including the main progress report.

(The above points were adapted from Anglia Ruskin University documentation.)

Some universities provide for an alternative way of indicating the scope and success of your work to date, through submission of actual completed work and parts of the PhD (see below).

As an exception, you may submit a minimum of two completed chapters of your proposed thesis in lieu of a progress report. One chapter should deal with theoretical foundations upon which the research is based, the other may be a chapter on either the methodology or the fieldwork.

Transfer to a PhD

- Transfer to a PhD provides a vital opportunity to receive constructive feedback on the research project and the plans to progress to PhD. It is the responsibility of supervisors to recommend independent referees who can provide specialist advice on the application to transfer and the viability of the proposed research.
- Your director of studies (or second supervisor) will be invited to attend the research degrees committee meeting to discuss your application. A member of the committee will act as the 'designated reader' to open the discussion. All members of the committee will have received copies of the application (but not the full progress report), plus the assessor's report.
- If appropriate, the research degrees committee will normally recommend approval of the transfer proposal. You will receive written notification of the outcome. In some cases, approval may be conditional on submission of additional material. In certain instances, the committee may decide that, in your bests interests, a revised application must be submitted.

(The above points were adapted from Anglia Ruskin University documentation.)

Transfer criteria

It is most important that you discuss with your supervisory team the criteria used in your discipline, to determine whether research is of a doctoral standard. Some evidence of the following is normally required:

- originality and/or creativity
- the exercise of independent critical powers
- a significant contribution to subject knowledge in the research field
- training in research techniques and methodology.

In particular, for a transfer application to be approved, a convincing case (with evidence) must be made that you have:

- chosen an appropriate doctoral research topic of sufficient scope
- gained satisfactory knowledge of the background literature, and are able to relate the project to existing scholarship and research in the field

- started to work at a PhD level, especially in terms of theoretical insights and conceptual frameworks
- planned a suitable research programme to achieve a successful doctoral conclusion.

You should also have reviewed the proposed doctoral programme in accordance with the ethical, legal and safety requirements set out by the university.

How to refocus and concentrate on scoping ready for writing your transfer document or progress report

At this stage, the focus and scope of the research possibly might be cut back realistically, extended or reshaped.

An extension might include another sample, another questionnaire, the addition of a focus group, adding interviews with individuals, considering the necessity of looking further into a different but related appropriate field of study, and so on.

More probably, you will be cutting back and reshaping. This is a time to look critically at the research, to see whether some of the work is possibly too ambitious or a little redundant – for example, too many questionnaires and tests planned on too many children. Often, then, at the *transfer document* or *progress report stage*, the research becomes more restricted and more clearly focused and defined.

This is a key moment in the development of your own work at postgraduate level. Certainly, taking time at this point to focus on what progress has been made and the scope of the research will help you, in particular, and also your supervisor, to:

- take stock
- check progress
- evaluate your work so far
- pull your work together
- see where it has been going
- see what has been achieved
- see what is still to be achieved
- see what has been successful
- see what has been unsuccessful
- see what needs to be dropped
- see what needs to be extended
- see what needs to be refocused.

Most of all, it is a way of capturing in a fully organised form what has been achieved to date and what is to be done in the future.

Transfer documents and progress reports have very much the same structure and aims. But for the transfer document, where it is used, there is a very definite sense of reapplying now for a higher level of postgraduate award, and so this is a formal resubmission moment.

Transfer documents

In the case of the transfer document, this is a critical moment. Referees are asked to comment on:

- the suitability of the candidate for transfer to a PhD
- the research progress achieved so far
- the planned work for the PhD programme
- other factors to bring to the attention of the research degrees committee, including guidance for strengthening the proposal.

Things to do

Transfer documents and progress reports; some questions to ask yourself about achievement so far

Consider:

- Looking back over the original proposal, how far have you achieved the overall aims and outcomes so far?
- What has been your research process – what have you done?
- What have you discovered, so far, from the literature in the subject that is feeding into the research?

Also:

- Indicate the literature themes
- Summarise your literature review chapter and, particularly, indicate how this has fed into your research planning and activities, and has helped you to contextualise your results to date
- What elements of the research activities have you carried out?
- What methods have you used?
- How appropriate and successful (or otherwise) have they been in

  - defining the field?
  - collecting the right kind of information?

- What have you found out regarding outcomes and findings so far?
- Have there been any surprises, problems or blocks to the research?

- Have you had to refocus your research, cut it back or extend it?
- What new avenues of thought and focus have you followed because of what you have found out to date?
- Why is this a PhD?
- Provide justification for the award. Look at the definitions of what constitutes an MPhil or a PhD.

Then, consider the following issues and jot down a short explanation or defence in relation to each.

In particular, for a **transfer** application to be approved, a convincing case (with evidence) must be made that you have:

- chosen an appropriate doctoral research topic of sufficient scope
- gained a satisfactory knowledge of the background literature and are able to relate the project to existing scholarship and research in the field
- started to work at a PhD level, especially in terms of theoretical insights and conceptual frameworks
- planned a suitable research programme to achieve a successful doctoral conclusion
- reviewed the proposed doctoral programme in accordance with the ethical, legal and safety requirements set out by the university.

In general, you need to think of the contribution your work has made to the field, and what you intend to do next. So, you need to ask yourself:

- What has your postgraduate research and writing up to date to do with 'originality'?
- What progress have you made towards achieving important outcomes?
- What are the critical ideas and information with which your research is providing the field/subject areas/discipline?
- What is the important work still to be done that will make your PhD a major contribution to the field of study?
- Where do you now think the research is going?

Plan – suggesting future developments and time scales

Once you have completed your progress report or transfer document, you will need to take stock of future work. For the EdD, the future work for the immediate future is the next progress report leading up to the final long report. For a PhD, you will be thinking of that long final piece of work now and will need to replan and scrutinise your time scales, and decide what is realistic, what new activities need planning in, and what parts of the original research plan can be carried out and when. You also need to decide what parts are unrealistic and where work has taken another direction due to interim findings, a change of sample, or other things that have affected your work since you began.

Things to do

Provide a detailed plan for the next year/to completion of the PhD/EdD and discuss the stages of this plan in detail:

- What do you hope to find out about now, and to continue finding out about?
- What do you intend to do?
- Which methods will you use?
- Indicate any need for further extended study, or curtailing of the study
- Indicate the need for refocusing because of any problems and contradictions or new lines of discovery.

Things to do

Produce a time plan – a critical path analysis – to help you to replan realistically, and indicate where your work is going to go in the next year and so to completion. Consider key dates, and key activities, such as collecting data, analysing it, writing it up and giving presentations. Think also, as you replan, about what else is happening in your life, what family, friends and work demands could affect your research and, so, what period of time might be less useful for undisturbed work. Some things you cannot plan in – the unforeseen activities – but you can plan some spare time just in case something goes wrong. Be realistic! Look back at Chapter 8 for an example of a critical path analysis and time plan.

You will probably be expected to submit your time and progress plan along with the full transfer document or progress report, but if not, keep it as a guide for yourself.

● MPhil, PhD and EdD – scope and differences

When considering transfer from an MPhil to a PhD, it is useful to consider the differences in scope between the two. It is also useful to consider the differences between progress reports demanded in a PhD a study and those in an EdD study.

What is the difference between an MPhil and a PhD thesis?

MPhil and PhD degrees are postgraduate awards gained by undertaking research with the submission of a thesis, normally assessed by an oral examination (viva voce). The PhD degree is the more advanced qualification, requiring a longer period of research and a thesis of greater length. The MPhil degree is an award of a higher degree in its own right.

Other general characteristics normally include the following:

MPhil degree – Candidates must submit a substantial thesis (maximum length 40 000 words) that shows evidence of instruction in research methods appropriate to the field of study, as well as sound knowledge of scholarship relevant to the student's particular subject.

PhD degree – Candidates must submit a substantial thesis (the university has a maximum word length of 80 000 words). It will have the various components of the MPhil, but also display research work of greater scope and creativity, and make an original contribution to knowledge in the field of study. Originally, the doctorate was seen as the passport into academic life as a university lecturer. While there are now wider career aspirations and other reasons for acquiring a PhD, the doctorate is still often associated with subject authority and the ability to push the frontiers onward and upwards.

(The above points were adapted from Anglia Ruskin University documentation.)

Your supervisor should discuss with you what makes a PhD. Often students have supervisors (usually one, sometimes two) who are external to the university awarding the degree, and it is therefore important to make sure that your supervisor is entirely familiar with the rules and regulations of the university awarding the degree (these do vary from university to university). You may find it helpful, therefore, to ask your supervisor to:

- familiarise him-/herself with the university's regulations on this issue – that is, what constitutes an MPhil or a PhD, the significant differences in level, and so on, between the two (as well as the regulations and codes of other universities, if they are going to be a PhD examiner)
- provide opportunities for you as an MPhil/PhD candidate to examine appropriate completed MPhil/PhD theses (some of these may be available in the library, while others, possibly those closest to your own field of study, can be borrowed on inter-library loan,

having first been identified by looking at abstracts of theses)
- discuss the nature of the PhD qualification with your (and other) supervisor(s), especially the concept of originality, where applicable, and also issues of what constitutes a PhD in your subject area.

What is the difference between an MPhil, a PhD and an EdD?

The **EdD** is characterised by its professional orientation, its substantial taught element, and its modular structure. The EdD is designed to meet the needs of professionals in education and related areas who are seeking to extend and deepen their knowledge and understanding of contemporary educational issues (hence the significant taught element), to develop appropriate skills in educational research and enquiry, and to carry out original research in order to contribute to professional knowledge and practice. (Extract from Open University documentation)

The series of progress reports required for the Open University EdD are matched by a series of long linking essays in other universities. Most EdD studies require a long progress report to ensure a move or transfer into the final stage, where the dissertation or thesis is written. In the EdD, the shorter and longer progress reports form a large part of both the work and the words towards this final dissertation or thesis, even as a progress report would form a part of the final write-up for a PhD thesis. However, note that progress report lengths differ for the EdD, and the progress report that enables a transition to the final stage of the EdD (when the final progress report or thesis is written) is likely to be much longer than any progress report required for the PhD (12 000–15 000 words for the Open University EdD progress report, enabling the student to move between Stage 1 and Stage 2.) For the Open University EdD, *the final* 'progress report', the tenth, at the end of the final stage, Stage 2 (40 000–50 000 words), is actually *equivalent* to the finished thesis for a PhD student. Do check length requirements carefully with your university, and also check the specific demands of each stage of the work, each kind of essay or progress report.

In this chapter, we have discussed the progress report – which contains a substantial amount of information about your work to date, your progress along your intended research – as a way of noting methods and findings, and a report that will contribute to the final thesis by being merged in with later work. It does not describe the kind of freestanding essay common in some EdD programmes.

● **Presentation issues to bear in mind as you carry on with your work**

MPhil, EdD and PhD theses (or the final long progress report/dissertation stage of the OU and similar EdD) must be the candidate's own work and presented in a satisfactory manner. This involves concentrating on your work throughout, and, as you move towards completion, on:

- grammar
- punctuation
- spelling
- clarity of expression
- logical argument
- appropriate language.

It is also important that a thesis has a technical apparatus to support it. This refers to the shape and organisation of the thesis and involves the following:

- abstract
- preface and acknowledgements
- footnotes/endnotes
- references
- appendices
- statistical tables
- diagrams
- illustrations
- bibliography.

These must be set out according to the conventions of the field of study. There are, for example, different conventions of referencing between literature theses and social science documents that provide layout and referencing guidelines for fields of study, and for that particular university. Look at past theses to see how these are organised and laid out, also, check with your supervisor.

One of the responsibilities of your supervisor is to draw these requirements to your attention and discuss how these can be met.

Particular attention must be given to the writing, editing and correction of the final draft before submission. Check issues of organisation and layout as you write up and submit to your supervisor. When you start to approach completion, check it out with a colleague as well – you could even use a professional proofreader, if that would be helpful. Most word-processing packages include good quality spell checks and even grammar, syntax and punctuation checks. Do use these, but do also ensure they are correcting the right things.

Use the writing of progress reports as a way of taking stock, seeing how your research and your writing up are progressing, and ensuring that all you do still fits in with the conceptual framework of your initial proposal.

Conclusion

We have looked at:

- ☐ Taking stock

- ☐ Transfer documents

- ☐ Progress reports.

● Further reading

Dunleavy, P. (2003) *Authoring a PhD* (Basingstoke: Palgrave Macmillan).
Murray, R. (2002) *How to Write a Thesis* (Buckingham: Open University Press).

27 Writing Up: Definitions and Qualities of a Good MA, MPhil, EdD and PhD Thesis

This chapter considers the features of successful research dissertations for the MA and theses for the MPhil, PhD and EdD, and looks at how you can turn your work into a successful thesis of merit. It concentrates on definitions and important elements of a successful thesis and dissertation, and contains advice on organisation, layout, editing and submission.

● The Master's dissertation or thesis

Both taught Master's and Master's by research require a dissertation or thesis. The differences lie in the length, breadth, depth and scope of the work being constructed and presented. For a taught Master's, coursework will comprise a large and regular part of the assessment, with possibly the equivalent of one 5000-word essay/report/video and an analytical/critical write-up each semester, or each 30-credit module. Usually, there is also a dissertation or thesis, which can be of 30 or 60 credits in length and would normally be substantial – perhaps 20 000 words for a 60-credit dissertation and half that for a 30-credit one. Every scheme has its own rules, so you would be well advised at this stage to look back at the rules on length and layout, and the house style in terms of presentation, references, diagrams, bibliographies and appendices. Issues such as how much of your quoted material counts in the word count really matter if you are about to produce a work that may go over length. Issues about the quality of diagrams matter if you have limited access to technology and are relying on hand drawing or photocopying.

You might also need to recruit help from friends at this late stage if there is an overwhelming amount of work to be done. I hand-drew dozens of graphs for a scientist friend in the late 1970s, and in the early 1980s another friend typed up my bibliography from index cards on the eve of the printer shutting for Christmas, with an early January deadline. Later still, another thesis found two of us photocopying in a north-London shop that hires out weird novelty costumes (the nearest photocopier), to get the work in on time. Checking the details of presentation as well as those of timing and submission can save you such awkward moments.

Quality in Master's work

The diversity of Master's programmes means that there are some difficulties in defining what a high-quality Master's award would comprise. While a more academic Master's course would demand research, creative output and independent study, a professional Master's, which sought to upgrade in a different or more practical area of the subject, would be more likely to seek a useful, practical, well-structured project or product from the Master's. One key issue is that the examiners of Master's programmes should recognise both the kind of Master's programme with which they are dealing, and therefore what constitutes quality at the different ends of the continuum and all points in between.

● The EdD

The EdD or doctorate in education is an increasingly popular route for education practitioners to gain a doctorate and it is generally characterised by its professional orientation, its substantial taught elements and its modular structure.

To undertake the EdD, you will first have completed the Open University's taught MA in Education (or similar), which acts as **Part A** of the EdD and comprises four taught modules.

Part B is the doctoral level work, and lasts for two years:

Stage One – literature reviews and progress reports (1 year, 60 points).
Stage Two – dissertation (2 years, 120 points).

The EdD is credit rated and the shape of any specific EdD on which you are studying will vary. For example, in the Open University this is 50 000 words, and it builds on a number of progress reports, each between 3000 and 15 000 words long.

Your writing of the progress reports can be guided by the comments in Chapter 22, while the final dissertation can be guided by comments on MPhil and PhD theses in this chapter.

● Definitions of a good dissertation or thesis

Things to do

Consider:

- ● What makes a good and successful Master's dissertation or thesis?
- ● What makes a good MPhil thesis?
- ● What makes a good PhD thesis?
- ● What makes a good EdD thesis?

Positive features towards which you can aim and advice on how to get there

Master's or doctorate – levels

Winter (1993) bases his definitions of doctorate-level work on statements produced by staff working with a variety of students on research by thesis, or taught by coursework in professional areas and in the more interdisciplinary areas. Winter's definitions of doctorate-level work builds developmentally upon Master's level work, so do look at his definitions of Master's work and then at the differences between this and doctoral-level work. This will help you make your case for the doctoral level of your own work. Critical reflectiveness is a key element in defining a Master's course outcome. Winter defines a Master's as having the following criteria:

- ● a balance is maintained between original and secondary material
- ● methodology and data analysis are clearly separated
- ● different investigative paradigms and their methodologies are understood
- ● it includes a critical self-appraisal of existing practices/beliefs
- ● it reaches a synthesis based on creative connections between different aspects of a problem/topic

- it is committed to/engaged with a project/discipline/body of reading ... set alongside theoretical and ethical grounding.

All of these elements of quality will also be found in an MPhil or PhD thesis, but, in Winter's accumulative model, there are also some extra, deeper and more complex outcomes which help define the higher level of the work.

Things to do

Look through the different categories of achievement and quality necessary in a Master's or MPhil/PhD and ask yourself the questions about relevance to your own work and thesis at MPhil, EdD or PhD level.

- Does your work have these positive qualities? If so, where could you prove/show they exist?
- If not, could you write up your thesis to ensure that these qualities do exist within it?

Winter (2000: 15–19)

● Positive features in a successful MPhil and PhD

There is a range of positive features of postgraduate work and additional elements present in a successful MPhil and PhD. The same elements will be present in an EdD.

Section 1 – positive features

Intellectual grasp is demonstrated by the candidate who:

- grasps the scope and possibilities of the topic
- shows diligence and rigour in procedures — catholic and multifactoral approaches to problems
- shows readiness to examine apparently tangential areas for possible relevance
- grasps the wider significance of the topic – how the analysis is related to its methodological and epistemological context
- shows iterative development, allowing exploration and rejection of alternatives
- possesses an internal dialogue – plurality of approach/method, to validate the one chosen
- treats a broad theoretical base critically

- demonstrates a coherent and explicit theoretical approach, fully thought through and critically applied – that is, noting its limitations
- gives a systematic account of the topic, including a review of all plausible possible interpretations
- demonstrates full mastery of the topic – that is, that the candidate is now an expert in the field
- indicates the future development of the work
- maintains clear and continuous links between theory, method and interpretation
- presents a reflexive, self-critical account of relationships involved in the inquiry and of the methodology
- connects theory and practice
- displays rigour.

Questions

Check your thesis against these criteria and ask the general summary questions of it:

- In what way does your developing thesis show coherence, rigour and reflective self-critical elements?
- How far does it connect theory and practice?
- How far does it indicate possible future work?
- How and where does it show mastery of the subject?
- How coherent is the argument, use of information, analyses, ideas, and so on?
- How far does it incorporate awareness of alternative arguments, incorporate and deal with alternatives?

Coherence is demonstrated by the candidate who:

- displays coherence of structure – for example, the conclusions follow clearly from the data
- skilfully organises a number of different angles – required by the extended length of the work
- is cogently organised and expressed
- possesses a definite agenda and an explicit structure
- presents a sense of the researcher's learning as a journey, as a structured, incremental progress through a process of both argument and discovery.

Questions

How far does your developing thesis show explicit structure, organisation and coherence and present a sense of your learning as a journey – that is, structured and directed development?

Engagement with the literature is demonstrated by the candidate who:

- displays comprehensive coverage of the field and a secure command of the literature in the field
- shows breadth of contextual knowledge in the discipline
- successfully critiques established positions
- engages critically with other significant work in the field
- draws on literature with a focus different from the viewpoint pursued in the thesis
- maintains a balance between delineating an area of debate and advocating a particular approach
- includes scholarly notes, a comprehensive bibliography and accurately uses academic conventions in citations.

Questions

How far does your developing thesis:

- show a comprehensive coverage of the field?
- show an ability to criticise, engage critically, debate, and advocate a scholarly approach?
- show awareness of other approaches?
- use bibliographies, citations, and so on, as appropriate?

Grasp of methodology is demonstrated by the candidate in whose work:

- the methodology is clearly established and applied
- the methodological analysis indicates the advantages and the disadvantages of the approach adopted
- uses several methodologies for triangulation.

Questions

- Does the methodology show itself to be clearly defined and aware of alternatives?
- Is it triangulated for greater quality assurance?

Good presentation is achieved by a candidate whose thesis:

- is clear, easy to read and is presented in an appropriate style
- contains few errors of expression
- displays flawless literacy.

Questions

How far can you say that yours is a well-presented thesis in terms of its articulation, literacy and expression?

Section 2 – originality and publishability

These two terms are often used as the fundamental 'criteria' for a PhD. This section attempts to give more guidance on how to interpret them. An MPhil might have less emphasis on these elements.

Originality is to be found in a thesis that:

- pushes the topic into new areas, beyond its obvious focus
- makes an original contribution to knowledge or understanding of the subject, in terms of topic area, method, experimental design, theoretical synthesis or engagement with conceptual issues
- solves some significant problem or gathers original data
- reframes issues
- is imaginative in its approach to problems
- is creative yet rigorous
- goes beyond its sources to create a new position that critiques existing theoretical positions
- uses the empirical study to enlarge the theoretical understanding of the subject
- contains innovation, speculation, imaginative reconstruction and cognitive excitement – the author has clearly wrestled with the method and tried to shape it to gain new insights
- is comprehensive in its theoretical linkages or makes novel connections between areas of knowledge
- opens up neglected areas or takes a new viewpoint on an old problem
- shows something new has been learned and demonstrated, such that the reader is made to rethink a stance or opinion
- shows 'a spark of inspiration as well as perspiration'

- shows development towards independent research and innovation
- is innovative in content and adventurous in method – obviously at the leading edge in its particular field, with potential for yielding new knowledge
- makes a personal synthesis of an interpretative framework
- shows depth and breadth of scholarship – synthesising previous work and adding original insights/models/concepts
- argues against conventional views – presents new frameworks for interpreting the world
- applies established techniques to novel patterns, or devises new techniques that allow new questions to be addressed.

Questions

Consider all the categories above generally and ask yourself in brief to what extent:

- is your thesis creative and original?
- does it provide a personal argument?
- does it apply established technique to new areas and problems?
- does it add something well planned and coherent, but original and creative?

Publishability is indicated when a thesis is:

- of publishable quality or has potential for publication
- publishable in a refereed journal with a good scholarly reputation
- written with an awareness of the audience for the work
- stylishly and economically written.

Questions

- How publishable is your thesis?
- Is it stylish?
- Is it directed appropriately at a chosen audience?
- Does it read fluently?

A thesis of merit will have all these aspects, or most of them, that is, publishability, coherence, sound methodology and a good grasp of the literature with which it engages. It will possess originality and a sound intellectual grasp of the issues, the reading, the concepts, and an original contribution to the fundamental and important arguments within the area.

● Writing up

The writing up process should be started as early a possible – you can always revise, develop and change, but trying to capture several years' worth of thoughts, analysis and processes all at once is too daunting a task for many students. In the past, this has led to non-completion – you have been warned. The significance of writing up your research from the start is very important. Another reason to continue to write about what you are doing is that it keeps up the writing momentum: if you leave it all until the end the task is overwhelming. Some people find it very difficult to commit thoughts and comments to paper, because this seems like a finished statement. Think of it as a draft, think of it as working out your thoughts, experiences and research more clearly by having to articulate them through the writing – it is an aid to a final write-up. Trick yourself into writing parts you feel you can handle first, and writing what you do perhaps in the form of a journal, so that there is a lot of written work before you start to formalise it into the shape of the thesis itself. These tricks should help you to clear up your thoughts by articulating them in writing, and overcome writer's block by having some elements written up as you go along.

If you look back at your research proposal, you should be able to consider the extent to which you are filling out the elements that you outlined in your contents page at the beginning. Perhaps the thesis has changed shape to some extent, and you need to acknowledge this. Your initial research 'map' laid out questions, the conceptual framework, methods, and so on; now, as you approach writing up, you will need to fill out each of these sections, and write up the analysis into findings. As you start to write up and as you go along, compile 'to do' lists reminding you of what you need to write next. Leave 'pick-up points' (Nightingale, in Zuber-Skerritt 1992: 115), memos in your writing to indicate how and where you left off and what needs to come next. These tricks all help you to structure, signpost and maintain the flow in the sections you are writing up. See if you can visualise these as a whole when written as a coherent piece. There are several tasks involved in the writing.

Coherence and the structure of the thesis

The thesis needs to be coherent overall – underpinning/driving questions need to be explicit and need to inform the exploration/investigation/examination that is the research. They need to be contextualised in terms of the field and in the theories that inform, underpin and drive the set of questions and the area of investigation. The research methodologies and methods need to flow obviously from the questions, the reading and the theories as being the clearest (defined) ways of investigating and asking the questions.

Then, the findings need to be discussed, figures, graphs and tables should be integrated into the discussion, explored and explained, analysed, thereby contributing to the overall argument. Finally, conclusions need to reiterate the introduction or produce the thesis in short, and round off and clarify the effects and the importance of what has been found, what it means, why it matters and what might be done with it. At this stage in the writing up, the level of the research should be clear – the justification for the award emerges from the coherence of the work, the importance of the questions, and the significance of the findings as finally tied together and made explicit in the conclusion.

Structurally there needs to be a logical flow of information and argument between the different sections of chapters and between the chapters themselves, and tables, figures and graphs need to fit comfortably with the text. They should be explored and explained rather than be left to stand alone or be laboriously described – use them to drive the argument and illustrate the points you make.

Headings and subheadings should indicate the significance and linking of different key parts of the chapters, so that a reader can see how the headings relate to each other and follow a flow between items or sections.

Avoid 'fog', or excessively complex language, when more straightforward and accessible language would suffice. This is not to deny the importance of technical terms – they do, after all, usually put an idea, concept or point in exactly the right form for the subject area. However, avoid unnecessary jargon that is there for its own sake, and avoid unnecessarily confusing language – think of your reader

Check on grammar and spelling, using the facilities on your word processor, but do check yourself as well, because word processors make mistakes and do not understand what you are saying in context. Some amusing errors (such as 'urinal' for 'journal') might be less amusing in the middle of a highly intellectual discussion in your thesis. There is nothing to be gained by confusing your reader, or writing in such an elevated way to impress that no one can really work out what you are saying.

Use of the first person

Many authors fear writing as 'I' or 'we', and you need to check the norms and conventions of your university and your subject in your choices. But there is a great difference between using 'I' when you are just asserting an opinion and using 'I' when you are recording the research you have actually carried out. 'I interviewed three people in order to discover ...' and 'we carried out a series of surveys of ...' are much better than, for example, 'a series of surveys was carried out to discover ...', which sounds a little distanced from the actual experience, not as active (it is in the passive form), and rather formal. It gives the impression that the words have been written by an unseen third person that observes and knows all. If you feel uneasy about writing in the first person, then remember that feminist researchers often argue that the subject (you – the self) needs to be replaced in experience, which is recorded. So, the first person is a sound device for this, and certainly, if you are using yourself as a case study in your own work, or researching your own creative or performative work in relation to theory, it would be absurd to hide this with a third-person record.

Presentation

Ensure the pages are numbered, check the visual layout so you do not have headings appearing at the bottom of some pages, and very carefully check all your referencing, being consistent throughout. Get a trusted colleague or friend to proof the whole thing – we often do not see our own mistakes when we are too close to the writing.

Thinking of your reader – the shape of the thesis

A thesis ideally represents an interaction and communication between you, your work, the field, and your reader(s). You need to explore:

Researcher/writer focus
⇩
What you set about to do
How and why you did it
What you did
What your results were
What the results mean in theory, what the results mean in practice
How other readers might link with and benefit from these results and findings
What they might want to go on and do further, or with your results
⇧
Reader focus

Robert Brown (1992) suggests that research students tend to write in a 'suspense' format and need to think, instead, of a journalist or report-writer format. In the suspense format, the thesis would start with a title, abstract, introduction, literature, research, methods, results and discussion, so leaving its finding, its importance and revelations to the end.

Actually, for the benefit of the reader, a different format might be preferable. In a chapter at the outset, outline what the major arguments and findings are and why they matter, and craft and build the elements of the thesis to highlight and relate to these main points. What are the key benefits and points of each chapter, and of the thesis as a whole? Brown talks about the 'journalist's pyramid', where a good journalist knows they must capture and retain the interest of their readers, so they put the main point first, followed by the next most important point, and so on, down. The reader is captivated by the main point and moves on to see what research methods and activities helped to produce it, but when they open the chapter they need to see immediately what it is about, what its punchline is, and the explanation of the key points. Actually, good report writing does this, since it starts by explaining who asked for the report and what it solves, what kind of problem or what kind of questions are being asked, and why they matter. Methods to ask the questions and interrogate the situation follow, and the summary and conclusion indicate what has been discovered. Any recommendations follow from that.

When you have looked through your thesis and seen whether or not and where it does fulfil these expectations, you can prepare a defence of its sound elements ready for the viva. Alternatively, and additionally, you can look at some of its weaknesses and work on them. Make it more coherent, with linking paragraphs, pointing out what seems obvious to you but is less so to a reader. Ensure that you have emphasised the original contribution, and what and how it contributes to the concepts, arguments and knowledge of the subject area. Make a case for your thesis and its contribution to the area of knowledge, skills, and so on. If you find that there are areas of weakness – such as coherence, originality or presentation quality – plan out how to tackle these now, and work on the weaknesses so that you end up with a good thesis that makes an original contribution.

Shape of the thesis

You might find it useful to look back over earlier advice about the shape of a thesis and see if yours is a variation on this or if anything is missing, if it is too short, too long, and so on. Consider this and, if you can, discuss it with your colleagues or a friend.

Elements of the structure of the thesis explained and variants discussed

The shape applies to the MA, MPhil and PhD – only the lengths will vary, so do be sure to check these out with your university and supervisor.

Do be aware that, if you are undertaking an arts or humanities dissertation/thesis, there are differences in their overall construction and structure. Look back at Chapter 17 for a more detailed discussion on why this is the case and for discussion of the actual structure of the thesis. Let us now discuss comment elements, that is, title abstract, introduction, the main body of the chapters, conclusion, references, bibliography, and so on.

Title – This should appear on a separate title page. Try to keep it to one or two lines and make it clear, suggesting the questions you are posing and assertions you are making, rather than just the field of study. Look at the example of an abstract below. Can you spot its qualities?

Abstract – Usually about 500 words, it answers the questions: 'What is this thesis about?', 'What does it argue, prove, contend?', and so on. Use the third person and passive verbs, that is, 'It is argued that … in discussing … using … evidence is presented which suggests that …'.

At the writing-up stage, the abstract is a very important part of your work. By offering a clear, coherent summary of the aims, developments, route and findings of the thesis, the abstract gives the reader, the examiner, your supervisor and yourself a clear idea of the plans, decisions and achievements of your research.

Note how it states the aim, focus and the field of study. It establishes a clear conceptual framework. It also states briefly what the major findings and contributions have been to date.

Things to do

Example of an abstract

Look this through and consider how it addresses the following areas:

- What the writer is/was aiming for
- What their research questions are/were
- How their methods and research activities flow from the questions
- How their findings follow from the research activities
- How the different parts of the dissertation/thesis represent and argue through this learning 'journey'
- Making the case for discoveries and the importance of findings, major points, what could be done with the findings/how the research contributes to knowledge and in the subject field.

Abstract

Recognising and overcoming dissonance in postgraduate student research

Action research conducted with Israeli and UK postgraduate students 1997–2001 indicates that dissonance in approaches to research as learning produces potentially significant difficulties for students at different stages in their work. These difficulties emerge principally when developing a proposal, deciding on research methodologies and methods, undertaking the research, and maintaining the links between findings, analysis and conclusions, specifically those that aim to lead to transformation. This research into postgraduate learning is grounded in well-established theories of how student approaches to learning affect learning outcomes (Entwistle and Ramsden 1983, Biggs 1993), including how students' concepts of what learning is – what are their perceptions of learning in scientific subject areas, how they go about their learning, how they know when learning has taken place, their outcomes and their motivation – affect the quality and kind of learning (Dahlgren and Marton 1978, Meyer and Shanahan 2001). Significantly, research into postgraduate learning is a relatively new field of exploration and yields interesting information related to levels of learning and movements between these levels. Inflections on learning relate to students' origins, particularly the experiences of international students whose 'tertiary literacy' could prove an issue in articulating and engaging in debate with complex concepts at postgraduate level (Marton, Dall'alba and Beaty 1993, Todd 1997, Meyer and Kiley 1998).

Quantitative and qualitative research vehicles (Entwistle and Entwistle 1992) have been employed in an action research format. The 'Reflections on Learning Inventory' (Meyer and Boulton-Lewis 1997) enables data to be gathered relating to students' conceptions of learning, knowing the learning has occurred, learning approaches, motivation and outcomes. The 'Research as Learning' questionnaire (Wisker 1998 – analysed using SPSS), specifically designed for this research, enables information to be gathered about students' perceptions of what research is as learning and how their own research operates as learning (seeing it as creative learning, cause and effect, finding out known facts, problem solving, and so on). Focus groups and workshop activities (taped, transcribed and analysed using NVivo) engage students as aware, reflective participants concentrating on the stages of their research and learning, and links between approaches to research as learning and outcomes. Supervisory dialogues (taped, transcribed and analysed used Nvivo) indicate different kinds of supervisor interactions that do or do not enable, empower and direct students, as appropriate, to continue with their research in effective and potentially successful ways.

The action research format enables the postgraduate students to be fully involved in shaping the research, and reflect on the implications for their own learning and research development of the research findings. For the researcher and colleagues working with postgraduate students, it enables a direct focus on the usefulness and success of research development and support programmes, and the appropriate forms of supervisory dialogues.

Findings have indicated that student research-as-learning approaches can lead to dissonance, particularly: (i) those taking accumulation approaches (acquiring numbers of facts) while seeking transformational outcomes; and (ii) those who take negative and postmodern approaches (seeing *everything* as relative and relevant). These approaches are at odds with the development of a cohesive focus and coherent, managed research. Other elements of dissonance have emerged in student/supervisor interactions when dialogues occur that *disable* students from writing their work and proceeding clearly with it in different stages. They also exist between the work carried out and findings developed in the context of the overall conceptual framework of the research itself. This can emerge when clear developmental links between the conceptual framework (the questions, theoretical background, underpinning methodology, methods, findings, and so on) and the conclusions made from the research are at odds or unclear.

Both development programmes and dialogues are focused on as sources of the research and, in their developmental stages, act as part products of the research findings. The development programme and the supervisory dialogues are being developed as models which, when refined, should help students to overcome the dissonance between approaches and outcomes, and empower them to be more effective and successful in their research, as appropriate.

This thesis details action research carried out with students between 1997 and 2000, and makes a case both for the importance of action research with students to identify, investigate and deal with dissonance in their approaches to learning and research, and to suggest possible models of developmental programmes and supervisory dialogues that assist in this supportive practice.

- Now you need to produce your own example of an abstract. Remember it must be in the third person, and should detail what was set out to be done and what was achieved, rather than suggest you are about to embark on this journey. It is the first thing a reader reads, and it suggests to them the main areas and claims of your work. It whets their appetite to read more.
- The abstract needs to be able to stand alone, as something to invite a reader into the work. It needs to make a case about the importance of the research and its findings, and how it contributes to the field of knowledge generally.

Preface and acknowledgements – Who do you want to acknowledge and to thank? Who helped you and enabled your work on the thesis, and on the research?

Introduction – The introduction:

- lays out the background to the thesis
- briefly describes other work in the area
- outlines general ideas and developments related to it
- moves on to lay down and explore the theoretical bases for the thesis and your work
- contextualises your arguments and findings in background, context and theory
- discusses your research questions and the hypotheses underlying the research
- sets out the main themes, and suggests what your work contributes to and develops in relation to these, and what your main arguments and contributions are
- usually tends to be written last as it provides a coherent introduction to themes, arguments and findings. This is difficult to do until the whole anatomy of the thesis has actually been constructed and flesh put on the bones of each chapter.

Review of the literature – Not all theses have a separate literature review. If your work develops logically and smoothly from the reading you have carried out, and if your research and findings follow on from a coherent body of established work in the field and have established informing theories, you will probably use a literature review at this point. It will establish the theories and arguments, and discuss the main debates, research and authors who contribute to the field, contextualising your own work. The literature review is liable to take up much of your introductory chapter as you interweave background reading, theories and critical views.

If, however, you will be moving stage-by-stage, and at different stages need to introduce and develop theories and reading, which is normal, then you might well find several chapters begin with and interweave the literature, theory and arguments. You need to decide which variation on these versions suits your work best. Remember that the literature review or survey is not just a collection of all you have read. You need to weave the reading and main points and arguments made into your own discussion, using them to back up or counteract some of your arguments. If you have found a few main themes developing logically and coherently through your reading, these can help form the basis for your main chapters.

Design of the study and methods – For social science, education and related research, the design of the study and methods is as crucial as it is for scientific research. You need to explain why and how you designed your studies, mentioning the pilot stage (if there was one), decisions taken about interviews, focus groups, questionnaires, samples, and so on (see Chapter 14).

If your research is based more in humanities or literature, you might well find that you have already described what your research questions are along with your main ideas and arguments. In this case, there is no specific study in logical stages, each depending on the data from the ones that have gone before, as such. Instead, each chapter takes a different theme, critical approach or point of view, or different author or book, and so on.

However, note that it is always preferable to interweave literature, texts and authors, rather than plodding through each one individually. Relate them and form your own way through them in relation to your arguments and information.

Presentation of results – This can be a clear, annotated record of what has been discovered in the areas of social sciences, education and health. You are unlikely to have this section in a literature or cultural studies thesis. In this case, your 'results', or discoveries and arguments, will form part of the discussions in separate chapters.

Discussion of results – For a social science, health or education thesis, there is often a logical place for working through different results, putting tables and statistics, bar charts and so on, either in the main text or referring to them in the appendices, and conducting a narrative that explores and brings in different results to develop arguments and present your coherent points and findings.

For a humanities or literature-based thesis – and also often for a social sciences-, health- or education-based thesis – there are often *several chapters* exploring different themes and issues in a linked discussion. The results, as such, will be your critically informed comments and arguments on the texts, images, your readings, and so on. You might find that the main themes identified in the literature review appear here as main topics in each of your chapters.

Summary – This chapter enables you to sum up your main findings and present an argued case for them, for your original contribution, for the creative element added to the field of study, and so on. In a humanities or literature-based thesis, there might well be a more *organic* structure of chapters, focusing on different themes and developing issues and authors, and a summary is not needed. The summary could also be part of the final chapter – the Conclusion.

Conclusion – All theses have a conclusion. This establishes the importance of your work, states its contribution clearly and summarises the main points you have made where, when and how. It rounds off your arguments, even if there are still points open for further work and for questioning. At this point – in theses that seek to suggest change or developments, to contribute new ideas and strategies, and so cause development and change – there could well be a section for recommendations, as there is in a standard report. If your work does indeed seek change, then it is essential that you think, throughout the research, *how* you are going to make constructive and realistic recommendations based on your findings.

Appendices, statistical tables, illustrations, and so on – These might appear in the main text where the argument using them appears. They may however, all appear in the appendices. Ensure each one is clearly labelled and referenced where it is used in the thesis. If they are not explained in the body of the thesis, explain them fully here.

References – If you are using footnotes, they appear at the foot of each page, and endnotes appear usually at the end of each chapter. Some writers leave all the endnotes to the end of the thesis, collected chapter by chapter at that point and integrated with the references. References can be signalled in the text by a number (1) that leads to the endnote and reference, or by a shortened form of the actual reference. For example, 'Phillips, E.M. and Pugh, D.S. (1994) *How to Get a PhD: A Handbook for Students and Their Supervisors*, 2nd edn (Buckingham: Open University Press)' (placed at the end of the thesis in the References section) can be signalled in your actual text as '(Phillips and Pugh 1994)'.

Bibliography – This is usually an alphabetical list of the books, journals, and so on that you have used. Not all theses have a bibliography, but it is a handy reference for any reader.

Ensure you have read the university guidelines about layout, typeface, presentation, binding, references, and so on, and that your work conforms to all of these. Many theses have difficulties just because of presentation, which is a waste if the hard work has been done and the presentation quality lets this down.

You will need to be able to pull together a clear and coherent defence of your thesis, ready for the viva. We will look at preparation of the viva next.

Please note: If you are undertaking an arts or humanities dissertation or thesis, you will find it useful to look back at Chapter 17. The shape of these works is different from those in the social sciences, although all contain:

- a title/abstract
- an introduction
- chapters defining the exploration/investigation/research
- a conclusion
- references/footnotes
- a bibliography.

Presentation – some final issues – You will need to pay particular attention to the quality of the presentation, since it would be a great pity to jeopardise your chances of attaining your PhD, MPhil, EdD or Master's because of slapdash bibliographical details, inconsistencies and poor presentation, which detract from the argument, coherence and originality of the thesis itself.

The greatest presentation problem is one aligned to rigour, cohesion and originality. If you have only gathered information – rather than moving the boundaries of the study onwards and having something original to add, contextualising your work – then this will show in the thesis, and its lower-level quality will be recognised. It is perfectly satisfactory to describe, relate, list and chart in some subjects at GCSE level – but certainly not at PhD level – rather, beyond that, it is necessary to concentrate on coherence, articulation and clarity.

Things to do

- Review your own dissertation or thesis so far.
- How far does it conform to the desirable qualities of work at this level?
- What will you still need to do to get it to conform to them?
- Organise a 'to do' list to bring your work up to the required level, including running it past a trustworthy, critical friend for comments on the content, coherence and presentation.
- Make sure you know the dissertation or thesis really thoroughly.
- Try producing a two-page outline of it, containing the abstract and a short version of methods, context and findings. Then answer the questions:

  - What has been discovered and developed?
  - Why does it matter?

- This will start to make it manageable for you to prepare for the viva.

Conclusion

We have looked at:

☐ The shape of a Master's, MPhil, PhD or EdD thesis

☐ Qualities of content, presentation to consider

☐ What makes a good MA, MPhil and PhD in terms of shape and content

☐ The structure of an effective thesis

Look at Chapter 24, for how to match the developed shape of your thesis against your initial proposal, and elements of writing style.

● Further reading

Brown, R. (1992) 'The "Big Picture" about Managing Writing', in O. Zuber-Skerritt and Y. Ryan, *Quality in Postgraduate Education* (London: Kogan Page).

Dahlgren, L. and Marton, F. (1978) 'Students' Conceptions of Subject Matter: An Aspect of Learning and Teaching in Higher Education', *Studies in Higher Education*, 3 (1).

Entwistle, A.C. and Entwistle, N.J. (1992) 'Experiences of Understanding in Revising for Degree Examinations', *Learning and Instruction*, 2: 1–22.

Entwistle, N.J. and Ramsden, P. (1983) *Understanding Student Learning* (London: Croom Helm).

Marton, F., Dall'Alba, G. and Beaty, E. (1993) 'Conceptions of Learning', *Journal of Educational Research*, 19 (3): 277–300.

Meyer, J.H.F. and Boulton-Lewis, G.M. (1997) 'The Reflections on Learning Inventory', University of Durham.

Meyer, J.H.F. and Kiley, M. (1998) 'An Exploration of Indonesian Postgraduate Students' Conceptions of Learning', *Journal of Further and Higher Education*, 22: 287–98.

Nightingale, P. (1992) 'Initiation in Research through Writing', in O. Zuber-

Skerritt, *Starting Research: Supervision and Training* (Brisbane QLD: Tertiary Education Institute).

Todd, L. (1997) 'Supervising Overseas Post-Graduate Students: Problem or Opportunity', in D. McNamara, and R. Harris (eds) *Quality in Higher Education for Overseas Students* (London: Routledge).

Winter, R. (1993) 'Continuity and Progression: Assessment Vocabularies for Higher Education', Unpublished research report data, Anglia Ruskin University Faculty of Health and Social Work, Chelmsford.

Wisker, G. (1998) 'The Research as Learning Questionnaire', Anglia Ruskin University, Cambridge.

28 Preparing Your Thesis and Dissertation – Coherence, Conclusions and Conceptual Level Work

This chapter looks ‹

▶ Completing your the‹
or dissertation
▶ Ensuring everything ‹
springs from and fit‹
with the conceptual
framework
▶ Reviewing the
proposal to define y‹
achievements and
complete the thesis‹
dissertation

You should have been writing up drafts of your work as you proceeded with the research, so that:

- You do not have to write the whole thesis or dissertation up in a rush at the end (a very daunting task)
- You will have worked out some of the difficulties and some of the complex thoughts and expression as you write
- Some of your work could be shared with a supervisor and some published or delivered at conferences/to your peers at 'work-in-progress' sessions.

Think about the writing of your thesis or dissertation as 'telling the story' of your aims, questions, the context in which your work has been set, the research methods and research work carried out, and the findings resulting from your research. It also makes a point about why you carried out the research and what kind of a contribution the research makes to knowledge in the field. It is like a story following a route or plan, and it shows development and achievement.

Most importantly, you need to ensure that your conceptual framework, the framework of the ideas, themes, questions and methods you have developed:

- relates closely to the main research question(s) you are asking and enables them to be asked
- is clearly underpinning, informing and 'driving through' the whole thesis so that all of it fits in with the conceptual framework, the

methods act as vehicles to discover what you set out to discover, and the findings and analyses all spring logically from it.

The conceptual framework is a framework of the thesis as a whole. As you near completion of your thesis, it is useful to look back at the original proposal. Of course, much of what you have completed will differ from that proposal because, in active research, our plans change, results make us change direction, and access to information and responses causes us to pursue variations on lines of thought and action. Not all of your research activities or your findings will conform to your original plan and proposal. In fact, if you have only found what you set out to find and there have been no risks, no revelations, surprises or developments in your thought along the way, your work might well be in danger of being neither demanding nor original enough for a PhD or EdD (if that is what you are problem solving and studying for. Originality can be less of an issue with an MA and MPhil). However, your supervisor will have been advising you about originality and development, and so you should have a good sense of how well developed and original your work is before you start to write up for the final time. The important thing now, at this final stage, is to review your proposal, capture the whole process of the research, and set about describing and explaining this, and then detailing, analysing and drawing conclusions from your findings.

Things to do

Look back at the requirements for the proposal – this will give you a sense of the actual structure of the thesis itself. Remember, you need to explore and express your plans about all these key areas. Thought-provoking comments – about how you can respond now to how the elements of the proposal relate to your work as you start to write up finally – should appear in italics.

● The proposal – revisited

In your proposal you needed to address the following areas (or similar):

- **Indicative title** – What will you call your thesis? It is better to pose questions and to make a suggestion about links in argument rather than to give a single word or area of study.

At the writing-up stage, you might want to refine your title but, before you do so, check whether this is possible in your university regulations. You might have to stick with the original title.

● **Aim and focus of the study** – This should suggest the underlying research area, and your main question and sub-questions. Hopefully, it will eventually form the abstract of your thesis. Think about it carefully. What are you really exploring, arguing, trying to find out, hoping to find out and then suggest? What links with what in your mind?

Has your focus changed? Can you explore this as you start to write your abstract and your introduction? It might well have changed for very good reasons in relation to what you have discovered and a need for a change in direction. You will need to talk about this in the early parts of your thesis.

● **Context for the research** – What issues, problems, history, background, others' questions and work carried out so far elsewhere in this field provide a context, an academic culture, and an ongoing set of questions, thoughts and discoveries for your own work? How is it contributing to academic work in this area?

Ask yourself now: How is it making a contribution? You will need to state this quite clearly in your abstract. The ground describing others' work and how yours will relate to it and take it on further will be laid in your literature review chapter and in your introduction (these might be one and the same). The closing parts of your thesis will make a case for your contribution to knowledge and thought in these areas. What your work adds to the field of knowledge is a key issue in deciding whether it is of Master's or of doctorate level.

● **Theoretical perspectives and interpretations** – From where have you taken your theories? From what kind of framework? What are the underpinning theoretical perspectives informing your ideas – for example, feminist theory or Marxist theory?

How clearly do you feel you have expressed your theoretical underpinning? How far does your work, as explored and described in the thesis, genuinely seem to be underpinned by theories and obviously flow from them? It is important to explain this in the abstract briefly, and in the introduction or theory chapter, and throughout the thesis it should be clear and logical. It is this kind of coherence that an examiner will be looking for.

- **Research design** – How will you go about collecting information, carrying out literature searches, and so on? Provide an outline of the different activities you will undertake at what points in your research, and do a critical path analysis of this.

  This will be explored in your methods chapter. You need to check that your research design underpins the whole process of the thesis and runs throughout the writing up. If you changed some of your research design as you proceeded with your work, you need to explore how and why this happened, and what it has led to.

- **Research methodology and methods** – What is the research methodology underpinning your research? What methods or vehicles and strategies are you going to use and why? How do they link with and help inform and develop each other?

  You will need to outline this briefly in the abstract and explore it in the methods chapter, if you have one. (If you are doing an arts thesis, you will probably not have a separate chapter for methods.) As with 'research design', above, it is important to ensure that you explain why and whether you have developed or changed your methods. The decisions you made to add/remove a questionnaire, add a focus group or expand into another area of work are important and need explaining and exploring.

- **Ethical considerations** – Many dissertations and theses have ethical considerations, and these will be particularly complex when you are using human subjects. Obviously, if you are involved in medical research this would be so, but it is also true of protecting the identities of those who give you information from questionnaires, focus groups or interviews. You will need to take care when asking certain sorts of personal questions or using documents that refer to people alive or dead, and so on.

  Your completion of an ethics statement might have to be in addition to the thesis and will also form part of your introductory discussion and inform the whole thesis. That is, the ethics need to be clearly in place and in practice in your work.

- **Outline and plan of study** – This part of the proposal asks you to indicate what you think would be the timeline for your research activities and/or the main features of each of your chapters. It would be useful to revisit this at different points in your ongoing research and consider how they are developing, whether any early findings are changing these.

Look back and see whether the chapters flow from this outline plan and, if not, you might well need to explore and explain why this is so, or even re-order some of them if this makes the thesis more coherent. You will probably talk about this in your abstract.

- **Justification for level of award** – An MPhil or PhD usually involves this question. You will need to describe and discuss what you feel your research will contribute to the field of knowledge, the development of arguments and the research culture. What kinds of practices, thoughts and arguments cannot move forwards? How can it make a difference? Why does it matter and why is it obviously at this level? Is it sufficiently serious, broad, deeply questioning and original? Such comments go into the abstract, and into your conclusion.

At this stage, you do not need to make a direct claim about the level of the award as this is assumed in your submission for an MPhil, PhD or EdD, but you do need to make sure that it is clear throughout your work, set out in the abstract and rounded off in the conclusion. The level of your research, its contribution to knowledge and thought in the field of study, its originality and its clear development are all important elements of your work. They need mentioning throughout the thesis and need to be very clear throughout the thesis by virtue of its organisation and logic.

- **Primary references** – There should be 10 or 12 of these included in your submission. You will need to check that you have all your references, placed either at the end of your chapters or the end of your thesis.

Things to do

On your own, then share with a colleague or friend (if you can), please consider your thoughts about your own work in relation to the areas of the proposal examined above. You will find it useful to consider each of them for about five minutes and then answer these questions.

Looking back at the outline for the proposal, at the shape of your own proposal, and at the thoughts and suggestions in italics, determine:

- How far has your work for this research achieved these aims?
- How far does its shape conform to the broad shape of the proposal?
- How far has it found out what it set out to find out, or found out other things?

- How far has it taken the expected decisions in the process of the research, or has it taken different decisions?
- How far has it pursued the expected route of the research and produced the kinds of results you expected? How far has it pursued different routes of research, in practice, and produced somewhat different results? Why?
- What do you feel you have achieved with your research?
- Does your work matter and, if so, how does it matter?
- What does it contribute to knowledge and thought in your field?

These are important questions.

As you start or continue to write up your thesis in its final form, you will need to think not only about the process of the research itself, but also the shape of the thesis. Again, looking back at the shape of the proposal will help you with this, since much of the outline work carried out at that stage will be similar to the shape of the completed thesis.

Conclusion

We have looked at:

☐ Ensuring a clear and coherent conceptual framework underpins all your dissertation or thesis as you finally write it up

☐ Rewriting elements of the proposal to see if they have been achieved in the final thesis or dissertation.

● Further reading

Murray, R. (2000) *Writing a Thesis* (Buckingham: Open University Press).

Murray, R. (2004) *Writing for Academic Journals* (Buckingham: Open University Press).

Winter, J. (1995) *Skills for Graduates in the 21st Century* (London: Association of Graduate Recruiters).

Wisker, G. (2005) *The Good Supervisor* (Basingstoke: Palgrave Macmillan).

29 Preparing for and Undertaking Your Viva

If you have been working for an MPhil, PhD or EdD in the UK, Europe, the USA and some parts of Australasia (but not Australia and much of New Zealand), you will need to be 'vivaed' on your work. This involves answering questions on, and defending, your work to examiners in an organised session based around your thesis.

It is important, as you prepare for your viva, that you know your thesis well and that you have had some experience in explaining, exploring and defending it.

Things to do

Think about the following questions as you prepare for your viva, and fill in some of the spaces below:

- What is really important about my work? What kind of contribution does it make to knowledge in the field in which I have been working? What might others do with it?
- What are the questions underpinning the research? (Try one or two short points.)
- What is the conceptual framework of my work?
- How are questions underpinned and asked by way of the theories and literature?
- How do the methodology and methods enable me to ask and consider the questions and deal with the ideas?
- How do the findings fit in?
- What methodology have I used (interventionalist or non-interventionalist, positivist or postpositivist ...)?
- What kinds of processes and methods have I used in my work? For example:

  – interviews
  – questionnaires, document analysis – asking questions

  – observations, case studies – observing and reflecting
  – reflective journal
  – experimentation, pre- and post-test, establish a test, models
    experimenting

Can I defend their use? Could I have used other methods
instead?

● What kinds of problems have I had in my research? What kinds
  of drawbacks, changes and new questions? How did I deal with
  and overcome any problems? Can I talk about moments of
  decision-making, surprises and problems and how I handled
  them?
● What have been the major findings from my research so far?
  (Try to establish a few *short* points.)

Now move on to speculate a little. You will need to know who your
examiners are in order to answer these questions:

● What might my examiners be interested in/want to ask about?
● What are their specialist areas?
● What is really typical in my field?
● Is there anything contentious in my work?

● Being prepared

You need to prepare to explain the conceptual framework, and how it underpins and drives everything in the research. This is conceptual-level work,
your research problematises given beliefs and ideas, and enables you to
contribute meaning and understanding to definable areas – emphasise and
explain this. Generally, you can describe the main issues and answer questions about interesting or strange problems. Describe the importance of your
findings, why the research matters and what it contributes to knowledge and
understanding in the subject.

Have some very brief notes handy for when you go into the viva (use the
sheet of questions you have just completed). Be sure you know where some
of your answers could be found in the thesis.

● Make reference points in your notes/answers; and
● Place post-its in the thesis where you think you could be asked
  questions, or where you want to make specific points.

There are many pieces of advice about the form and functions of the viva and ways of handling it. Joe Wolfe (School of Physics, University of New South Wales, Sydney) has some advice for those of his students who undertake vivas; wise suggestions for handling examiners and their questions by somewhat flattering them without entering into a *real* argument, as distinct from a discussion, unless there is nothing to lose. There *are* awkward examiners – this is a human interaction – but a respectful exchange is what you hope for, and usually get. Joe Wolfe notes:

- The phrase 'That's a good question' is exceedingly useful. It flatters the asker and may get him/her onside, or less offside; it gives you time to think; it implies that you have understood the question and assessed it already and that you have probably thought about it before. If necessary, it can be followed by the stalwart 'Now the answer to that is not obvious/straightforward ...' which has the same advantages.

- If the nightmare ever did come true, and some questioner found a question that put something in the work in doubt ... mind you this is thankfully very rare ... then what? Well, the first thing would be to concede that the question imposes a serious limitation on the applicability of the work: 'Well, you have identified a serious limitation in this technique, and the results have to be interpreted in the light of that observation.' The questioner is then more likely to back off and even help answer it, whereas a straight denial may encourage him/her to pursue more ardently. Then go through the argument in detail – showing listeners how serious it is while giving yourself time to find flaws in it or to limit the damage that will ensue. In the worst case, one would then think of what can be saved. But all this is hypothetical because this won't happen.

Source: http://www.phys.unsw.edu.au/%7Ejw/viva.html)

You might find it useful to consider some of the questions that Peter Hartley of the University of Bradford and I have developed for a CD-ROM 'Interviewer: Postgraduate Viva', which are explored fully in *The Good Supervisor*. My own students have found the exercise of asking and answering these broad question areas most useful as a way of developing confidence ready for the viva. But please note – a health warning – while they enable confidence-building because they give you the chance to articulate your ideas and arguments, they in no way offer the opportunity to explore the specific features of your own piece of research – they are general and generic. Still, I hope they can be useful to you.

● Postgraduate viva

Think of asking yourself some of the following questions:

Choosing your topic

1   Tell me how your research area and topic/career has developed?
2   What made you choose this research?
3   What was your research question?
4   What attracted you to work in this context?
5   If you were starting again today, would you change your research question in any way?

Concepts and theories

6   Could you explain briefly your conceptual framework?
7   What are the main theories you have chosen to underpin your work?
8   Why did you choose these main theories?
9   Did you consider other theories or approaches?
10   In retrospect, are there any other theories or approaches you could have considered?

Your research methodology

11   What methodologies and research methods did you select and why?
12   Why did you not select other methodologies/methods?
13   How did you gain access to your sample(s)?
14   In retrospect, are there any other theories, approaches or research methods you could have considered?
15   What is the most important thing you have learned about research methodology from doing this work?

How the research progressed

16   What stages did your research go through?
17   Were there any particularly problematic moments that caused difficulties? How did you overcome these?

18   Did you need to make any changes to your methods when you were designing or carrying out your research? Why and how?

19   Did you have any particularly revelatory or surprise moments? What did you do?

20   If you were given the opportunity to start again, would you do anything different?

Your research results

21   How did you analyse your data?

22   Why did you choose this form of analysis?

23   What were your main findings?

24   How do these findings relate to your previous work in this field?

25   What is the most important implication of these findings?

The importance of your work

26   How would you justify your work as being at the level of a PhD?

27   How do you feel your work fills a gap in knowledge?

28   Why does your work matter?

29   Are you going to take this work any further?

30   Would you suggest any further work for other future researchers?

What follows are extracts from the 'Interviewer: Postgraduate Viva' CD-ROM (Wisker and Hartley 2006) as examples of questions, tips and what is expected. These could provide extended activities for a mock viva or insights for a student working alone. Extended versions of this material can be found in *The Good Supervisor* (2005).

You could:

- look at and listen to the question
- answer
- tape yourself answering
- then look at the hints, tips and examiners' views on your own or with a friend/your supervisor, and *reflect* on the quality of your response and how you can improve the response. Consider what else you might say, what expressions to avoid and how to be absolutely clear in your answers.

These are some of the questions on the CD-Rom, which you might like to try out. To add to these, discuss with your supervisor what other questions might come up at the viva. Some will be about the decisions made, the design and experience of the research, choices made, problems met and overcome, and how you might undertake the work differently next time. Do remember that the questions given here are very generic. While they most probably come up in each viva in some form or other, they will be differently phrased and the body of the questions you will meet is much more likely to engage specifically with YOUR thesis and its subject matter, its contribution to knowledge, So, these questions are just a beginning – you need to devise and try out the answers to a few more specific questions. Even then, the viva could well surprise you beyond these practice questions, as each examiner has his or her own issues and own views about your thesis. So, you cannot memorise answers and hope to reel them off – each viva is different.

Having said that, the generic questions can help you prepare, and very many of the students who have used them (my own and other people's supervisees) have found them useful, to help them gain confidence in speaking, and to gain fluency in the more conceptual kinds of language and comments, so please try them out.

● Generic questions

Choosing your topic

1 How has your research career developed?

Hints and tips

- Did you explain what choices you have made to reach this point?
- Did you look at what kind of research you have been doing and why this interested you?
- Did you demonstrate your enthusiasm for research?
- Did you show how your interest in the present topic/area developed?

Examiner's view

I *am asking this general question to give the candidate a chance to relax and become less nervous before the really important questions start.*

Concepts and theories

4 Could you explore for me your conceptual framework?

Hints and tips

- Did you explain how the research question(s) relate to or involved some key concepts?
- Did you explain how the research question(s) relate to or involved some key ideas?
- Did you explain how you selected theorists and reading that informed your understanding of the concept and helped you to ask the question(s)? How they provided theoretical perspectives and helped you to engage with debates in the field?
- Did you explain how the methodologies and methods you have used arose from the question and how the theoretical perspectives you have read about developed the question and helped you ask it?

Examiner's view

I am looking to see if you have a thorough sense of the structure and design of your work, and of the concepts underlying it. You need to be able to show how the key concepts or ideas in your work are underpinned by reading in the appropriate theorists and experts, and that the questions you are asking can be asked using the vehicles, the methodologies and methods selected. I am looking for overall coherence throughout the research and an expression of it in the thesis that you can explore here in discussion.

5 Can you explore any particularly problematic moments that caused difficulties? How did you address and overcome these?

Hints and tips

- Did you explain any stages that caused problems for you and how you overcame or addressed these?
- Did you explore any moments when the research met difficulties, such as an inability to discover appropriate theories and theorists, to work at a conceptual level to draw conceptual conclusions, or other kinds of difficult moments when the sample disappeared or you were refused access, when a specific methodology or method did not yield the information and ideas needed and so you had to redesign the research approach differently and to express it differently?

- Did you explain how you identified problems and what problem-solving strategies you used to overcome them and proceed with the research?

Examiner's view

This question seeks to discover how you deal with problems such as scientific experiments not working, the sample disappearing, difficulties with analysis and so on. It shows me that you can spot, deal with and solve problems, and so can take a creative, responsive, developmental questioning and problem-solving attitude to your work.

These are fleshed out versions of some of the questions asked, and tips towards answers on the CD-ROM 'Interviewer: Postgraduate Viva' (Wisker and Hartley 2006). You might like to develop your own further, and/or ask these of your student, exploring the expected kinds of response. Students at a distance can be asked to send written responses to the mock viva questions and to rehearse them with a friend or a colleague, and with you in a last minute mock viva before they go into the real thing. However, although these questions have been put together based on research and experience – my own, that of Peter Hartley, John Hartley (Hartley and Fox 2003), Trafford and Leshem (2002), and Wisker and Robinson (2002) – students need to be made aware that there is no guarantee these will be asked, though some almost certainly will.

These are generic – that is, *not* the subject- and thesis-specific questions that will very probably also be asked. It is useful to work with your student over these latter kinds of questions based on the following thoughts:

- Is there a particular 'take', interpretation, approach, conceptual interpretation of knowledge or any key issues in the subject underpinning this thesis that will need clarifying and defending? What are the competing conceptualisations or versions?
- Is there a particular reading of a key theory, belief, ideology or text that needs clarifying and defending?
- Are there any relatively controversial choices, interpretations or arguments about the subject matter that need defending?
- Are there any relatively controversial choices about the use of specific methodology or methods?

(*Source*: *The Good Supervisor*, Wisker 2005)

● Stress management

A viva is a potentially stressful experience. Think about ways of managing your stress so that you can perform well in the actual viva. Persuade a friend to undertake a mock viva with you, so you can practice your defence and learn to manage any stress. It is possible that your university offers training in preparation for the viva. If so, do take advantage of this. Although it is not an interview, it has similar stresses, and being prepared will help you deal with these.

- Make sure you are not stressed, let your stress drive you, rather than overwhelm you
- Control your breathing consciously, breathe deeply and slowly
- Practise relaxation
- Concentrate on repeating and rehearsing your main points, so that you are engaged and coherent
- Make sure you are well rested and have ingested food and drink appropriately
- Do not wear clothes that are awkward or too tight, you need to be alert but also relaxed
- Remember that you would not have got this far if your work was not passable and interesting
- Relax before you go into the viva, get some fresh air, and sit quietly and reflectively
- Take with you a copy of your thesis, with annotations (for example, on post-its – but not too many – stuck in the thesis) and a summary sheet of your main points, and so on
- Make sure you really know your own work – its conceptual framework, how each part fits together and what you have achieved.

● The viva voce – a brief outline

Present: Two external examiners (or one internal and two external)
             Possibly chaired by a university research degrees committee member or similar
             The candidate (and translator)
             Supervisors – at the discretion of the candidate.
             Supervisors may not speak.
Duration: Unspecified – 30–90 minutes or more

Room:	A comfortable and informal setting (tea, coffee and water should be available)
Atmosphere:	Friendly, collegial and non-inquisitorial
Purpose:	To examine the academic content and scholastic level of the thesis
	To provide candidates with the opportunity to defend their thesis
	To explore and explain the design, methodology and outcomes of the research
	To discuss the research from the perspective of 'experts in the area'
	To provide evidence to help the external examiners arrive at a judgement about the defence of the thesis
	To enable the external examiners to make a recommendation to the university about the thesis.

(Adapted from a handout by Dr Vernon Trafford, Anglia Ruskin University, 1999.)

Useful tips during the viva

You might find these ideas and tips useful:

- Sit down and place the thesis at hand, but do not open it
- Thank the examiners for the opportunity to talk with them about your work
- Answer questions clearly and concisely
- Use the arguments, ideas and examples from your thesis in answering the questions
- Back up your cohesive and coherent piece of research by making it clear how the conceptual framework links questions, themes, methodology, methods, fieldwork, findings and conclusions
- Be able to refer to key texts you have used, and agree or disagree with
- Use eye contact
- Do not fumble through your thesis – use bookmarkers to allow you easy access to pages you feel might be useful (but not all of the pages, mark key chapters, problem points and any original points you would like to discuss)
- If the examiners do not seem to mention what you think are key issues, new findings or important contributions, mention them and ask what they think about these issues, engage them in conversation

- If they point out problems, think on the spot and let them know if you do not know/agree/disagree/or indicate that these issues led to further work beyond the scope of this thesis
- Do not try to answer questions that you do not understand; ask them to clarify them
- Do not introduce new information and new ideas that are not in the thesis (this could lead to suggestions that you go off and do more work now) but do recognise (and say) that other people might be interested in pursuing these ideas and areas, or that you might do so at postdoctoral level
- Make sure you relate to and answer the questions of each examiner
- Thank the examiners at the end of the session
- It is rather like a job interview – but you are not in competition with other people: it is all about your work
- If everyone relaxes and talks as intellectual equals about your work, you will probably have very little else to do to it
- Good luck.

Remember – many candidates have to make revisions (some large, some small), so do not be dismayed if you are asked to revise. You will need to clarify the work required, schedule it in and get on with it.

Conclusion

In this chapter we have looked at:

☐ Preparing for the viva – knowing your thesis and the viva process

☐ How to do well in your viva

☐ Managing revisions.

● Further reading

Hartley, J. and Fox, C. (2003) *Assessing the Mock Viva: The Experience of British Doctoral Students* (Keele, UK: Keele University).

Holbrook, A., Bourke, S., Lovat, T. and Fairbairn, H. (2006) 'PhD Thesis Examination: Overview on an ARC Discovery Grant Project 2003–06' SORTI Group, University of Newcastle Australia, HERDSA News, 38 (2).

Kiley, M. and Mullins, G. (2005) 'Examining the Examiners: How Inexperienced Examiners Approach the Assessment of Research Theses', *International Journal of Educational Research*, 41 (2): 121–35.

Trafford, V. (1999) Handout, Anglia Ruskin University.

Trafford, V.N. and Leshem, S. (2002) 'Starting at the End to Undertake Doctoral Research: Predictable Questions as Stepping Stones', *Higher Education Review*, 35: 31–49.

Wisker, G. (2005). *The Good Supervisor* Basingstoke: Palgrave Macmillan.

Wisker, G. and Hartley, P. (2006) 'Interviewer: Postgraduate Viva', CD-ROM.

30 Dealing with Corrections – Life after the Viva . . .

See the viva as a:

▶ Turning point, a cata-
lyst in your working
life to enable you to
move on
▶ Rite of passage for
further entry into the
academic community
and beyond
▶ Development process
▶ Prelude to a period c
relief and celebratior
of your efforts, what
ever the result

The viva feels like, and in many ways is, the end of the PhD process. It is the culmination of years of research, writing, editing and polishing, re-reading and owning all aspects of your work. In one sense, it is an end to this stage of your work, but it is also a turning point in your work, and your development as a researcher. For comments on the shape of a viva, see Trafford and Leshem (2002). Universities have several categories of response following PhD assessment, and these usually range between:

- Award without any modifications
- Award with minor modifications
- Award with modifications that could take up to 6 months (some universities do not have this central category, and so decisions may seem either very generous or a little unkind)
- Major modifications (also known as resubmission in some instances)
- Fail (usually with opportunities for resubmission).

Since as few as 12 per cent of UK PhDs are awarded without any work at all to do to the thesis (the first category), it is psychologically helpful to expect there will be some modifications and improvements to carry out on your thesis following the viva, whatever the response. In fact, it is a good idea to consider the viva as a developmental stage in the production of a really good thesis that does justice to your hard work and contribution to knowledge. In this developmental process, the thesis will be enormously aided in its improvement by the experience of being read, commented on and discussed between yourself and academic colleagues (the examiners), experts in the field (or methodology) acting (one hopes) as critical friends, as well as judges and assessors of your work.

Use your supervisor and support wisely – It is useful to work with your supervisor to be ready for the viva, experience mock vivas with friends and colleagues, use generic viva preparation sessions and materials (for example, the CD-ROM 'Interviewer: Postgraduate Viva' 2006 – Peter Hartley, Bradford University, and Gina Wisker, University of Brighton, or Rowena Murray's book (2003) and video on the viva).

Supervisor involvement ranges from being one of two examiners, through being a silent observer to being excluded from the viva. In all but the last instance, your supervisor can take notes throughout the viva and, more specifically, in the examiners' summing up of advice/requirements, in order to identify and clarify the exact areas of work that are needed to finalise or resubmit the thesis. Some universities issue the full formal response of required changes immediately, others take longer. The full verbal response usually has a final status and will be repeated in the written response. Check this, and work with your supervisor immediately after the viva to use the verbal, then written, response to develop an agenda for tidying up, revision, further work or whatever is required. Be careful to get full final instructions and a clear sense of when the work is due, and by whom it will be assessed and agreed, so that you can proceed to the award. The sooner you agree an agenda and can realise, plan for and start on the work, the more you will feel this is a developmental stage – the end is in sight – rather than a vague state with some indistinct insurmountable hurdles in between, and you can congratulate yourself on all that has been achieved so far. If you need to re-register with the library and renegotiate supervisions with your supervisory team, now is the time to do this as you agree the work agenda and timings.

● What next?

The completion of the research project is an exciting moment, but it can also leave you feeling somewhat adrift – this is what you have been heading towards, working towards for such a long time, it has taken your life over – what next?

Continuing the supervisor–colleague relationship

The supervisory process does not end with the successful dissertation, or thesis. Indeed, what you might well have established with your supervisor is an ongoing academic working relationship. Certainly, you can expect some hints, tips, suggestions and invitations to carry out further work, further research, publications, information about conferences, or suggestions of furthering your academic career.

Sharing your work with others

One of the major gains from a successful piece of research is your (further) entrance into the academic community. Research students develop and share their work with others and this peer exchange and support helps to build academic communities. Getting your work published while you are working on a thesis is a desirable and necessary part of research, as it enables you to contribute to the research culture in which your work is placed, as well as getting your name known in the field among other specialists. Getting work published from it afterwards is essential. You might not have the whole thesis published as a book – it could perhaps be better used and more widely read as a series of articles or other contributions. You will almost certainly have to work on any thesis for publication as tone, length, structure and audience are different for a publication than for a thesis, so do not be put off by publisher and editor comments – these, too, are developmental.

Transferable skills

Cryer (1997) suggests doctoral students should recognise that generic, postgraduate skills developed during their study could equip them for employment in a variety of contexts, while Francis (1997) and Leonard (2001) point out that personal expectations are more likely to be achieved than are career expectations.

> Surveys suggest students' personal expectations are more likely to be fulfilled by doing a doctorate than career aspects. Few regret doing a doctorate, or what it has cost to them. Of course, the most disgruntled may get left out of samples; there are certainly horror stories of bad supervision, wasted time, too heavy teaching requirements on low pay, and exploitation in labs; and initial hopes may have been changed and modified along the way. Nonetheless, 'a self forged through tackling the difficulties of research, especially when stress from other sources is high, is a new self. So is the self that overcomes the doubts about ability to do the work'. (Francis 1997: 18, Leonard, 2001: 59)

Contribution to developing knowledge in the disciplines, professional practice and more generally in society is a very important product of research. You should be encouraged to continue with research if this has been something you enjoy and for which you have developed/are still developing the skills. You might find it useful to identify the kinds of skills that have developed during the course of your research, since many of these are directly transferable into paid work, and the achievement of others suggests to yourself and employers your ability to undertake a whole variety of projects and roles. Indeed, in the light of the UK Quality Assurance Agency requirements following the Roberts review in 2002, and with the increased emphasis on research training in Australasia, you will be expected to have undertaken research development programmes and processes that enable you to develop and be aware of the development of a range of transferable skills and attributes, some practical, some concerning attitudes, lifelong learning, career planning. Identification of transferable graduate and post-graduate research-related skills also enhances self-esteem, as well as opportunities on the job market.

● Celebrate

Finally, whatever the result, whatever future work and sharing is involved, celebrate – reward yourself for the long hard journey of problem solving, painstaking foraging, analysis and writing up, and exciting revelations. This is a real turning point, your life will never be quite the same again. Make the most of it. Well done.

● Further reading

Cryer, P. (1997) *The Research Student's Guide to Success* (2nd edn) (Buckingham: Open University Press).

Francis, H. (1997) 'The Research Process', in N. Graves and V. Verna (eds) *Working for a Doctorate: A Guide for the Humanities and Social Sciences* (London: Routledge).

Leonard, D. (2001) *A Women's Guide to Doctoral Studies* (Buckingham: Open University Press).

Murray, R. (2003) *How to Survive Your Viva* (Buckingham: Open University Press).

Trafford, V. and Leshem, S. (2002) 'Questions in a Doctoral Viva', in UK Council For Graduate Education Research Degree Examining Symposium (London).

Wisker, G. and Hartley, P. (2006) 'Interviewer: Postgraduate Viva' (CD-ROM developed as the result of National Teaching Fellowships).

31 Presentations, Conferences and Publishing

An important part of your work as a research student is sharing and presenting your work in progress with others. Research is a contribution to knowledge and to ideas in the subject(s) and, as a researcher, you are part of a larger research community that shares its ideas and moves forward through that sharing. Additionally, sharing your work with others helps you to clarify, control and evaluate it. It also enables you to seek analytical responses from others, and this can help you develop in your work. You might well be worried that such sharing can show up the faults in your work, and you could also be rather apprehensive about the public appraisal presentation seems to offer. But a well-planned presentation of work in progress can provide immensely useful feedback to help you in your research work. Attending the presentations of others can enable you to stand back from your own work, advise them on points in theirs, and reflect on the ways in which you can develop your own, illuminated by strategies others have adopted. Sharing your work in a research community is not about giving it away but, rather, about supportive, analytical critique for constructive purposes. If you decide to become involved in work-in-progress seminars, it is important to ensure that a structured, constructive response is part of the ground rules.

Give: (i) work-in-progress presentations; and (ii) conference presentations at various points during your research, as it is useful to share your work with your peers, and probably also your supervisor. It is also important to share your work with the wider academic community once you feel you have a contribution that they will find useful (do not be too modest, and do not wait too long to do this). There are both informal and formal opportunities to make presentations, as there are a number of differences in terms of formality, length and activity involved. Let us explore these in the first instance:

Work-in-progress presentations – These are essentially a matter of you sharing the work you have carried out to date, the ways you have approached it and why, and what you have discovered. The presentations provide an opportunity to ask questions and to seek support from your peers on some of the developments, issues, points and problems you might have come across. Certain information is possible and some interaction would be a good idea.

Conference presentations – These take several forms. You might be giving a whole paper or running a seminar that consists of a formal paper, followed by questions and prompts for a reaction – rather more like presenting to your peers. You might also be running an interactive workshop session in which, after you have introduced some of your work, you can involve participants in active questioning, trying out activities, engaging with and reflecting on some of your ideas or findings.

Poster presentations – The idea behind a poster presentation is to produce a visually striking and appropriate summary of the main issues, questions and findings of a piece of research or other development. The content is often rather like an abstract with summarised findings. Your role at a conference is to present your point to whoever is interested in hearing about your work and discuss it with them, so you need to put up your poster, stand by it, and talk about it to whoever shows interest.

Whatever the type of format or context of your presentation, you need to:

- define the area of your research that you wish to share and explore
- clarify the questions that this addresses
- contextualise this piece of research in relation to questions for your research so far
- clarify the research strategies and methods you are using
- define and clarify the investigations, questions and findings to date
- organise your information and arguments into the format of a presentation
- invite appropriate others/join in a series of seminars and offer your presentation
- plan to deliver your work several weeks or months ahead so that you have plenty of time to prepare the whole presentation
- decide who else needs to be involved to help you with OHTs (overhead transparencies) and handouts.

In the more conventional presentations you should find the following presentation tips helpful:

Things to do

Decide on an element or part of your research that could form a short presentation. Look below at the planning, preparation and presentation stages and consider what you would need to think of and produce to present your work.

Consider the four Ps

- Plan
- Prepare
- Practise
- Present.

● Plan

Decide when and where you want to present, and to whom. Find out all you can about your audience and their interests and needs. In the case of a research community, find out who else works in your area. Who else is using similar research methods? Who might be interested in your research? Who might be only marginally interested and who might know much more than you do? Who will need introducing to basic concepts before the full presentation?

Decide on the plan and aim of your presentation: (i) to introduce others to your work, select a part of your work and explore it as an example; (ii) to enable you to explore the full shape of your research to date. Be precise.

- Commit yourself to a title and a date for your presentation, select an area that will be of interest to you and to others
- Select a coherent part of your work
- Decide what kinds of questions you hope can be approached in the work
- Decide what kinds of questions about your work in progress can be answered or agreed with by your audience
- Select a manageable part of your research work to date
- Decide on the main point of your presentation or argument
- Carry out a critical path analysis, assessing what work you need to carry out and when, in order to produce a good quality presentation of part of your work to date.

● Prepare

Gather together all the information you need. Carry out the appropriate research to help you answer your questions and fill in facts and information. Ask questions, investigate on the Internet, carry out any research needed, and consult your notes and drafts of papers to date. Carry out any necessary extra reading, but do not become so embroiled in extensive new work that you lose sight of the subject of the paper to be presented.

There are many shapes to a presentation, as is indicated in the many different purposes suggested above. There are also many different ways to organise yourself for this presentation. The two main ways are:

1   to collect and produce an outline and headings, then fill them in with information;
2   to produce a full paper, with headings, and so on, then to extract these.

Either way, you need a more or less full (but not necessarily finished) text with some elegant phrasing and a shorter way of presenting it, so that you can speak from it. Remember, a written text is not in presentation format. Spoken language is much simpler than written language, and you can ensure the more complex parts of your talk/'presentation' are delivered through handouts, and so on, rather than word for word in the talk itself. Audiences find it difficult to follow the complexity of written prose when it is read out rapidly in a presentation.

Audience

Thinking about your audience is not just a matter of working out who could be there and what their interest might be. It also involves producing spoken English at the level at which people can hear and understand your main points, if necessary providing written handouts as back-ups.

- Organise your points under headings, starting with an introduction and selecting main points.
- Decide how to structure your presentation: what will come first, what follows, where to place OHTs, charts and handouts, where to show slides, play video clips or music, and whether to use a visualiser to show a model.
- Organise the charts, slides, video clips, handouts and OHTs as necessary, and write up the presentation.
- You would be well advised to organise your arguments and ideas

under headings in the main text and then to separate them from the main text, perhaps on index cards or in bold, and to collate your points separately on OHTs.

OHTs are very useful for highlighting main points but they need to be carefully produced, as do handouts.

Handouts

We all use handouts if we teach, and also when we give presentations, but why and to what ends? What types are there?

- Lecture/presentation outlines
- Full lecture/presentation note handouts
- Background information
- Examples, samples, cases, extracts and images
- Gapped handouts for completion of notes and answers to questions considered in the course of the presentation
- Interactive handouts that ask audiences to complete a task.

Some dos and don'ts in putting handouts together

Do ensure handouts are:

- legible in terms of copying, layout and clarity of images and words
- laid out in the most appropriate format and shape to make movement around and use of them straightforward and appropriate to the format of the class
- logical in layout, for example, first things first, then what follows, then summaries and further work.

Don't produce handouts that are:

- ugly or badly designed
- cluttered and confusing
- irrelevant to the task, content and context
- illegible – retype and re-copy.

Design a one-page handout that would be suitable for these design needs in this context. In a rough plan, indicate layout, shapes and content. Then define and evaluate why it is useful and appropriate and what, if any, were the difficulties and questions raised while designing and producing it.

Things to do

- Choose any element of your research so far, or a favourite topic not connected to your research
- Decide on a specific context for presenting your work
- Consider the reason for the handout – for example, information and so on (see p. 396)
- For how long would you like this handout to be used – in interaction, as a record forever, or just to provide shape to a talk for now?
- Do you want to use colour, images and interaction?
- What kind of layout, shape, amount and kind of content would best suit your audience in terms of the context and your own presentational strategies?

Design and layout – Decide:

- Who is this handout for?
- When is it for?
- What are the learning outcomes it serves?

Are the content and the shape intended:

- to inform
- to illustrate
- to prompt thought
- to prompt individual or group interaction
- to aid a record/act as the full record, or prompt some further record
- to encourage further study
- for another purpose?

Do you want to use:

- colour
- images
- bullets
- large fonts
- spaces to complete interactions
- desktop publishing formats?

Designing and using OHTs

For a 20-minute talk you need to have no more than four or five OHTs, otherwise all anyone will do is read them. If you want to show charts, statistics, and so on, these can be produced separately or on handouts for people to look at later. One thing to remember is that audiences learn and respond immediately through what they hear and see, and later use the material in their own work if it has been delivered in a transportable fashion with paper and handouts. They do not want to be copying down complex figures and notes, so keep this to a bare minimum. This is why photocopies of your OHTs are useful, to enable audiences to follow the flow of the points you are making when they review the session later, as well as while they are listening and jotting down the odd key point.

The rules for designing and using OHTs are very similar to those of handouts. It is important that they should serve the learning outcomes, be pitched at the right level for the audience, be clear, legible, visible, and well laid-out, uncluttered and totally appropriate.

OHTs can be used to:

- provide an overall shape to a talk or session
- indicate main points and key moments to summarise and move on
- give instructions and the essential information
- suggest reading and suggest interactions and activities
- trace development and movement – for example, through overlays.

How to use them

- Do ensure that the projector is clean, clear and focused. Ensure that there is a spare bulb in case the bulb blows.
- Never project an OHT onto a white board as this reflects, and also can intermingle with your previous writing on the board. Project onto a screen.
- Ensure that the distance between the OHT and the screen is suitable to make the words readable and clear at the back – adjust the clarity of the OHT when you move it, and avoid 'keystoning' – a shape that disfigures the wording and is caused by a flat rather than a slightly angled screen.
- Indicate on the OHT using a pen or pointer, and avoid looking at the screen or blocking the screen while doing so. If you are happy using pointers on the screen – for example, the magic eye of a laser pointer – then do use one, but try not to move it around

confusingly. Normally you would not be pointing at the screen but facing the audience and pointing at the OHP.

- Keep a paper copy of your transparencies to read from, so that you are not turning round to squint at the screen.
- The ideal font size is 24 point – no smaller, and preferably a font that shows up well, such as Times or New York, with gaps between words, well laid-out. If using bold throughout helps, use it.

Using PowerPoint

The ability and opportunity to use PowerPoint is increasing today. PowerPoint can be used to construct whole layouts of OHTs for sessions. It will help you to order these and run off a shrunken version of the OHTs so that they can sit alongside your notes.

PowerPoint can also be used in conjunction with a laptop to deliver a lecture onto a screen, making notes on the screen and interacting with the presentation.

It can enable you to update your notes and OHTs, and to add comments from the session onto the originals as you proceed.

Drawbacks

- It is rather static and pre-prepared. You need to proceed at the pace of your individual OHTs, which can be too slow.
- The tendency to make a separate headline for each transparency means it can take an age to get on to anything complex.
- Running a PowerPoint presentation from an OHP in the dark can reduce concentration.

Your script

Organisation

Write out your opening paragraph clearly, with well-chosen words, and memorise it. This will enable you to feel comfortable, to maintain eye contact with your audience without depending on notes, and to get into your stride. You would be well advised to write out a closing paragraph to which you can jump when your time is up, in the event this might happen before you have completed all you have to say. A neat closing paragraph summing up your main points can enable you to round off the presentation and leave a lasting and positive effect in the minds of the audience.

● Practise

It is important to practise the presentation – not to memorise it and practise too much so that you will feel artificial, but enough to ensure that it is not too long and that the points flow logically and clearly.

If there is enough time for you to use the OHTs and slides, and so on, you might prepare by identifying in your master text (the version with all the headings on) exactly where you might show a slide. Annotating your master script as if it were a production copy of a drama is a good idea – for example:

> 'OHT 2 here'
> 'now refer to handout 3'

and so on. When you are in full flow you might forget key elements, so the wise thing to do is make notes while the timing does not matter. Then, when the timing is crucial, you can jog your mind with such notes and so stick to the coherent organisation you have planned.

You need to assure yourself that if all the technical equipment fails you, you still have the handouts and your script, with bold headings, in colour or underlined, or on card index files. You can speak from this.

As you practise, consider all the elements of the actual presentation.

● Presentation

- Just prior to the presentation, you need to check the room, the projector, other audio-visual aids, the quality of your handouts, and ensure your notes and OHTs are in order.
- Make sure you know where to stand in relation to any audio-visual aids so that you are not blocking them, do not get yourself hemmed in behind too much machinery and too many bits of furniture Give yourself the kind of space you feel you will need. If this is not possible (that is, you are in a group of four, each of whom will speak, and you will have to negotiate getting around each other to the OHP), talk to yourself about the negotiations so that none of it upsets you when it is your turn to speak. Plan what you will do to overcome any physical difficulties that might be thrown in your way.

In the presentation you will need to:

- Engage the attention of the audience. Introduce yourself and your topic, thank them for being there and explain what you hope to achieve in your short presentation.

- Ensure they have sufficient copies of any handouts. Check with them that they can see the OHT and hear you at the back (if it is a big auditorium, this is essential).

- Speak clearly. Try not to gabble your information, or speak so slowly that little is said.

- Place your notes in a position so that you can see them. A lectern seems to cut you off from an audience, however, it does ensure that your notes stay at eye level so that you can see them. During your presentation, it is important to maintain eye contact with the audience, so a lectern it is a good place to put your notes, even if you walk around.

- Ensure your OHTs, and so on, are in the right order and are accessible to the place where you will show them when the time comes.

- Speak very clearly and write, spell, or have handouts for difficult words, terms and names.

- Emphasise the main points by repetition and by indicating them on the OHT with a pencil, pointer or your finger.

- Do not face the OHP screen or any other screen, instead stand slightly behind the projector.

- Try not to block it. Indicate which part of the OHT you are speaking about. Some people learn to reveal parts of an OHT one by one but, potentially, this can be irritating. However, if you put up a very cluttered slide, the audience might spend the whole time trying to decipher and copy it down. So, do keep the OHT slides very clear and simple.

- Try not to read the text out, although, if you mention it very briefly, then it does actually give you the kind of visual structure on which you can depend.

- Ensure that you keep eye contact with the audience. This means not fixing your gaze on one single person, however positive their responses might be, and ensure that you at least give the impression that you can see all around the audience and are trying to engage their attention.

- Avoid appearing like a nodding dog, or a spectator watching a game of tennis, looking from side to side, when making eye contact. Avoid unnecessary personal habits, such as jangling keys and change in your pockets (men), adjusting necklaces and dropping beads (women), pacing back and forth, swaying from side to side, marching, tapping or mangling paper clips and Blu-Tac that may happen to be lying around.

- Avoid irritating speech habits, such as saying 'in a manner of speaking' or making 'um' every other word. Audiences tend to concentrate on the mannerisms rather than the content if there is an excess of mannerism over content. These mannerisms are often just personal traits. So, you do not want to be superhuman or faceless – an automaton – but ask yourself whether you have any mannerisms that are excessive and, if so, whether they might be distracting to your audience, rather than helpful in emphasising what you are saying. If this is so, try and keep a voice in your head that warns you off them and tells you to concentrate on eye contact, pace, tone of voice and presenting your arguments clearly.

Time yourself and try to ensure that you do not run beyond your allotted time, especially if there is someone speaking after you. Ensure that you finish with an organised conclusion, so that you feel you have rounded off your points. It is possible, even if you have prepared and practised, that the timing of the presentation will be different, especially if anyone asks questions.

After the presentation, you can invite questions and be prepared to answer them. Quite often, a rather stiff presentation becomes much more lively at this point, when you are asked about your findings and some special issues, and engage directly with the audience. This can be most rewarding. Think about how to deal with difficult questions, however.

Dealing with difficult questions

There are several sorts of difficult questions and difficult questioners, so do be prepared.

1   There are the difficult questioners, who are merely there to ask you to explain what you have said, or a part of it. It is a matter of being well rehearsed and familiar with your work. This is not the real difficulty. The really difficult questions are from people who want to take issue with your points or with your statistics, and you need to think how to deal with these frequently mischievous interruptions.

2   If someone asks a question part of the way through – and this is not the conventional response in these circumstances – ask them to wait until the end or you will lose your flow – unless it is a simple question that is easily answered. Consider not only the questioner,

but also the other listeners who want to hear you develop your thesis and back it up.

3   If questioned about your statistics, which you cannot actually explain there and then, or if the questioner raises a substantive issue that is not covered in your research (it can happen), you would be well advised to thank them for this and to suggest that you discuss it later as, otherwise, it will hold up the presentation. This prevents them from taking over. You will need to use your initiative to spot whether you feel this is the case, but there are people out there who are good at asking awkward questions – do not be put off by them. Say you have noted their interest and will tackle it later.

Be prepared to give or send members of the audience your whole paper after the presentation. Make sure they have your full referencing details so they can cite you, should they use your work in their own.

Publications

- Why publish?
- Where to publish?
- What to publish?

Getting your work published while you are working on a thesis is desirable, and probably a necessity, but it needs careful managing and steering. It is a necessary part of research, as it enables you to contribute to the research culture in which your work is placed, as well as getting your name known in the field among other specialists.

You will need to start thinking about publishing articles from your thesis as you write it. There is a safeguard here of which to be careful, that is, that only a proportion of your work submitted for the thesis can actually be published (otherwise it is considered to be an already published work rather than a thesis). Also, beware that you might be sacrificing the coherence of your thesis to a desire to get in print. You need both thesis and publications. Producing publishable articles and conference publications while also writing your thesis will require very careful time planning and a particular ruthlessness. Once you have finished your work, submitted it and passed, then you may publish as much of it as you can.

Getting published

Things to do

If you have already published, identify:

- What were the stages of getting published?
- What were the problems and pitfalls?
- What are the tips and guidelines?
- What one specific piece of advice would you give a colleague seeking to be published?

Stages of getting published

Some practical guidelines, tips and examples of good practice developed and shared:

- Be clear about the area(s) in which you wish to write
- Your favourite subject might not be topical and interesting to others
- Can you give a favourite subject a topical spin?
- Can you find something else that is topical and interesting, or of major importance, on which you are working?

Your PhD or Master's thesis or your lecture will not be published as it stands.

Find at least one suitable outlet or forum. Read carefully through any work already published there and identify:

- what sort of area of work they usually publish
- any special treatment and angle likely, any particular flavour or preferred kind of writing
- the tone
- the audience
- complexity and specialist elements
- length, presentation, layout, footnotes, endnotes, referencing, and so on.

Approach these outlets/forums with a suggestion.

- Identify whom to contact – specialist areas and specialist responsibilities.
- Some publishers appreciate a personal approach first to discuss areas of interest.

- Some appreciate recommendations from someone they know.
- Some accept papers/books out of the blue (but this is pretty rare).

Draft a proposal and include specimen material or the draft paper/a chapter and send it to the commissioning editor/relevant person.

Eventually, you will possibly want to publish your work as a book. One main tip is that very few (if any) dissertations or theses go straight into print. They all need reshaping for a different audience.

Draft outline/frequently expected elements of a book proposal

Proposal/outline

This is an introductory piece outlining the main area of argument and interest in the book. Make this accessible in style but ensure it contains the main arguments and main conceptual points you wish the book to put across.

Rationale and audience (can be separate)

Explain why is the book will be:

- topical and interesting. What kinds of readers it might expect (be as full as possible and relevant).
- worth doing right now. What it will contribute to the field of knowledge and ideas.

Market

Carry out market research

What other books, articles, conferences, and so on are there on this? Identify, list and evaluate them, and detail why your work is different, how it adds to existing literature and how it improves on it.

Draft chapters and contents

Include a draft contents page, outlining the major chapters in your book.

Give information on topics and the arguments they develop, some of the work they will refer to (a short paragraph for each).

Include a draft chapter. This can be the introduction, but more usually it would be a chapter from the body of the book.

What happens next?

Absolutely nothing:

Chase it up.

If it all comes back months later, turned down flat, with a shallow excuse (irritating you):

- Contact them to thank them and ask for ways in which it might be better directed at their market. Then redo it.
- Or dump it.
- Or find another outlet and start to gear it all up again towards this outlet. Look back through the stages and see if you can spot where it went wrong.

Where could it have gone wrong?

- The editor you sent it to was too busy skiing/moving/working on another topic.
- The commissioning editor is conservative/radical/it is not their field.
- They have someone else working in this field already and have invested in this/they are more important than you/they have a track record.
- You did not make it clear how topical and appropriately written your book was going to be.
- It needs a sponsor.
- It was a bad idea anyway.
- It was not well worked-out in the proposal.

If they like it and they want you to write more about it so they can judge it better:

- Weigh up the investment. Carry out the writing unless you do not want to go any further (intuition and long conversations help here).
- Send them the next version with a letter.
- Usual wait time, and so on.
- Follow up with a call.
- Follow up again.

If it is accepted:

- Be very clear about the terms and conditions of any contract.
- Who owns the copyright?
- Is there an advance?
- How do you get royalties? Will you have to pay the advance back out of your own pocket if the book is pulped within six weeks?
- Are there any overseas rights and what is your cut of these?
- Do they intend to go into paperback too?

- What is their practice with regard to publicity, marketing and distri-
  bution?
- How many free copies will you get?
- Can you complete an author's form to detail referees? Who would
  like to hear about it?
- Is there advance publicity and, if so, can you get hold of it?

Writing your book

- Time your planning and critical path analysis so that you can work
  out how long each phase might take.
- Carry out research and start to draft in parts.
- Contact anyone whose information is needed in advance. Leave
  plenty of time for gathering information that is crucial but time-
  consuming to gather.
- Do you know the field very well? Or will you benefit from a litera-
  ture search?
- Do you need any new skills or de-rusting?
- Whether you work directly on a PC or whether it needs typing up
  will affect timing.
- Leave plenty of time for graphs, statistics and so on to be drawn up
  appropriately.
- Draft and redraft.
- Test it out on a friend and colleague for sense and interest.
- Test it against your market, colleagues and students, for accessibil-
  ity and interest.
- Ensure the references are all in the same format and the layout is
  the same.
- Edit, edit and edit.
- Ensure it looks really well presented.
- Photocopy it twice. Send two copies of the manuscript to the editor
  and keep one for yourself. Do you need to send a disk too?

Writing for a journal or other outlet

- The main advice is to select your outlet, your journal, and find out
  about the tone, the audience, find a sponsor who will write a letter.
  Read the journal to gauge the kind of pitch, the kind of essays it
  usually publishes.
- See if they are interested in the idea of the essay first and send an
  A4 outline to them, with a copy of other work you have done, if
  relevant and well presented.
- Some never get back to you – chase these.

- Others send out to the referees even for the proposal/for the essay.
- When comments return, decide how to deal with them. Most will need to be taken on board, but sometimes intuition will tell you that this is a hint that they do not want it.
- In this case, find another outlet and possibly rewrite for it.
- And/or, when you do get the paper accepted, ensure you know all about their guidelines for layout, length, timing, and so on.
- Write it.
- Check it.
- Edit it.
- Test it.
- Send off two copies. (Do they need a disk?)
- They will probably contact you with other minor changes and some proofing questions. You will probably be asked to sign a contract. Check if you will receive payment, offerings or a copy of the journal.

Things to do

Please identify the kind of help and ideas that have emerged from reading through these materials.

- Which elements of your work could you usefully develop now to publication?
- What would you need to do to your current work in order to carry out the writing?
- Where might you send it? Why?

Conclusion

We have looked at:

☐ Organising your work for presentation at conferences and work-in-progress seminars

☐ Organising your work for publication in books and journals.

Further reading

Murray, R. (2004) *Writing for Academic Journals* (Buckingham: Open University Press).

Websites accessed

www.askoxford.com/betterwriting/osa/givingpresentations/
www.mmu.ac.uk/academic/studserv/learningsupport/studyskills/
presentations.html

32 Life After the Research

● **'Is there life after the research?'**

Depending on where you are in your research project, you will probably want or *not* want to consider what happens when you finish. Indeed, 'Is there life after the research?' is not such an ironic question. A research project that lasts the best part of a year (MA) to up to eight years (PhD – but preferably three years) quite simply takes over your life, or part of it. Once you have been successful in your submission and assessment and in your viva, and if necessary, resubmitted or revised, you will probably feel all or some of the following:

- Elated – this is *the* major achievement
- Ready to rejoin the human race – the family and your friends
- Ready to do all those things you have been putting off
- Bereaved.

You live with your research and your thesis for a long time, like a recalcitrant pet animal. For some people it is actually impossible to stop, give it up, hand it over, bring it to a close. There was no life after research for the nineteenth-century British novelist George Eliot's Casaubon in *Middlemarch*. He could not imagine completion and he never completed. But you have finished and the world awaits you.

If you are looking ahead to this chapter at the *beginning* of your research career, you will see that the planning and time-management issues stressed throughout should include some planning of work and ongoing activities that take you beyond the research. Research-based degrees are, after all, *not* an end in themselves. They are qualifications that recognise achievement, but also confer a kind of licence to practice. They are a training ground for, and an indication of, the future likelihood of further research. So, do think about staging your withdrawal, celebration and future development based on your research degree.

First of all, celebrate. Then, take a holiday, or at least an intellectual break, or you will become stale. Friends and family, expecting your return to normality, will have calculated tasks both physical and emotional for you to be engaged in, and/or you will find they are piling up for you by your own planning. Obviously, they include things such as painting the kitchen or cooking regular meals again. But they also should include developing elements of the research, following up avenues, picking bits out – and publishing, giving conference papers and seminars, and putting in for research method posts and research funding. You might find you need quite a long break before you get on with this last area of work but you might also find that, unless you *do* throw yourself into some projects (*after* a break), you will feel rather bereaved. After my own PhD, within 18 months I moved house, moved to a new job, started an advanced diploma, and had a first baby. Not everyone needs to be quite so obsessive, of course. For me, publication approached gradually and the entire thesis has never seen the light of day in publication, though its ideas have fed into much of what I do daily, and into my teaching. So, in terms of the work/research areas involved, do consider:

- selecting elements of the thesis or dissertation to develop and rewrite for publication
- selecting elements of the thesis for conference presentation (do these two quickly)
- update your CV and gradually look for openings/seize immediate openings for job improvement (if that is your aim).

If none of these necessarily appears immediately:

- update your CV
- appear at conferences.

Then, when you are ready – but do not wait too long, even research into ancient history becomes superseded by newer research into ancient history – seek research funding, and – with or without it – carry on.

If you have been involved in Personal Development Planning during the course of your engagement with your research, and have identified ways in which you have developed various transferable skills and approaches that can be used beyond the PhD, you are ready now to market yourself in a career. Remember that while you have completed a single piece of research, you have developed a host of skills in problem solving, project mapping, balancing priorities, time management, project planning, communication, writing and presenting.

Things to do

Draw up a brief plan of 10 things you intend to do upon completion of the research. Make some of these just for your own benefit, some for friends and/or family, some work-related and some research-related. Do ensure some are easily managed, and others less easily obtained. Once you have drawn up the list, consider what you can do to work towards them.

Life after research list

Things to do – goals	What to do to achieve this
1	
2	
3	
4	
5	
6	
7	
8	
9	
10	

Conclusion

We have looked at:

☐ Life after your research

☐ Celebrations

☐ Further work.

● Further reading

Mullins, G. and Kiley, M. (1998) 'Quality in Postgraduate Education: The Changing Agenda', in M. Kiley and G. Mullins (eds), *Quality in Postgraduate Education: Managing the New Agenda* (Adelaide: Advisory Centre for University Education): 1–14.

Nerad, M. and Cerny, J. (1999) 'From Rumors to Facts: Career Outcomes of English PhDs Results from the PhDs – Ten Years Later Study', *Communicator*, 32 (7), Fall: 1–11.

Newman, J. (2001) 'The Shape of Graduate Studies in English', in *Issues in English: Doctor Doctor Doctoral Studies in English in Twenty-first Century Britain*, 1: 15–24 [16–17].

Patterson, A. (2001) 'Overproduction', in *Issues in English: Doctor Doctor Doctoral Studies in English in Twenty-first Century Britain*, 1: 5–13 [8].

Pearson, M. and Brew, A. (2002) 'Research Training and Supervision Development', *Studies in Higher Education*, 27 (2), 135–50 [138].

Shinton, S. (2007) 'What Do PhDs Do?', UK Grad report – a product of the UK Grad programme, http://www.grad.uk.ac/downloads/wdpd.pdf

Bibliography

Alavi, C. (ed.) (1995) *Problem-based Learning in a Health Sciences Curriculum* (London: Routledge).

Allan, G. and Skinner, C. (1991) *Handbook for Research Students in the Social Sciences* (London: Falmer Press).

Anderson, G., Boud, D. and Sampson, J. (eds) (1996) *Learning Contracts: A Practical Guide* (London: Kogan Page).

Andresen, L.W. (1997) *Highways to Postgraduate Supervision* (Sydney: University of Western Sydney).

Ashenden, Dean (2002) *The Good Universities Guide to Postgraduate and Career Upgrade Courses* (Cambridge: Hobsons).

Atkinson, P., Delamont, S. and Hammersley, M. (1988) 'Qualitative Research Traditions: A British Response to Jacob', *Review of Educational Research*, 58 (2) (Summer): 231–50.

Bales, R.F. (1950) *Interaction Process Analysis: A Method for the Study of Small Groups* (Cambridge, MA: Addison-Wesley).

Bell, J. (2005) *Doing your Research Project* (4th edn) (Buckingham: Open University Press).

Biggs, J. (1993) 'From Theory to Practice: A Cognitive Systems Approach', *Higher Education Research and Development*, 12: 73–85.

Biggs, J.B. (1978) 'Individual and Group Differences in Study Processes and the Quality of Learning Outcomes', *British Journal of Educational Psychology*, 48: 266–79.

Biggs, J.B. (1999) *Teaching for Quality Learning at University: What the Student Does* (Buckingham: Open University Press).

Biggs, J.B. and Rihn, B.A. (1984) 'The Effects of Intervention on Deep and Surface Approaches to Learning', in J.R. Kirby (ed.), *Cognitive Strategies and Educational Performance* (London: Academic Press): 279–93.

Blaxter, L., Hughes, C. and Tight, M. (1993) *How to Research* (Buckingham: Open University Press).

Boice, R. (1990) *Professors as Writers: A Self-Help Guide to Productive Writing* (Stillwater, OK: New Forums).

Brew, A. and Peseta, T. (2005) 'Is Research Higher Degree Supervision Teaching or Is It Research? What Difference Does It Make?', Paper presented at the Society for Teaching and Learning in Higher Education (STLHE) Conference, University of Ottawa, Canada, 16–19 June.

Brookfield, S. (ed.) (1986) *Self-Directed Learning: From Theory to Practice* (New Directions for Continuing Education 25) (San Francisco: Jossey-Bass).

Brookfield, S.D. (1986) *Understanding and Facilitating Adult Learning: Comprehensive Analysis of Principles and Effective Practices* (Milton Keynes: Open University Press).

Brown, Robert (1992) 'The "Big Picture" about Managing Writing', in O. Zuber-Skerritt and Y. Ryan, *Quality in Postgraduate Education* (London: Kogan Page).

Buchanan, D., Boddy, D. and McCalman, J. (1988) 'Getting In, Getting On, Getting Out and Getting Back', in A. Bryman (ed.), *Doing Research in Organisations* (London: Routledge).

Burkitt, I., Husband, C., McKenzie, J., Torn, A. and Crow, S. (2001) *Nurse Education and Communities of Practice* (London: ENB).

Carr, W. and Kemmis, S. (1986) *Becoming Critical: Education, Knowledge and Action Research* (London: Falmer).

Cooper, H.M. (1985) *The Integrative Research Review: A Systematic Approach* (London: Sage).

Cooperrider, D.L. and Srivastra, S. (1987) 'Appreciative Inquiry into Organizational Life', in W.A. Passmore and R.W. Woodman (eds), *Research into Organizational Change and Development*, vol. 1(Greenwich, CT: JAI).

Cottrell, S. (2003) *The Study Skills Handbook* (2nd edn) (Basingstoke: Palgrave Macmillan).

Cousin, G. (2006) 'Threshold Concepts, Troublesome Knowledge and Emotional Capital: An Exploration into Learning about Others', in J.H.F. Meyer and R. Land (eds), *Overcoming Barriers to Student Understanding: Threshold Concepts and Troublesome Knowledge* (London and New York: Routledge).

Creswell, J.W. (2002) *Research Design: Qualitative, Quantitative, and Mixed Methods Approaches* (2nd edn) (Thousand Oaks, CA: Sage).

Cryer, P. (1997) *The Research Student's Guide to Success* (2nd edn) (Buckingham: Open University Press).

Dahlgren, L. and Marton, F. (1978) 'Students' Conceptions of Subject Matter: An Aspect of Learning and Teaching in Higher Education', *Studies in Higher Education*, 3 (1).

Davies, M.B. (2007) *Doing a Successful Research Project* (Basingstoke: Palgrave Macmillan).

Delamont, S., Atkinson, P. and Parry, O. (1997) *Supervising the PhD: A Guide to Success* (Buckingham: Open University Press).

Denscombe, M. (1998) *The Good Research Guide* (Buckingham: Open University Press).

Denzin, N.K. and Lincoln, Y.S. (1998) *The Landscape of Qualitative Research, Theories and Issues* (Thousand Oaks, CA: Sage).

Dewey, J. (1963) *Experience and Education* (New York: Collier).

Dunleavy, P. (1986) *Studying for a Degree* (Basingstoke: Palgrave Macmillan).

Dunleavy, P. (2003) *Authoring a PhD* (Basingstoke: Palgrave Macmillan).

Elbow, P. (1973) *Writing Without Teachers* (Oxford: Oxford University Press).

Eliot, G. (1965 [1871]) *Middlemarch* (London: Penguin).

Entwistle, A.C. and Entwistle, N.J. (1992) 'Experiences of Understanding in Revising for Degree Examinations', *Learning and Instruction*, 2: 1–22.

Entwistle, N.J. (1998) 'Improving Teaching Through Research on Student Learning', in J.J.F. Forest (ed.) *University Teaching: International Perspectives* (New York: Garland): 73–112.

Entwistle, N.J. and Ramsden, P. (1983) *Understanding Student Learning* (London: Croom Helm).

Evans, L. (1998) *Teaching and Learning in Higher Education* (London: Cassell).

Evans, P. and Varma, V.P. (1990) *Special Education* (London: Falmer).

Fisher, J. (1996) *Starting from the Child: Teaching and Learning from 4 to 8* (Buckingham: Open University Press).

Fisher, S. (1994) *Stress in Academic Life* (Buckingham: Open University Press).

Flanders, N.A. (1970) *Analysing Teacher Behavior* (Reading, MA: Addison-Wesley).

Francis, H. (1997) 'The Research Process', in N. Graves and V. Verna (eds) *Working for a Doctorate: A Guide for the Humanities and Social Sciences* (London: Routledge).

Gibbs, G. (1981) *Teaching Students to Learn* (Buckingham: Open University Press).

Gibbs, G., Wisker, G. and Bochner, B. (1999) 'Supporting More Students', (Oxford: Oxford Brookes University).

Glaser, B. and Strauss, A. (1967) *The Discovery of Grounded Theory* (Chicago: Aldine).

Gordon, William J.J. (1961) *Synectics: The Development of Creative Capacity* (New York: Harper).

Graves, N. and Varma, V. (eds) (1997) *Working for a Doctorate: A Guide for the Humanities and Social Sciences* (London: Routledge).

Greenfield, T. (2002) *Research Methods for Postgraduates* (London: Arnold).

Hart, C. (1999) *Doing a Literature Review: Releasing the Social Science Research Imagination* (London: Sage).

Hartley, J. and Fox, C. (2003) *Assessing the Mock Viva: The Experience of British Doctoral Students* (Keele, UK: Keele University).

Hildreth, P., Kimble, C. and Wright, P. (2001) *Computer Mediated Communications and International Communities of Practice,* Proceedings of Ethicomp '98, March 1998 (Erasmus University, Netherlands).

Hodge, B. (1995) 'Monstrous Knowledge: Doing PhDs in the New Humanities', *Australian Universities' Review,* 38 (2): 35–9.

Holbrook, A., Bourke, S., Lovat, T. and Fairbairn, H. (2006) 'PhD Thesis Examination: Overview on an ARC Discovery Grant Project 2003–06', SORTI Group, University of Newcastle Australia, *HERDSA News,* 38 (2).

Holland, J. (1991) *Learning Legal Rules: A Student's Guide to Legal Method and Reasoning* (London: Blackstone).

Holland, J. and Ramazanoglu, C. (1994) 'Coming to Conclusions: Power and Interpretation in Researching Young Women's Sexuality', in M. Maynard and J. Purvis (eds), *Researching Women's Lives from a Feminist Perspective,* pp. 125-48. (London: Taylor & Francis): 125–48.

Holloway, I. and Walker, J. (2000) *Getting a PhD in Health and Social Care* (London: Blackwell).

Holloway, W. and Jefferson, T. (2000) *Doing Qualitative Research Differently, Free Association Narrative and the Interview Method* (London: Sage).

Honey, P. and Mumford, A. (1986) *Using your Manual of Learning Styles* (Maidenhead: Peter Honey Publications).

Horn, R. (1996) 'Negotiating Research Access to Organisations', *The Psychologist,* December.

Hughes, J. (1990) *The Philosophy of Social Research* (2nd edn) (New York: Longman).

Hussey, J. and Hussey, R. (2003) *Business Research* (2nd edn) (Basingstoke: Palgrave Macmillan).

Kiley, M. and Mullins, G. (2005) 'Examining the Examiners: How Inexperienced Examiners Approach the Assessment of Research Theses', *International Journal of Educational Research*: 41 (2): 121–35.

Kolb, D.A. (1984) *Experiential Learning: Experience as the Source of Learning and Development* (Englewood Cliffs, NJ: Prentice-Hall).

Lacey, C. (1976) 'Problems of Sociological Fieldwork: A Review of the Methodology of "Hightown Grammar"', in M. Shipman (ed.), *The Organisation and Impact of Social Research* (London: Routledge & Kegan Paul).

Lave, J. and Wenger, E. (1999) 'Legitimate Peripheral Participation in Communities of Practice', in R. McCormack and C. Poechter (eds), *Learning and Knowledge* (London: Paul Chapman).

Lawton, D. (1997) 'How to Succeed in Postgraduate Study', in N. Graves and

V. Varma (eds), *Working for a Doctorate: A Guide for the Humanities and Social Sciences* (London: Routledge).

Lee, R. (1995) *Dangerous Fieldwork* (Thousand Oaks, CA: Sage).

Leonard, D. (2001) *A Women's Guide to Doctoral Studies* (Buckingham: Open University Press).

Leshem, S. and Trafford, V.N. (2006) 'Overlooking the Conceptual Framework', *Innovations in Education and Teaching International*, 43 (2), December.

Mailer, N. (2000) *Why Are We in Vietnam?* (USA: Picador).

Marton, F. (1986) 'Some Reflections on the Improvement of Learning', in J.A. Bowden (ed.), 'Student Learning: The Marysville Symposium' (University of Melbourne: Center for the Study of Higher Education): 31.

Marton, F., Dall'Alba, G. and Beaty, E. (1993) 'Conceptions of Learning', *Journal of Educational Research*, 19 (3): 277–300.

Marton, F., Hounsell, D., Entwistle, N. and Mckeachie, W. (eds) (1984) *The Experience of Learning* (Edinburgh: Scottish Academic Press).

Marton, F. and Säljö, R. (1976) 'On Qualitative Differences in Learning. I – Outcome and Process', *British Journal of Educational Psychology*, 46: 4–11.

May, T. (1997) *Social Research: Issues, Methods and Process* (Buckingham: Open University Press).

Melamed, L. (1987) 'The Role of Play in Adult Learning', in D. Boud and V. Griffin (eds), *Appreciating Adults Learning: From the Learner's Perspective* (London: Kogan Page).

Metcalfe J., Thompson, Q. and Green, H. (2002) 'Improving Standards in Postgraduate Research Degree Programmes', October (Bristol: HEFCE).

Meyer, J.H.F. and Boulton-Lewis, G.M. (1997) 'The Reflections on Learning Inventory', University of Durham.

Meyer, J.H.F. and Kiley, M. (1998) 'An Exploration of Indonesian Postgraduate Students' Conceptions of Learning', *Journal of Further and Higher Education*, 22: 287–98.

Meyer, J.H.F. and Land, R. (2004) 'Threshold Concepts and Troublesome Knowledge: 2 Epistemological Considerations and a Conceptual Framework for Teaching and Learning', *Higher Education*, December.

Meyer, J.H.F. and Land, R. (eds) (2006) *Overcoming Barriers to Student Understanding: Threshold Concepts and Troublesome Knowledge* (London and New York: Routledge).

Meyer, J.H.F. and Shanahan, M.P. (2001) 'A Trianguated Approach to Modelling of Learning Outcomes in First Year Economics', *Higher Education Research and Development*, 20 (2): 127–45.

Mezirow, J. (1985) 'A Critical Theory of Self-directed Learning', in S. Brookfield (ed.), *Self-Directed Learning: From Theory to Practice* (New Directions for Continuing Education 25) (San Francisco: Jossey-Bass).

Mezirow, J. (1990) *Fostering Critical Reflection on Adulthood: A Guide to Trans-formative and Emancipatory Learning* (San Francisco: Jossey-Bass).

Miles, M. and Huberman, M. (1994) *Qualitative Data Analysis* (London: Sage).

Morrow, R. and Brown, D. (1994) *Critical Theory and Methodology: Contemporary Social Theory* (Thousand Oaks, CA: Sage).

Moses, I. (1984) 'Supervision of Higher Degree Students – Problem Areas and Possible Solutions', *Higher Education Research and Development*, 3: 153–6.

Moses, I. (1985) *Supervising Postgraduates* (Sydney: HERDSA).

Mullins G. and Kiley, M. (1998) 'Quality in Postgraduate Education: The Changing Agenda', in M. Kiley and G. Mullins (eds), *Quality in Postgraduate Education: Managing the New Agenda* (Adelaide: Advisory Centre for University Education): 1–14.

Murray, R. (2000) *Writing a Thesis* (Buckingham: Open University Press).

Murray, R. (2002) *How to Write a Thesis* (Buckingham: Open University Press).

Murray, R. (2003) *How to Survive Your Viva* (Buckingham: Open University Press).

Murray, R. (2004) *Writing for Academic Journals* (Buckingham: Open University Press).

Murray, R. and Moore, S. (2006) *The Handbook of Academic Writing* (Buckingham: Open University Press).

Nerad, M. and Cerny, J. (1999) 'From Rumors to Facts: Career Outcomes of English PhDs Results from the PhDs – Ten Years Later Study', *Communicator*, 32 (7), Fall: 1–11.

Newman, J. (2001) 'The Shape of Graduate Studies in English', *Issues in English: Doctor Doctor Doctoral Studies in English in Twenty-first Century Britain*, 1: 15–24 [16–17].

Nightingale, P. (1992) 'Initiation in Research through Writing', in O. Zuber-Skerritt, *Starting Research: Supervision and Training* (Brisbane QLD: Tertiary Education Institute).

O'Leary, Z. (2004) *The Essential Guide to Doing Research* (Thousand Oaks, CA: Sage).

O'Neill, J. (1993) *Ecology, Policy and Politics: Human Well-being and the Natural World* (London: Routledge): chs 1–2.

Oliver, P. (2003) *The Student's Guide to Research Ethics* (Berkshire: SRHE and Open University Press).

Orna, E. and Stevens, G. (1995) *Managing Information for Research* (Buckingham: Open University Press).

Over, R. (1982) 'Does Research Productivity Decline with Age?', *Higher Education*, 11: 511–20.

Patterson, A. (2001) 'Overproduction', *Issues in English: Doctor Doctor Doctoral Studies in English in Twenty-first Century Britain*, 1: 5–13 [8].

Pearson M. and Brew, A. (2002) 'Research Training and Supervision Development', *Studies in Higher Education*, 27 (2), 135–50 [138].

Phillips, E.M. and Pugh, D.S. (1994) *How to Get a PhD: A Handbook for Students and Their Supervisors* (2nd edn) (Buckingham: Open University Press).

Piantanida, M. and Garman, N. (1999) *The Qualitative Dissertation: A Guide for Students and Faculty* (Thousand Oaks, CA: Sage).

Prosser, M. and Trigwell, K. (eds) (1999) *Understanding Learning and Teaching: The Experience in Higher Education* (Buckingham: Open University Press).

Quinn, J., Thomas, E., Slack, K., Casey, L., Thexton, W. and Noble, J. (2005) 'From Life Crisis to Lifelong Learning: Rethinking Working-class "Drop Out" from Higher Education, Rethinking Working-class "Drop Out" from University', Joseph Rowntree Foundation (http://www.jrf.org.uk/book shop/eBooks/1859354130.pdf), accessed 25 January 2006)

Ramsden, P. (1979) 'Student Learning and the Perception of the Academic Environment', *Higher Education*, 8: 411–28.

Ramsden, P. (1992) *Learning to Teach in Higher Education* (London: Routledge).

Rendel, M. (1986) 'How Many Women Academics 1912–1977?', in R. Deem (ed.), *Schooling for Women's Work* (London: Routledge).

Roberts, Sir G. (2002) *Set for Success: The Report of the Sir Gareth Roberts Review* (London: HM Treasury) (available at http://www.hmtreasury. gov.uk/media/643/FB/ACF11FD.pdf).

Robson, C. (1993) *Real World Research* (Oxford: Blackwell).

Roesch, R. (1998) *Time Management for Busy People* (New York: McGraw-Hill Professional).

Rogers, J. (1989) *Adults Learning* (Buckingham: Open University Press).

Ryan, Y. and Zuber-Skerritt, O. (eds) (1999) *Supervising Postgraduates from Non-English Speaking Backgrounds* (Buckingham: Society for Research into Higher Education and Open University Press).

Säljö, R. (1994) 'Minding Action–Conceiving of the World versus Participating in Cultural Practices', *Nordisk Peadagogik*, 14 (4): 71–80.

Säljö, R. (1997) *Learning and Discourse: A Sociocultural Perspective* (Leicester: British Psychological Society).

Salmon, Phillida (1992) *Achieving a PhD: Ten Students' Experiences* (Stoke-on-Trent, UK: Trentham Books).

Savin-Baden, Maggi (2003) *Facilitating Problem-based Learning* (Maidenhead: Open University Press).

Savin-Baden, Maggi and Major, Claire Howell (2004) *Foundations of Problem-based Learning* (Maidenhead: Open University Press).

Savin-Baden, Maggi and Wilkie, K. (2004) *Challenging Research in Problem-based Learning* (Maidenhead: McGraw-Hill and SRHE).

Schmeck, R.R. (1988) *Learning Strategies and Learning Styles* (New York: Plenum Press).

Schön, D. (1983) *The Reflective Practitioner* (San Francisco: Jossey-Bass).

Sherman, R.., Kutner, M., Webb, L. and Herman, R. (1991) 'Key Elements of Adult Education Teacher and Volunteer Training Programs' (Washington, DC: Pelavin Associates).

Sherman, R. and Webb, R. (1988) *Qualitative Research in Education* (London: Falmer Press).

Shinton, S. (2007) 'What Do PhDs Do?', UK Grad report – a product of the UK Grad programme, http://www.grad.uk.ac/downloads/wdpd.pdf

Shipman, M. (ed.) *The Organisation and Impact of Social Research* (London: Routledge & Kegan Paul).

Smith, L.T. (1999) *Decolonizing Methodologies: Research and Indigenous Peoples* (London: Zed).

Somekh, B. (2006) *Action Research: A Methodology for Change and Development* (Oxford: Oxford University Press).

Strauss, A. (1987) *Qualitative Analysis for Social Scientists* (Cambridge: Cambridge University Press).

Strauss, A. and Corbin, J. (1990) *Basics of Qualitative Research: Grounded Theory Procedures and Techniques* (London: Sage).

Svensson, L. (1977) 'On Qualitative Differences in Learning. vol. III – Study Skills and Learning', *British Journal of Educational Psychology*, 47: 233–43.

Svensson, L.G. (1987) *Higher Education and the State in Swedish History* (Stockholm: Almqvist & Wiksell).

Swinnerton-Dyer, H.P.F. (1982) *Report of the Working Party on Postgraduate Education* (London: HMSO).

Tenopir, C. and Lundeen, G. (1988) *Managing Your Information* (New York: Neal Schuman).

Thomas, P.R. and Bain, J.D. (1982) 'Consistency in Learning Strategies', *Higher Education*, 11: 249–59.

Tight, M. (1983) *Education for Adults Volume 2: Opportunities for Adult Education* (London: Routledge).

Todd, L. (1997) 'Supervising Overseas Post-Graduate Students: Problem or Opportunity', in D. McNamara and R. Harris (eds) *Quality in Higher Education for Overseas Students* (London: Routledge).

Trafford, V. (1999) Handout, Anglia Ruskin University.

Trafford, V. and Leshem, S. (2002) 'Starting at the End to Undertake Doctoral Research: Predictable Questions as Stepping Stones', *Higher Education Review*, 35: 31–49.

Trafford, V. and Leshem, S. (2002) 'Questions in a Doctoral Viva', in UK Council For Graduate Education Research Degree Examining Symposium (London).

University of Queensland Calendar (1984) University of Queensland

Walliman, N.S.R. (2005) *Your Research Project* (London: Sage).

Watkins, B. (1981) *Drama and Education* (London: Batsford).

Watkins, D. and Hattie, J. (1981) 'The Learning Processes of Australian University Students: Investigations of Contextual and Personological Factors, *British Journal of Educational Psychology*, 51 (3), November: 384–93.

Wenger, E. (1998) *Communities of Practice* (Cambridge: Cambridge University Press).

Wenger, E. (2000) 'Communities of Practice and Social Learning Systems', *Sage*, 7 (2): 225–46.

Wenger, E. and Lave, J. (1991) *Situated Learning* (Cambridge: Cambridge University Press).

Williams, D. (2005) *The Essential Guide to Postgraduate Study* (Thousand Oaks, CA: Sage).

Winter, J. (1995) *Skills for Graduates in the 21st Century* (London: Association of Graduate Recruiters).

Winter, R. (1989) *Learning from Experience: Principles and Practice in Action Research* (London: Falmer).

Winter, R. (1993) 'Continuity and Progression: Assessment Vocabularies for Higher Education', Unpublished research report data, Ruskin Anglia University, Faculty of Health and Social Work, Chelmsford.

Winter, R. (2000) 'Assessment Vocabularies for Higher Education: Practice-based PhDs', *Journal of Further and Higher Education*, 1.

Winter, R. and Guise, S. (1995) The Ford ASSET Project: The Report of a Two-year Collaborative Project to Introduce Work-based Learning within an Honours Degree Level Award in Engineering Undertaken Jointly by Ford Motor Company Ltd and Anglia Polytechnic University (Chelmsford: Anglia Polytechnic University).

Winter, R. and Sabiechowska, P. (1999) *Professional Experience and the Investigative Imagination* (London: Routledge).

Wisker, G. (1998) 'The Research as Learning Questionnaire', Anglia Ruskin University, Cambridge.

Wisker, G. (1999) 'Learning Conceptions and Strategies of Postgraduate Students (Israeli PhD Students) and Some Steps Towards Encouraging and Enabling their Learning', Paper presented to the Quality in Postgraduate Research Conference: Developing Research, Adelaide.

Wisker, G. (2000) 'Good Practice Working with International Students', SEDA Occasional Paper 110 (Birmingham: SEDA).

Wisker, G. (2005) *The Good Supervisor* (Basingstoke: Palgrave Macmillan).

Wisker, G. and Hartley, P. (2006) 'Interviewer: Postgraduate Viva' (CD-ROM developed as the result of National Teaching Fellowships).

Wisker G., Kiley, M. and Aiston, S. (2006) 'Making the Learning Leap: Research Students Crossing Conceptual Thresholds', Paper presented at the Quality in Postgraduate Research Conference, Adelaide.

Wisker, G. and Robinson, G. (2002) *Getting There in the End: Contributions to the Achievement of the PhD* (available at http://www.qpr.edu.au/).

Wisker, G., Robinson, G. and Trafford, V. (2003) HERDSA Conference.

Wisker, G., Robinson, G., Trafford, V., Warnes, M. and Creighton, E. (2003) 'From Supervisory Dialogues to Successful PhDs: Strategies Supporting and Enabling the Learning Conversations of Staff and Students at Postgraduate Level', *Teaching in Higher Education*, 8 (3), July: 383–97).

Wisker, G. and Sutcliffe, N. (eds) (1999) 'Good Practice in Postgraduate Supervision', SEDA Occasional Paper 106 (Birmingham: SEDA).

Wisker, G., Tiley, J., Watkins, M., Waller, S., Maclaughlin, J., Thomas, J. and Wisker, A. (eds) (2000) 'Discipline-based Research into Student Learning in English, Law, Social Work, Computer Skills for Linguists, Women's Studies, Creative Writing: How Can It Inform our Teaching?', in C. Rust (ed.), *Improving Student Learning through the Disciplines* (Oxford: Oxford Brookes University): 377–97.

Zuber-Skerritt, O. (1992) *Action Research in Higher Education* (London: Kogan Page)

Zuber-Skerritt, O. (2004) 'Quality in AR Research' conference from DBA Associates in the Business School Netherlands, Johannesburg.

Websites accessed

Article (2004), t magazine online http://www.tmag.co.uk/articles/July04 Pg20.html, 26 January 2006.

http://carbon.cudenver.edu/~mryder/ltc_data/pract_res.html

http://utoronto.ca/writing/litreview.html

http://www.anglia.ac.uk/research/gradsch/gshome.shtml

http://www.ecu.du.au/ses/research/CALLR/Writing

http://www.gwu.edu/~litrev

http://www.phys.unsw.edu.au/%7Ejw/viva.html

http://www.qualitative-research.net/

http://www.qualitativeresearch.uga.edu/QualPage/

Renewal.net (2006) 'Increasing Participation in Education and Training' (http://www.renewal.net/Documents/RNET/Overview/Education/ Increasingparticipationedcation.doc, accessed January 2006).

www.askoxford.com/betterwriting/osa/givingpresentations/
www.grad.ac.uk
www.mmu.ac.uk/academic/studserv/learningsupport/studyskills/
    presentations.html
www.thegoodguides.com.au

Index